NEW NARATIF:
THE FIRST YEAR

New Naratif: The First Year

© New Naratif

ISBN 978-981-11-9727-7

Published for New Naratif (www.newnaratif.com)

By Pagesetters Services Pte Ltd

28 Sin Ming Lane #06-131

Singapore 573972

Editors: Kirsten Han & Thum Ping Tjin

Cover design by Izyanti Asaari

Layout and design by Bayu P. Nugroho

Printed by Ho Printing Pte Ltd

6 5 4 3 2 1   22 21 20 19 18

CONTENTS

INTRODUCTION

KIRSTEN HAN & THUM PING TJIN

A year passes very quickly. It feels not so long ago that the three of us (including Sonny Liew, our co-founder) were sitting in a cafe, trying to figure out a name for our new website and company while our coffee got cold, or standing in front of a whiteboard trying to sketch out a business model and value proposition.

On 9 September 2017, we launched crowdfunding to a packed audience at The Projector in Singapore. It was a nerve-wracking time. The website didn't work properly, and so we launched with just a PDF preview. PayPal didn't work properly and we couldn't collect funds. It later emerged that this was due to an obscure Singapore regulation that required a special license for Singaporean accounts to send money to a foreign non-profit organisation. Because of our non-profit, no advertising business model that tried to put ethical considerations first, we had very little money and all of it went straight out to pay our freelancers and editors. Kirsten worked unpaid until March 2018. PJ still hasn't drawn a salary. The company has no shares, so there's no equity.

Our plan was to open offices through Southeast Asia, starting with Singapore. The Singapore government torpedoed that by effectively banning our company in April 2018. Our attempt to register a wholly-owned subsidiary in Singapore was rejected by the Accounting and Corporate Regulatory Authority on (frankly, ridiculous) grounds that we "would be contrary to Singapore's national interests." Our appeal against this decision was rejected by the Minister of Finance in late September 2018. We had to cease public activities in Singapore and shut down our physical office. This was on top of a sustained smear campaign and a lot of harassment and abuse.

Will Nguyen, author of "North/South", was arrested and beaten by Vietnamese police while attending a public protest in Ho Chi Minh City. A Vietnamese-American, he was, fortunately, released after pleading guilty to charges of disturbing the peace following about two months in jail. We were very worried the whole time he was behind bars, wondering if what he'd written for us could have contributed to his treatment by the authorities. Despite the happy ending, it was a sobering reminder that our contributors face threats to their safety across Southeast Asia,

It has, by any measure, been a tough year.

And yet… it also has been a wonderful and successful year. In the past year—between 1 November 2017, when we started publishing, and 30 October 2018, we've published a total of 231 articles:

- 188 total journalism articles, including:
  - 98 unique articles
  - 65 translations, in Bahasa Indonesia, Bahasa Malaysia, Vietnamese, and Chinese.
  - 25 "Akan Datang" articles—a look ahead to the week's most important stories in Southeast Asia.
- 20 Research articles, including 3 articles in Bahasa Malaysia.
- 10 Comics
- 2 Videos
- 11 Podcasts, for over 9 hours of total audio content

Some of these articles have really gained a wide audience and hopefully helped change the narrative around important issues. Our most read journalism article was "The Making of a Female ISIS Bomber" by Febriana Firdaus, our Consulting Editor for Jakarta and Papua. It was widely shared in Indonesia, and shed light on the dehumanising effects of the system of migrant labour. Our most read research article, "How Malaysia's Election is Being Rigged", was published in the days before Malaysia's groundbreaking election in May 2018 and went mildly viral, despite being nearly 6,000 words. We'd like to think it made a small contribution to the outcome of the election.

"Remembering Coldstore: Former Detainees Speak" helped to humanise and contextualise a group of people who had been demonised by the Singapore government for over 50 years: men and women detained without trial under Singapore's draconian internal security laws. The photos, reproduced in this book, showed a group of gentle elderly men and women who had fought for Singapore's independence from colonialism and tried to help build a new country. The photos were juxtaposed with quotes from the former detainees, notes from their arrest documents, and historical explanation, giving new context to their politically-motivated detentions. We were very proud of the juxtaposition of the visual, written, and historical presentations in this article.

Collectively, these articles also showed that there is a market out there for well-written, in-depth, long-form, evidence-based articles on important issues. All these stories are included in this anthology.

Our comics have also done well—Sonny's "The Select Committee on One Tight Slaps" was a wonderfully Singaporean take on a not-so-wonderful Singaporean political exercise. "Malay in the Modern World" was thought provoking on the nature of identity in the modern era. "No One Should Have to be Super in Order to be Human" touched many raw nerves with its look at inequality in an era of unprecedented wealth.

The crowdfunding was a big success. It ended on 2 September 2018 with a total of 544 crowdfunding members who contributed a total of US$42,710 after transaction fees and exchange rate losses. With these proceeds, we rebuilt the website, raising the paywall on 9 September 2018, and creating a new payment system and membership database. We received a grant from the Open Society Foundation, which enabled us to stabilise our financial situation and put it on a sustainable footing.

In response to the de facto ban in Singapore, we accelerated our timetable to open our Kuala Lumpur office, successfully launching it in October 2018. We've moved our regional headquarters to KL, and will be basing our Southeast Asian operations out of that city. Our goal of opening an office in every Southeast Asian country remains, although it may be a long time before we can open an office in Singapore.

The most positive outcome from this year, and what sustains us the most, is the sheer level of support that we've received. People have stepped up to fund New Naratif, to volunteer with us, or just to give us food. People stop us in the street to thank us for our work and encourage us to keep going. Freelancers thank us and praise us for the simple (and yet very rare) act of paying their invoices promptly and in full. We receive messages from across Southeast Asia from people affected by our stories, who have learnt something new about the world around them and about themselves.

We're proud of our work, and we're proud of our home region. In reading this anthology of stories from our first year, we hope you will appreciate the wonderfully complex and diverse region that is Southeast Asia.

NEW NARATIF— A PLATFORM FOR SOUTHEAST ASIA

KIRSTEN HAN | 09 SEP 2017

New Naratif's Editor-in-Chief Kirsten Han on why we need you to join us in creating space for Southeast Asia and Southeast Asians to speak for ourselves.

When it comes to finding our own voices and telling our own stories, Southeast Asians face two major challenges.

In the international media, we exist as the backdrop for the sorts of stories editors think people in the West want to hear: an arena in which global superpowers play chicken, a location for colourful *Eat, Pray, Love* fantasies, or a source of weird-looking fruits and "kooky Asians".

At home, we run into obstacles when it comes to speaking up. Authoritarian governments and repressive laws restrict our options and reduce the space in which we can frame our own issues and craft our own narratives. Many across Southeast Asia have already paid the price for standing up for their beliefs.

I've encountered both these problems myself, as a freelance journalist and as an activist. It's frustrating. The issues that we need to grapple with and the stories that we can tell are numerous and complex. There is insufficient space to address them in the international press, and insufficient political will to address them in the local media.

That's why it was a no-brainer when historian Thum Ping Tjin approached me with the idea that would become the site you're now looking at—the need for a principled website dedicated to studying and reflecting Southeast Asia in all its glory was immediately clear. Award-winning comics artist Sonny Liew later joined us, because this need for platform and authorship for Southeast Asians isn't just limited to journalism and academic research, but the arts too.

New Naratif was born of our love for and fascination with Southeast Asia, and our unwavering belief that the region's stories aren't just entertaining exotica for Western audiences, but are in and of themselves important and worth telling. This is our home; we want to tell its stories on our own terms, in ways which are meaningful and important to us.

This isn't a vanity project to indulge ourselves: this is a journey for all of us, and you are an integral member of the team. By becoming subscribing to *New Naratif*, you're not just supporting our work; you're contributing to a collective effort to build Southeast Asian identity and solidarity, and to nurture a platform for journalism, research, and art where Southeast Asians can recognise ourselves and our truths.

Subscribers don't just get access to our content. We aren't selling you a product. We're asking you to join a movement. Our subscribers are part of the conversation, participating in discussions and having a say in the sort of themes and issues you would like the site to explore. We believe that everyone has their own area of expertise, and we invite you to weigh in on subjects and attend our offline events. *New Naratif* belongs to all who support it, and you will always have access to our editors.

None of this is for profit—all the money you commit to the project goes into the running and sustaining of the website. We pay our contributors—be they writers, photographers, researchers or artists—because we know from personal experience how unfair it is to be asked to work for "exposure". We embody the governance that we want to see in this region, and pledge to be honest and transparent about the way things are run at *New Naratif.*

The international media limits our stories, the local political contexts restrict them. But those stories are still out there. Help us bring them to you—join *New Naratif* today.

BEING LGBTQ IN SOUTHEAST ASIA

"A NATIONAL COMING OUT": 10 YEARS SINCE REPEAL 377A

KIRSTEN HAN | 01 NOV 2017

10 years after an attempt to repeal an anti-gay law, Singapore's LGBTQ activists are still seeking equality.

It's been 10 years and Siew Kum Hong still remembers the walk from his seat to the Clerk of Parliament: "I was so worried I'd stumble and fall! I was relieved to get it done without messing up."

Parliamentary sessions are usually important yet mundane events, but the petition Siew had in his hands was significant and unprecedented: it was the first time in Singapore that a parliamentary petition was being submitted with popular support.

The petition called for the repeal of Section 377A of the Singapore Penal Code. The law criminalises sex between men, even if the act is consensual and occurs in private. Its existence has side-effects; by effectively criminalising gay men, 377A affects government policies and positions, such as the representation of the lesbian, gay, bisexual, transgender and queer (LGBTQ) community in the media, and the inclusion of LGBTQ issues in sex education in schools.

"An overt discrimination"

Following a comprehensive review of the Penal Code, the Ministry of Home Affairs tabled amendments in September 2007. Among the long list of suggested changes was the decriminalisation of oral and anal sex between heterosexual couples, as covered in Section 377. Section 377A, however, was left untouched.

The discrepancy leapt out at George Hwang. "This was an overt discrimination. And I thought that it went against the grain of the formation of Singapore," he told *New Naratif*, referring to promises of equality enshrined in declarations such as the national pledge, which commits to building "a democratic society, based on justice and equality".

Hwang, with the support of Stuart Koe—founder of the prominent LGBTQ website Fridae—approached then-Nominated Member of Parliament Siew Kum Hong with the idea of submitting a parliamentary petition.

Independent of Hwang and Koe's efforts, another group of LGBTQ activists were finding their way towards what would become the Repeal 377A campaign. According to campaigner Alan Seah, there was an indirect push from an unexpected source: "We were a little bit inspired by Sir Ian McKellen [who was touring with the Royal Shakespeare Company]... he did a whole thing on *Channel News Asia* where they asked him, 'What do you hope to do in Singapore?' and he said, 'Well, I hope to go to a gay bar!' They all didn't know what to do, it was the morning show and [broadcast] live! I won't say he's the inspiration, but he definitely encouraged us to be a bit more mischievous."

Seah and a couple of friends set up Repeal377A.com. The campaign took shape around the parliamentary petition and an open letter to Prime Minister Lee Hsien Loong. Local celebrities appeared in a video, their calls for repeal set against a pop beat.

Seah remembers going around gay bars collecting signatures. "It's always difficult to try and get people activated when you're at a club!" he said with a laugh. "But I remember the response was generally pretty good."

Some local businesses put up boxes where people could deposit their signatures; individuals with no direct connection to the campaign collected signatures from their peers. Hwang had set a target of 200 signatures, but the response exceeded his expectations tenfold. On 22 October, Siew submitted a petition with 2,341 signatures to Parliament. The open letter, submitted to the Prime Minister's Office, had 8,120 signatures.

Straws and noses

In Parliament, Siew's speech quoted comments left by signatories to the open letter, including one from a mother:

> My son... came out to me when he was 22. And I was upset and I blamed myself for why my son is gay... I blamed myself all the time. But he is my son. ... I love him for who he is, for what he is. It sickens me that people think... just because he is gay, our family is not what it is. We are a family... He does not know I am doing this but I support this repeal. He is my son and he is not a criminal. If I

can accept him, his mother who gave birth to him, who are these people who so quickly judge him and condemn him?

Some Members of Parliament, including those from the ruling People's Action Party (PAP), spoke supportively of repeal. But others argued strongly for 377A's retention. Nominated Member of Parliament Thio Li Ann gave the most memorable speech of the debate—still referenced by activists today—accusing "homosexual activists" of trying to "hijack human rights initiatives to serve their political agenda". She likened anal sex to "shoving a straw up your nose to drink" and spoke approvingly of efforts to help gay people get rid of their same-sex attraction and "fulfill their heterosexual potential".

"It was quite jaw-dropping," Seah said. "And the fact that [other MPs] applauded her, that was really disturbing."

"[T]he whole Section 377A saga in 2007 gave me a rude awakening that there is a segment of the Singapore population that is not only conservative but bigoted to the extent that they advocate imprisonment for sex between two consenting adult males in the privacy of their own home," Hwang said.

"Out of the closet"

All the arguments, media coverage and celebrity videos weren't enough to shift the law. There was resistance; a counter-petition urging the retention of 377A accumulated over 15,000 signatures. The government was reluctant to move, and Parliament voted to retain the law.

"If you try and force the issue and settle the matter definitively, one way or the other, we are never going to reach an agreement within Singapore society," said PM Lee Hsien Loong.

But the activists and their allies don't consider Repeal 377A a failure. "It might be hard to imagine today, but back then, there were a lot more people bashing LGBTQ folks in public than there were people defending their freedom to be who they were in public," Siew said. "The debate around 377A in 2007 in and outside Parliament took place very publicly and openly, and a lot of people, especially straight allies, stood up in public to oppose anti-LGBT discrimination for the first time."

"While we didn't succeed, for the first time, we united and organised," said Indulekshmi Rajeswari, project leader of a legal guidebook for LGBT families in Singapore. "Alliances and relationships were forged in that attempt which still have an impact on LGBTQ activism today."

"It brought our community out of the closet at a national level," Seah said. "And I do think—without taking anything away from previous efforts—it galvanised our community. I'm not sure Pink Dot would have happened the way it happened [without Repeal 377A]."

Pink Dot and beyond

10 years after Repeal 377A, Hong Lim Park—a modest green space next to Singapore's Central Business District—was packed on July 1, 2017, a heaving sea of pink in the tropical heat.

In its ninth iteration, Pink Dot* had dancers, singers, community booths, celebrity ambassadors and over 100 Singaporean company sponsors; its organisers, Seah included, have been careful to present the event as a family-friendly festival, to better reach protest-phobic Singaporeans.

It'd come a long way from its inception in 2009. "They didn't allow us to use the stage," Hwang recalled. "[Actress and singer] Pam Oei brought a stool, stood on the stool and had a loudhailer. That was the first Pink Dot."

The annual event's astonishing growth might give the impression that much progress has been made for LGBTQ rights in Singapore, but the reality isn't so simple. "There have been overtures [from the government], acknowledgement that we are valuable and that we shouldn't be despised," said Seah. "But institutionally, 377A really chops off our hands and feet. And makes it really hard."

Constitutional challenges mounted against 377A were dismissed by the Court of Appeal in 2014. Pink Dot has also not been left alone; new rules introduced this year forbade foreign companies like Google or Barclays—companies that had been sponsors in previous years—from supporting the event, and required organisers to erect a barricade around the park so that only citizens and Permanent Residents would be allowed entry.

Although LGBTQ issues have gained visibility, the pushback has grown too. Groups like "We are against Pinkdot in Singapore" and "Singaporeans Defending Marriage and Family" have popped up online, monitoring and flagging any perceived move towards equality or "pro-LGBT" content, be it a brief same-sex peck in a touring production of Les Misérables or the existence of children's books featuring different family types—including gay families, as represented by a couple of male penguins in And Tango Makes Three—in the National Library. The government has been accused of pandering to these groups: following complaints, the authorities demanded the kiss be excised from the musical, while the children's books were only saved from being pulped after a public uproar, including a "read-in" where young parents read the books to their offspring outside the library building.

"Once you're given certain dog-whistles or certain cues to let that sort of speech… flow so freely, then it really does," Seah said. "So definitely by the government not repealing 377A back then, the constitutional challenge being unsuccessful, the restrictions on Pink Dot, I think all those things embolden such speech. Hate speech; let's call it for what it is."

As with all movements, there are a variety of perspectives on strategy and advocacy, but the LGBTQ movement shows no signs of throwing in the towel. "I quite appreciated what happened this year with Pink Dot, because then it slaps [young Singaporeans] awake and they finally understand that Pink Dot is not about just coming and having a picnic," said Eileena Lee, founder of LGBTQ community space Pelangi Pride Centre. "We really need protest! And we're not free to do whatever we want to do; it's just a matter of time before they use the laws against us."

A new generation of LGBTQ activists is set to pick up the baton from the veterans. Observers say they're more aware of the need for diversity, which is good news for those who have felt that Singapore's LGBTQ movement has historically skewed too much towards Chinese gay men. "Things are changing in the younger generation of activists and students, who are a lot more open to diversity, who know what intersectionality means, and demand a lot more in terms of gender and sexual diversity inclusion," said Indulekshmi.

There's still no indication of 377A budging from Singaporean law; the prime minister continues to argue for status quo until society changes. This issue continues to lie at the heart of the struggle for LGBTQ equality in Singapore, challenging activists to continue searching for creative and courageous ways to fight for their freedom to love.

* NOTE: *The writer of this piece was a speaker in Pink Dot 2017's Community Voices segment.*

intersectionality: how aspects of a person's societal and political identities might combine to create unique modes of discrimination and privilege
- race, disability, sex, gender, nationality

MORE DANGEROUS THAN NUCLEAR WAR
KATE WALTON | 06 NOV 2017

Despite historical tolerance of different sexual orientations and gender identities, Indonesian politicians are using LGBTQ rights as a wedge issue in their power play.

In 2015, lesbian, gay, bisexual, transgender, and queer (LGBTQ) people suddenly became Indonesia's most hated community. It seemed to come out of nowhere—even queer people themselves were surprised. Government ministers began issuing statements saying that LGBTQ people were in opposition to Pancasila, the state's ideology; universities began banning LGBTQ students from campus; Muslim leaders wrung their hands about LGBTQ people corrupting children; one Minister even described queer people as more dangerous than nuclear war.

"This is a kind of modern warfare," said Defence Minister Ryamizard Ryacudu in February 2016. "It's dangerous because we can't see who our foes are, but out of the blue everyone is brainwashed. Now the [LGBTQ] community is demanding more freedom. It really is a threat."

Minister Ryamizard described the "war against LGBTQ people" as a "proxy war", in which "another state might have occupied the minds of the nation without [us] realising it. In a nuclear war, if a bomb is dropped over Jakarta, Semarang will not be affected. But in a proxy war, everything we know could disappear in an instant. It's dangerous."

"Catching" queerness

The trigger for the Minister's comments was social media debate sparked by a poster from the Sexuality and Gender Resource Centre (SGRC), a student group then-associated with the University of Indonesia. The poster was a draft, released too early, and advertised peer counsellors for people with questions about sexuality and LGBTQ issues. The poster went viral on social media, accompanied by warnings that LGBTQ people were infiltrating university campuses and "converting" students to homosexuality.

"SGRC collaborated with Melela [an NGO] to have LGBTQ peer counsellors to answer questions, and give people information and [build] understanding," explained Ferena Debineva, Founder and Chairperson of SGRC. "The people involved were basically champions [for LGBTQ issues]. They were already out and wanted to talk to you about anything—challenges, depression, or even your happy moments. They were like friends with competencies to say that 'you are not alone and you can also be someone'."

Ferena sighed. "We hadn't finished the poster… And suddenly it was out there, circulating in one night, and creating a backlash. All because of the stigma towards LGBTQ people, [the belief] that providing information means teaching people about LGBTQ, which leads to making LGBTQ accepted and normal, which leads to converting people to LGBTQ."

Misconceptions that people can be converted and "catch" queerness, as though it were an illness, are widespread across Indonesia.

"The idea that LGBTQ is an 'infection' is based on people's ignorance," said Ferena. "[People] believe that LGBTQ is a mental disability or pathological condition. The lack of understanding of religion [also contributes], so the approach is 'prevent or cure', which, unfortunately, is also supported by Indonesian medical professionals."

It's not always been like this

The strangest part of the controversy is that historically, Indonesia has been relatively accepting of LGBTQ people. Violence against queer people is rare, and while many people admit they would not want their child to be gay or transgender, different sexual orientations and gender identities have traditionally been tolerated as long as people kept their activities relatively private.

Transgender women and cross-dressing men (both referred to as *waria*, a portmanteau of the Indonesian words for woman [*wanita*] and man [*pria*]) frequently perform on television and at weddings as comedians, singers and dancers, and are met with uproarious applause. Some of Indonesia's most famous entertainers are transgender or perform as the opposite gender, such as dangdut singer Dorce Gamalama and Javanese dancer Ninik Didik Thowok. Many traditional art forms also involve cross-dressing, such as *ludruk*, an East Javanese comedic performance in which all roles, including female roles, are played by men.

According to Dede Oetoemo, a senior LGBTQ activist, academic, and founded of GAYa NUSANTARA, *waria* have historically been accepted in Indonesia because they "occupy a known social niche" and don't pose a risk to broader society; many people even prefer going to *waria*– or gay-owned salons for haircuts and beauty treatments. Queer language has also had a massive impact on mainstream slang, with hundreds of terms previously only used in queer communities—such as "*alay*" to describe something as over the top or "*jijay*", meaning "disgusting"—now common across the archipelago.

One Indonesian culture even has five different genders. The Bugis people of South Sulawesi recognise cisgender men (*oroane*); cisgender women (*makkunrai*); transgender men (*calalai*); transgender women (*calabai*); and an androgynous third gender reserved for religious figures (*bissu*). *Calalai* are assigned female at birth but live as heterosexual men, dressing in traditionally masculine clothes, working traditionally male jobs such as mechanics and engineers, and living with female partners. *Calabai* are assigned male at birth but live as heterosexual women, and are deeply involved in traditionally feminine activities such as wedding planning. *Bissu*, on the other hand, are considered to possess the aspects of all genders, and perform religious duties in Bugis society. *Calalai*, *calabai*, and *bissu* live as they please: they able to move about freely, entering most male and female spaces, and can marry and adopt children within their community, even though this is not officially enshrined in Indonesian law. All five genders live in peace and each has an important societal role to fulfil.

A convenient political football

Nevertheless, activists point out that there has always been discrimination towards LGBTQ people in Indonesia, even before *reformasi*, the post-1998 "reform" period in which politics and society became more democratic, liberal and open. "The difference is that since *reformasi*, the previously hidden LGBTQ organisations became braver and began organising publicly," said Agustine, founder of Ardhanary Institute, a research and advocacy organisation for lesbian, bisexual, and transgender (LBT) people. "The movement became better co-ordinated and started focusing on [LGBTQ] human rights. Technology has also made the movement more visible."

"[The reactions to this] visibility opened our eyes [and showed us] that hate and discrimination towards LGBTQ people… has actually always existed, and has become embedded in society," Agustine continued. "This happens whenever a social or political issue intensifies in Indonesia: groups trying to gain power use sensitive issues, such as ethnic, religious or LGBTQ issues, as commodities for their own political interests. This opens up space for groups who reject plurality and diversity to act out towards minorities, persecuting them, pushing them out of communities, and becoming violent towards them."

Yuli Rustinawati, head of LGBTQ organisation Arus Pelangi, agrees, saying the issue has become a political football. "It is beneficial [to make this a political issue]," she said. "It will be used to make a profit, to get people's votes in elections. [Politicians] will be seen as heroes, as though they created public order, a healthy and safe society."

Some politicians are even encouraging hatred towards LGBTQ communities by equating them with radical Islam. One recent example came from the head of Parliamentary Commission VIII, Ali Taher Parasong. Commenting on the banning of extremist Islamic group Hizbut Tahrir Indonesia (HTI) in July following a new mass organisation law, Ali was quoted by Merdeka.com as saying that the banning was inappropriate, since "radicalism doesn't only emerge out of religious radicalism, but also secularism". He argued that if HTI was to be banned, LGBTQ organisations should be as well, explaining that "the LGBT problem is a huge one, as are drugs, so why are other mass organisations [being banned]?"

It's not just politicians doing this, either. "Both directly and indirectly… all elements—political parties, mass organisations, even the Indonesian Ulema Council [the country's top Muslim clerical body]—have been pushing LGBTQ people into a corner," Yuli explained. "They do this by [attacking us] personally, by limiting our freedom of association and by issuing fatwas and laws that threaten to criminalise us."

"They say that LGBTQ [people] are a threat to the nation, that we are destroyers of society's morals," Yuli added. "And the statements made have become the weapons of intolerant groups, mass organisations supposedly acting in the name of religion, to perpetrate violence towards us. We are worried about our safety."

Evidence of these changing attitudes can be found across the archipelago. A *waria*-only Islamic school for adults in Yogyakarta was forced to shut in February 2016 after repeated threats from local fundamentalist groups, despite police promises to protect the students. The school had been operating without problems since 2008. More recently, in January 2017, a four-day-long event celebrating *waria* and *bissu* in Soppeng, South Sulawesi, was disbanded by police, ostensibly because organisers did not have a permit. The head of the group told BBC Indonesia that they had tried to obtain a permit, but had been "ping-ponged" around for two weeks: "They purposely made it difficult for us."

Further clampdowns—but not all hope is lost

The latest worrying development is a bill from the Parliamentary Legislative Body, which on 28 September agreed to ban all LGBTQ content on television, including cross-dressing and men displaying "feminine traits".

Andreas Harsono, Indonesia Researcher for Human Rights Watch (HRW), says the bill was successful because of bias, ignorance and belief in rampant propaganda. Lawmakers are "not learning enough about human rights, science and so on," he argued. "They believe this nonsense [that homosexuality is contagious], but some are also doing this to appease the increasingly-conservative community."

Also concerning is a proposed revision to the Criminal Code. The current draft Code plans to outlaw sex outside of marriage as well as the practice of *kumpul kebo*, where unmarried couples (of any gender) live together under the same roof. A fine and jailtime of up to one year is being discussed, and could become law as early as the end of 2017.

Despite this, activists are tentatively positive about the future, if somewhat subdued. In late September, after much bluster, the Indonesian government accepted most of the recommendations made during the UN's Universal Periodic Review in May 2017, among which were two recommendations relating to the protection of LGBTQ people.

When asked if she thinks they can change people's minds on LGBT, Ferena responds hesitantly: "We can at least change how [the debate] affects people, by having inclusive participation."

"Perhaps what people are afraid of is not the LGBTQ person itself, but the imaginary ideas," she said. "Because they don't think they have to interact with them, so they don't feel that LGBTQ people are as human as they are. We must change it so that there are LGBTQ people are not seen as imaginary ideas, ghosting around us."

THE ONGOING STRUGGLE FOR LGBTQ EQUALITY IN VIETNAM

CALUM STUART, DAM XUAN VIET | 09 NOV 2017

LGBTQ rights in Vietnam have improved in recent years, but traditional social norms and stigmas still make life difficult for queer individuals in the country.

"Everyone push together, please! Make room for each other!" the organisers shout above the chatter of over a thousand people cramming into a hotel ballroom clearly too small for their number. It's mild chaos as they rush to find somewhere to sit or stand, and all free space in the room quickly disappears.

Although squashed together, the attendees of the final day of VietPride 2017: Saigon in late September are excited and enthusiastic. Waving rainbow flags and sporting matching face paint, the young crowd—most of whom appear to be under the age of 30—cheer the oncoming acts on stage: dance groups are followed by same-sex couples playing games of "how well do you know your partner?", the US ambassador to Vietnam introduces his husband and gives an uplifting speech in broken Vietnamese, and drag queens, in dazzling attire, march proudly up and down the room.

With its over-the-top colours and styles, VietPride's big day is living up to the expectations of any gay pride event around the world, but behind the scenes, the organisers are becoming increasingly anxious. The venue's lack of space has forced attendees to congregate at the front of the hotel while waiting for the upcoming street parade. The crowd has attracted the attention of the authorities, who have threatened to shut down the entire event. It's a situation the organisers are already familiar with, having experiencing something similar just two days ago.

"The Rainbow Night [musical show] was cut short by the police," says one of VietPride's organisers, Nguyen Thien Tri Phong, a project assistant from the Ho Chi Minh City-based lesbian, gay, bisexual, transgender and queer (LGBTQ) rights group Information, Connecting and Sharing (ICS). "They cut the music midway through, even after we showed them the permits, saying they would punish [fine] us, and the venue we hired too, if we didn't go home. They gave some vague reasons, like they were worried we were going to spread 'bad propaganda'."

Progress?

On paper, the last decade has brought big changes for Vietnam's LGBTQ community. Headlines in the international media paint an image of a more progressive country, decriminalising same-sex weddings (even though legal recognition of same-sex marriages or civil unions has not yet materialised) and allowing those who have undergone gender-affirming surgery to legally register under their assigned gender. These developments are even more pronounced when compared to Vietnam's neighbours—such as Singapore, Indonesia and Malaysia—where restrictions range from laws forbidding male-on-male sex, to the public floggings of alleged homosexuals.

Although the communist country is often lambasted for its woeful human rights and free speech records, Vietnam has sometimes been portrayed as a shining light for LGBTQ equality in Southeast Asia.

"Back in 2007, LGBTQ people were considered a social evil, a bad influence or a disease which could be fixed," says Vuong Kha Phong, an LGBTQ Rights Program Officer for the Institute of Study, Economics and the Environment (iSEE). This largely changed via the Internet, which offered a space for LGBTQ people to share stories and compare ideas. From there, friendships and communities evolved into groups that organised and steadily worked their way into the public eye. "It happened from the bottom up, starting from the community, then the public, and then the government.

"LGBTQ issues are often seen in the government's eyes as peaceful—it's not politically sensitive for them. We don't want to fight or to start a revolution, so they are often supportive or ready to listen to us."

Vietnam's LGBTQ movement has come a long way in a short time. But despite progress on the legal front, LGBTQ people in Vietnam still face widespread discrimination and harassment, often stemming from social stigmas. At home, at school and at work, people who are openly gay or transgender face daily reminders that they are somehow "different", or living outside of acceptable social norms. "There are strict gender roles placed on the male and the female [in Vietnam]," says Vuong.

"The male has to be strong; he has to be the breadwinner. He has to get a wife and be financially reliable. The female has to bear children, she has to have a family, she has to listen to the husband.

"We see a lot of problems, especially for young transgender people. They dress as their gender identity and face a lot of abuse—verbal abuse—from their family and their friends. We recently had a suicide of a young transgender guy because he couldn't handle the pressure of his family telling him to dress up 'normally', as a girl. It's very upsetting."

At home, in school, at work

Bullying against LGBTQ students remains rampant in Vietnam's schools. Over 70% of gay or transgender high school students surveyed in 2016 said they had suffered from physical and/or verbal abuse. The problem runs deeper than childish or adolescent teasing, as there are few incentives among educational establishments to teach inclusivity or offer information on different sexual orientations. Many LGBTQ students drop out of school early as a result.

These attitudes often continue into the workplace, with few domestic businesses are wary of hiring openly LGBTQ employees. There are also currently no provisions in Vietnam's Labour Code to prevent discriminatory employment policies. Studies show that many gay men and women choose to remain closeted so as not to draw attention or ire from their colleagues.

Even gay or gay-friendly bars are often hesitant to make their support for the LGBTQ community widely known. "Our Rainbow Night—a very peaceful musical night—was cut short by the police just because it was LGBTQ-themed," says Nguyen. "Make that comparison to a local business, and they wouldn't stand a chance. If you market [your establishment] as a gay bar the authorities will notice you and that might make a lot of people afraid, not to mention the fuss you'll get [from the authorities]. They can just come to your place and ask for a bribe or give you a hard time."

These problems are magnified in provinces outside of the country's urban centres. Over 60 million people—about two-thirds of Vietnam's total population—live in more conservative rural areas, which the largely urban-based LGBTQ groups struggle to reach. "A lot of our resources and a lot of our events are happening in Hanoi, Ho Chi Minh City or Danang," says Vuong. "So the people living in other far away provinces don't really have access to resources or information."

"Oftentimes, [LGBTQ activists] from the cities go to the provinces, but they don't listen to us. To them, LGBTQ rights are pretty much a Western value or ideology—they say that in Vietnam we don't have LGBTQ people; we don't have these Western values."

Targeting the rural areas has become one of the focal points for LGBTQ activism in Vietnam, a goal aided by the economic growth the country has experienced in recent years. The boom in urbanisation has led to more people moving from the provinces to the cities, where they come into contact with established support and advocacy groups. They later bring the knowledge that they've picked up back to their hometowns, thus extending the reach of these city-dwelling groups.

"I think this is crucial to the movement… if we want to target people who are living far away," says Vuong. "The thing that will change their minds is the personal stories—of their friends, of their families, of their neighbours—who are LGBTQ."

The challenge of organising

There has been tangible progress in advancing the cause, but LGBTQ activists are quick to acknowledge that the nuts and bolts of Vietnam's legal statutes still presents a major obstacle.

Although LGBTQ groups aim to work with, rather than protest, the government's authority, the movement is still a challenge to the status quo. The country's authoritarian system—which curtails the ability of advocacy groups to increase public visibility or organise properly—essentially hobbles the movement's long-term progress. "In Vietnam we don't really have freedom of speech, we don't have freedom of association or of assembly," says Vuong. "LGBTQ groups still can't legally register, they can't legally march, they can't legally protest. So a lot of legal framework prohibits the LGBTQ groups [which] can't really develop into an organisation or an institute without the law allowing them."

Events such as VietPride are a very recent occurrence. While officially permitted, large assemblies of people remain a contentious issue for the local authorities, and continue to run into difficulties on the street level. "We've been 'pinged' by the authorities since 2015," says Nguyen. "VietPride [that year] attracted thousands of people in a public space, and they were afraid of large gatherings. As a result, in 2016 we couldn't hire any outdoor public space whatsoever! There's no document or order prohibiting the event, but the authorities could be interfering 'behind the scenes' so that every location is scared of having us."

Getting bigger every year

As one of 2017's main VietPride events draws to a close, the attendees proceed outside; despite the threat of police closure, the street parade is about to go ahead as scheduled. For about an hour, hundreds of people, making show of support for LGBTQ equality, parade up and down the main boulevard in Vietnam's biggest city. This is something which would have been unheard of in Vietnam barely a decade ago.

The community is still very much in a nascent stage, working to change entrenched societal norms and a conservative legal system. It'll be a long, uphill battle, but despite the obstacles, LGBTQ activists remain cautiously optimistic, and hopeful that the networks which have been established will allow the movement to gather momentum.

"We do have a good position; we have a good foundation," says Vuong. "There are a lot of the community-based groups all over Vietnam… which I think is a good foundation for the movement. It is getting bigger and bigger every year."

HOW DISCRIMINATION KILLS GAY MEN IN SINGAPORE

JOHN LEE | 19 NOV 2017

Contrary to the Prime Minister's stated position of "Live and Let Live", cradle to grave discrimination in Singapore results in gay men being economically poorer and less healthy, and consequently leading shorter and more impoverished lives.

T he gay man, or more precisely, someone perceived as a cisgender male person who is attracted to one or more cisgender male person/people, is the target of systemic cradle-to-grave discrimination in modern Singapore. This essay discusses five aspects of such discrimination—law, military, housing, education, and health—and explain how gays attempt to retain agency, dignity, and autonomy in the face of these respective constraints.

Law

Over the past decade, many activists and academics repeated this clause *ad infinitum*: Section 377A of the Penal Code stipulates that "any male person who, in public or private, commits, or abets the commission of, or procures or attempts to procure the commission by any male person of, any act of gross indecency with another male person, shall be punished with imprisonment for a term which may extend to two years." Because of the wide-ranging interpretations and implications of this law, which was drafted and introduced to the Straits Settlements in 1938 and subsequently into the Penal Code of Singapore, it is not unreasonable to say that every single aspect of a gay person's life is thereafter affected through and through.

Activists have tried thrice in the past decade to repeal the law without success. The first time was in October 2007 when Nominated Member of Parliament Siew Kum Hong put forth a petition to amend the law through parliamentary action. A counter-petition and rebuttals from other members of parliament ensued. Consequently, Prime Minister Lee Hsien Loong declared for the status quo to remain on the grounds of a heteronormative society and the assurance not to actively enforce the law.[1]

The parliamentary promise failed to effect changes in the law enforcers' operations. At least twice in 2010, culprits accused under Section 377A given amended charges. This time, one of the criminals, Tan Eng Hong, decided to raise a constitutional challenge that triggered a furore in traditional and social media. These public and private debates were sustained by a subsequent challenge from a gay couple, Lim Meng Suang and Kenneth Chee Mun-Leon in November 2012.[2] While both cases were unsuccessful, they surfaced in the media and over conversations multiple aspects of being gay. They revealed the multifaceted nature of being gay: like everyone else, some gay men have sex in public, and some in private; some are monogamous and others promiscuous; some are rich and powerful, but many are poor and powerless. More than anything else, they revealed both how banal and typical the lives of gay men are.

These national events aggrandize the influence of gay people. In fact, gay men bear little hope of the law changing towards their favor. Unless they are themselves lawyers, the legal jargon and cost of proceedings are major obstacles. As for garnering social acceptance, long-term sociological surveys over the past decade continue to affirm the conservative tenor of the population. One such survey argues that conformity to norms, intrinsic religiosity, Western orientation, interpersonal contact, mediated exposure and perception of homosexuality as a choice are all factors salient in forming and changing attitudes towards gays and lesbians.[3]

Military
While the ban on gays serving in the Singapore Armed Forces was only lifted in 2000, the Armed Forces adapted the Category of 302 from the International Classification of Diseases (9th revision) and continued

---

1 Lim Puay Ling, "Penal Code Section 377A", http://eresources.nlb.gov.sg/infopedia/articles/ SIP_1639_2010-01-31.html.

2 George Baylon Radics, "Section 377A in Singapore and the (De)Criminalization of Homosexuality", Reconstruction 15(2), 2015.

3 Detenber, B. H., Ho, S. S., Neo, R. L., Malik, S. and Cenite, M., Influence of value predispositions, interpersonal contact, and mediated exposure on public attitudes toward homosexuals in Singapore. Asian Journal of Social Psychology 16, 2013, 181–196.

to inquire into the sexual orientation of all prospective enlistees.[4] The specific clause considers the "exclusive or predominant sexual attraction for persons of the same sex with or without physical relationship" as a sexual deviance or disorder. In other words, the Armed Forces believes that there is something wrong with gay men merely because they are gay.

During the pre-enlistment health assessment, new recruits are asked about their sexual orientation. Upon the declaration of oneself as a homosexual or transgender, the personnel undergo a round of psychological inquiry and are classified under the category of "302". The classification of the conscripts determines their vocation and reporting hours. Soldiers labelled "302" are given non-commissioned positions and are not allowed to stay overnight. Regardless of fitness condition, they are excused from two out of five physical test stations.

The military community behaves similarly to most other civil communities, such as corporate organizations and factory assembly lines, in the prevalence of how certain characteristics are considered desirable or objectionable, and those who display them are picked out to be admired and/or bullied. As social attitudes toward sexual orientation change, lines between homosexuality and homosociality are blurred within the armed forces. Here after all is where the principles of social bonding and national cohesiveness are supposed to be inculcated.[5] Discounting the self-declaration, the military is perhaps the best equalizer of all Singaporean men, regardless of sexual orientation.

Housing and Space

Space, according to the official narrative, is scarce. Living spaces are planned and constructed skyward and underground. With sand from neighboring countries such as Cambodia and Indonesia, reclamation has steadily expanded Singapore's land area. Existing areas are frequently redeveloped. National planners distribute this space among

---

4 Sexual and Gender Identity Disorders 302. http://www.icd9data.com/2012/
    Volume1/290-319/300-316/302/default.htm

5 Chris K. K. Tan, "Oi Recruit! Wake Up Your Idea!": Homosexuality and Cultural Citizenship
    in the Singaporean Military', in Jun Zubillaga-Pow and Audrey Yue (eds.) Queer Singapore:
    Illiberal Citizenship and Mediated Cultures, Hong Kong: Hong Kong University Press, 2012,
    71-82.

the population according to discrete demographics—e.g. race, marital status, household income, and citizenship status. These urban planning and housing policies aim for an idealized form of society, as envisioned by the state, and hence discriminate against gays and lesbians, who are excluded from this ideal vision.

Same-sex partnerships are not recognized by the state. The permission to acquire public housing, subsidized or otherwise, is granted almost exclusively to married heterosexual couples with or without children. Before the introduction of the Singles Scheme (which permits unmarried individuals above the age of 35 to purchase a two-room flat), gays who could not afford properties available on the private market either remained in their parents' apartments or rented rooms from others. Thus, real estate privileges accorded to married couples are denied to same-sex or unmarried cohabitants. In this vein, families with homosexual children have less access to state resources, financial or otherwise. Furthermore, gays face the frequent closing and depopulation of heterotopia, that is, differentiated spaces patronized not by the mainstream but mostly by homosexuals—"safer spaces" where gays can socialize without fear.[6] These include bars, clubs, saunas and cruising grounds. The common notion of the public display of affection and intimacy—a basic right that is taken for granted by many people—are, for gay people, relegated to other secretive spaces, such as motels and private residences.

Ditto with everyday expression of intimacy. Physical gestures, such as kissing, hugging, and the holding of hands, are perceived as awkward when performed in view of the public. The fashion and actions that gay and gay couples can do in public belongs to a limited vocabulary. In general, contemporary Singaporean society implicitly dictates a certain conservative form of dressing and acting; gays have overtime toned down the colors and tightness of their clothes and reduced the amount of bodily accessories lest being discriminated at work or in public. This personal negotiation between the political distribution of space and the communal management of the body represents a psychological and social translation from real homophobia to imagined homophobia.

Gays are resigned to little public space carved out for them so much so that they eventually adapt their behavior to suit the environment.

<hr>

6 Jun Zubillaga-Pow, 'Foucault v. Singapore: Biopolitics and Geopolitics in Contemporary Queer Films', in Stephen Teo and Liew Kai Khiun (eds.), Singapore Cinema: New Perspectives. London and New York: Routledge, 2017, 129-143.

Gays understand they have drawn the short straw with respect to their habitation and mobility; they recognize that some places accommodate them better than the others. As the city constructs more shopping malls and park grounds, gays are secretly gentrifying suburban locales beyond the public gaze. Led by their inner yearnings for safer spaces, they have, through their instincts, identified certain quiet spots conducive for making contact and hanging out. Some venture onto these places for a quick thrill, but most frequent these locations in search of like-minded individuals for friendship or relationship.

Education and Culture

Gay people are rendered invisible within the education curriculum: gay people or topics related to them are almost completely absent from school textbooks. Except for the definition and legal provisions regarding homosexuality, other important issues such as attachments and abuses, coming out to family and friends, and sexual health are not included in the sexuality education programs. In 2009, a moral panic broke out between the Ministry of Education and various communal vendors of Sexuality Education programs. After an internal review, the "abstinence" version substituted the "comprehensive" one.[7]

Growing up in such a heteronormative environment, the young gay person has no role model to emulate or reflect upon. On mainstream media, positive portrayal of gay men, lesbian and transgender characters are heavily censored. Films and plays with homosexual and transgender themes are automatically classified unsuitable for patrons aged under 21-years-old; and such television programs are aired during later slots with a "Parental Guidance" warning on the corner of the screen. The Media Development Authority upholds the ambiguous guideline where "alternative lifestyles" must not be glamorized or promoted on print, radio and screen.

The modern gay man is forced to be adroit to locate the relevant entertainment for his own pleasure on a daily basis. Social media, web chatrooms and video-sharing portals have satisfied the leisure and education of the gays (as they have been for everyone else). Gays have set up their own versions of most media and digital applications, encompassing

---

7 Warren Mark Liew, 'Sex (education) in the City: Singapore's sexuality education curriculum', Discourse: Studies in the Cultural Politics of Education, 2014, 705-717.

the entire spectrum from Christian cell groups to pornographic group chats. Gays also benefit from international exchanges with foreigners in multinational companies and global conglomerates, such as Huawei and Facebook, some of which are equally active in sponsoring local activist events. The increasing geographical mobility of local and foreign gays inevitably generates vast opportunities for cross-cultural interactions.

Bangkok is one such destination frequented by gays. The anonymity of being in a foreign land allowed gays to escape the prying gaze of an erstwhile homophobic nation-state.[8] Bars, clubs, strip-shows, go-go boys, cheap hotels: all of these provide the freedom that gay men so crave for. They can also find affordable apparel, undergarments, erotic literature, pornographic videos, and sex toys. With the introduction of budget air travel, Bangkok became and remains the liberal haven for gays to be emancipated from their everyday repressions. Equally accepting of gay people and behavior, the other city that attracts countless gays is Taipei. Chinese Singaporeans share cultural similarities with the Taiwanese and feel very much at home in the city. With heavy influence from the USA, the gay culture there is diverse and vibrant. In addition to the mainstream tourist attractions in the food and scenery, gays are drawn to the city for the local boys (who also undergo military conscription) and the many gay-friendly amenities and large-scale themed events.

Health

Like everyone else, gays fall sick and grow old. Despite paying the same level of taxes, gay men receive only minuscule amount of the state benefits in comparison to those doled out to married heterosexual couples with children. In terms of integrated healthcare, gays receive far less support. Unless bestowed with inheritance, neither can gays rely on the savings (via the Central Provident Fund) from his partner nor distant relatives. Almost all of their medical expenses have to be borne by themselves, without which an early demise could be inevitable. Some international studies in developed countries have shown that the life expectancy for

---

8 Alex Au, 'Speaking of Bangkok: Thailand in the History of Gay Singapore', in Peter A. Jackson (ed.) Queer Bangkok: 21st Century Markets, Media, and Rights, Hong Kong: Hong Kong University Press, 2011, 181-192.

homosexuals is very much shorter than that of heterosexuals.[9] Judging from the lack of communal visibility of older gay men, it is most likely to be the case in Singapore as well. A lamentable point to be raised within an Asian cultural tradition is that very few of the gay man's descendants will pay respect at his grave or tomb after his decease.

In the past, gays with potential health risks and symptoms would hesitate before visiting their General Practitioners for fear of being reported to the medical or criminal authorities. Sexually-related diseases also received little specialist intervention up until the early 2000s, when the DSC (Department of Sexually Transmitted Infections Control) Clinic was the only clinic dealing with heterosexual and later to include homosexual clients. Subsequently, Action For AIDS (a Singaporean charity) began anonymous services thrice a week for men who have sex with men and that saw an increase in testing and correspondingly HIV-positive numbers. Today, more private clinics are offering the most up-to-date testing technology and medicine for HIV and STI. Costs are also substantially subsidized by the state accordingly to the household income of the patient. That said, the social stigma attached with people living with HIV remains strong. Attitudes towards belittling and rejection, say, in the contexts of employment or friendship, are two of the most severe discriminations that continue to trouble HIV-positive gays today.

Like within the medical sector, social workers have in the past decade been adapting their profession with the counselling of gay clients. The understanding of the basic life courses of the gay person living and working in Singapore is essential to the successful management of the clients' social and psychological issues whether they are related to his sexual orientation or otherwise. Growing up and being discriminated at every stage in one's life can bear a heavy emotional strain on the mental well-being of a person. (The multiple façades that gays have to put on to pass off as heterosexual in the military, the workplace and, most crucially, at home with the family, create complicated emotional vicissitudes, often resulting in internalized homophobic feelings.) As with

9 P. Cameron, K. Cameron, W. L. Playfair, 'Does homosexual activity shorten life?', Psychological Report 83(3), 1998, 847-66; Marten Frisch and Henrik Bronnum-Hansen, 'Mortality Among Men and Women in Same-Sex Marriage: A National Cohort Study of 8333 Danes', American Journal of Public Health 99(1), 2009, 133-37.

other cultural differences, counsellors and social workers would have to gradually address these psychosocial phenomena as a fundamental part of their practice.

Intersectional Futures

As society progresses and diversifies with the influx of international migrants, figures and voices previously not seen or heard become more visible and audible within enclaves of the gay communities. Rather than belonging to the more apparent demographics of a middle class, English-speaking ethnic-Chinese Singaporean, the "new gays", who have "come out" as poor, physically challenged, or an ethnic minority, have thwarted the conventional stereotype of the liberal-minded, high-maintenance dandy. Gays with hearing impairment want to be seen attending public gay events, such as the Pink Dot protests and outdoor gay parties on Sentosa island; as do some Malay men who like men, positioning themselves at the forefront of youth, health and international community activism. Gay residents from international corporations as well as other Southeast Asian countries, such as Malaysia, Myanmar, and the Philippines, have also made their presence felt, participating in cultural and social activities and volunteering their expertise in business and legal matters.

The government has however maintained their reservations about repealing the 377A law, most probably to remain in accordance with the intrinsic beliefs of the political elites as well as the constitutions of neighboring India, Indonesia, and Malaysia.[10] The claim that, social values, vis-à-vis the issue of homosexuality, will have to be the final arbitrator of its legitimate status, remained contentious. For a majority to determine the acts and thoughts of the minority already presupposes homosexuality as a deviance, criminological or otherwise. In addition, any gay-friendly speech or identity may jeopardize the reputation and profession of the speakers and place them at significantly personal risk, raising the stake for prospective change-makers. Muslim and civil servants who have come out as gay have experienced death threats and job terminations/career stagnations respectively.

---

10 Parliamentary Debates Official Reports, Parl. 11, Session 1, Vol. 83, Sitting 15, 23 October 2007, Bills. https://sprs.parl.gov.sg/search/topic.jsp?currentTopicID=00002031-WA& currentPubID=00004748-WA

The future for gays will continue to be grim unless they can circumvent the social prescriptions of compulsory heterosexuality and homosexual norms. Many have resigned to placate the demands of the family and society by getting married and having children, while others seek out an alternative of "silent acknowledgement"—that is, keeping one's sexual orientation and relations as ambiguous as possible giving the allowance for others to make their own conclusions—as a survival tactic against other challenges in life. Among these is the ascendency of the conservative gay—someone who does not counter the discrimi- nations but leads a neoliberal and self-centered lifestyle. The increasing prevalence of this materialistic outlook will inevitably lead to the continued suppression of gays, whether self-imposed or otherwise. As the Prime Minister Lee Hsien Loong reiterated in the 2007 Parliamentary debates: 'the [Singaporean] attitude is a pragmatic one—we live and let live.' However, as I have shown in this essay, such a moral stance has not been put into practice by the various government ministries. Contrary to the Prime Minister's stated position of "live and let live", cradle to grave discrimination in Singapore results in gay men being economically poorer and less healthy, and consequently leading shorter and more impoverished lives. Discrimination is, quite literally, killing gay men, both spiritually and physically.

The greatest irony is the unconscious internalization of pragmatism for a majority of the gay men. By accepting (and even embracing) the status quo, gay men have given implicit consent to state control and discrimination from cradle to grave, thereby contributing to their own suffering and deprecation. Any form of personal autonomy is a tall order even in the near future.

BEHIND TIMOR-LESTE'S PRIDE

SOPHIE RAYNOR | 07 JUN 2018

Timor-Leste's first Pride parade last year was heralded in international headlines as a major win for LGBTQ equality, but advocates and activists say there's still a long way to go to shift mindsets.

O n a sunny afternoon by Dili's waterfront in June last year, throngs of activists in T-shirts crowded onto blocked-off streets, milling behind bright banners as they waited for the band to start. A pause, a shared intake of breath… then, the sharp *rap-rap-rap* of a snare drum and hundreds took that first step together, marking the beginning of Timor-Leste's first-ever LGBTQ Pride parade.

One small step, one giant leap; the joyous, historic march garnered Timor-Leste international attention[1], a televised endorsement from the Prime Minister, and catapulted its charismatic organisers to brief media fame. The march was heralded a victory for an overwhelmingly Catholic nation neighbouring a country suddenly turning on its LGBTQ community.[2]

Reading rhapsodic coverage of the march, you'd be forgiven for thinking Timor-Leste an LGBTQ paradise, an oasis of tolerance in a region of surging discrimination.[3] Praise for the community is doubtlessly hard-fought and well-deserved, but as queer activists prep for the next march—planned as part of a three-day festival in July—the shine of a single event belies a grittier day-to-day.

Rejection and reconciliation

"I hate you. I looked up to you, and now I don't even know you. Gay people are monsters."

---

1 https://mashable.com/2017/07/04/pride-parade-east-timor/

2 https://newnaratif.com/journalism/more-dangerous-than-nuclear-war/

3 https://theaseanpost.com/article/lgbt-community-threatened-asean

The message came over Facebook while Natalino Guterres—the coordinator of the youth-run social inclusion network that organised the Pride march—was studying abroad. His brother had shared a homophobic Facebook post, so Guterres took the moment to come out in a private message. The men didn't speak for two years after the exchange.

Moments before the drums started up that day last June, the brothers, long reconciled, embraced before the crowd.

Guterres had asked his brother to attend the march, but his hopes weren't high. "He was working as an election observer, and they didn't finish until 10, so he said he'd try to come, but, you know," he says on a warm night in Dili, nearly a year after the now-famous embrace.

That moment was a long time coming for Guterres, who was bullied for being different growing up. Just last year, the activist got into arguments over a newspaper article declaring that transgender people bring shame upon Timor-Leste.[4]

"My father saw it, he said, 'Everyone looks up to you and I just hope you're not like that'," Guterres says. "'And if you are, are you willing to change?' He made me promise."

A nervous laugh belies his next comment. Feeling as if he would never be accepted at home, Guterres had previously considered moving abroad permanently, or even committing suicide.

"Beyond the joyous performance of Pride lies a deep-seeded problem area where culture, religion and rights clash," confirms Ryan Silverio, the regional coordinator of ASEAN's Sexual Orientation and Gender Identity/Expression (SOGIE) Caucus. While Timor-Leste is a secular state, approximately 97% of the population identifies as Catholic.[5]

Guterres is a reluctant spokesperson, quick to acknowledge that Timor-Leste's queer community is more than just one gay man, and anxious to emphasise that he can only speak to his own experience. He's aware of his privileged position: fluency in English, an overseas education and a plum job in development consulting places him firmly in a group of Timorese elite not representative of the country's majority rural population. This sensibility anchors his activism; the social inclusion network he coordinates is named Hatutan, which means to pass on or hand down.

4 https://timoragora.blogspot.com/2017/04/kazamentu-trans-jender-kontra-doutrina.html

5 https://cathnews.co.nz/2017/10/26/timor-leste-government-church-partner/

Sharing experiences for the first time

A pioneering study published in November 2017 by researcher Iram Saeed and her activist partner Bella Galhos reveals the context and challenges experienced by lesbian and bisexual women and transgender men in Timor-Leste. The report captures statements of queer people in the country, several of them hiding their sexual orientation by living outwardly heterosexual lives.[6]

"I was raped by my own uncle who believed he could change my sexual orientation by pushing me into a heterosexual relationship," one lesbian woman told researchers. "I got pregnant but I found traditional medicine to get it aborted. After that I left home."

Women interviewed in the study speak of being assaulted, burnt, slapped; one said she'd been tied up in the back of a car and dragged across a road for everyone to see. Others shared experiences of leaving school and work because of teasing and ridicule.

"It was believed that I like to have sex with children and all children in the family were kept away from me," one trans man said.

For many, the terminology used by the researchers was utterly foreign—both because they'd never heard it, and also because Tetun, Timor-Leste's most widely spoken local language, lacks the vocabulary to describe queer people in neutral or positive terms. The researchers instead used Portuguese words.

Guterres says that a perception exists of gay men as predatory.

"I feel like, um, people sort of, people sort of compare you to… just *that*." He laughs, shifting hesitantly in his seat. His reference to "that" is undefined, but the negative connotations are clear.

"That's all that we had. It's like, do you want to be one of *those*?"

"Bringing shame to us"

Until as recently as two years back, Romiaty da Costa Barreto had to wear masculine clothing when returning to her village to visit family. A transgender woman who works for CODIVA, a diversity coalition established as the country's first LGBTQ group, she's faced confusion, harassment and abuse for her gender expression.

---

6 https://aseansogiecaucus.org/images/resources/publications/ASC%20-%20Rede%20
Feto%20-%20LBT%20Womens%20Lives%20in%20Timor%20Leste.pdf

"If I was wearing women's clothing the neighbours used to say that I was bringing shame to them," she says. "So I adapted and tried to become closer with them, tell them about my experiences, so they can understand and accept it. If people are discriminating against you and you distance yourself, they will continue."

She cites legal reform that will allow transgender people to change their legal names and genders as a key priority for Timor-Leste. "It will be hard, but that's the plan."

On paper, Timor-Leste's LGBTQ community appears already well-protected from discrimination. The country's constitution enshrines human rights for all, and its representative to the United Nations has enthusiastically signed a suite of recommendations and resolutions confirming the rights of the LGBTQ community.[7] In March 2017, Timor-Leste informed the Human Rights Council it was accepting two recommendations made on sexual orientation and gender identity.

But a push to explicitly guarantee equal rights for LGBTQ people in the constitution's 2002 drafting was voted down.[8] Opponents of the clause variously said its inclusion would create conflict with the Catholic Church, that the country isn't ready to deal with the issue, and that its inclusion would "give people ideas".[9]

Iram Saeed says an explicit constitutional guarantee would require policymakers to consider the LGBTQ community's needs as part of their regular decision-making process. Too often, she says, organisations and individuals in positions of power see LGBTQ rights as a separate issue or area of consideration; in this way, human rights organisations are able to derogate responsibility towards queer people whose struggles should fall within their remit.

"[W]hen [LGBTQ people are] not continuing their education because they're being bullied on account of their gender identity, when it affects their job prospects, because they don't have the education to get a good job, these things are affecting them," Saeed says. "It's affecting them as well. But [human rights organisations] don't see it as their issue."

---

7 https://aseansogiecaucus.org/images/resources/publications/ASC%20-%20Rede%20Feto%20-%20LBT%20Womens%20Lives%20in%20Timor%20Leste.pdf

8 https://aseansogiecaucus.org/images/resources/publications/ASC%20-%20Rede%20Feto%20-%20LBT%20Womens%20Lives%20in%20Timor%20Leste.pdf

9 https://press.anu.edu.au/publications/timor-lestes-bill-rights

International support

While local groups are dogged in their efforts, support from international institutions have given the issue a significant boost. Saeed's report was published through local women's network Rede Feto and funded by the United Nations Development Programme's Being LGBTI in Asia project[10], and the United Nations Human Rights Advisor funds activities in Timor-Leste.

"Some people think [that the concept of LGBTQ] is a foreign import, so it's good that we ran [the Pride march], but it's still important to have credibility from these big organisations," says Guterres of the march, which he and a UN Women staffer discussed for the first time a mere two weeks before the event.

Hatutan had moved quickly, organising the 500-person-strong march and concert, including wrangling worldwide media coverage and producing branded shirts still seen today on the streets of Dili. "I accept and respect people's differences," read the shirts, which were provided free to Hatutan through an international donor network. "How about you?"

"Despite the many positive efforts and progress being made to advance gender equality, [LGBTQ] people continue to face considerable violence, discrimination and exclusion because they do not conform to perceived norms of gender as binary and fixed, and attitudes which assume all people are heterosexual," Sunita Caminha, UN Women's Head of Office in Timor-Leste, tells *New Naratif*. For UN Women to realise its mandate for gender equality, she says, LGBTQ people must be seen and heard.

Work by the ASEAN SOGIE caucus has also increased regional support for Timor-Leste's LGBTQ community. Its 2017 country assessment, *Building a Rainbow in Timor-Leste*[11], laid out the context and challenges faced by the community, and recommended a consolidated national response and investment in LGBTQ youth. The caucus supported Saeed and Galhos' research, and helped Guterres and Hatutan prepare their documentary *The Road to Acceptance*, which showed families accepting their LGBTQ siblings and children.

---

10 http://www.asia-pacific.undp.org/content/rbap/en/home/operations/projects/overview/being-lgbt-in-asia.html

11 https://aseansogiecaucus.org/images/resources/publications/Building%20A%20Rainbow%20in%20Timor%20Leste.pdf

"Such cross-country collaboration between Timorese activists and comrades in the region is putting Southeast Asian solidarity in action again," says Silverio.

Building momentum

Last year's march wasn't actually Timor-Leste's first gay rights event. The previous year, CODIVA organised[12] an LGBTQ conference, and HIV activists have been advocating for decades.[13] But the march was Timor-Leste's first groundswell—a national moment emboldened by an affirmation from then-Prime Minister Rui de Araújo of the LGBTQ community's worth.[14]

While organising the march, Hatutan volunteers had decided to try and record a message of support from the prime minister. They wrote to his media advisor on a Monday in early June, then settled back to wait, expecting to be kept on tenterhooks for the customary couple of weeks.

They received a positive reply later that same day. When they went to his office to shoot the video, not a single word of their proposed draft had been changed. The message was screened on national television two days before the march.

Barreto says the video was widely shared on social media, and helped increase awareness and tolerance of LGBTQ people in the country. "The general community who didn't yet understand the lives of LGBT people could start to understand," she says.

When it comes to raising awareness, individual stories and public faces are crucial in the struggle to get people thinking and talking.

"We need more strong voices," says Saeed. "We need more women coming out to talk about their issues and challenges and how their lives can change when people start accepting them. Right now, there's only one voice. She was the first one and she's still alone."

As if on cue, Bella Galhos enters the living room, barefoot and carrying an open pot of yogurt. She came out publicly at CODIVA's 2016

---

12 https://aseansogiecaucus.org/images/resources/publications/Building%20A%20 Rainbow%20in%20Timor%20Leste.pdf

13 https://aseansogiecaucus.org/images/resources/publications/Building%20A%20 Rainbow%20in%20Timor%20Leste.pdf

14 https://aseansogiecaucus.org/news/external-news/106-official-statement-of-his- excellency-prime-minister-of-the-democratic-republic-of-timor-leste-on-lgbt-acceptance

Pride event, and is one of just a handful of out-and-proud queer people in Timor-Leste. Her participation in the resistance against Indonesia's occupation of Timor Leste—which lasted from 1975 to 1999—is well-documented, harrowing, and deeply inspiring.[15]

"My brother tried to kill me," she says, matter-of-factly, spoon in hand. "Right here in front of this house. He hid behind the wall and threw stones at me when I came in with the car. He wanted to kill me because I brought shame to the family."

A pause; a mouthful; a shrug. "I'm over it now."

On top of the not-for-profit environmental school and a new government-contracted hotel that Saeed and Galhos run together, they've also recently formed an LGBTQ organisation, Arcoiris, which takes its name from the Portuguese word for "rainbow". Headquartered near their house in Dili's suburbs—a safe area where Galhos' status protects visitors—the organisation serves as a safe space for young queer women and non-binary people.

"Many have horrible experiences of being kicked out and having no support from their families," says Saeed of the centre's first visitors, some of whom were employed by the pair to conduct interviews for the research report.[16] "They have these issues, but nowhere to go."

The pair's report makes a series of compelling recommendations, calling for sweeping reform to violence-response services, the creation of leadership and economic opportunities for LGBTQ people, and the establishment of physical safe spaces for queer people.

Ignorance, not bigotry

Despite the significant challenges faced by Timor-Leste's LGBTQ community, hope burns bright.

Galhos, busy with the hotel, recalls a weekend spent surveying the site not too long ago. "There were these big guys there, and we spent over an hour talking about LGBTQ rights," she says.

---

15 https://magdalene.co/news-1497-in-east-timor-activist-bella-galhos-challenges-norms-fights-patriarchy.html

16 https://aseansogiecaucus.org/news/asc-news/112-new-publication-a-research-report-on-the-lives-of-lesbian-and-bisexual-women-and-transgender-men-in-timor-leste?highlight=WyJ0aW1vciIsInRpbW9yJ3MiLCJsZXN0ZSIsInRpbW9yIGxlc3RlIl0=

"No one had ever talked to them about it before. They all hugged me at the end of it; it was the first time someone had explained. I always have a lot of patience when I talk to people because I know I'm talking to an ignorant, so I talk with them full of respect, full of manners." She switches from English to Tetun, mimicking her own politeness, grinning as she imitates the responses she gets: *sorry, sister, I ask forgiveness.* "We need to have opportunities for healthy discourse."

The mental image of a five-foot-tall woman talking down burly builders is as compelling as the thought of Guterres' brother racing from polling booth to Pride parade, or of Barreto's previously disapproving neighbours sharing Pride videos on Facebook. The road is long, but these instances are signs of Timor-Leste's true promise, of a community embattled, but never broken.

WEAPONISING SCIENCE: MALAYSIA'S LGBTQ "RESEARCH"

SAMANTHA CHEH | 23 JUL 2018

LGBTQ-focused research academics and organisations might sound like a good idea on the surface, but some of this work in Malaysia is actually about pushing homophobic messages disguised as scholarship.

In 2008, Seksualiti Merdeka, a sexual rights festival, was held in Kuala Lumpur. Frequently cited as the first major piece of activism for sexual rights in conservative Malaysia, the event boldly proclaimed: "If one of us ain't free, none of us are!" Although celebrated as a landmark moment for LGBTQ activism, the festival also marked the moment the government attitude towards LGBTQ issues took a turn for the worse. In 2011, the festival—which featured talks, workshops and performances by activists—was banned by the police for inciting public disorder.

Since then, the relationship between the state and the LGBTQ community has continued to be fraught. In recent years, homophobic attitudes have also sought the cover of academia and scholarly "research" in Malaysia.

Conflating queerness with illness

"It's important for us to acknowledge that LGBT bodies have always been medicalised, always been framed in some medical way—we are mentally ill, we need surgery," says Thilaga Sulathireh, a prominent LGBTQ activist working with the pro-trans NGO Justice for Sisters.

Lesbian, gay, bisexual, transgender and queer (LGBTQ) communities have long been treated as a serious public health issue by Malaysia's public authorities. In 2017, the Ministry of Health organised a video contest encouraging people to submit videos on topics such as gender dysphoria and ways LGBTQ individuals can "prevent, control and seek help"—implying that being queer was something undesirable that required treatment. The contest, worded in a way that framed sexual orientations and identities as public health concerns, incited huge public backlash.

Despite the outcry, Sulathireh believes that there still are "concerted and organised" efforts by both state-backed and independent organisations to stigmatise the LGBTQ community, portraying them as victims of mental illness and disease.

"There is a lot of panic about the global conversation around LGBTQ people," she says. "There is definitely a shift in people discussing gender and sexuality, and many countries have changed their policies and legislation so that there is better enjoyment of human rights for LGBTQ people, which I think is creating some panic and pushback around LGBTQ people."

Religious conservatives often draw connections between being LGBTQ and suffering from some form of illness or disease: a forum organised by the Ma'aruf Club of the International Islamic University Malaysia referred to the existence of queerness as the "chronic cancer of society", while the state's own religious authorities consider gay or transgender people as having "abnormal instincts."

The Ma'aruf Club's forum was relatively small, but Islamic authorities in Malaysia have become extremely influential in recent years, in large part thanks to the politicisation of religion by political elites. Religion has been used by the former Barisan Nasional government as a tool to delegitimise its multi-ethnic political rivals and clamp down on rising dissent. In the 2018 Budget, it was revealed that MYR1.03 billion (US$252 million) had been allocated for "Islamic development", with the lion's share going to the controversial Islamic Development Department (JAKIM).

Although homosexuality was officially removed from the Diagnostic and Statistical Manual of Mental Disorder published by the American Psychiatric Association in the 1970s, it's still common in Malaysia—and the wider Southeast Asia—to encounter the belief that anything falling outside the cis-gendered, heterosexual "norm" is a form of mental illness.

"It's a way for authorities to consolidate power... [which] definitely has an Islamic dimension," says Dr Alicia Izharuddin, a gender studies scholar from Universiti Malaya. "People who are in between, those who are progressive or those who claim that this isn't true Islam—I'm just worried that these voices disappear and get shouted down because those on the polarising ends are getting louder."

State connections and power play

In 2016, it emerged that JAKIM—a federal office tasked with governing the implementation of Islam in public life—had been collaborating with the government, particularly the Ministry of Health (MoH), to produce an action plan[1] to address LGBTQ individuals, building on the work of existing committees who focus on treatment and rehabilitation plans for LGBTQ people.

"The Ministry of Health works *very* closely with JAKIM," says Vee, a transwoman and community organiser based in Selangor. "We have a module called 'HIV in Islam' targeted at key populations, but it is very repentance focused. While the MoH programme does provide testing and condoms, that [particular] module is all about how these 'key populations' are sinful."

Instead of working to address issues such as poverty or a lack of public information—which have been shown to have an impact on HIV transmission—authorities are actively focusing their resources and attention on criminalising "key populations".

"What we are seeing is that sexual transmission of HIV is high. So what is the government's response? Is it right to say that all LGBTQ people should be corrected? That approach is not only misguided, it increases harm to those people," says Vee.

Some of JAKIM's programmes have been compared to "conversion therapies" used by Christian evangelicals in the United States; the most well-known is the *mukhayyam*[2] programme, which was designed as a form of outreach to the transgender community. Sulathireh notes that these conversion programmes commonly use "a very passive aggressive approach, using love and compassion in a toxic way with a community that already faces a lack of acceptance."

Vee relates how *mukkhayam* organisers never directly urge participants to conform to their assigned-at-birth gender, but instead rely on gaslighting tactics to "psycho your mind".

---

1 http://www.islam.gov.my/berita-semasa/34-bahagian-keluarga-sosial-komuniti/629-bicara-usrati-jannati-majlis-pelancaran-portal-piswi-pelan-tindakan-keluarga-sakinah-dan-pelan-tindakan-menangani-gejala-sosial-perlakuan-lgbt

2 https://www.malaymail.com/s/788375/jakims-spiritual-camp-tried-to-change-us-lament-muslim-transgenders

"It's bit by bit. [They will say,] 'Oh your hair is so nice, it's long'but why don't you cut it shorter, to your shoulder? You will look so good with shorter hair, you still look pretty! [Their approach] is not harsh, but we were so naïve," she says.

The *mukhayyam* programme—whose format has now been replicated by other religious groups such as state religious councils—is an indication of the religious community's position on LGBTQ issues: that homosexuality or transgenderism is a personal choice or a mental defect, and those afflicted must "*balik ke pangkal jalan* (return to the path)".

Following the wide influence of JAKIM's tactics, a cohort of scientists, researchers and ostensible scholars are now bringing anti-LGBTQ discourse and rhetoric into the realm of science and academic research, causing a subtle but notable shift in public discourse.

Academia takes a stand

In late March 2018, Universiti Sains Malaysia's (USM) alumni club organised a forum entitled "Back to the Fitrah: *Menyantuni LGBT Kembali ke Jalan Allah*", which loosely translates into "Back to human nature: Returning LGBT [people] to God's path".

The forum sparked protests from pro-LGBTQ groups; a coalition of LGBTQ advocacy groups, including Justice for Sisters, Pelangi, Sisters in Islam, and Women's Aid Organisation released a press statement[3] in response: "Despite claims of '*menyantuni*' or 'politely approaching' LGBTQ persons, many documented cases have shown that such attempts resulted in an invasion of privacy, increase of lack of personal security and safety, increase of targeting and harassment of persons based on gender expression and actual or perceived sexual orientation and gender identity, increase of isolation, all of which can have severe long term impact on the student's academic performance, health and well-being."

Tensions were further heightened after Universiti Sains Islam Malaysia (USIM) announced the establishment of an "LGBTQ research academy" to study the LGBTQ community through the lens of medical and scientific research. The academy is small, currently consisting of five individuals, and is led by Dr Rafidah Hanim Mokhtar, whose actual area of medical expertise is in cardiovascular biology.

---

3 https://justiceforsisters.wordpress.com/2018/03/23/open-letter-education-institutions-must-be-safe-spaces-for-all-students/

Dr Rafidah's lack of concrete experience in sexuality or gender research, while worrying, is simply par for the course in Malaysia where many academics commenting on LGBTQ issues tend to lack the relevant credentials. For example, Dr Ahmad Jailani, invited to represent the academic point of view at the "Back to the Fitrah" event, has a PhD in Islamic finance.

The research academy is governed by USIM's World Fatwa Management and Research Institute (INFAD), formed as a "research and consultation institution [and] information centre on fatwa," academy director Dr Irwan Mohd Subri tells *New Naratif*. INFAD has close ties with JAKIM and various state-backed Islamic scholars or muftis. Although these people have no authority to issue fatwas—a non-binding but authoritative pronouncement on Islamic law—they are regularly consulted in relation to such decisions.

Both Dr Irwan and Dr Rafidah say that Islamic tenets could bring real benefits to scientific research, especially in issues of public health and medicine. "It is very important for Islamic scholars today to do field or academic research rather than referring to traditional textbooks," Dr Irwan says. "Islamic scholars today have to contribute to new things but still within an Islamic, or syariah, framework and [in line with] general Islamic principles."

Dr Rafidah points to Western publications on issues of science and religion, such as the *Journal of Religion & Health* and *Zygon: Journal of Religion and Science*, but the academy's work also follows a long-established practice in Malaysia of religion exerting influence over public health policies and studies. For instance, the Health Ministry turned to the National Fatwa Committee in 2009 to adjudicate on issues around female genital mutilation (FGM)[4] despite opposition to the practice by the World Health Organisation, which classifies[5] the practice as having no medical benefits.

Dr Rafidah says that her goal is to integrate religion in a way that "is acceptable to the scientific community", but also states that there are no-go zones in which science cannot enquire—such as *aqidah* (belief in God).

---

4 https://www.themalaysianinsight.com/s/36377

5 http://www.who.int/en/news-room/fact-sheets/detail/female-genital-mutilation

Old sentiments in new clothes

Dr Rafidah's research academy forms only a part of INFAD's research, but stands at the centre of the debate between religious parties and pro-LGBT groups. Dr Rafidah herself seems an odd choice to lead the academy; a medical practitioner by training, her focus area up until around 2015 was cardiovascular physiology.

She explains that her close relationships with colleagues at USIM were a major influence in her interest in "the underlying factors which [lead to the] embrace [of] this lifestyle."

"For the first time, I was able to see health issues from a social perspective and the university gave me a platform for that," she tells *New Naratif.* "It was also partly a public interest issue, and I've always been curious to learn about [the] phenomenon of LGBTQ people."

Dr Rafidah's characterisation of being queer as a "phenomenon" and a "lifestyle" is a common refrain often heard amongst anti-LGBTQ groups in Malaysia and beyond. Such framing has been criticised[6] for delegitimising queer identities, implying that they are reversible choices.

International study suggests otherwise: despite years of research, scientists have been unable to "conclude that sexual orientation is determined by any particular factor or factors," says the American Psychological Association. The group adds that "most people experience little or no sense of choice about their sexual orientation."

To date, Rafidah and her five-person team have only published one article related to healthcare for LGBTQ people: a 2017 paper entitled "Addressing Muslim Transgenders' Health Issues Using Religious Approach in the Malaysian Setting"[7]—published in *Advanced Science Letters*—based on a two-year research project that assessed JAKIM's "religious approach"; essentially, the *mukhayyam* programme.

"We studied their knowledge, attitude and practice before they embarked on the classes and the three-day *mukhayyam*, or *ibadat* (behaviour) camp," she says. "My study covers those transgenders who have already started religious classes, including reading the Quran and prayers. Our study assesses the before and after [effect] of the programmes."

---

6 https://www.glaad.org/reference/offensive

7 https://www.ingentaconnect.com/content/asp/asl/2017/00000023/00000005/art00239

Dr Rafidah explains that the central question of her research was an inquiry into whether the "religious approach would be able to tackle health issues [in LGBTQ communities]" through the prevention of "high-risk behaviour" such as "having multiple sexual partners" and drug-taking, activities often associated with the LGBT community.

"[It's] just the same as we approach a normal person to embrace religion so as to change their lifestyle, in the same way that we seek to correct other bad habits like smoking," she says.

The peer-reviewed paper concludes that transgender individuals suffer from medical issues such as HIV and "debilitating mental health conditions", and that "Islamic preachings" could have a major impact in reducing its risk factors. There is little in the way of recommendations and actionable solutions, but the paper does include a brief rundown of "integration programmes" gleaned from JAKIM's *mukkhayyam* structure.

Legitimising forces

[The emergence of research like Dr Rafidah's signals a shift in tactics on the part of conservative groups, where higher education institutes are used to legitimise their efforts.] Since publishing her paper, Dr Rafidah has made the rounds in local media, penning op-eds that arouse anger or support, and using her scientific and academic backgrounds to position herself as an authority on the subject.

One such piece, entitled "The regressive left: Human rights extortionists"[8] and co-written with Azril Mohd Amin, implied that "gay-rights activists and left-wingers" were fascists and argued that homosexuality is a "chosen behaviour" that should be "subject to laws that regulate public behaviour."

In another piece, entitled "No room for secular Malaysia"[9], she stated that "[t]he accorded human rights to gays, bisexuals and transgenders not to be discriminated against, abused or harmed should not be mixed with our duties and obligations to ensure the health of the population is taken care of", going on to point out that men who have sex with men and transgender individuals are among the populations most affected by HIV/AIDS in Malaysia.

---

8 https://www.malaymail.com/s/1561301/the-regressive-left-human-rights-extortionists-azril-mohd-amin-and-rafidah

9 https://www.freemalaysiatoday.com/category/opinion/2018/05/18/no-room-for-a-secular-malaysia/

In doing so, Dr Rafidah brings attitudes that have often been dismissed as quaint rural ignorance into the authoritative spaces of academia. "[Dr Rafidah is] using her background in medicine as a legitimiser of her research, as well as her statements about LGBTQ people," Dr Izharuddin says.

Such output isn't limited to USIM's LGBTQ research academy. In February 2018, an article[10] in a prominent Malay daily featured a list of "ciri-ciri LGBTQ (LGBTQ characteristics)[11]" written by the prominent evangelical Muslim, Hanafiah Abdul Malek, as a series of markers to identify and study LGBTQ people. He also provided a guide for identifying dominant genitalia for intersex people.

According to Sulathireh, such arguments aren't just based on bad science that ignores globally accepted standards; they're actively harmful because they perpetuate a mindset that views non-binary and sexually diverse bodies as being in need of medical intervention. "[Sex normalising surgeries] create more trauma for people and they are embedded in a very patriarchal ideation that our bodies must be either a male or female cisgender body," she says, referring to surgical medical interventions for intersex individuals.

[Yet the establishment continues to endorse and legitimise such attitudes, using the veneer of respectability accorded by scholars and academia to further influence mainstream mindsets.]

Hope for change?

The result of the 9 May general election has given progressive advocacy groups cause to hope for reforms to counteract the regressive policies of the last few years. But while Prime Minister Mahathir Mohamad and his Cabinet have made significant commitments to review and perhaps even abolish oppressive laws like the Peaceful Assembly Act, the Anti-Fake News Act and the mandatory death penalty, there's unlikely to be significant movement in the realm of LGBTQ rights.

The new government has so far declined to clarify what lies ahead for JAKIM, and also all the other organisations under its umbrella. Mahathir has said that the organisation will come under review but

---

10 http://www.sinarharian.com.my/mobile/sinar-islam/dekati-lgbt-kena-dengan-caranya-
1.795868

11 https://www.malaysiakini.com/news/412107

those hoping for extensive reform will likely be disappointed. After all, an Islamist party is still a significant member of the new ruling coalition.

Homophobia is also still alive and well in the "new Malaysia". When Numan Afifif Saadan began working as the interim press officer for Syed Saddiq, Minister for Youth and Sports, it sparked a fierce backlash, with detractors insisting that a "champion of LGBTQ causes" couldn't serve as a government officer. Numan has since quit[12] as press officer.

"Trust me, we have never felt [that] any government of Malaysia [has] ever been encouraging for LGBTQ people here," says Pang Khee Teik, a prominent LGBT activist, in a widely disseminated[13] social media post debunking claims that a "*Gabungan Gay* (Gay Coalition)" was protesting outside Syed's offices. Pang speculated that the false claim might have been an attempt by "anti-Pakatan Harapan parties" to "make it appear that the government is encouraging LGBT people to be bolder."

However, many still see the new government as its best chance for change. Members of Parliament, such as Charles Santiago and Lim Yi Wei, have spoken up for LGBTQ rights, giving voice to a community that has long lacked champions in the House. Meanwhile, Malaysian LGBTQ allies and advocates continue to push on; as long as they are around, there will always be voices to counter homophobia presented as science.

---

12 https://www.thestar.com.my/news/nation/2018/07/09/lgbt-activist-numan-afifi-quits-as-syed-saddiq-press-officer/

13 https://www.facebook.com/pangkheeteik/posts/10156668878498092

BEING LGBTQ IN BRUNEI

ZAINA ABDUL | 30 JUL 2018

The implementation of the syariah penal code attracted the attention of the international media to the treatment of LGBTQ people in Brunei, but the reality is more complex than what's been reported thus far.

"I came out to my parents last night," Ros* tells me nonchalantly. "It was probably the eighth time I came out to them in the past fifteen years."

Ros is gay, or, as they prefer to describe themselves, "a raging homosexual". It was something they'd known since their teenage years. Ros' repeated coming out story is common to LGBTQ people in Brunei—a country that looks down upon anything that falls outside of the heterosexual norm. Like many, Ros' parents refuses to acknowledge their homosexuality.

The stories of LGBTQ lives in Brunei are often hidden from the public eye. Love stories written and celebrated in the country are usually between men and women. Social media influencers are usually in heterosexual relationships; the one openly gay DJ keeps their Instagram account private.

This suppression of LGBTQ representation and experiences is the result of an institutionalised oppression, trickling down from Brunei's lawmakers and religious elite to individuals choosing to stay in the closet out of fear of repercussions from not only family, but peers and society at large.

Laws and regulations

It's technically not illegal to be gay in Brunei, but many LGBTQ individuals are fearful of expressing their sexuality. Salmah* says she wishes she could be open about the fact that she's bisexual, but she's afraid of the Internal Security Department. She was shocked to discover that it wasn't actually illegal to be bisexual; she hadn't known that the law only outlaws acting on sexual urges, both in terms of premarital sex between heterosexual couples and intercourse between same-sex couples.

It's unsurprising—Bruneian society has long projected the impression that just *being* queer is wrong, so many assume that homosexuality itself is criminalised.

Like other former colonies, Section 377 of Brunei's penal code was inherited from the days of British rule. The law criminalises any form of penetration between men. If found guilty of this "unnatural offence", individuals can be punished with up to 10 years' imprisonment and/or a fine.

This regulation is also reflected in the new syariah penal code, which attracted the attention of the Western media[1] regarding Brunei's treatment of LGBTQ people as it was being introduced and implemented. The syariah penal code, first announced in 2013, criminalises adultery and sodomy by punishing those involved with a fine, whipping or death by stoning. It also forbids *musahaqah*, acts of sexual nature between women. Punishment for these acts can include fines of up to BND40,000 (USD29,903), or a maximum of 10 years' imprisonment with 40 strokes. The code is currently in the process of being implemented.

A more complicated reality

The international media were quick to jump on Brunei—usually a much-overlooked country when it comes to global news coverage—during the early phases of the syariah penal code's introduction, painting a picture of the country as out to punish LGBTQ people in public, but the reality is more complex.

Despite Section 377 remaining on the books, there has been no known case of an individual brought to court on sodomy charges, whether under the statute or the new syariah penal code. It's also not that easy to prove that illegal sexual acts under the new syariah law—both heterosexual or homosexual—have taken place. Four male witnesses must be present during the conduct of the sexual act before there can be a conviction; video recordings are considered invalid as proof.

But the very *presence* of such laws can have an impact. "[S]uch penalties are there to act as a deterrent and there is no greater deterrent than the fear of what might happen if you get caught," writes Matthew Woolfe, founder of The Brunei Project in an email to *New Naratif*.

Another possible reason for the lack of prosecutions could be the community's own reticence. "Just like the broader Bruneian society, the

↳ reserve

1 http://www.msnbc.com/msnbc/brunei-sharia-penal-code-gay-stoning

LGBTQ community is much more conservative than in many other countries and are much less visible, therefore attracting less attention," Woolfe explains. However, with increasing number of individuals outing themselves on social media, a change in how authorities deal with LGBTQ people in the future is possible, particularly with the full implementation of the syariah law.

There are concerns that "the authorities will become more stringent in enforcing laws that directly impact LGBTQ Bruneians," Woolfe says, pointing to instances of LGBTQ individuals being fined for cross-dressing under the syariah penal code. Transgender individuals are forbidden from changing their gender on official documents, putting them in a difficult position.

Despite these penalties, a well-known comedian who dresses up as a woman for his performances has not faced any legal action. This discrepancy has led to questions about when the line is crossed, and who gets to make that call. Why is cross-dressing illegal in everyday life, but considered entertainment when it's up on a public stage?

A wider lack of awareness and education has also proven to be a stumbling block to acceptance. "Unless they know someone who identifies as LGBTQ, most Bruneians know very little about what it means to be LGBTQ because there are no education programs in schools or in the community that help people to understand ideas around diversity and the challenges faced by those who do not conform to a certain mold," says Woolfe.

With so much stigma and uncertainty, it's not always easy for LGBTQ people to find each other. Some say they make compromises or find ways to work around society's strict gender norms. There are cases of queer people entering straight marriages; while many might have been forced into marriage by their families, some are also the result of agreements between gay men and women to maintain a facade of social acceptability. A lesbian woman interviewed by *New Naratif* got married because she wanted a child; she and her husband maintain an open relationship based on mutual understanding.

The political climate   ⌐ scarcity

Despite all these issues, there's a dearth of activism and advocacy on LGBTQ issues in Brunei. It's not necessarily a lack of interest in LGBTQ equality, but indicative of the Bruneian political landscape—a culture of fear keeps Bruneians from speaking out and challenging authority.

It's a wariness that perhaps goes back to the failed 1962 Brunei Revolt, where a group of insurgents who opposed the monarchy of Brunei, as well as the plan to join the Malaysian Federation, took up arms to attack police stations, government facilities and the oil town of Seria. Over five decades later, the insurrection is still seen as a taboo subject in the country; there's a sense that openly talking about this period of history might lead to questions over one's loyalty.

This taboo extends to any form of critique towards government and royal institutions; individuals have been charged with sedition for speaking ill of the monarchy or critically on religious matters. As part of its Freedom in the World 2018 report, Freedom House categorised[2] Brunei as "not free", with an aggregate score of 28 out of 100 (100 being the most free).

"There is a very real fear in Brunei about publicly speaking out and even about raising genuine concerns because of the perceived repercussions if caught," Woolfe says.

[Fear of repercussion isn't the only thing keeping Bruneians from speaking out. A wealthy nation blessed with extensive petroleum and natural gas fields, the government has been able to provide a comfortable life for most of its population: there's free healthcare and education, subsidies for fuel and certain foodstuffs, an affordable national housing scheme and welfare for the poor and people with disabilities. With most of their basic needs met (and more), it's unsurprising that many choose not to rock the boat.]

There's therefore a lack of official or established institutions within the country working on not only on LGBTQ rights, but *any* form of human rights. But there have been small initiatives and efforts to get the stories of LGBTQ people in Brunei out, employing subtle methods to avoid becoming targets.

---

2 https://freedomhouse.org/report/freedom-world/2018/brunei

Small, careful efforts

"There are no formal organisations or support networks dedicated to LGBTQ advocacy in Brunei and such are the laws and regulations concerning the formation of formal organisations that any attempt to establish such an organisation is most certainly guaranteed to fail," Woolfe tells *New Naratif.*

"As such, social media remains the primary avenue for advocacy and provides a degree of security for advocates by allowing them to protect their identities, while also reaching a wide audience."

Songket Alliance[3], an indie webzine, has been publishing stories of minorities in Brunei for several years now, under the column "Bruneian Me[4]". A handful of those stories, as well as a several others outside the column, touch on the lives of LGBTQ people in Brunei.

The Brunei Project[5] is also works to highlighting human rights issues in Brunei, mainly through Facebook. On 8 March 2018, the page published[6] a story from Khairul, a gay man demanding acceptance from Bruneian society.

"Sadly, support services for people like Khairul who are coming to terms with their sexuality or who may be confused about their identity and what they are feeling are lacking in Brunei," The Brunei Project wrote in its post before referring those in need of support to Oogachaga, a Singapore-based LGBTQ-friendly counselling service.

Both Songket Alliance and The Brunei Project do not openly advocate for the repeal of laws or the legalisation of same-sex marriage, but choose instead of provide space for personal narratives to humanise LGBTQ individuals to encourage understanding and empathy among Bruneians as a first step.

At the end of the day, the thing that LGBTQ individuals interviewed by *New Naratif* want the most is the freedom to be themselves, whether it's being open about their sexual orientation in society, or at peace with their faith. "I am actively seeking acceptance with my family

3 https://songketalliance.com/

4 http://songketalliance.com/tagged/column%3A-bruneian-me

5 https://www.facebook.com/thebruneiproject/

6 https://www.facebook.com/thebruneiproject/posts/1867511910205634

and religion," Ros states. "I am gay. I am a Muslim. I can exist in this world. My faith is strong, but my family thinks that my gayness makes me less religious. I feel more religious knowing that my gayness is my struggle in this complex world."

Names have been changed to protect identities

CORRECTION: *The article had originally mistakenly stated that the syariah penal code was in its third and final phase of implementation. It's now been corrected—thank you to a* New Naratif *reader for pointing it out!*

STRUGGLING WITH STIGMA: INDONESIA'S LGBTQ "EXORCISMS"

TEGUH HARAHAP, AISYAH LLEWELLYN | 06 AUG 2018

Under intense pressure to conform, members of Indonesia's LGBTQ community are turning to religious exorcisms in the hope of finding a "cure".

Daniel (not his real name) has tried everything to live a "normal" life in Indonesia. At first glance, he's nothing more than your average 25-year-old. He lives in Medan, North Sumatra, and is finishing law school in the hope of becoming a notary. He's also married to a woman who used to be his neighbour. No one would suspect, from just looking at him, that he's guarding a deep secret about himself.

For the sake of being considered "normal" in Indonesia, Daniel pretends that he isn't gay. Closeted homosexuals aren't uncommon in Indonesia, a country where being queer still carries a huge amount of stigma, but Daniel feels, deep down, like he's been banished from his own life. With his true self suppressed, he can only dream that one day he'll be free to live the life that God gave him—as a gay man.

"There's nothing wrong with my life now, only that I'm not being true to myself by living in Indonesia. I have a dream of moving to Bangkok, I think that's where my life would be normal and I could be myself every day," he says wistfully.

Homosexuality in Indonesia

Homosexuality is not illegal in Indonesia—home to the largest Muslim population of any country on earth—except in Aceh Province, a semi-autonomous part of Indonesia that follows syariah law. But a bill being discussed in parliament is likely to result in laws that would criminalise homosexuality across the whole of the archipelago. Despite this, President Joko "Jokowi" Widodo has made a number of public statements stressing that there's no discrimination against minorities in Indonesia. If anyone is threatened because of their sexuality, the police must act to protect them, he said in an interview[1] with the BBC in 2016.

It sounds reassuring, but this often isn't the reality for Indonesia's LGBTQ community. In fact, the situation for LGBTQ people in Indonesia has worsened in recent years; in 2016, a government minister even declared[2] that the LGBTQ community is a "threat" against which "a kind of modern warfare" is being waged.

The number of arrests of members of the LGBTQ community by religious organisations, acting as unofficial community police officers, has increased in recent years. One of the most controversial was the arrest of a group of transgender residents in Tanah Jambo Aye, North Aceh, on 27 January 2018. A total of 12 transgender residents were detained[3] at a salon where they worked; the police forcibly cut their hair and demanded that they put on "masculine" clothing. The video of their detention and enforced head shaving went viral on Indonesian social media. Then-North Aceh Police Chief Utung Sangaji told a local newspaper[4] that the increasing number of lesbian, gay, bisexual and transgender residents in Aceh was a bad influence on the younger generation.

While many people in Aceh applauded the move to publicly shame the transgender salon workers, the incident was criticised in other parts of Indonesia. The Indonesian Legal Aid Foundation's (YLBHI) Chief of Advocacy, Muhammad Insur, said that the police had failed to respect the rule of law in that case. "What was the crime of the transgender residents? These people were punished because of who they are. There is no legal punishment for being transgender. They don't need any 'intervention'. If you want to help, then help them to prosper," he told Indonesian website *Tirto*[5] in February 2018.

Dealing with the social stigma

But what's often considered worse than the legal consequences of being gay in Indonesia is the pressure that comes from both friends and family.

---

1 https://www.bbc.com/indonesia/indonesia/2016/10/161019_indonesia_wwc_jokowi_lgbt

2 https://newnaratif.com/journalism/more-dangerous-than-nuclear-war/

3 https://www.theguardian.com/world/2018/jan/29/indonesian-police-in-aceh-province-cut-hair-of-transgender-women

4 https://tirto.id/aksi-akbp-untung-sangaji-di-aceh-soal-lgbt-menuai-kritik-ylbhi-cEdo

5 https://tirto.id/aksi-akbp-untung-sangaji-di-aceh-soal-lgbt-menuai-kritik-ylbhi-cEdo

Daniel admits that he sacrificed his own feelings when he was forced to marry a woman he's sexually uninterested in. But he feels that the decision had to be made, whether he liked it or not, so that the people around him wouldn't start thinking that there was something "wrong". He can't imagine what would happen if people knew of his sexual orientation; he's convinced that if his friends found out, they would mock him or, worse still, that he would be rejected by his family.

"I'm sure that I can't stop these feelings, but I also have to think about my family," he explains. "How would they feel if they knew I was gay, especially my mother?" His voice breaks as he says this. He looks away.

Adi Sujatmika, a lecturer in the social psychology department of the University of Surabaya, explains the impact of the stigma against the LGBTQ community in Indonesia. "Mostly people don't want to be gay in Indonesia because of social norms and religious values," he tells *New Naratif*. "They think that heterosexual people consider homosexuality a sin which will be damned by God. And almost everybody wants to fit into society. Indonesia has a strong collective culture."

Daniel reveals that he's so desperate to be rid of his homosexuality that he's tried several methods said to "cure" LGBTQ people, including traditional counselling, hypnosis and a visit to a *ruqyah* expert. *Ruqyah*, practised by some religious scholars, is like a form of exorcism.

Exorcising "demons"

Rudiawan Sitorus isn't the one Daniel visited to "solve his homosexuality problem", but the 35-year-old *ustadz* (Muslim teacher) is known as an expert in the field of *ruqyah*, and is a member of Community Care Ruqyah Syar'iyyah—a community group that provides training to anyone who's considered suitable and has an interest in learning about the world of *ruqyah*.

Sitorus opened his own *ruqyah* practice in his home three years ago, and reveals that the number of LGBTQ patients has been steadily increasing. In Indonesia *ruqyah* is also used for anything from health problems like arthritis and asthma, to issues such as a failed business or struggling relationship—all of which are said to be caused by the same kinds of "demons" that cause homosexuality.

Sitorus says that *Ruqyah Syariah*, which uses recitations of verses from the Quran and the hadiths, is permissible in Islam. "I believe that LGBTQ behaviour is a sickness and that it's caused by a physical and mental disturbance from *jinn*(demons) who have succeeded in controlling the patient's body," he explains. "Therefore we read short verses from the Quran and the hadiths, which we believe will make the *jinn* who control the patient afraid and they will then leave the patient's body."

It's clear that Sitorus thinks homosexuality or gender incongruence (the term the World Health Organisation uses to refer to people who are transgender or genderqueer) is caused by a demon-triggered mental health disorder, as opposed to a natural part of one's identity that cannot be "cured". It's a commonly held belief in many societies that don't affirm LGBTQ identities, including in neighbouring countries within Southeast Asia[6].

Growing up in such an environment, LGBTQ people themselves might internalise such beliefs; Sitorus says his patients come to him because they want to "recover" from being gay, and believe that their behaviour can be "corrected". For many people, *ruqyah* is a favoured choice of conversion therapy as it's considered permissible in Islam, as opposed to visiting a traditional Indonesian shaman known as a *dukun*—a practice prohibited in the Muslim faith as shamans are said to use sorcery.

Most LGBT patients who go to Sitorus' practice for "treatment" usually come alone—after hiding their sexual orientation from everyone around them, there's no one who can accompany them. Others might bring one person to support them throughout the process. With privacy a major concern, LGBT patients who ask for consultations or go through *ruqyah* are seen by Sitorus alone.

When the process begins, Sitorus reads verses from the Quran in a loud voice, then puts his hands on the patient's chest and back. He slaps them hard to get the *jinn* to leave their body, as he demands that the dreaded demons leave their mortal hosts.

"The *jinn* like to hide in the arteries," he explains. "So I have to pull them out by massaging the circulatory system of the patient."

Sitorus gives a demonstration of the *ruqyah* process with the help of one of his students, Mustafa. They sit cross-legged next to each other on the floor. Sitorus puts his hands on Mustafa's back and chest and slaps him, then moves his hand up Mustafa's chest to his throat, which Sitorus claims is the demons' preferred hiding spot. If this were a real session, Sitorus says, the patient would writhe around, as if in pain, and

---

6 https://newnaratif.com/journalism/weaponising-science-lgbtq-scholarship-malaysia/

start to vomit, which is meant to be a firm indication that the demons are being expelled. After the *ruqyah* process is complete, Sitorus washes the patient with salt water laced with *bidara* (Chinese date) leaves and splashes them with the water while reciting more holy verses.

An ineffective "treatment"

Although he went to a different *ustadz*, Daniel's *ruqyah* process was similar to the one witnessed by *New Naratif*—he was also pummelled, massaged, and then bathed in holy water mixed with salt and *bidara* leaves. "But it had no effect whatsoever," he says, shaking his head and laughing at the memory.

Sitorus claims he's managed to cure a number of LGBTQ patients in Medan. His fame has grown, and he was even invited to act as a consultant for the local TV station, Trans TV, on a programme called *Jinn Interference in the Sodom Community*. He shows *New Naratif* the videos on his phone—episodes feature a number of purportedly gay patients going through the *ruqyah* process. Several of them are shouting, crying and screaming, and in one video a supposed LGBT patient is shown trying to escape from the *ustadz* performing the *ruqyah*.

It's unclear whether the videos are staged, but the *ruqyah* patients appear extremely distressed. Sitorus insists that when people cry and shout, it doesn't come from the patient themselves—they, apparently, don't feel anything at all—but from the *jinn* who has been crippled with pain as a result of the *ruqyah* treatment.

After the *ruqyah* process is complete, Sitorus follows up with spiritual guidance for his patients, explaining to them that, according to the Quran, homosexuality is a sin.

Ruqyah failed to give Daniel the "cure" he sought; he says it hasn't worked for a number of his friends either. Despite this he still wants to seek more spiritual help, because he just can't find a way to reconcile his homosexuality and his faith.

But homosexuality and religion is not that clear cut. According to Lailatul Fitriyah, a Muslim academic who spoke to7 the Indonesian feminist online magazine *Magdalene*, Islamic teachings or "fiqh" [Islamic jurisprudence] actually give a lot of space to the LGBTQ community.

7 https://magdalene.co/news-1259-quran-tak-ajarkan-membenci-kelompok-lgbt-akademisi-muslim.html

"An assistant in the Prophet's house who helped to take care of his wives was known to be transgender. And many men who exhibited female characteristics became artists in the palaces of the caliphs," Fitriyah said.

Hera Diani, the Managing Editor of *Magdalene*, also points out that the LGBTQ community in Indonesia has the support of a number of Muslim scholars and religious leaders who don't see conversion therapy as either necessary or useful. "Musdah Mulia, Lailatul Fitriyah and Aan Anshori are all LGBTQ-friendly Islamic scholars. Also Ustadz Abdul Muiz Ghazali frequently counsels transgender people," she tells *New Naratif*.

"I'll probably never be 'cured'"

Daniel acknowledges that homosexuality isn't a mental health issue, and he's now able to laugh about the *ruqyah* treatment that made no difference to his life. But for some, conversion therapy can have serious consequences.

According to a report8 by the American Psychiatric Association, conversion therapy or "reparative therapy" like *ruqyah* can have a serious impact on patients, even if they voluntarily sought such therapy. The report states that "[t]he potential risks of 'reparative therapy' are great and include depression, anxiety, and self-destructive behavior, since therapist alignment with societal prejudices against homosexuality may reinforce self-hatred already experienced by the patient."

Still, the pressure to conform is great. Although Daniel knows that other therapies are just as likely to fail as the *ruqyah* he'd already experienced, being gay in Indonesia is not something he wants to face in his life, given the stigma. He's currently focused on starting a family with his wife, but there are obstacles as he's not sexually attracted to her and often has problems with sexual intercourse. However, he hopes that having a baby will give him a real purpose in life and stop his homosexual desires for good.

"I know that I'll probably never be 'cured'", he says. "The best I can hope for is that I can learn to control it."

8 https://www.hrc.org/resources/the-lies-and-dangers-of-reparative-therapy

FREEDOM OF EXPRESSION

THE USE OF HUMILIATION AS A POLITICAL TOOL

THUM PING TJIN | 04 DEC 2017

Singapore's Vandalism Act (1966) was designed, from the beginning, as a political tool to humiliate those who fight to exercise their right to free speech and political expression.

On Tuesday, Singaporean human rights activist Jolovan Wham was charged by prosecutors with three counts of holding unauthorised public assemblies, three counts of refusing to sign his statements to the police, and one count of vandalism. This drew swift condemnation from within and without Singapore.[1] While most commentary focused on the absurdity of Singapore's laws on public assemblies and the government's willingness to suppress free expression, many also expressed puzzlement on the charge of vandalism.

This charge stems from the second of Wham's three peaceful protests. In June this year, Wham held a "silent protest" on the Singapore subway. That event marked the 30th anniversary of Operation Spectrum, where 22 social activists and volunteers were arrested and detained without trial, accused of an alleged Marxist plot to subvert the Singapore government.

---

1 See, for example:

Function8, Statement, 30 November 2017, https://www.facebook.com/function8ltd/
photos/a.350454085131572.1073741847.350013055175675/865386370305005/;

Human Rights Watch, "Singapore: Drop Case Against Peaceful Protester", 29 November 2017,
https://www.hrw.org/news/2017/11/29/singapore-drop-case-against-peaceful-protester;

Amnesty International, "Urgent Action: Activist Faces Seven Charges For Peaceful
Protest", 29 November 2017, https://www.amnesty.org/download/Documents/
ASA3675162017ENGLISH.pdf;

New York Times, "Charges Cast Spotlight on Singapore's Strict Rules on Public Gatherings",
29 November 2017, https://www.nytimes.com/2017/11/29/world/asia/singapore-arrest-
protests-gatherings.html; and

The Online Citizen, "HK Activist Joshua Wong expresses solidarity with Jolovan
Wham", 2 December 2017, https://www.theonlinecitizen.com/2017/12/02/
hk-activist-joshua-wong-expresses-solidarity-with-jolovan/.

The detainees were deprived of sleep, kept in freezing rooms, physically assaulted and harshly interrogated. The Singapore government has never produced evidence linking them to any conspiracy, let alone any crime; more broadly, it has never produced evidence to substantiate any of the approximately 1,000 formal detentions without trial (and a further 1,000-1,500 informal detentions) it has made since the governing People's Action Party (PAP) took power in 1959.[2]

As part of his protest, Wham taped two sheets of paper on the wall of a subway car. The sheets read "MARXIST CONSPIRACY?," "#nodetentionwithouttrial", and "JUSTICE FOR OPERATION SPECTRUM SURVIVORS". There was no damage to the wall, but this led to the vandalism charge.

After this was announced, Facebook users began sharing photos of indelible advertisement stickers (in particular, by locksmiths), leaflets advertising rooms to let, and other assorted posters, to which police have routinely turned a blind eye. What was most shocking to many was that the punishment was so disproportionate to the crime: under Singapore's law, vandalism is punishable by a maximum fine of SG$2,000, up to three years in prison, and three to eight cane strokes, depending on the severity of the offence.

Wham's prosecution under the *Vandalism Act*, however, is no accident. The *Punishment for Vandalism Act* of 1966 (amended in 1970 to the *Vandalism Act*) was written deliberately to punish political dissidents, by demarcating certain expressions of political opinion as criminal and anti-national. This not only suppressed free speech, but consolidated the power of the state to decide what constitutes the 'nation'. This was part of the broader British colonial strategy for control upon which the PAP expanded.[3]

---

2 For a list for formal detentions, see https://fn8org.wordpress.com/advocacy/political-detainees-in-singapore-1950-2015/. "Formal detentions" refers here to those detained under section 8 of the Internal Security Act, which permits detentions (indefinitely renewable) up to 2 years. "Informal detentions" refers here to being held under section 74 of the Internal Security Act, which permits people to be held without a warrant by the Internal Security Department merely on suspicion of being a security risk for up to 28 days. Many such detainees were released after 28 days and immediately re-arrested when they stepped out of the ISD compound.

3 See "Justifying Colonial Rule in Post-Colonial Singapore", https://newnaratif.com/research/justifying-colonial-rule-in-post-colonial-singapore/

By monopolising the meaning of the 'nation', the government can justify all manner of authoritarian action by simply defining its opposition as 'anti-national', and hence a threat to the 'nation' and the 'people'. Central to the *Vandalism Act*'s effectiveness was that it ignored the principle that the punishment should be commensurate to the crime, instead using excessive and humiliating punishment to break opposition political activists.

Crushing Dissent and Closing Down Public Space

The *Punishment for Vandalism Act* was a response to several challenges faced by the People's Action Party in 1966. From 1962, the PAP had sought to cripple its political opposition through a variety of tactics. This included:

- Harassment, by spying on opposition activists and raiding opposition gatherings;
- Distraction, including entangling opposition activists in court cases;
- Squeezing the opposition out of public space, including suppressing media reporting of the opposition and banning opposition rallies; and
- Outright coercion, including detaining opposition leaders through detention without trial, declaring lawful activities to be illegal, and deregistering or banning opposition trade unions and other organisations.

It was hoped that this would provoke frustrated opposition activists into unlawful and unconstitutional action. The government could then use it to justify further and more direction action against them.[4]

Despite having severely crippled the political opposition, the opposition grassroots remained substantial. It continued to present alternative accounts and inconvenient facts about the PAP through its use of posters and other public displays. Furthermore, the PAP found that its use of detention without trial turned detainees into martyrs, winning them greater public affection and following (the same problem colonial authorities faced throughout their empires, including Gandhi, Sukarno, and in Singapore, Lim Chin Siong).

---

4 For more on the criminalisation of legitimate politics, see Christopher Tremewan, The Political Economy of Social Control in Singapore (London: Macmillan, 1994), 194-199.

This situation intensified following the arrival of US troops into Singapore for the first time in April 1966. They had been serving in South Vietnam and arrived for rest and recreation leave. For a Singaporean public whose memories of the depredations of British colonialism, the Malayan Emergency, and Konfrontasi were still fresh, the prospect of being drawn into another conflict was extremely unwelcome. Likewise, a fundamental plank of the opposition Barisan Sosalis' policy was to keep Singapore non-aligned, and avoid getting drawn into a Cold War conflict between the two imperialist blocs. They also recognised the Vietnam War as an anti-colonial conflict between a colonised people and a colonial power. The United Nations charter and the Bandung declaration recognised the right of the all people to self-determination and their own choice of government, and not to have one imposed on them. The Barisan's position was that the Vietnamese were no exception, and that Singapore should not be enabling oppression.[5]

Consequently, the Barisan and left-wing trade unions launched a campaign against the presence of US troops in Singapore and against US military action in Vietnam. As they were denied public space in the form of rallies and coverage in the media, they put up posters in the middle of the night. This followed in a long tradition of protest, from Roman graffiti, to Martin Luther's theses, to Chinese "Big Character Posters", where posters are used to express dissent against an authoritarian power.

On 13 April 1966, Singapore awoke to find red anti-American slogans painted on bus-stops and walls. Subsequently, on the eve of Labour Day (1 May 1966), despite a heightened police presence, constant surveillance of opposition activists, and public announcements *every half an hour* warning people not to take part in rallies or demonstrations, anticolonial activists managed to put up "Yankee Go Home" posters on the streets leading to the American Embassy and around the offices of left-wing trade unions.

The government prosecuted 23 men and boys for putting up the posters, but they ran into a legal obstacle. The 1906 *Minor Offences*

---

5 For more on the Barisan's position on self-determination and soverignty, see Thum Ping Tjin, "The Malayan Vision of Lim Chin Siong: Unity, Non-violence, and Popular Sovereignty", Inter-Asia Cultural Studies, 18:3 (2017), 402-408. http://dx.doi.org /10.1080/14649373.2017.1346167 or https://www.academia.edu/34683473/ The_Malayan_vision_of_Lim_Chin_Siong_Unity_Non-Violence_and_Popular_Sovereignty

Ordinance classified vandalism as a minor nuisance, with a maximum penalty of a $50 fine and a week in jail. It was non-seizable, so all the police could do was summon people to court. It was barely a deterrent to a determined democracy movement.

The government tried to pre-empt the placing of posters. Three days before Singapore's first National Day (9 August 1966), Internal Security Department (ISD) officers raided the Barisan Sosialis headquarters, seizing documents and posters. However, they knew that they could not stop every single instance of political posters this way; they needed to deter activists from placing posters.

Ten days after the raid, on 16 August, the *Punishment for Vandalism Bill* had its first reading in Parliament.

The Punishment for Vandalism Bill 1966

The government moved with great haste. A further ten days after its first reading, on 26 August, the Bill had its second and third readings and was passed into law.

The narrative presented to Parliament at the second reading followed the same pattern that the British colonial government and the PAP had used against their opponents:

First, they would characterise legitimate political protest as illegitimate public disorder;

Second, they would characterise the people who practise political protest as "anti-national" and thus not only subversive but also enemies of the people;

Third, they would smear these people by questioning their motives and spreading partial truths or even outright falsehoods about their actions, reducing these people to a subhuman "Other" for which the normal rules of law and civilisation need not apply.

This created a narrative in which the government could argue it was compelled to pass more and more restrictive laws. In order to take effective action, it had to create laws which gave it the maximum discretion to exercise its power. This then created a large amount of arbitrary power which the government could wield selectively against its opponents.[6]

Accordingly, the introducer of the Bill, Minister of State for Defence Wee Toon Boon, described vandalism as being done by 'anti-social and anti-national elements in the name of democracy'.[7] Frequently repeating the term 'anti-national', Wee further emphasised that such 'anti-national elements were 'damaging or destroying public property which is provided for the benefit of the people'… these people find 'cruel joy in destroying and damaging public property. In the interests of the nation, it is therefore necessary that the minority who cause damage should be dealt with severely.'[8] Prime Minister Lee Kuan Yew described vandalism as 'a particularly vicious social misdemeanour, like taking a pot of paint and going to every bus stand and chalking up anti-American or anti-British or pro-Vietcong slogans'.[9]

It is clear that what they were actually describing was not vandalism but *legitimate dissent* – and in particular, anti-colonial pro-democracy expression which, in the face of determined PAP attempts to obstruct and regulate legitimate political expression, had resorted to acts of disobedience in order to find space for expression.

In her analysis of the PAP's argument for the law, legal scholar Jothie Rajah notes important sub-texts to the language used by the PAP.[10] Firstly, it infantilised the people. "We have a society which, unfortunately, I think, understands only two things – the incentive and the deterrent," said Lee[11], while Wee argued for caning as appropriate punishment by applying an analogy comparing the state and the people to a parent and

---

6 See "Justifying Colonial Rule in Post-Colonial Singapore" for a broader discussion on how the PAP elaborated on British policies of control.

7 Why the Minister of State for Defence was introducing the Bill, and not the Minister for Law, is not known. Singapore Parliamentary Debates, vol. 25 col. 291, 26 August 1966. The full report for the 26 August 1966 sitting of Parliament is at https://sprs.parl.gov.sg/search/report.jsp?currentPubID=00069148-ZZ

8 Ibid.

9 Singapore Parliamentary Debates, vol. 25 col. 295, 26 August 1966.

10 Jothie Rajah, Authoritarian Rule of Law: Legislation, Discourse, and Legitimacy in Singapore (Cambridge: Cambridge University Press, 2012), 65-80.

11 Singapore Parliamentary Debates, vol. 25 col. 296, 26 August 1966.

a child.[12] This is in line with the myth of vulnerability that is frequently repeated by the PAP – that the people are helpless, and vulnerable, and only the PAP can protect them.[13]

Second, sweeping assertions were used to attribute sinister motives to the people who committed vandalism. "It is common knowledge to Members that anti-national elements use children and other young persons to smear and mar public and private property," declared Wee.[14] This double smear described vandals as both 'anti-national' and as taking advantage of children. Wee and Minister of Law E. W. Barker also both drew a moral equivalence between those who permanently damaged property (emphasising damage which potentially placed lives at risk) and those who did non-permanent damage, such as writing slogans with delible ink or hanging up posters.[15]

The net effect, notes Rajah, was to set up the logical chain:

If those who commit vandalism oppose the PAP;

and those who commit vandalism oppose the nation and seek to hurt the people;

and those who commit vandalism are subhuman and must be punitively dealt with;

therefore those who oppose the PAP also oppose the nation, seek to hurt the people, are subhuman, and must be punitively dealt with.

'The sub-text of the *Punishment for Vandalism Act*', writes Rajah, 'suggests that the distinguishing feature of the population declared to be "subhuman and a public danger" is ideological dissent. The question thus becomes: Is ideological compliance to the ruling party necessary for membership in the category "the people" and the resulting protection of "the nation"?'[16]

From the PAP's perspective, the answer was a resounding yes. Furthermore, as the people were helpless and vulnerable, their enemies had to be dealt with by the PAP through any means possible. Thus armed, the PAP proceeded to cast aside legal principle and precedent in the *Punishment for Vandalism Act*.

---

12 Singapore Parliamentary Debates, vol. 25 col. 293, 26 August 1966.

13 "Justifying Colonial Rule in Post-Colonial Singapore".

14 Singapore Parliamentary Debates, vol. 25 col. 291, 26 August 1966.

15 Singapore Parliamentary Debates, vol. 25 col. 298-99, 26 August 1966.

16 Rajah, 78-79.

First, the law mandated punishment that was completely disproportionate for what was hitherto legally classified as a minor property offence. It was made a seizable and non-bailable offence, and the maximum punishment was increased from a SG$50 fine and a week in jail, to SG$2,000, three years in jail, and, most crucially, a minimum of the three strokes of the cane, up to a maximum of eight strokes. Aware of this, Lee's argument reveals how the conduct that the state sought to contain was not conventional vandalism:

> '[A] fine will not deter the type of criminal we are facing here. He is quite prepared to go to gaol, having defaced public buildings with red paint. Flaunting the values of his ideology, he is quite prepared to make a martyr of himself and go to gaol. He will not pay the fine and make a demonstration of his martyrdom. But if he knows he is going to get three of the best, I think he will lose a great deal of enthusiasm, because there is little glory attached to the rather humiliating experience of having to be caned.'[17]

The "vandal" is described as being motivated by political ideology, yet is categorised as a criminal, not a political activist. If the "vandal" were to be recognised as a political actor, then their right to dissent would have to be recognised. Instead, they are categorised as criminal, and the punishment of caning is mandated to deliberately humiliate.

Second, the Bill departed from the general principle that a criminal conviction requires guilt in terms of both action and intention. Following on from his unsubstantiated assertion that 'anti-national elements use children and other young persons to smear and mar public and private property' Wee argued that the law had to take punitive action against those 'actually responsible'.[18] The Bill thus not only criminalised the commitment of an act of vandalism and any attempt to vandalise, but also, most crucially, it also criminalises anyone who 'causes' an act of vandalism to be done.[19]

---

17 Singapore Parliamentary Debates, vol. 25 col. 296-97, 26 August 1966.

18 Singapore Parliamentary Debates, vol. 25 col. 293, 26 August 1966.

19 '... any person who commits any act of vandalism or attempts to do any such act or causes any such act to be done shall be guilty of an offence'. Vandalism Act (Cap. 341, 1985 Rev. Ed. Sing.) s.3. http://statutes.agc.gov.sg/aol/search/display/view. w3p;ident=436b1cad-8743-4166-9c0d-ab4976bd18d6;page=0;query=DocId%3A%2222e3d 9bf-886f-48fe-b02f-205dbe5f9570%22%20Status%3Ainforce%20Depth%3A0;rec=0#legis

Third, the *Punishment for Vandalism Act* shifted the definition of vandalism and greatly expanded the parameters of the offence. Under the *Minor Offences Ordinance*, it was the act of marking a surface or putting up a bill or poster that constituted the nuisance. Nothing in the *Minor Offence Ordinance* paid attention to the message that was being written or the information conveyed by the mark upon the surface. However, the *Punishment for Vandalism Act* prioritised communication:

(i) writing, drawing, painting, marking or inscribing on any public property or private property any word, slogan, caricature, drawing, mark, symbol or other thing;

(ii) affixing, posting up or displaying on any public property or private property any poster, placard, advertisement, bill, notice, paper or other document; or

(iii) hanging, suspending, hoisting, affixing or displaying on or from any public property or private property any flag, bunting, standard, banner or the like with any word, slogan, caricature, drawing, mark, symbol or other thing;[20]

"Word, slogan, caricature…poster, placard, advertisement… flag, bunting, banner." The intent of the Bill was not about the damage caused by the act (as with most laws addressing vandalism around the world), but the attempt to communicate information. Expanding the definition of vandalism so widely enabled to PAP to eliminate all other communication of information from our public space, allowing them to assert a monopoly over the information that we see and hear.

Finally, both Lee and Barker were careful to point out that the law distinguished between permanent and non-permanent damage, and mandated caning only for the former.[21] However, this is only for the first offence. From the second offence onwards, the law effectively treats both permanent and non-permanent damage equally. Given the extremely broad latitude of the definition of vandalism, it is extremely easy to fall afoul of the law. Earlier this year, for example, the High Court ruled that merely leaning a placard against a wall could be vandalism:

'There may have been no permanent alteration let alone any damage to the properties in question. However, for as long as the items

20 Vandalism Act (Cap. 341, 1985 Rev. Ed. Sing.) s.2.

21 Singapore Parliamentary Debates, vol. 25 col. 296 and 298-99, 26 August 1966.

were being displayed, there certainly was "defacement" of the property. The appellant's conduct constituted anti-social behaviour of the type the [*Vandalism Act*] seeks to address.'[22]

Thus, returning to Jolovan Wham, while it is unlikely that Wham will be subjected to caning for this offence, Wham could easily be charged with vandalism a second time in the future. Under the law, he does not even need to commit vandalism himself. As Wee made clear in Parliament in 1966, it merely needs to be shown that Wham 'caused' someone else to commit vandalism. Given the massive breadth of what can be considered vandalism in the city-state, and in light of what the *Vandalism Act* is intended to achieve, the possibility of Wham being charged with vandalism again cannot be ruled out.

Conclusion

The public response to the charge of vandalism against Wham – the ridicule of the prosecutors and the sharing of photos of advertising posters and stickers – is understandable, but is based on a misunderstanding of the *Vandalism Act*. The Act was not meant to punish people who damage property. The Act was meant to give the PAP a monopoly over the information displayed in our public space; to conflate the 'nation' with the 'PAP'; to criminalise and smear political opposition to the PAP as being subhuman and anti-national; to deter people who might dare exercise their constitutional right to free speech and political expression in opposition to the PAP; and, ultimately to humiliate through caning anyone who might persist in standing up to the PAP in public. In this regard, Jolovan Wham is exactly the type of person that the *Vandalism Act* is designed to target.

---

22 Ng Chye Huay v Public Prosecutor [2017] SGHC 224, 14 September 2017. http://www.singaporelawwatch.sg/slw/attachments/109020/%5B2017%5D%20SGHC%20224.pdf

Bibliography

Chris Lydgate, *Lee's Law: How Singapore Crushes Dissent*. Victoria: Scribe Publications, 2003.

Poh Soo Kai, Tan Kok Fang, and Hong Lysa, *The 1963 Operation Coldstore in Singapore: Commemorating 50 Years*. Petaling Jaya: SIRD and Pusat Sejarah Rakyat, 2013.

Jothie Rajah, *Authoritarian Rule of Law: Legislation, Discourse, and Legitimacy in Singapore*. Cambridge: Cambridge University Press, 2012

Francis Seow, *Beyond Suspicion? The Singapore Judiciary*. Petaling Jaya: SIRD, 2006.

Thum Ping Tjin, "Justifying Colonial Rule in Post-Colonial Singapore", https://newnaratif.com/research/justifying-colonial-rule-in-post-colonial-singapore/

———, "The Malayan Vision of Lim Chin Siong: Unity, Non-violence, and Popular Sovereignty", *Inter-Asia Cultural Studies*, 18:3 (2017), 391-413.

Christopher Tremewan, *The Political Economy of Social Control in Singapore*. London: Macmillan, 1994

VIETNAM'S SOCIAL MEDIA BATTLE

MICHAEL TATARSKI | 22 JAN 2018

Social media platforms like Facebook are giving people access to information and reports outside of the Vietnamese government's control. Are the authorities fighting a losing battle, or will social media users see their online spaces shrink?

Look around the streets of Vietnam, and you'll notice crowds of young people glued to their smartphone screens. Such scenes are no different from elsewhere, but here, more than in almost any other country, there's a good chance they're interacting on Facebook.

Statistics put Vietnam in seventh place for its number of Facebook users, with 64 million accounts out of a population of nearly 93 million.[1] In Southeast Asia, only Indonesia and the Philippines have more users. YouTube is also hugely popular among Vietnamese internet users. This means tens of millions of Vietnamese are accessing news and information online without having to go through state-backed news outlets, though major newspapers such as VnExpress and Tuoi Tre have large online followings.

Recent stories have highlighted the stark divide between news reported by foreign publications and the state press. Last August Trinh Xuan Thanh, a former government official seeking asylum in Germany, was kidnapped by Vietnamese agents in central Berlin and ferreted back to Hanoi to stand trial for corruption. State newspapers reported Germany's allegations, but stressed the Ministry of Foreign Affairs' assertions that Thanh had voluntarily turned himself in. In the pre-Facebook era, few in Vietnam would have known better, but articles featuring detailed accounts of the kidnapping from publications such as The New York Times and Reuters were widely shared on Facebook.

---

1 https://www.statista.com/statistics/268136/top-15-countries-based-on-number-of-facebook-users/

Aware of this challenge to their domination over the flow of information, Vietnam's government has taken action: over the past six months officials have ramped up both their rhetoric and proposed actions against social media. The Ministry of Public Security introduced draft legislation in November which would require foreign tech companies such as Facebook and Google to set up servers inside Vietnam. This would have theoretically allowed the government to better monitor the flow of information across these networks and track certain users or posts. The proposal was recently dropped, but Google, in particular, is still facing official pressure to establish an office in the country so that the internet giant can better respond to requests from the government.

Truong Minh Tuan, the Minister of Information and Communications, has also voiced his displeasure with Facebook's alleged failure to remove content which the government considers "toxic".[2] Facebook responded a month later by deleting 159 anti-government accounts, while throughout 2017 Google removed 6,423 of the 7,140 videos that Vietnamese officials had flagged on YouTube.

Perhaps the most striking move regarding Vietnam's internet, which is classified by Freedom House as "Not Free"[3], was the December revelation of Force 47. This 10,000-member cyber warfare unit has been tasked with countering "wrong" views online, but their exact mandate and scope is unclear.

According to Reuters, Lieutenant General Nguyen Trong Nghia, deputy head of the military's political department, told a conference in Ho Chi Minh City: "In every hour, minute, and second we must be ready to fight proactively against the wrong views."[4] This phrase—"wrong views"—covers a broad range of discussion topics, from advocating for democracy to criticising economic policies.

It's not uncommon to see Vietnamese Facebook or Twitter users blame communism or the government for the country's maladies, but this harder line on social media could change that.

---

2 https://e.vnexpress.net/news/news/vietnam-unhappy-with-how-facebook-handles-requests-to-remove-toxic-content-3672127.html

3 https://freedomhouse.org/report/freedom-net/2017/vietnam

4 https://www.reuters.com/article/us-vietnam-security-cyber/vietnam-unveils-10000-strong-cyber-unit-to-combat-wrong-views-idUSKBN1EK0XN

Some Facebook users have even been punished recently for harmless posts, such as a young man who claimed it was snowing in a town that never sees snow, or a phone shop owner who compared holiday decorations in a Mekong Delta city to women's underwear. Facebook hoaxes are not new to Vietnam, but strident official reactions to them are.

All of these actions received extensive coverage in Vietnam's English- and Vietnamese-language press, but the reaction of the populace has been relatively muted.

Everyday users

"I don't really worry about it," says Diep Nguyen, who has run businesses in Ho Chi Minh City through both Facebook and Instagram. "I think it will change, but we will find a way. Sometimes when it's a very sensitive time and Facebook and Instagram are blocked, you can always use a VPN."

Vietnam has demonstrated both its capability and willingness to shut down social media. Following an enormous environmental disaster involving the Taiwanese company Formosa Plastics on the north-central coast in April 2016—several poor coastal provinces were devastated by a steel mill chemical release which wiped out fish stocks—protestors took to the streets around the country. The government allowed the demonstrations at first, but cracked down once anger turned towards the country's leadership.

Facebook, YouTube and Instagram were blocked for several successive weekends, though Twitter, which is not widely used by Vietnamese, remained available. Once the protests ended, access to all social media sites returned to normal. This was the first time in recent memory that multiple social networks were completely blocked at the same time.

Thinh Pham, an entrepreneur based in Ho Chi Minh City, sees these actions as a cautionary tale. "It's not something I'm thinking about, but I can totally see them doing it," he says. "I talked to a couple of people and they brought that [blocking Facebook] up and said, 'Oh, there's no way they could do it,' but they can."

But while the government's actions in mid-2016 demonstrated its ability to block access to social media platforms like Facebook, it might be too late for them to make this a permanent policy.

"Many Vietnamese get their news from the internet that the government just can't control," says Zachary Abuza, a professor at the National War College in Washington D.C. who specialises in Southeast Asian political and security issues. "They know that if they completely cracked down and create a closed internet like China that people would be on the warpath."

Zalo, a privately-owned messaging app, is the only social media platform created in Vietnam that has attracted a respectable user base, but it still pales in comparison to its American rivals. "Vietnam does have Zalo, but I don't use it much," Nguyen says. "I think it's because it's very local, and it's just a copy of WeChat, and only Vietnamese use it."

Online activists

The most intense digital battle this year will likely be between the Vietnamese government and activists who use Facebook and other platforms to shed light on issues such as corruption and environmental degradation.

For activists like Phong[5], this access is key, and he too believes it's too late for Vietnam to move against a free internet.

"I don't worry about that," he asserts. "The same story happened in China a long time ago, and their government… is more powerful and they have a longer vision than our government. When they saw that they could not control Facebook, they built another one, Weibo… and they forced their residents to use that platform only."

Vietnam had tried to emulate the Chinese model, partially restricting Facebook—back when it was still fairly new to Vietnam—in the hopes of creating its own alternative native platform. "They did it back in 2008 or 2009, trying to create an indigenous alternative to Facebook and it was a dismal failure," Abuza explains. "The government invested tens of millions of dollars and not a person used it because everyone knew why the government did it."

Following this failure, the Vietnam government could only watch as the number of Facebook users in the country ballooned. "From that time, I always knew that they cannot do anything to prevent it anymore," Phong says. Facebook quickly became the default site for everything

---

5 Not his real name, due to security concerns.

from keeping in touch with your parents to shopping and keeping up with the latest news from the BBC.

He recounts the weeks following the 2016 Formosa disaster. "It was a bad time for me, my friends and family," he says. "They did it [blocked Facebook and Instagram] because of that disaster only, but it affected lives. Our world was closed."

Many people, he explains, were simply trying to go about their daily lives and weren't involved in any protests, but their access was blocked anyway. Frustrations were voiced in personal interactions, and the fact that the disruptions were limited to weekends suggested that the government was aware of how upset people would be if access was blocked for a longer period.

"To me and many of my friends who really cared about the disaster, at that time the only thing we could do is talk about it," Phong adds. "We wanted to talk about it and share our opinions, we wanted the government to listen to the young people."

Phong was detained during a protest following the disaster and held with hundreds of other people for eight hours before his local police collected him. He was questioned for two more hours, though Phong says he was treated very well, and ultimately sent back home. His Facebook page is still monitored, he says, and he has received text messages from the police asking him to remove certain posts.

But even if he complies with the official requests, the news is out there in the international press. "They cannot prevent people from getting in touch with that data, that information, and the truth is the truth," he says.

Battle lines drawn

The stage is set this year for a collision between the popularity of social media and the Vietnamese government's desire to reign in what it sees as an unruly public space.

"You'll probably see the government try to compel Facebook to open up offices and research centres in Vietnam physically, which will give them a little more criminal vulnerability," Abuza says. "China has played this game with all of the internet companies for years, and more recently Indonesia forced Telegram to open up an office there so that they have some legal skin in the game if they do not comply with government laws."]

While the young Vietnamese interviewed for this story are optimistic that they won't lose Facebook, Vietnam's conservative leadership has consolidated power through a ruthless ongoing purge carried out under the banner of an anti-corruption drive and appears supremely confident.[6]

Vietnam's huge population of internet-savvy social media users has the upper hand for now, but 2018 is shaping up to be a crucial point in the country's digital history.

---

6 http://www.latimes.com/world/asia/la-fg-vietnam-corruption-2018-2018-story.html

TOGETHER, WE CAN: FIGHTING HATE SPEECH AGAINST THE ROHINGYA

BRENNAN O'CONNOR | 26 FEB 2018

As the crackdown against the Rohingya continues in Rakhine State, Rohingya in Yangon come forward to combat misinformation and promote peace.

Facing antagonism from many in Myanmar, Rohingya Muslims living in Yangon often hide their ethnic identity to avoid discrimination, but keeping silent is not always easy. Disturbed by the uptick in hateful comments following attacks on their community by the military in Rakhine State, some educated Rohingya living in Yangon feel compelled to speak out, at least in the digital realm.

"We found [that] what the media was reporting about the Rohingya was totally biased," says Soe Ko[1] from the headquarters of the youth group Together, We Can, situated in a high-rise flat in one of the Yangon's Muslim quarters.

"It was our idea to write the real news about what's really happening in Rakhine State, [accompanied with] a peace message in Burmese."

Together, We Can created a Facebook group[2] to voice their concerns about the torrent of hate speech and fake news about the Rohingya that has circulated online. They've also launched a website[3] to publish articles on issues affecting not only their community, but other minority groups as well.

---

1 Some names have been changed for security reasons.

2 https://www.facebook.com/peoplesvoicetd (in Burmese)

3 https://www.peoplesvoice.today/

Blending in, speaking out

Rohingya in Yangon live in daily fear of harassment by extreme nationalist Buddhists, or arrest by police. Even though many have National Registration Cards that allow them to stay in Yangon, most hide their identity by blending into the greater Muslim community. With the government, police and ultra-nationalists cracking down on the Rohingya and making life difficult, many just want to keep a low profile and stay out of trouble. "Only those that are close to them know who they are," Ko says, even though their accent sometimes gives them away.

Most of the Rohingya in Yangon moved there from Rakhine State before the 1990s; it was still possible to change family registries with immigration then, Ko says. The citizenship law with regard to the Rohingya has a convoluted history: although Rohingya had been granted citizenship under an old law from the 1940s, subsequent legislation and official lists of "national races" in Myanmar excluded the Rohingya from official recognition as an ethnic group. Selective and arbitrary processes to replace identity documents under the more recent law led to many Rohingya losing full citizenship. Various other measures, such as restrictions on movement, marriage and childbirth, or frequent policing and "spot-checks" on residences, continue to make life difficult and precarious for the ethnic minority group, particularly back in Rakhine State.[4]

According to Ko, identifying as Rohingya in Yangon wasn't an issue before 2012. The violence that broke out in Rakhine State between Rohingya Muslims and Rakhine Buddhists that year was accompanied by the growing prominence of an extremist Buddhist nationalist movement. Some Buddhist monks—most famously Ashin Wirathu, who TIME magazine described as "The Face of Buddhist Terror"[5] in 2013—started preaching hate against all Muslims, and encouraged the boycott of Islamic businesses under the nationalist 969 movement, instigating attacks on Muslim homes and businesses across the country.

Having largely achieved their goal of seeking better salaries and higher education for their children, Rohingya families in the city are often reluctant to risk their hard-earned gains by getting involved in political or sensitive issues. But as things got worse in their home state—including an outburst of violence in October 2016 that shook many of the urban-dwelling Rohingya—Ko says that more are coming forward.

---

4 http://www.fortifyrights.org/downloads/Policies_of_Persecution_Feb_25_Fortify_Rights.pdf

5 http://content.time.com/time/magazine/article/0,9171,2146000,00.html

"After continuous human rights violations they are becoming more aware of what is going on there, and they feel the need to do something," Ko says.

The violence in Rakhine State

Since late August, a systematic military campaign in Rakhine State on the western coast of Myanmar has forced more than 655,000[6] to flee their homes and seek refuge in cramped, squalid camps in neighbouring Bangladesh. Numbers at the camps continue to grow. Survivors bring with them harrowing accounts of gang rape by soldiers, torched villages and being shot at while escaping.

The military denies targeting civilians, instead blaming insurgents from the Arakan Rohingya Salvation Army (ARSA) for burning villages after the rebel group attacked multiple police posts and an army base in northern Rakhine State. But in-depth investigative reports have found otherwise; a story published by the Associated Press on February 1, 2018, confirmed mass graves and painted a picture of "a systematic slaughter of Rohingya Muslim civilians by the military, with help from Buddhist neighbours".[7] About a week later, Reuters published the story two of their journalists—Wa Lone and Kyaw Soe Oo—had been investigating when they were detained "for allegedly obtaining confidential documents relating to Rakhine" and later charged under the Official Secrets Act.[8] Their investigation confirmed the Burmese military's involvement in the campaign to clear Rohingya out of the coastal village of Inn Din.

Options are limited for the beleaguered Rohingya. Those with relatives in Yangon find it difficult to join them. The police arrested ten people travelling in a vehicle in October last year after it was suspected to be part of a smuggling operation to Yangon from Rakhine State, according to *Irrawaddy* magazine.[9] Seven of those arrested were Rohingya. A Rohingya man found sleeping on the street—Ko suspects he was a recent arrival from Rakine State—was beaten by Burmese nationalists and then arrested.

---

6 https://reliefweb.int/sites/reliefweb.int/files/resources/weeklysitre10cxbban1.pdf

7 https://apnews.com/ef46719c5d1d4bf98cfefcc4031a5434

8 https://www.reuters.com/article/us-myanmar-rakhine-events-specialreport/special-report-how-myanmar-forces-burned-looted-and-killed-in-a-remote-village-idUSKBN1FS3BH

9 https://www.irrawaddy.com/news/burma/police-arrest-seven-self-identifying-rohingya-irrawaddy-region.html

Last May, the police had to fire shots in the air to disperse a mob of extremist monks and their followers who had gathered around a block of flats in a predominantly Muslim neighbourhood.[10] The group, which calls itself the Patriotic Monks Union, claimed that Rohingya were being illegally sheltered in the apartment block. A police search turned up nothing.

The discrimination and prejudice doesn't just affect new arrivals; even Rohingya who have lived in Yangon for years have been on the receiving end. A few years ago, Ko was forced to resign his high-level position at a prominent international non-governmental organization (INGO) after a government clerk discovered he was Rohingya. Although his employment was legal, it was decided that it would be the best if he left the INGO, so his status would not hamper the organisation's operations.

The skills that he's picked up in INGO work, such as team organisation and collaboration, has come in useful. Even before Together, We Can, Ko and other Yangon-based Rohingya were already involved in organising secret meetings between the Rohingya and other communities as a way to build bridges, keep lines of communication open, and counter the antagonism being spread by nationalists. When the group came together last June, they were able to tap on not just his experience, but the knowledge of other members who have also worked for international organisations.

Fighting online vitriol

Neither the police nor the military have interfered with Together, We Can so far. However, their Facebook group, named Pyithu Ahtan—"Peoples' Voice" in English—is at times littered with hate speech from trolls.

Some people use bad language, Ko says, or post photos of pork. Comments use the term "kalar"—a racial slur against dark-skinned complexions that's now most often directed at Muslims. Under a video of Rohingya fleeing to Bangladesh, one person wrote that they should go back to their country—a common argument by ultra-nationalists who consider the Rohingya to be interlopers from Bangladesh, despite the fact that the majority of them have lived in Myanmar for generations.

---

10 http://www.thesundaily.my/news/2017/05/10/police-fire-shots-break-myanmar-nationalist-muslim-scuffle

Ko says it's rare for the moderator to delete comments or block people from the Facebook group. They prefer to try reasoning with them, he explains, writing things like "we are trying to promote peace" or "give a voice to the victim".

It might come as a surprise to anyone who has ever engaged in a heated argument on social media, but this approach sometimes works. Once, after the moderator responded to a negative comment, the sender had a change of heart and later thanked the group for its good work.

Separating the fake from the real

Ko was unhappy to find that his friends from university were also writing hateful messages about the Rohingya and condoning the military campaign in Rakhine State, but attributes their participation to the prevalence of misinformation, often spread by the Burmese military themselves. "You can see the intention of what they [the army] are doing. Totally releasing the fake news and hate speeches," he says. "Demonising the victim, it's what they are doing to get the support from the public and increase the support [for] the military."

This spread of false information and propaganda has been a big problem in Myanmar, where media literacy is still low.[11] Doctored images quickly go viral, creating a false picture of what's happening in Rakhine State. Journalists on a rare government-organised trip to Rakhine State were handed photographs were later discovered to have been faked[12] to support the government's claim that Muslims were the ones who had burned down homes and villages. Accusations of "fake news" fly in all directions.[13]

With contacts on the ground in Rakhine State and Bangladesh, Myint Yaza*, a second-year law student and member of Together, We Can, says the group is able to find out what's really going on. For example, whenever a Rohingya is killed by the military in Rakhine State, it's often reported in the state media that the deceased was a terrorist and member of ARSA. But the youth group can quickly verify this with their contacts, then report their findings on their Facebook or in an article on their website.

---

11 http://unesdoc.unesco.org/images/0024/002447/244760E.pdf

12 http://www.bbc.co.uk/news/world-asia-41222210

13 http://www.bbc.co.uk/news/world-asia-41170570

Together, We Can also makes sure not to focus exclusively on human rights abuses against the Rohingya. They've also drawn attention[14] to recent deaths in Mrauk U township in northern Rakhine State, after police opened fire on Rakhine demonstrators, killing seven and injuring 12 on January 16. The protesters had gathered in the thousands, without prior permission from the government, to protest the government's decision to ban celebrations of the 233rd anniversary of the fall of the ancient Arakan Kingdom.

"Everyone needs to know the real situation in Myanmar and that is what we are trying to do," Yaza says.

Disappointment with the Lady

There are fears that violence against Rohingya and other Muslims will spread to Yangon, says Jessica Olney, an American humanitarian working with Together, We Can. Last September, the youth group cancelled an evening meeting after a rumour spread that Buddhists planned to attack Muslims in the commercial capital. A mob of seventy people attacked a Muslim goat slaughterhouse in central Myanmar's Magwe division around the same period; the police used rubber bullets to disperse the crowd after they gathered outside a mosque.

Like many international observers, Olney doesn't understand why human rights icon and State Counsellor Daw Aung San Suu Kyi has been silent about the Rohingya. "It just seems like no one really knows the reason why she doesn't speak up," she says. "It's just presumed that its fear of losing power."

Ko disagrees that Suu Kyi risks losing her popularity if she spoke positively of the Rohingya: "If she says something that is reasonable, and which is understandable, the public will listen to her. Many people admire her."

Although Suu Kyi has little control over the Burmese military, Ko says she's also been releasing biased information about its activities in Rakhine State. He speculates that she might be trying to avoid a confrontation with the military while her party tries to amend the 2008 Constitution—which allows the military to retain significant amounts of power in the country—but thinks that the Rohingya are simply not a priority.

---

14 https://www.facebook.com/peoplesvoicetd/posts/364387380639565 (in Burmese)

"It's like she is sacrificing the Rohingya for the majority," he says.

Yet Olney says members of the youth group still support the state counsellor. "There is no other alternative," they tell her. "We have to keep hoping that the NLD [Suu Kyi's ruling National League for Democracy) will do something beneficial for us in the long run."

Ko's parents are still in northern Rakhine State. Their neighbourhood in Maungdaw had moved out for a month during the army's crackdown, just in case they were targeted. They returned after hearing that their home had looted, despite being located right next to a police post.

Bribes have to be paid to the police and the ward administration, for protection; Ko has to keep sending money home so his family can continue to pay the police the amounts that they demand.

Ko worries about them; his mother is old and suffers from hypertension and other medical conditions. On top of that, he says that they've been traumatised by the ongoing crisis. He hopes to bring them to Yangon, but acquiring the necessary documents will be no easy feat.

THE DECAY OF PRESS FREEDOM UNDER AUNG SAN SUU KYI

VICTORIA MILKO | 05 MAR 2018

Many expected more democratic freedoms in Myanmar under Aung San Suu Kyi's National League of Democracy, but journalists have learnt the hard way that things are not getting better.

Burmese journalists Wa Lone and Kyaw Soe Oo were just doing their jobs, meeting sources and digging deeper into the story they were working on. That's what they thought, anyway. But the Burmese government saw it differently. In December 2017, the two Reuters journalists were arrested and charged for breaching the Official Secrets Act.

For decades the press in Myanmar operated under the oppressive rule of the military junta. Publications faced heavy censorship and journalists who wished to write articles critical of the government were forced to do so in secret; the threat of either imprisonment or exile hung over their heads.

When former President Thein Sein's government took power in 2011 in a high-profile transition towards a nominally civilian government, the situation began to improve. Private daily newspapers, for instance, were allowed to be published for the first time in decades. Although restrictions still remained in place, the victory of Nobel Laureate Aung San Suu Kyi's National League for Democracy (NLD) in the 2015 elections gave many hope that greater press freedom would soon follow.

[Yet in the time since the NLD took power, it's become chillingly clear that freedom of the press is far from a priority for those in power. There has instead been an uptick in the persecution of members of the press: colonial and junta-era laws have been deliberately kept intact by the government, and authorities stifle reporting on a growing range of topics.]

The media under assault

"Myanmar's media, both local and foreign, is under heavy assault as security measures used to suppress the press under military rule are reactivated under Suu Kyi's quasi-democratic regime," writes Shawn Crispin, the senior Southeast Asia representative for Committee to Protect Journalists. "It marks a dramatic reversal in recent press freedom gains and augurs ill for the country's delicate transition from military to elected rule."[1]

It didn't always seem like this was going to be the case. Within the first year of the newly elected parliament, the government amended 19 and enacted 23 laws in total, including abolishing the notorious 1950 Emergency Provisions Act—a law used by the former military regime to target dissidents and journalists—which carried penalties as extreme as life imprisonment or even death.[2]

But hopes of further progress towards press freedom quickly diminished after that promising start.

In June 2017, three journalists photographing a routine drug-burning ceremony by an armed ethnic group were arrested and charged under the Unlawful Associations Act, a provision used against journalists during military rule to discourage reporting on the Myanmar's numerous armed ethnic conflicts. The journalists were held without bail for several months before being released after the charges were dropped.

A few months later, in October 2017, two journalists working for Turkish media TRT World were arrested and charged with the 1934 Burma Aircraft Act after flying a drone through the capital city of Naypyidaw. Their local driver and fixer were also arrested and held without bail, despite being found to have never operated the drone.

The case of the two Reuters journalists, Wa Lone and Kyaw Soe Oo, has attracted plenty of international attention. They had been working on an extensive investigation that proved the involvement of the Burmese military in the killing of Rohingya civilians in Rakhine state. The story, later published by the wire agency as a special report[3], has triggered calls

---

1 https://cpj.org/blog/2018/02/threats-arrests-and-access-denied-as-myanmar-backt.php

2 https://www.irrawaddy.com/opinion/guest-column/burma-one-year-daw-aung-san-suu-kyi-press-freedom-lags-behind-democratic-progress.html

3 https://www.reuters.com/investigates/special-report/myanmar-rakhine-events/

from the United States for an independent probe.[4] The journalists are currently being held in prison pending trial; if found guilty, they could be sentenced to up to 14 years in prison.

Aung San Suu Kyi, Myanmar's de-facto leader, has voiced support for the reporters' pre-trial detentions. Veteran US diplomat Bill Richardson claimed that she had been "furious" when he brought up the journalists' case during a meeting of an international panel on the Rohingya crisis.[5] He later quit the panel.

Ambiguous laws

Since the NLD came to power in January 2016, there has also been an increase in the use of Article 66(d) of the 2013 Telecommunications Law, a law which Human Rights Watch describes as having "opened the door to a wave of criminal prosecutions of individuals for peaceful communications on Facebook and has increasingly been used to stifle criticism of the authorities."[6]

Article 66(d) stipulates that people can be jailed for up to three years for "extorting, coercing, restraining wrongfully, defaming, disturbing, causing undue influence or threatening any person using a telecommunications network." The language of the law is ambiguous—a deliberate feature of many junta-era laws—and thus allows police and officials to enforce it selectively.

According to Free Expression Myanmar's analysis of the 106 criminal complaints made under the article between November 2015 and November 2017, 81 cases took place since January 2016. Between 2016-17, every person charged under the article was convicted and sentenced to prison.[7]

In August 2017, following a three-day debate over proposed amendments to the 2013 Telecommunications Law, President U Htin Kyaw signed into law changes that restricted the lodging of cases under 66(d) to those directly impacted by the action in question. The amendment

---

4 http://www.straitstimes.com/asia/se-asia/call-for-independent-probe-into-atrocity

5 https://www.theguardian.com/world/2018/jan/25/
    aung-san-suu-kyi-lacks-moral-leadership-us-diplomat-bill-richardson-quits-rohingya-panel

6 https://www.hrw.org/news/2017/06/29/burma-repeal-section-66d-2013-
    telecommunications-law

7 http://freeexpressionmyanmar.org/wp-content/uploads/2017/12/66d-no-real-change.pdf

also enabled defendants to be granted bail and reduced the maximum penalty to two years.

These changes fell short of the expectations of activists and human rights organisations that called for a full repeal of the law. Critics of the amendment say that the legislation still contains broad and undefined language that enables the continued prosecution of the press.

"It is widely used against journalists and activists. Some media even refuse to publish articles which criticize the military or the government to avoid being sued and jailed," Burma Campaign UK said in a statement. "The law puts such control on the media that it leads to self-censorship."[8]

Barriers to reporting

Arrests and legal action are just one aspect of the barriers to independent reporting in Myanmar today. Access to large parts of the country remain restricted; this includes the majority of Rakhine State, where over half a million Rohingya Muslims have fled a brutal crackdown by the Burmese military. Journalists can only visit the region via state-run media trips curated by the government and military.

"The space in which journalists can operate in Myanmar has been getting smaller and smaller since the Rakhine conflict kicked off again in August 2017," says Katie Arnold, a freelance journalist who worked in Myanmar for two-and-a-half years. "Places journalists can travel in-country are limited, and government officials who are willing to speak to you are [growing fewer in number]. There's such a small space in which we can effectively work, which then limits the quality of the work we can produce."

Freelance and staff journalists have been subjected to much longer wait times for visas to work in the country, as well as additional mandatory paperwork that requires applicants to sign documents promising not to travel to restricted areas. Other journalists who have routinely worked in the country have been denied visas entirely, including reporters who have worked with the BBC. Yet many are reluctant to go on record with their experience, for fear of being blacklisted and blocked completely from reporting within the country.

8 http://burmacampaign.org.uk/media/Repressive-Laws-Section-66-d.pdf

Self-censorship and repercussions

Like in many other authoritarian states, journalists often find themselves in positions where refusals to exercise self-censorship could lead to potentially severe consequences.

In late 2016, Fiona MacGregor, then the investigations editor at *The Myanmar Times*, was fired after writing an article about the Burmese military reportedly raping citizens during operations in the country's western Rakhine State.

Her report led to presidential spokesperson Zaw Htay blasting her on social media for being "biased" against the government. MacGregor says she was fired by the newspaper for breaching company policy by "damaging national reconciliation and the paper's reputation."[9]

Several staff members of the English edition quickly responded on social media to MacGregor's termination. Others privately reached out to professional contacts to share their discontent with the paper's actions. The English edition staff ran an ad apologising to readers for the lack of a clear editorial policy.

"I felt like I didn't know what else to do," says Robert Vogt, who had been a reporter at the paper when MacGregor was fired. "I didn't feel courageous enough to quit my job but did feel courageous enough to let other people know what was going on—and I wasn't the only person there who felt this way."

Despite reporters' efforts, things remain grim at *The Myanmar Times* and in Burmese media in general, says Vogt.

"I don't think things got any better," he says. "The owner runs the paper however he likes and it seems no one is stepping up for those writing about Rakhine State or other tough issues. It feels like journalists are powerless at the hands of this government, which has no respect for journalism."

The recent appointment of former Reuters reporter Aung Hla Tun as the Deputy Minister for Information has not inspired much confidence. He has been critical of the international media's coverage of the Rohingya crisis, stating in a press conference that "the greatest responsibility of media today in Myanmar is safeguarding our national image." With such a clearly stated priority, there is little expectation of him facilitating a more open and transparent relationship with the press.

9 https://www.theguardian.com/world/2016/nov/04/myanmar-times-journalist-fired-fiona-macgregor

On top of all this, threats to one's physical safety remain. Journalists receive death threats on social media networks from irate trolls, threatening comments are regularly made against media workers by nationalist monks, and members of the press are often tailed by government and private officials while in the field. CPJ reported on February 12, 2018, that Associated Press journalist and Pulitzer Prize winner Esther Htusan fled her home country in late 2017 in the face of increasing threats to her safety.[10]

"The basis of democratic freedom is freedom of speech," Aung San Suu Kyi once said in 2010, but it seems as if free speech has quickly fallen to the wayside for her administration.

"I think that she has proven herself less dedicated to free press being part of a democracy than many had hoped," says one journalist who used to work in Myanmar, and wishes to remain anonymous due to the sensitivity of criticising the government. "It may have been naive… the way a lot of journalists heralded her rise and sacrifice, expecting her to act as human rights advocate instead of a politician."

But being the figurehead of a struggle for freedom is vastly different from playing politics, and many have been disappointed in Aung San Suu Kyi's performance thus far. If the National League for Democracy wishes to stand for democracy, institutional and cultural changes promoting free expression will be imperative, but don't appear to be forthcoming so far.

---

10 https://cpj.org/blog/2018/02/threats-arrests-and-access-denied-as-myanmar-backt.php

RED LINES AND (SELF-)CENSORSHIP: JOURNALISM IN SOUTHEAST ASIA

KIRSTEN HAN | 03 MAY 2018

On World Press Freedom Day, New Naratif's contributors highlight the obstacles they've faced working in and reporting on Southeast Asia.

Reporters Without Borders (RSF) didn't have much good news to share when it released its 2018 World Press Freedom Index. Somewhat predictably, China took the a large chunk of the spotlight. But RSF pointed out the implications for Southeast Asia: "Internationally, the Chinese government is trying to establish a 'new world media order' under its influence, by exporting its oppressive methods, information censorship system and Internet surveillance tools," said RSF in its regional press release.[1]

A list of Southeast Asian countries—Vietnam, Cambodia, Thailand, Malaysia and Singapore—were identified as having emulated the Chinese model, while Myanmar and the Philippines received special mentions for the decline in media protections and safety of journalists.

There's been a depressing number of high-profile breaches of press freedom in Southeast Asia over the past year. After 24 years of operations, the *Cambodia Daily* announced in September 2017 that it was shutting down less than two weeks after Cambodian Prime Minister Hun Sen described the publishers as "thieves", alleging that they had failed to pay a hefty tax bill (which the publication disputed).[2] In January 2018, the Filipino Securities and Exchange Commission ordered the

---

1 https://rsf.org/en/rsf-index-2018-asia-pacific-democracies-threatened-chinas-media-
control-model

2 https://www.cambodiadaily.com/news/cambodia-daily-announces-immediate-closure-
amid-threats-134283/

closure of Rappler Inc. by claiming that it had violated restrictions on foreign ownership of local media.[3] In Myanmar, court proceedings are ongoing against two Reuters' journalists, Wa Lone and Kyaw Soe Oo—proceedings in which a police officer admitted that that he'd been ordered to entrap them.[4]

Last month, *New Naratif*'s managing director Thum Pingtjin and myself made the headlines[5] in Singapore when the Accounting and Corporate Regulatory Authority (ACRA) publicly refused an application to register a Singapore subsidiary of Observatory Southeast Asia, which publishes this website. ACRA said that allowing the company's registration would be contrary to Singapore's national interest and implied that we were "being used by foreigners to pursue a political activity in Singapore"—an allegation that we refuted.[6]

But one doesn't need to be shut down or jailed to face threats to press freedom. Behind the headline-grabbing cases, journalists across the region face daily challenges. On World Press Freedom Day, *New Naratif* contributors talk about the obstacles in their way.

"Red lines"

All too often, issues over what can or can't be said emerge even before anything's been written. In most Southeast Asian countries, there are "red lines"—sensitive subjects that can make it difficult for journalists to say very much at all.

Some of these are well-known. Thailand's lese majeste laws can make writing or speaking about the monarchy extremely difficult, and perhaps even dangerous, for everyone in the country. As of January this year, at least 94 people have been prosecuted on lese majeste charges since the May 2014 coup.[7] Writing about the royalty in other Southeast Asian countries, like Malaysia and Brunei, can also be a risky business.

---

3 http://newsinfo.inquirer.net/960631/sec-orders-closure-of-rappler-site

4 https://www.reuters.com/article/us-myanmar-journalists/
   myanmar-police-set-up-reuters-reporters-in-sting-police-witness-idUSKBN1HR12Q

5 https://www.channelnewsasia.com/news/singapore/acra-rejects-bid-by-thum-ping-
   tjin-kirsten-han-to-register-10127496

6 https://newnaratif.com/journalism/statement-new-naratif/

7 https://www.reuters.com/article/us-thailand-king-insults/thai-court-jails-blind-woman-
   for-1-1-2-years-over-royal-insult-idUSKBN1ET0UA

In Myanmar, the media is blocked not only from Rakhine State, where the Rohingya crisis continues to unfold, but also from many other restricted areas in the country. Other boundaries are not so literal. According to Victoria Milko—who's covered the erosion of press freedom in Myanmar—reporting on military activities, ethnic armed insurgencies, or anything critical of the government, on top of the current sensitivities related to the Rohingya crisis, requires journalists to tread with great care.[8]

But other countries' "danger zones" might be less well-known to outsiders. In countries like Malaysia, Singapore and Brunei, covering race and religion can be dicey, particularly when legislation like Singapore's Sedition Act defines something as being seditious if it has the tendency "to promote feelings of ill-will and hostility between different races or classes of the population of Singapore".[9]

Febriana Firdaus, *New Naratif*'s consulting editor for Jakarta and Papua, identifies three sensitive areas when it comes to reporting in the country: the massacre of communists (or alleged communists) in 1965–1966, LGBT issues, and the matter of Papua, where there's ongoing conflict between the Indonesian government and particular segments of the population.

"Reporting on the 1965 story can be dangerous, especially when we talk about the controversy of the murky history behind the anti-communist propaganda during the Cold War," says Firdaus. "It's a no-go for people to publicly discuss why communism has been banned in this country."

Writing or reporting anything that might question (or be perceived to question) the established narrative could attract threats and harassment. The sensitivity around communism is still so present in Indonesia that accusations of being "pro-communist" can lead to concerns of safety. In 2016, Firdaus was subjected to threats and intimidation[10] while covering an anti-communist symposium, and also became the target for an onslaught of violent threats online[11] that pushed her to go into hiding.[12]

8 https://newnaratif.com/journalism/decay-press-freedom-aung-san-suu-kyi/

9 https://sso.agc.gov.sg/Act/SA1948?ProvIds=pr3-.

10 https://en.tempo.co/read/news/2016/06/03/055776685/AJI-Condemns-Intimidation-against-Journalist

11 http://www.freemedia.at/indonesia-reporter-in-hiding-after-harassment-campaign/

12 https://www.hrw.org/news/2016/06/10/dispatches-indonesias-journalists-under-threat-militants

LGBT issues in Indonesia have also become more and more sensitive. "I was interrogated by immigration recently about my activities here. Most of the topics they asked me about were predictable —Papua and so on—but I was surprised that I was questioned about whether I wrote 'about LGBT', as they phrased it," says Kate Walton, a Jakarta-based journalist who has written about gender[13] and LGBT issues[14] for *New Naratif.*

"Since a few years ago, I've even refused to comment on the topic to foreign journalists for fear of retribution [both from the government/police and the community]," she adds. "Journalists reporting on LGBT issues have been threatened with violence and reported to the police and to immigration for allegedly violating the Pancasila [Indonesia's five founding principles]."

The issue of access

Press freedom isn't just about the journalists' physical safety, but the entire climate in which reporters have to operate. Outside of prosecutions or threats, there are far more mundane ways in which reporters are impeded and obstructed.

One example is to, quite literally, stop journalists from being present, or block them from accessing newsmakers. "In a country where most media outlets are owned by the government, Malaysiakini has long been accused of being a tool of the opposition," says Koh Aun Qi, a sub-editor at *Malaysiakini* who wrote one of *New Naratif*'s earliest articles.[15] "Our journalists continue to be banned from attending (or, in some cases, asked to leave) certain government events."

Another way, particularly in countries that lack freedom of information legislation, to put up roadblocks to critical or investigative reporting is to restrict access to full or reliable data. Without the ability to access the information—and lacking in resources to conduct independent large-scale studies themselves—journalists, particularly freelancers, are stymied in attempts to do in-depth work.

"As a business/economic journalist working in Malaysia, my main grouse is with the department of statistics," says Emir Imrantski, who

---

13 https://newnaratif.com/journalism/perils-spg-jakarta/

14 https://newnaratif.com/journalism/more-dangerous-than-nuclear-war/

15 https://newnaratif.com/journalism/penang-hokkien-and-its-struggle-for-survival/

wrote for *New Naratif* about Malaysia's bumiputra policy.[16] "There have been numerous occasions where I need fact and figures to support my story and the official statistics are outdated. In other cases, the data published by the government may not be in line with the ones available in the previous year; the ethnographic breakdown might be removed or the grouping of the data has been simplified."

Safety and self-censorship

The challenges journalists face aren't always straightforward: the lack of press freedom often means that problems and dangers are neither consistent, nor always clearly identifiable. But the effects of this are often very relative—foreign and local members of the press often grapple with different issues and risks.

"As an American freelance journalist working in Southeast Asia, I have a certain level of protection—my family is far away, my income comes mostly from foreign media outlets, and I can always go home and be safe," says Nithin Coca, who often reports on Indonesia.[17] "But for the people I work with—local journalists and sources—this is not the case, and I always have to be aware that what I report on could have consequences far beyond a single story."

This doesn't mean foreign journalists don't have worries of their own: for those settled in Southeast Asia, the lack of citizenship can be a reminder of a particular precarity. "As a foreign journalist in Indonesia, the price of writing an article saying the wrong thing is steep: arrest, detention, deportation and blacklisting," says Aisyah Llewellyn, *New Naratif*'s consulting editor for North Sumatra. I've observed a similar concern in Singapore among non-citizen reporters, where stories of foreign journalists unable to renew their employment passes circulate within industry circles.

Such difficult environments tend to trigger anxieties that encourage self-censorship, particularly when one's job depends on it.

"In Malaysia, there are two camps, at least that's the way I look at it, of journalists. Ones who write for their owners and the others who write for their audiences," says Susan Tam, *New Naratif*'s consulting editor for Malaysia. "Self-censorship is a real problem for journalists who have to

---

16 https://newnaratif.com/journalism/malaise-malaysian-malays/

17 https://newnaratif.com/journalism/indonesias-ongoing-democracy-project/

work for their media owners, while access to information and security obstacles [are issues] for the ones that have bit more independence. It is frustrating when those in power who want to avoid accountability push out more repressive laws or buy up more outlets of expressions."

"Every local journalist knows where *not* to cross the line, powerful people or evil corporations you can't mess with, what to report and what can't be reported," says Yen Duong, who contributed a story on Vietnamese youth.[18] "What I'm often told is that if I want to work in this field in the long run, I'll just have to 'compromise'."

It's a situation that can lead to disillusionment and disappointment. "Being a local journalist in Vietnam means being underpaid, under-appreciated, and undervalued for the job that many of my colleagues, I believe, choose to follow out of passion," she adds. "But will that passion die or survive if you decide to submit to control?"

Sources and responsibility

Then there are the times when the issue isn't about the journalists, but about sources—the people who share bits of their lives and provide information to substantiate a story or contribute crucial context. Finding good sources is an uphill battle in societies where people are afraid of speaking out.

"It's widely known that writing about sensitive issues in Vietnam is difficult, meaning that I sometimes have to leave information out of stories," says Michael Tatarski, who's written for *New Naratif* about environmental issues[19] and online regulation[20] in the Communist state. "Worryingly, even discussing mundane topics can leave interviewees scared of talking out of line. I once tried to interview someone associated with Saigon's river bus service, and when I pulled out my recorder he reacted as if I had pulled out a weapon."

Protecting and being responsible for sources is an issue that occupies the thoughts of every ethical journalist, and rightly so. But it's a minefield in contexts where the powerful have wide-ranging options to exert costs, and where the boundaries of what's "safe" might not always be clear.

The stories that journalists tell can have very real consequences on sources. "I spoke to villagers about pollution and health impacts of a

---

18 https://newnaratif.com/journalism/the-political-apathy-of-vietnamese-youth/

19 https://newnaratif.com/journalism/backed-banks-vietnam-embraces-dirty-coal/

20 https://newnaratif.com/journalism/vietnams-social-media-battle/

nearby factory, a factory that was also providing them with some basic temporary jobs. I found, a few months later, that the factory had stopped giving work to villagers because they had spoken to me openly, and they were upset about losing a vital source of income," recalls Coca.

"In Southeast Asia, we can't just be reporting, we have to do our very best to ensure the safety and well-being of everyone around us, something that, at times, can be impossible."

Journalists don't just need consent from sources, but _informed_ consent. It's important that sources—particularly those who lack power or capital—are aware of the potential risks and repercussions before agreeing to put their comments on record, but this isn't always easy in contexts where people aren't very media-savvy. Journalists are then left to wonder if they know what they might be getting themselves into.

"People here, especially in North Sumatra, will tell you anything. I enjoy amazing access and almost everything is on record. But this comes with its own set of issues," says Llewellyn. "Because people are so open, it's up to me to filter out what may be too sensitive to publish. I worry, like many journalists, that interviewees often don't appreciate the consequences of some of the things they tell me."

What this means for Southeast Asia

"Every morning when I wake up in my Yangon apartment I think about the illegal acts I'll be potentially committing for work that day," says Milko. "For example, when I meet and interview the leader of an armed ethnic group about human rights abuses by the Burmese military will I be charged with the Unlawful Association Act?"

She adds: "The list of laws—both modern and colonial-era—that have been deliberately left intact in the country directly impact my ability to work while simultaneously threatening my safety, thus forcing me to make daily choices about just 'how much' I'm willing to risk in order to provide a voice for those who have been intimidated or silenced by authorities across the country."

When journalists are forced to operate within such a climate, the impact is felt by the readers and audiences they serve. When the press is afraid to broach particular "no-go" subjects, societies end up being less informed about crucial institutions and issues, and the powerful continue to operate with little need to be accountable for their actions. When access to governments, influential actors, and data is blocked, the lack of in-depth, investigative work leaves everyone in the dark.⌉

Ultimately, it isn't just about the livelihood and daily routines of a bunch of reporters—when the press is not free, everyone is the poorer for it.

CIVIL LIBERTIES

DISAPPEARED IN MALAYSIA

KATE MAYBERRY | 30 MAY 2018

The families of four individuals who have disappeared in Malaysia are pressing for answers in a public enquiry with few leads.

In a conference room in a Kuala Lumpur office tower, Susanna Liew waited anxiously for a decision from the Malaysian human rights commission on its enquiry into the disappearance of her husband, Raymond Koh—a well-known social worker and Christian pastor—almost a year before.

Under discussion was a surprise development in the case. The police had just informed the commission that they were about to charge a suspect in court; a man they had previously ruled out of their investigation. Citing a clause in the legislation relating to the conduct of the commission's enquiries, the police wanted proceedings to stop.

The minutes ticked by. Journalists played with their phones. Lawyers and enquiry officials milled about. Notices taped up on the walls warned against taking photos.

Liew sat quietly.

Frustrated and disappointed at the seemingly glacial pace of the police investigation into the 62-year-old's abduction, Liew and her adult children had turned to Suhakam, as the commission's known in Malaysia, to provide them with some of the answers they so desperately wanted. Now, three months after the enquiry had begun in October 2017, the opportunity appeared to be slipping away.

As the three commissioners—led by lawyer and retired Court of Appeal judge Mah Weng Kai—returned to the room, everyone rose from their seats.

"We have decided we will immediately cease the enquiry (into Raymond Koh's case), until further notice," Mah announced to the room. "We will continue with the other two cases."

At a hastily organised press conference with their lawyers, the family was unable to hide their disappointment.

"It's very shocking for us," Liew told journalists as she struggled to hold back her tears. Her two eldest children—Jonathan and Esther—sat close by. "Our hope in coming to Suhakam was to find some answers to the many questions we have of Pastor Raymond's abduction, and we are very disappointed that even this hope of exercising our human rights to truth and justice is being denied to us."

"It's not easy not knowing where he is"

A month later, Liew is selling jewellery at a weekend market in a Kuala Lumpur shopping mall not far from where her husband disappeared. The semi-precious stones and pearl necklaces sparkle under the lights and one of her regular customers is trying on a necklace. "She brings in the best things," the woman says, smiling and admiring the chain in the mirror.

Liew shows little outward sign of the anguish she must have endured since her husband's disappearance (when the enquiry visited the street where he was snatched, Liew found it so upsetting she had to take a moment for herself, holding back from the crowd and finding comfort on a friend's shoulder).

Today she's dressed in an elegant floral dress and cardigan, her hair neatly bobbed and a string of pearls at her neck, as she chats with the customers and the friend who's come to help her out with the stall.

But over a cup of green tea latte, Liew admits some days are better than others.

"It's not easy; not knowing where he is or how he's being treated," she says of the man she married in 1983. "Sometimes I just don't want to go there, imagining what's happened to him.

"How I cope is actually my deep faith in God," she continues. "There's a verse in the Bible—Romans 8.28—that God has his purpose. We don't necessarily understand why or how he's going to work out everything, but I believe that Raymond is in God's hands. I just have to release Raymond to God. Whether he's alive or dead, he's a hero to me." Liew's voice cracks. She stops to wipe away the tears that have trickled down her cheek.

The kidnapping

The couple first met at a Christian conference in Singapore back in 1977. Liew was 20 and Koh a couple of years older. She was drawn to the "quiet and humble" young man and they started chatting. Even then, his commitment to his faith was strong.

After getting married, the couple moved to New Zealand where Johor-born Koh spent nearly four years studying theology. When they returned to Malaysia in 1994, he got a job as a pastor at the Evangelical Free Church of Malaysia before devoting himself full-time to Komuniti Harapan, the community centre he had set up as a way to help Malaysia's more vulnerable people. Liew, meanwhile, ran the home and looked after the couple's three children: Jonathan, Esther and Elizabeth.

The last time the two saw each other was the morning of 13 February 2017, the day Koh disappeared. Liew had left their home for a friend's place while her husband was still asleep, inadvertently taking with her a box of *sambal belacan* (a spicy shrimp paste) that he was supposed to be selling that afternoon. It was the kind of "good deed" that appealed to Koh, his wife says.

Koh stopped off to collect the box on his way to the office. "I love you," he told Liew as he left. They expected to see each other later that afternoon when he was going to pick up his wife for a meeting in Klang, about an hour's drive away.

The pastor set out from the apartment in his ageing silver Honda Accord on his usual route to the office, joining the vehicles jostling for space on one of the busiest highways in suburban Kuala Lumpur. Turning left onto a narrower road, he passed a school playing field, a few blocks of police apartments—the paint peeling and mouldy in the humidity—and rows of terraced single and double-storey houses. The road wasn't particularly busy compared with the highway, but there was still plenty of traffic.

Shortly afterwards, Roshan Gomez, a 25-year-old trainee lawyer, turned into the road too. He and a friend had just come from a funeral and were on their way to the crematorium, but they could see something strange ahead of them—a few cars stopped on the side of the road and a group of people dressed in black, their faces covered with balaclavas. At first, the two friends thought it might be a movie shoot. As they got closer, they got the feeling it was something more sinister. Gomez's friend reached for her mobile phone so she could film what was happening.

"An Indian man appeared in front of us," Gomez recalled as the enquiry opened. "He stood in front of our car. He seemed agitated and was pointing at my friend."

Fearful, Gomez put his car into reverse. His friend put her phone away.

Although they didn't know it at the time, they were the main witnesses to a kidnapping. Koh's Honda had been forced onto the grassy verge and was surrounded by black vehicles. Motorcyclists milled about. One man was apparently videoing the scene, as another, his face covered, struggled with Koh. In less than a minute, the social worker was gone, forced into one of the other vehicles, while another of the kidnappers jumped into the car and drove it away. The incident was captured on security cameras installed by some of the nearby homeowners, but neither Koh nor the Honda have been seen since.

Liew had no idea that anything had happened to her husband until the late afternoon when he failed to collect her for the meeting. Calls to his mobile went straight to voicemail. For someone with a reputation for being reliable, it was unusual, but Liew didn't yet suspect anything untoward had happened.

Just over an hour later, Jonathan was on the line to say that the police had called the registered owner of Koh's car to tell him the vehicle was suspected to have been used in the "kidnapping of kids". It then emerged that Koh had missed the meeting. As Liew set off for the police station around 9pm that night, she says she had a "bad feeling" about what might have happened to her husband.

A rare abduction and the search for answers

Such brazen abductions are rare in Malaysia—between 1980 and 2016, the UN's Working Group on Enforced or Involuntary Disappearances received only two cases of enforced disappearance from Malaysia, and both were resolved—but Koh's disappearance came at a time when a number of other people had also gone missing in strange, and still unexplained, circumstances.

Amri Che Mat, a Muslim community worker in the northern state of Perlis, was apparently abducted by a group of men about half a kilometre from his home in November 2016, while Joshua and Ruth Helmi, the former a Christian pastor and the latter an Indonesian Christian, haven't been seen since November last year.

The incidents were unusual enough to raise concerns about enforced disappearances—defined by the UN as involving three cumulative elements: the deprivation of a person's liberty against their will, the involvement of officials, at least by acquiescence, and a refusal to acknowledge the deprivation of liberty or concealment of the fate or location of the missing person.[1]

"It is extremely troubling that the spectre of enforced disappearance has reared its ugly head in Malaysia," Dimitris Christopoulous, FIDH president said in a statement in May last year.[2] "Malaysian authorities must immediately investigate the disappearances of Amri Che Mat and Raymond Koh in order to determine their whereabouts and safely return them to their families."

It was the concern about enforced disappearance—and the infrequent reports to the families—that led to the Suhakam enquiry. Explaining its decision, the Commission noted the apparent lack of progress in the investigation "created public anxiety" while the "lack of information or regular updates by the authorities led to (the) allegation that these disappearances are indeed enforced or involuntary."

From the beginning, Liew says questioning focussed more on Koh's work with Komuniti Harapan and young Muslims than on his abduction. Even when she went to report her husband missing the police seemed more interested in "Christianisation and proselytisation," she recalls. "I was wondering, "Why are they treating me like a suspect? I'm the victim."

After five hours, she had had enough. "I said to the investigating officer, 'What is important is that we go and find my husband.'" It was three o'clock in the morning.

Supported by friends and civil society, the family began organising vigils and publicising the case in the local media. A MYR100,000 (approx. USD25,129) reward was offered to anyone who provided information leading to Koh's recovery, but relations with the police were becoming increasingly strained.

Difficulties with law enforcement

According to their lawyers, Koh's family had just two briefings with the police after the pastor's disappearance, even as senior officers spoke to reporters about developments in the case. Both took place in March.

At one of them, in the Chinese restaurant of Kuala Lumpur's Hilton Hotel, Liew says then-police chief Khalid Abu Bakar expressed sympathy

---

1 http://www.ohchr.org/EN/Issues/Disappearances/Pages/DisappearancesIndex.asp

2 https://www.forum-asia.org/?p=23893

over Koh's disappearance, but told the family not to publicise the case or speak to the media because it would put the pastor at risk.

Even at the enquiry, there were testy exchanges between the police, lawyers and commissioners. Officers often declined to provide answers, saying Koh's disappearance was still under investigation or subject to the Official Secrets Act.

When Inspector Ali Asrar, the first officer to visit the crime scene, insisted[3] he could not hand over his investigation diary without first consulting the Attorney-General's Chambers, Mah, who was leading the inquiry, told him that Suhakam was legally entitled to see the diary and sent the commission's officials to retrieve it.

Khalid, who retired in September, often replied that he "couldn't remember" and prompted incredulous looks in the public gallery when he suggested the kidnappers weren't necessarily professionals and could have worked out what to do from watching a few Hollywood films.

"The difficulty that Suhakam is facing is the same problem everyone in Malaysia is facing," says Rama Ramanathan from the Citizen Action Group on Enforced Disappearance (CAGED), a non-profit set up to help the families of the missing. "A police force that's not accountable to anyone."

An additional complication: religion

Religion adds to the complexity. According to Malaysia's Constitution, Islam is the country's official religion with other religions to be practised "in peace and harmony". About 61% of the country's population—mainly the Malay majority—are Muslims, while just under 20% are Buddhist and about 7% Hindu. Around 9% of the population are Christian.

Proselytisation of Muslims and apostasy *(renunciation of religion)* are both crimes in Malaysia, and Komuniti Harapan's activities—offering a learning centre for children, some of them Muslims, to read and take classes, as well as support to single mothers and people living with HIV and AIDS—drew attention.

Matters reached a head in 2011, when enforcement officers from the Islamic affairs department appeared unannounced at a fundraising dinner the NGO was holding in an evangelical church hall.

Video footage of the raid uploaded online shows officials wearing baseball caps and reflective jackets questioning the organisers about the presence of Muslims. Koh later released a statement questioning the religious department's decision to "disrupt a peaceful and harmonious charity event."

At the Suhakam enquiry, Zaaba Zakaria, a state religious affairs officer, testified that the event was seen as "insulting" to Islam. Some 15 religious enforcement officers and 20 members of the police were involved in the raid, he added. Meanwhile, the police revealed some 78 reports had been lodged against Koh between 2011 and 2012.

In the weeks following the raid, Koh received death threats and bullets through the post. Liew says she was sent an envelope containing white powder. On it, scrawled in red in Malay were the words, "We want to kill you." The police told Suhakam that tests showed the two bullets to be live, but that they had made no progress in finding the culprits.

Former police chief Khalid, meanwhile, revealed that Koh had been interviewed at least ten times over the religious nature of his activities.

Sri Ram KS Gopala Iyer, a director at Komuniti Harapan, testified that the police visited the group's centre a number of times after the pastor disappeared—on one occasion going through documents, taking photographs and ripping out a student register—even though they had no search warrant. They later interviewed some of the youngsters who were regulars at the centre about whether they read the Bible there or were ever taken to church. Among them was a 12-year-old girl, but the interviews took place without parents or guardians present, Sri Ram said. While the police were interviewing the girl, they agreed to allow a female Komuniti Harapan administrator to sit outside with the door open.

Religion has also been at the centre of the three other cases being investigated by Suhakam.

Like Koh, Amri, who was reportedly abducted by as many as 15 people travelling in a five-vehicle convoy, caught the attention of religious authorities through his work with the poor and vulnerable. Amri wasn't Christian, but he was Shia, considered a "deviant sect" in Malaysia.

The founder of an NGO called Perlis Hope, he was visited at home by the mufti of the state accompanied by about 20 police and Islamic officials, his wife, Norhayati Ariffin, told Suhakam.

The mufti, giving evidence later, said he had received complaints about Amri because he had expressed a belief in Shia. The social worker was free to follow its teachings, he told the enquiry, but only within the confines of his own home.

Much less is known about the cases of Joshua Helmi and his wife Ruth, both aged 49. Last seen in November 2016, they were reported missing by a friend when he hadn't heard from them for a couple of months. While Ruth was born a Christian in Indonesia, Joshua was working as a pastor. Suhakam has still to hear the evidence of their disappearance.

"We are not giving up"

The enquiry took a break as Malaysia geared up for its 14th General Election, preparing to meet again a week after the May 9 vote, with police officers from the northern state of Kedah scheduled to take the stand.

But by the time the commissioners returned to the conference room of the Suhakam office, Malaysians had voted out the previous administration—for the first time since independence in 1957. Almost overnight, the fear of the past had been replaced with a new mood of optimism with talk of far-reaching institutional reforms, democratisation and freedom of expression.

To the delight of Koh's family, the commissioners' first move was to resume the enquiry into the pastor's disappearance, saying the issues being addressed by the enquiry, and those under discussion in court, were different.

But there was more. Norhayati said she'd been visited at home by an informant on the night of May 12, who claimed police officers were involved in the disappearances of Amri and Koh. Three days later she made a statement on what she'd heard to police headquarters in Shah Alam, the capital of Selangor state.

"I urge the police to investigate these serious allegations with urgency, and to find my husband, Amri Che Mat, and also Pastor Raymond Koh and return them to their loved ones immediately," she said.

After more than a year of uncertainty, this month's developments have revived hopes that had been almost extinguished by January's suspension. Koh may still be missing, but together with Norhayati, Liew believes they are inching closer to the truth.

"We need to support one another and press on to find the truth about what happened to our husbands," she says. "Who has taken them? Where are they? All these unanswered questions in our minds. We are not giving up."

FREEDOM OF ASSEMBLY ON TRIAL IN VIETNAM

VI TRAN | 19 JUL 2018

Vietnamese–American Will Nguyen was arrested at a protest in Ho Chi Minh City in June. He will stand trial on 20 July, despite freedom of assembly being a constitutionally protected right in Vietnam.

UPDATE at 1pm, 20 July 2018: The Vietnamese authorities have said that Will Nguyen will be released and deported from Vietnam.

With a dismal Freedom House score[1] of 20 out of a 100 (100 being the most free), Vietnam is often seen as an authoritarian country where one breaks the law by participating in protests. But when the Vietnamese authorities arrest people for demonstrating, it's not actually about illegal assemblies; it's about the government acting unconstitutionally and ignoring its own obligations and responsibilities when it comes to political and human rights.

The arrest of Will Nguyen

In a May 2018 article, *Culture Trip* identified "13 Ways to Get Arrested in Vietnam"[2], listing things to steer clear of, ranging from trafficking drugs to distributing "anti-Vietnamese" propaganda, taking photos of demonstrations, and posting about politics on social media.

This highly simplistic list was seemingly validated a month later when William Anh Nguyen was arrested in Ho Chi Minh City. Nguyen, a Vietnamese-American who contributed a personal essay[3] to *New Naratif* on Vietnam's North-South divide, had been visiting Vietnam shortly before graduating from his Masters degree in Singapore. While in the

---

1 https://freedomhouse.org/report/freedom-world/2018/vietnam

2 https://theculturetrip.com/asia/vietnam/articles/13-ways-to-get-arrested-in-vietnam/

3 https://newnaratif.com/journalism/north-south/

southern Vietnamese city, he joined a large demonstration against two controversial draft bills regarding on cybersecurity and the creation of special economic zones on 10 June 2018, posting photos and comments on Twitter[4] as he went.

Ho Chi Minh City wasn't the only place with protests; people gathered across Vietnam to oppose the highly unpopular bills. The turnout—the largest in over four decades—was a striking turnout for a country where civil liberties are often curbed.

Later in the afternoon, the authorities decided that enough was enough. The police began to break up the protest, blocking the roads and arresting protesters. As people shared developments and news on social media[5], photos popped up of Nguyen standing on a police vehicle with the caption: "Pics at the scene when @will_nguyen_ beaten and got arrested."[6]

Video footage[7] later emerged showing Nguyen bleeding from his head and being dragged along the road by a group of men who were reportedly plainclothes police officers. Apart from an appearance on state television about a week after his arrest—an appearance that many believe to be a forced confession as he expressed "regret" for his actions—Nguyen has not been seen by the public since. He is due to go on trial on 20 July[8] for "disturbance of public order".

Nguyen's predicament reinforces certain beliefs about authoritarian Vietnam: that it's illegal to protest or post political content on social media, for instance. But this isn't reflected in Vietnamese law.

"Demonstration": a politically sensitive word

Strict censorship and the Vietnamese government's reaction to protesters give the impression that Vietnamese laws don't protect individual rights. But Article 25 of the country's Constitution clearly states that all citizens "shall enjoy the right to freedom of opinion and speech, freedom of the press, of access to information, to assemble, form associations and

---

4 https://twitter.com/will_nguyen_/status/1005651466776805381

5 https://twitter.com/AnhChiVN/status/1005637939517259776

6 https://twitter.com/AnhChiVN/status/1005769525634035714

7 https://www.facebook.com/freewillnguyenNOW/videos/462951327496977/

8 https://thinkprogress.org/u-s-citizen-william-nguyen-faces-trial-detained-in-vietnam-34849598faf1/

hold demonstrations", promising that the "practice of these rights shall be provided by law". [Vietnam has also ascended[9] to the International Covenant on Civil and Political Rights (ICCPR) since 24 September 1982, and the Constitution maintains that it will conform "to the Charter of the United Nations and international treaties in which the Socialist Republic of Vietnam is a member".

But if participating in demonstrations is a right protected by the Constitution in Vietnam, why is Nguyen being put on trial for exercising it? The answer may not lie in the commission of any illegal act, but is instead embedded in the Vietnamese government's sophisticated, but unconstitutional, system of rights abuse, developed over the years.

Despite what the Constitution says about the right to peaceful assembly, the Vietnamese government issued Decree 38/2005/NĐ-CP (Decree 38)10 to regulate "public gatherings", requiring public gatherings of more than five people to seek approval from the Provincial People's Committee, allowing law enforcement to disperse crowds and mandating11 the police and army to cooperate with local authorities "to ensure the public order in case of need". This ordinance was not passed by the country's legislative body—the National Assembly—but was an order issued by the administrative branch of the government.

At the same time, the word "demonstration" has become taboo. It's a word that puts the government in a bit of a fix; while they want to suppress dissent and protests, banning demonstrations outright would contradict the words of the late revolutionary leader Ho Chi Minh when he enacted Presidential Order 31[12] in September 1945, guaranteeing all people the right to assembly. As a result, the Vietnamese authorities have grown sensitive to issues related to public demonstrations and assemblies.

This sensitivity has been put on display over the past month. On 19 June 2018, President Tran Dai Quang—who is also part of the

9 https://treaties.un.org/pages/ViewDetails.aspx?src=IND&mtdsg_no=IV-4&chapter=4&lang=en#EndDec

10 https://luatvietnam.vn/an-ninh-trat-tu/nghi-dinh-38-2005-nd-cp-chinh-phu-17055-d1.html

11 https://books.google.com.sg/books?id=RTYrDwAAQBAJ&pg=PA120&lpg=PA120&dq=decree+38/2005/N%C4%90-CP+vietnam&source=bl&ots=hMknO0q8cB&sig=KJyfMyuJ1OAprP2qcv6Z8ca66Jo&hl=en&sa=X&ved=0ahUKEwjpwufsw6fcAhUafX0KHdk3D7QQ6AEIODAD#v=onepage&q=decree%2038%2F2005%2FN%C4%90-CP%20vietnam&f=false

12 https://thuvienphapluat.vn/van-ban/Quyen-dan-su/Sac-lenh-31-buoc-khai-trinh-bieu-tinh-truoc-24-gio-Uy-ban-nhan-dan-so-tai/35875/noi-dung.aspx

delegation of National Assembly members representing Ho Chi Minh City—met his constituents in the city. Tuoi Tre, the largest newspaper in the country, reported on its Vietnamese website that Quang had expressed his support for the National Assembly to begin a discussion on a "Law on Demonstration"—expected to enshrine the right to protest while laying out clear guidelines on what behaviour or activity is or isn't allowed—during its next meeting. The headline triggered a dramatic response from the public, especially given the fact that the country had witnessed the largest countrywide protest since 1975 just two weekends prior.

The online article was swiftly taken down by Tuoi Tre; a move that prompted snarky comments on Facebook that even the President of Vietnam himself had been censored for daring to mention legislation related to demonstrations. Slamming the paper's report as "untrue" and causing "severe impacts", and highlighting a "nationally divisive" comment left by a reader on another article, the government suspended[13] Tuoi Tre's permit for its Vietnamese website for 90 days, and ordered that the paper pay a total fine of VND220 million (close to USD10,000).

Curbing freedom of assembly in Vietnam

Many lawyers and scholars in Vietnam find Decree 38 to be problematic and unconstitutional. In November 2011, Dr Nguyen Quang A, a prominent rights activist and a well-respected public intellectual, told[14] RFI Vietnamese that "just by replacing the word 'public gathering of a crowd' with 'demonstration', then we could see right away that Decree 38 is unconstitutional, and that it directly violates the people's right to protest as prescribed in our Constitution."

Earlier that same year, during a three-month-long nation-wide protest against China's actions in the South China Sea, Tran Vu Hai, an attorney in Hanoi, petitioned[15] the Standing Committee of the National Assembly to exercise their power to "interpret the Constitution". While

---

13 https://e.vnexpress.net/news/news/major-online-newspaper-suspended-for-three-months-in-vietnam-3778939.html

14 http://vi.rfi.fr/viet-nam/20111128-nhung-tro-ngai-trong-viec-xay-dung-luat-bieu-tinh-tai-viet-nam

15 https://www.bbc.com/vietnamese/mobile/vietnam/2011/06/110630_tranvuhai_protest.shtml

Vietnam does not have a constitutional court, the Standing Committee is entrusted with the responsibility of judicial review, allowing them to interpret the "Constitution, the law, and decree-laws".

But Trinh Huu Long, a Vietnamese jurist and democracy activist who had participated in the 2011 protests, says that "the National Assembly has yet to respond to [the] request to decide on the constitutionality of Decree 38", adding that he believes that the Standing Committee never actually exercised their power of judicial review. With the Vietnamese Communist Party's dominance in the National Assembly—they control close to 95% of all the seats, with no other political party in the country to oppose them—it seems as if the constitutional battle for human rights and civil liberties has come to a standstill.

But the human rights violations don't just stop with Decree 38. Vietnam has also enacted laws, such as Article 318 of the 2015 Vietnam Penal Code[16], to punish those whose conduct have been deemed to be "disturbing public order"—the very offence that Nguyen has been charged with—giving the government legal grounds to prosecute people who participate in protests.

Article 318 is worded broadly, giving the authorities plenty of discretion in its application. Instead of a clear definition of what a "disturbance of public order" entails, Article 318 simply frames it as an act that "negatively impacts social safety, order, or security".

Under Clause 1 of Article 318, the penalty is either a fine of VND5 million to VND50 million (USD250 to USD2,500), up to two years' of community service, or three to 24 months in jail. But state media reports say that Nguyen has been charged under Clause 2—for cases with aggravating circumstances, such as inciting others to "cause disturbance"—which means he's potentially facing a penalty of two to seven years' imprisonment, in a country whose prison system has been reported[17] as being rife with maltreatment and lacking in accountability.

---

16 https://www.bbc.com/vietnamese/mobile/vietnam/2011/06/110630_tranvuhai_protest.shtml

17 https://www.amnesty.org/en/latest/news/2016/07/the-secretive-world-of-viet-nam-torturous-prisons/

A failure to live up to obligations

Although cloaked in the language of public order and safety, both Decree 38 and Article 318 are red herrings—they aren't laws that protect the right to freedom of assembly, nor do they clearly stipulate legal or illegal behaviour during public demonstrations. Their existence merely diverts attention from the fact that Vietnam still has no law providing for the right to peaceful assembly as required by the Constitution.

During its second cycle of the Universal Periodic Review (UPR) before the United Nations Human Rights Council in 2014, Vietnam accepted[18] Australia's recommendation to "enact laws to provide for and regulate freedom of assembly and peaceful demonstration in line with ICCPR." But the government has yet to fulfil this commitment.

Despite constitutional protection and international commitments, Vietnam regularly and routinely uses vaguely worded and overly broad legal provisions to prosecute those who exercise their human rights and freedoms, especially human rights defenders and activists. It also uses disproportionate force. In its 2018 World Report on Vietnam, international NGO Human Rights Watch reported[19] that "police used excessive force while dispersing protesters in front of the entrance of a Hong Kong-owned textile factory in Hai Duong province" in September 2017, leaving many injured. It also reported[20] that, in 2017, Vietnam "arrested at least 41 rights advocates and bloggers for joining protests or other events or publishing articles critical of the government."

"Disturbing public order" is a very convenient catch-all for a government eager to suppress dissent. But without any law explicitly regulating freedom of assembly and protest, the act of participating in a demonstration can't be said to be illegal; there simply isn't a legal definition to prescribe what constitutes a legal or illegal protest.

What now for Will Nguyen?

Will Nguyen now finds himself in the same fix as many Vietnamese human rights defenders; six Vietnamese nationals have already been sentenced to two-and-a-half years' imprisonment for a similar charge.

---

18 https://www.upr-info.org/sites/default/files/document/viet_nam/session_18_-_

january_2014/recommendations_and_pledges_viet_nam_2014.pdf

19 https://www.hrw.org/news/2018/06/07/vietnam-withdraw-problematic-cyber-security-law

20 https://www.hrw.org/news/2018/06/07/vietnam-withdraw-problematic-cyber-security-law

There is, however, one crucial difference: Nguyen is not a Vietnamese citizen, but an American citizen of Vietnamese descent. This allows him some, albeit limited, "privileges": with the permission of the Vietnamese authorities, he has been allowed access to US consular officers, and the authorities have said that his family will be allowed to attend his trial.

These are luxuries withheld from many Vietnamese political prisoners, who are often held incommunicado for months—even years—before standing trial. Although all trials in Vietnam are supposed to be public, family members have had to fight for the right to be present at court hearings.

Yet Nguyen's case has received fairly limited attention in the American media. Although the US State Department confirmed[21] that Secretary of State Mike Pompeo had raised Nguyen's case with his Vietnamese counterparts during a visit to Hanoi earlier this month, encouraging "a speedy resolution" to the case, Pompeo made no public mention of Nguyen during his visit.

"Secretary of State Pompeo missed a golden opportunity in Hanoi to publicly raise Will Nguyen's case and demand his immediate release," says Phil Robertson, Deputy Asia Director of Human Rights Watch. "Trump has become perhaps the most anti-human rights president in modern US history and activists like Will Nguyen are collateral damage in Trump's mad dash to overturn the international order."

It's highly likely that the verdict in Nguyen's case will not be a matter of law, but the outcome of a political decision. According to the 2017 US State Department human rights report: "The law provides for an independent judiciary and lay assessors, but the judiciary was vulnerable to influence by outside elements, such as senior government officials and [Communist Party of Vietnam] leadership."

Nguyen's family and friends have worked hard to secure his safe release, running the Free Will Nguyen campaign[22] on social media with the hashtag #FreeWilly.

"Regardless of the outcome of the trial, Will's family is just desperate to get him home as soon as possible," Nguyen's college friend Kevin Webb told[23] NBC News.

---

21 https://www.state.gov/r/pa/prs/ps/2018/07/283897.htm

22 https://www.facebook.com/freewillnguyenNOW/

23 https://www.nbcnews.com/news/asian-america/u-s-citizen-arrested-during-protest-vietnam-scheduled-stand-trial-n891296

In Singapore, Nguyen's peers had to graduate without him last Saturday, but keep their fingers crossed for the best outcome.

"Missing Will at graduation sucks because we worked so hard and he is not here due to his detention for exercising his freedom of speech," says his classmate Azira Aziz.

Inkar Aitkuzhina, another friend, agrees. "It was extremely sad and heartbreaking that a poster with his picture was there instead of him, but we are hoping that the trial ends well and that he is released very soon."

REMEMBERING A REVOLUTION

OLIVER SLOW | 13 AUG 2018

It's been 30 years since the 8 August 1988 uprising that saw Aung San Suu Kyi emerge as the face of the pro-democracy movement. Today, Myanmar faces new challenges amid calls for transitional justice.

On a Saturday afternoon in September 1987, Ba Htoo Maung walked the short distance from his university housing to a restaurant in northern Yangon, then known as Rangoon. As he was ordering his lunch, an announcement came over the government-run radio declaring that three banknotes—25, 35 and 75 kyats—would be demonetised, effective immediately. In a country that was already undergoing economic turmoil, three-quarters of the currency was instantly wiped out.

"I looked down and I couldn't believe it," Ba Htoo Maung recalls more than 30 years later. "I had three 35 kyat banknotes, then suddenly I had nothing."

This devastating decision was made by the military general Ne Win, the strongman who had ruled the country then known as Burma since launching a coup in 1962. After taking power, Ne Win had immediately introduced his Burmese Way to Socialism—a superstitious, xenophobic approach that saw the country go from one of the richest in Southeast Asia to one of the poorest in just a few years.

"I knew nothing about politics, but I knew socialism was not good," says Ba Htoo Maung, who at the time was a student at Rangoon University. "I knew that since Ne Win had ruled the country the people had become poorer, but the officials got rich."

That evening Ba Htoo Maung and a handful of fellow students organised a small protest, marching the short distance from their lodgings to the main Rangoon University campus on Pyay Road, the city's main thoroughfare. It was perhaps the first demonstration of a series of protests that swept across the country the following year, which saw thousands killed and a new pro-democracy movement formed.

"That small protest created the virus inside of me. I was biding my time for another spark," he says with a cheeky laugh.

A growing movement

That spark would come the following March following a seemingly innocuous argument at a tea shop in Rangoon's Insein Township.

A fight had broken out between three students from the Rangoon Institute of Technology (RIT) and some members of the local community. After the fight, one of the members of public was arrested, then quickly released.

The next day, students at the nearby RIT campus learned that this individual was the son of a senior member of Ne Win's hated regime, and held a protest. Keen to quell dissent, Burma's brutal riot police cracked down heavily, shooting into the crowd and killing at least one student.

Protests—led mainly by students from RIT and Rangoon University—continued over the next few days, then spread throughout the country over the next few months.

To the surprise of many, Ne Win stood down on 23 July 1988, admitting that those taking part in the protests lacked "confidence in the government and the party leading the government."

But Ne Win's resignation came with a clear threat. Towards the end of his speech, which was broadcast live on national radio and television, he warned: "If the army shoots, it hits—there is no firing into the air to scare."

Any hope of meaningful change was dispelled a few days later when Ne Win announced his replacement as Sein Lwin, a man so brutal he earned the moniker "the Butcher of Rangoon". In his book *Outrage: Burma's Struggle for Democracy*, which focuses on the 1988 protests, journalist Bertil Lintner wrote that Sein Lwin was "probably the most hated man in Burma" at the time.

8 August and beyond

Up till that point, protests had largely been led by students, but a nation-wide protest began at 8am on 8 August 1988—a time considered to be particularly auspicious. People from across the country and all walks of life joined the demonstration, including government employees and Buddhist monks.

"8 August was a huge turning point in that movement," says Ba Htoo Maung. "Before that we didn't know if what we were trying to achieve could be achieved."

Thousands descended on Rangoon, the then-capital, and marched towards Sule Pagoda in the heart of the city. "I stood on the roof of a bus and looked behind me; I couldn't see the end of the procession. There were people everywhere," Ba Htoo Maung recalls.

The army allowed the protest to continue at first, standing aside idly throughout the day. They finally made a move in the evening, firing into the huge crowd at Sule Pagoda. The number of people killed remains unknown till today.

Heavy crackdowns continued around the country in the following days; although protests continued, they never reached the heights of 8 August again. Sein Lwin relented to public pressure on 12 August and resigned, replaced by Ne Win's biographer Maung Maung.

Throughout the protests, leaders had been holding aloft portraits of Bogyoke Aung San, the country's independence hero who was gunned down by a political rival in 1947. His daughter, Aung San Suu Kyi, had spent most of her life abroad, but happened to be in the country caring for her ailing mother when the protests began. She was swiftly swept up in the tumult.

On 26 August, tens of thousands gathered at the Shwedagon Pagoda, the country's holiest site, to hear Aung San Suu Kyi speak. It was in this moment that she emerged as the leader of the country's pro-democracy movement, despite criticism that she was married to a foreigner and knew nothing of Burmese politics.

Protests continued over the next few weeks, but on 18 September the military launched a coup "in the interests of the people". Maung Maung was replaced by Saw Maung, who established a new body known as the State Law and Order Restoration Council (SLORC). A brutal army crackdown brought any lingering protests to a halt, and over the next year and a half the country edged towards an election promised by the military.

The National League for Democracy (NLD), with Aung San Suu Kyi as its leader, was formed to contest the vote, but most of the its leaders were arrested in the build up to the elections. Despite this, the party still won convincingly, taking 392 of the 492 available seats. The military then refused to honour the result, issuing an order saying it needed to take control in order to prevent the break-up of the country.

Myanmar today

Little changed for the people of Myanmar over the next few years, and the country continued under the control of the military, headed by Than Shwe. In May 2008, 20 years after the protests—and a year after another anti-government uprising known as the Saffron Revolution which had also been met with state violence—the military pushed through a new constitution in a sham referendum. The vote was held weeks after Cyclone Nargis, which devastated the country's south and saw an estimated 140,000 people killed.

Despite the quick turnaround, official results claimed that 90% of the population had approved the new charter. The 2008 Constitution secured the military's role in the country's politics, guaranteeing them a quarter of all parliamentary seats and control of three key ministries. So when the military-backed Union Solidarity and Development Party (USDP) won a landslide in the 2010 general election, which the NLD boycotted, no one expected change to come any time soon. Even when Aung San Suu Kyi was released a few days after the vote, and Than Shwe announced he would be replaced by a general named Thein Sein, only the most optimistic of observers thought there was any real change on the horizon.

It's not entirely clear how much of a back seat Than Shwe took during the first few years of USDP rule, but changes did start happening. Thousands of political prisoners were released, economic reforms were introduced, and the NLD was allowed to register as a political party. Aung San Suu Kyi's party entered Parliament for the first time following a 2012 by-election, and swept the polls in the 2015 general election, coming to power a year later.

Constitutionally barred from becoming president—because her two sons and late husband are British citizens—Aung San Suu Kyi effectively rules the country today as State Counsellor, a clever workaround of the country's constitution engineered by renowned lawyer Ko Ni, who was gunned down outside Yangon International Airport in January 2017. Those accused of plotting the gruesome murder, carried out in broad daylight as Ko Ni held his infant grandchild, remain on trial. They include former members of the Myanmar Army, known as the Tatmadaw.

Constitution challenges

Although Aung San Suu Kyi is seen as the country's leader and her party holds an absolute majority of seats, the military continues to play an important role in Myanmar's politics. Most notably, it remains in control of defence, which oversees the country's police and military, the latter which has been accused of brutality towards the country's ethnic minorities, most notably the Rohingya in Rakhine State.

Last week, events were held to commemorate the 30th anniversary of the protest that's today remembered as 8-8-88, including inside the Yangon University campus, the leafy compound that played such a huge role in the movement.

"The political situation is better today, but we have many steps to move forward," says Kyaw Soe Win, a former political prisoner, speaking at the university. "The main thing is that we need to amend, or abolish the Constitution, and make a new Constitution; one that supports development and peace."

Despite the military's continued role, there have been questions about the NLD's capacity. Under their leadership, the economy has struggled, and there are still political prisoners in the country's jails. Press freedom remains an issue too; at least seven journalists have been arrested under NLD rule, most notably the two Reuters reporters, Wa Lone and Kyaw Soe Oo, who remain on trial for their coverage of the crisis in Rakhine State.

Some of the most prominent figures from the 8-8-88 protests have also failed to speak up on behalf of the Rohingya, a largely stateless population who have suffered oppression at the hands of the state for decades.

After the crisis broke out in Rakhine State in 2012, Ko Ko Gyi, who emerged as one of the student leaders of the 1988 movement, blamed the crisis on "illegal immigrants from Bangladesh" and "mischievous provocation of some members of the international community".

"Genetically, culturally and linguistically Rohingya is not absolutely related to any ethnicity in Myanmar," he said[1] in comments carried in local outlet *The Irrawaddy*.

Since the reforms began in 2011, activists have been calling for some form of transitional justice, either in the form of accountability from those who committed some of the worst crimes when the country was

---

1 https://www.irrawaddy.com/news/burma/analysis-using-term-rohingya.html

under military rule, or reparations for former political prisoners and their families.

The NLD, though, appears reluctant. After her party won the election, Aung San Suu Kyi said she wouldn't be calling for "Nuremberg-style" trials, a reference to the hearings that brought Nazi Germans to justice following the Second World War.

"Talking about transitional justice is still taboo in our politics," says Letyar Tun, who spent more than a decade in jail for his role in the pro-democracy movement. "We want acknowledgement, not only for victims but more importantly for the perpetrators. Otherwise they would never get the chance to repent, and future generations will be ignorant about the value of a real sense of justice. Without such values, how can we build a better society?"

THE DANGERS OF ACTIVISM IN CAMBODIA

GEORGE WRIGHT, MECH DARA | 15 AUG 2018

Tep Vanny has spent two years behind bars, away from her family and community. The challenges that she faces highlight how difficult it is to fight for one's rights in Cambodia.

On an overcast afternoon two years ago, Tep Vanny was doing what she knows best. The land rights activist was protesting in her neighbourhood, alongside a couple dozen others, against what she perceived as grave injustices committed by the Cambodian government. The 38-year-old was bundled into an unmarked police car and driven away.

The peaceful vigil, which included candles and effigies of court officials, was in Vanny's eviction-hit Boeung Kak neighbourhood and formed part of the "Black Monday" campaign calling for the release of jailed rights officials. Campaigners were also pushing for a full investigation into the murder of Kem Ley, a political commentator and government critic who had been gunned down a month before in what was widely thought to have been a politically motivated assassination.

After Vanny was taken away, many people assumed that the country's most recognised activist would be given a ticking off before being released. But 730 days later, she remains in a cell with around 70 other women in Phnom Penh's notorious Prey Sar prison.

"She often catches flu, fever, diarrhea. She's always sick," says her 69-year-old mother, Sy Heap.

Vanny's moods swing up and down. While she sometimes can be upbeat, Heap says, there are times she worries about her daughter's state of mind.

"I'm afraid that sometimes she seems hopeless and sometimes I'm worried she might harm herself. I'm afraid she loses hope when she isn't released," Heap says as she stands beneath photos of her daughter at protests, on family trips and posing alongside former US Secretary of State Hillary Clinton.

"When I go to see her I have to encourage her. I don't dare to speak a lot though because people are listening. We cannot talk about politics in the prison."

Deterring others

Despite initially being handed a six-day sentence for "insulting public officials" with fellow activist Bov Sophea over the innocuous "Black Monday" protest, Vanny was kept behind bars as authorities started pulling long-dormant cases out of the woodwork.

One six-month sentence was handed down over a scuffle that broke out with security forces in 2011, while another 30 months were added for allegedly inciting violence at a protest outside Prime Minister Hun Sen's residence in 2013.

The charges have been slammed by rights groups as a cynical political move by the Cambodian government to silence one of their loudest critics, while sending out a warning to others.

Human rights defenders, political commentators and the independent press have come under pressure in the country as Prime Minister Hun Sen clamps down on dissent. Two reporters from Radio Free Asia are facing up to 15 years behind bars on espionage charges widely believed to be politically motivated, while James Ricketson, an Australian filmmaker and outspoken critic of Hun Sen, is facing 10 years for similar charges after flying a drone at an opposition rally. Members of the public have been arrested for "crimes" including calling the government "authoritarian" on Facebook and throwing a sandal at a ruling party billboard. Other critics, including election monitor Koul Panha, are currently living in exile due to fears of arrest after being accused of serving foreign powers, and press freedom has taken a nosedive[1] in the run-up to the election.

Activists, journalists and analysts are now thinking twice before speaking out. "I really want to go out and protest but we can't do it. I'm scared they'll beat me if I go out. We talked about it together and we are all scared of arrest," says Nget Khun, a 79-year-old activist from Boeung Kak better known as "Mummy".

"If the authorities arrest us, who's going to look after our children?"

---

1 https://newnaratif.com/journalism/end-cambodias-free-press/

The Boeung Kak struggle

Despite receiving a land title three years ago, Khun says the Boeung Kak activists want to help others who have faced similar evictions as her community. In 2007, thousands were forced off their land after Boeung Kak lake was leased to a private developer with close ties to the government. The Boeung Kak activists grew out of this struggle.

Peaking around 2011 and 2012, the movement turned into a real force to be reckoned with. Mostly driven by women, dozens from the community came out in force to protest the seizing of their land, often facing the wrath of armed security forces.

However, the community began to splinter shortly after as factions were accused of being bought off by the government. One member of the community, who requested anonymity for fear of retribution, tells New Naratif that local authorities prevented her from continuing construction on a new home until she agreed to join the ruling Cambodian People's Party (CPP). Despite agreeing, she stayed away from the polling booth in last month's widely discredited general election.

Khun draws out a poster of one of those alleged "defectors", Toul Srey Pov, from inside the taupaulin room she's currently living in. Under a photo of a stern looking Srey Pov text reads: "The side that separated from the community use violence while authorities stand and watch" in Khmer. Khun accuses Srey Pov of pelting her with rocks during one altercation, one of which split her forehead open.

Sitting inside her three-storey home a few hundred yards from Khun's makeshift home, 41-year-old Srey Pov denies she was ever co-opted by the government. She claims she decided to step away from protesting after getting locked up with Vanny in 2012.

"Upon leaving prison, it was clear we had different visions. I don't want to be involved in politics and the opposition kept getting involved," Srey Pov says. "I'm just a normal housewife, not a politician. You must have a high education to be involved in politics."

Srey Pov calls Vanny "arrogant" and claims she was seeking fame. Now working as an estate agent, she accuses Vanny's clique of spreading rumours that she was a spy. She also claims she only threw rocks at the elderly activist in self-defence.

"After I heard that word was going around I was a spy I lost all my strength. These words made me not sleep for one year. I had to take anti-anxiety pills," Srey Pov claims.

"If I knew this before I would have let the company pump sand to flood all the villages and everyone would have suffered."

Despite her relationship with Vanny turning sour, she calls the detention of her former friend "unjust." Her tone switches between bitterness and fond nostalgia when flicking through an old photo album of them on holiday together.

"I miss then, I miss the old memories that we have in the past. We shouldn't have become enemies," she says.

"Bogus" charges

Vanny's lengthy imprisonment is a clear message to any budding activists thinking of standing up to Hun Sen's increasingly authoritarian regime, says Phil Robertson, deputy director of Human Rights Watch's Asia division.

Since Vanny's imprisonment, the Cambodia National Rescue Party, the only electoral threat to Hun Sen, was dissolved and its leader, Kem Sokha, thrown in jail on charges that many believe to be politically motivated. There was also a widespread crackdown on independent media and civil society ahead of the sham July 29 election, which saw the CPP take all 125 seats in the National Assembly.

"At the most basic level, the Cambodia government is following the brutal adage of 'killing the chicken to show it to the monkeys', meaning to make an example of one activist to cause fear so others will not dare say anything," Robertson says.

"Seizure of land by government and security officials, their crony business friends, and foreign investment partners is an important path to wealth in Cambodia, and Tep Vanny stands in the way of that—so it's no surprise that she is languishing in prison on bogus charges."

It's now vital that the US and EU governments make Vanny's release a "top priority," Robertson adds.

Future anxieties

Back in Boeung Kak, Vanny's mother Heap says that her daughter isn't hoping for a pardon. In fact, her sentence could be further extended if the courts drag up another case against her.

The situation is having an increasingly negative effect on Vanny's two children, ages 13 and 12, who regularly skip school. "It's impacting on the children's education because they miss their mother. The children are not themselves, it's like they are somewhere else," Heap says.

But although she's languishing in a cramped cell away from her children and community, Heap is certain that her daughter will never cave in to the ruling party, and is likely to continue her activism upon release.

"I don't think she'll stop… people have tried to get her to join the CPP in jail," Heap says. "If she followed and obeyed [the ruling party], she would not be in jail. She's very strong, she can't betray the people and sell her conscience. She's also stubborn and this makes me concerned."

"Vanny knows the difference between right and wrong. It's impossible to buy her."

POLITICS AND RELIGION

DERADICALISATION SCHOOLS: THE ANSWER TO TERRORISM?

AISYAH LLEWELLYN | 04 JAN 2018

The Al-Hidayah Islamic Boarding School seeks to break the cycle of generational terrorism in Indonesia.

Khairul Ghazali explains how he was deradicalised: it happened when he was arrested for his roles in a 2010 bank robbery in Medan, North Sumatra, and a terrorist attack on a police station. He hadn't been directly involved in either incidents but was one of the masterminds behind the plots (including harbouring those who carried out the attacks). He was sentenced to six years in prison.

"I was interrogated every day for hours on end," he says. "When I was asked to go through the details of what I had done and the reasons behind it all, I started to realise how flawed my radical thinking had been."

Ghazali now runs Al-Hidayah Islamic Boarding School on the outskirts of Medan in Deli Serdang. It's a small establishment with just 20 pupils, but what makes it different from the thousands of other schools across the archipelago is that all its students are the children of convicted terrorists. Ghazali opened the school upon his release from prison after seeing the effects his incarceration had on his own family, and the families of other inmates convicted on terror-related charges.

["The inmates always talked to me about their families," he says. "Most of their children had dropped out of school because of the stigma of having a parent who is a terrorist. They were no longer accepted as part of the local community."]

This stigma alone is highly damaging, but Ghazali explains that it goes deeper than just being bullied at school: "The children usually drop out of school at an early age. They then lack education, particularly religious education. This means that they have no good role models and don't have the intellectual ability or historical context to understand that terrorism is wrong."

This leaves these young, impressionable children more vulnerable to following in the footsteps of the only role models they have—parents or other relatives who have been radicalised. Thus begins a cycle of generational terrorism.

"Becoming a terrorist was like my inheritance"

Generational terrorism is not a new phenomenon in Indonesia. Many of the most well-known terrorists in Indonesian history have come from "terrorist families". Ghazali himself is an example: his father, grandfather and other relatives were all members of Negara Islam Indonesia (NII), a group dedicated to transforming Indonesia—which recognises religious pluralism—into an Islamic state. Offshoots of NII include the militant extremist group Jemaah Islamiyah.

"Becoming a terrorist was like my inheritance," Ghazali says.

He also points to other famous examples, like Iman Samudra, who received the death penalty for his part in the 2002 Bali bombings; his son later joined the Islamic State (ISIS) in Syria, where he was killed. Another is Abu Jibril, a hardline Indonesian preacher implicated in the 2009 bombing of the JW Marriot Hotel in Jakarta; his son, Muhammad Ridwan Adburrahman, also died in Syria fighting for ISIS in 2015.

Ghazali realised the importance of breaking this cycle of generational terrorism while held in solitary confinement in prison. Once removed from an environment where everyone held the same deeply-entrenched extremist views of Islam, he was able to look at his radicalisation objectively and start questioning his choices.

For children of terrorists, deep reflection is usually not an option. If they drop out of school, they tend to stay at home with family members who will continue exposing them to the same thought processes and ideologies. Isolated from and disillusioned with the local community which they feel has rejected them, these children have nothing to emulate other than their family's radical legacy, often stretching back generations. Without intervention, it's very difficult to break them out of this cycle.

Ghazali explains: "The idea of 'lone wolf' attacks or someone waking up one day and suddenly wanting to be a terrorist or join a terrorist organisation is largely a myth in Indonesia. It happens, but people who commit terrorist attacks are far more likely to be people who have family members who are convicted terrorists or who come from areas known for having high numbers of residents who believe in radical ideology."

Many youngsters also have little motivation to turn away from terrorism, Ghazali says. Many of the children at his school were present when their parents were arrested. They saw them, in some cases, being shot by Indonesian police officers and dragged away in handcuffs. Many swore they would avenge their parents' treatment at the hands of the police, who have increasingly become terrorist targets in recent years. Add this to social problems like low levels of education, poverty that keeps children isolated in rural areas, and failure to integrate into wider society and Al-Hidayah's significance becomes clear.

"We can't cure social problems," Ghazali says. "They will always be here and will always be a factor in terrorist recruitment. But we can tackle other issues and start with a grassroots approach when the children are young."

Al-Hidayah's deradicalisation programme

The study of deradicalisation is a fairly new one. There are still only thought to be around 40 deradicalisation schools around the world, and Al-Hidayah is one of the few focused solely on the children of terrorists. Studies are now being undertaken[1], such as research by social psychologist and co-director of the National Consortium for the Study of Terrorism and Responses to Terrorism (START) Arie Kruglanski. According to Kruglanski's research into deradicalisation programmes in countries such as Egypt, Iraq, Saudi Arabia and Indonesia, most share a set series of initiatives. These usually include intellectual, emotional and social initiatives to provide a full programme of support.

At Al-Hidayah the intellectual component of the training comes in the form of classes that teach the students the true meaning of the Qu'ran, which has often previously been misrepresented by their parents.

"We teach the students how the Prophet Muhammad protected other religions in Medina and taught his followers not to threaten other people," says Ghazali.

The emotional component comes from providing students with a stable home life—they all live in the boarding school—as well as providing emotional support while their parents are still in prison. The students call Ghazali "Ayah"—Indonesian for "Father" instead of the more formal "Bapak"—and he says he considers all of them to be like his own children.

1 http://www.apa.org/monitor/2009/11/terrorism.aspx

When it comes to the social component, Ghazali helps the children reintegrate into the local community by, in some cases, sending them to local schools on top of their classes at Al-Hidayah if he feels they need more support like learning basic writing and arithmetic skills. The students also grow corn and beans—which they then sell at the local market—and raise fish in a large pond on the school property, which Ghazali describes as the "Life Skills" portion of the children's education. They also interact with members of the local community such as teachers sourced from neighbouring schools.

But even those who are hopeful about the effectiveness of deradicalisation programmes have to qualify their optimism. As John G. Horgan, the director of the Center for Terrorism and Security Studies at the University of Massachusetts, said in an op-ed in the *Los Angeles Times*:

> It is not a silver-bullet solution, nor can it ensure 100% success, but there is no doubt that de-radicalization programs can be tremendously effective in countering terrorism. Although they are becoming more common around the world, such programs remain an experiment in progress. Indeed, some operate in secret, waiting to see whether they are successful before the outside world learns of their existence.[2]

Horgan also called for creativity in seeking solution to combating extremism. Al-Hidayah has risen to the challenge, doing things a little differently from other programmes by focusing on the next generation.

But the issue with such programmes is that they are too new for anyone to come to any conclusion about success or failure. Al-Hidayah's youngest pupil is only 11 years old, and there's no knowing for sure what path he'll take as he grows up.

This 11-year-old student didn't want to give his name for fear of further stigma, as he is one of the children who also attends a local community school, but he's thriving in the school so far. When he came to Al-Hidayah a year ago, he couldn't even write the letters of the alphabet. His father is incarcerated in Nusa Kembangan, an island prison known as the Indonesian version of Alcatraz. According to Ghazali, the boy hardly spoke when he arrived at the school and was suspicious of strangers, but now he cheerfully asks us to join him for lunch. He

---

2 http://www.latimes.com/opinion/op-ed/la-oe-0215-horgan-terrorist-deradicalization-20150215-story.html

says, like many of the other pupils, that he wants to become a police officer, which Ghazali sees as a sign of changing attitudes towards the local authorities.

At this early stage, Al-Hidayah appears to have a lot going for it. And when asked whether deradicalisation programmes like this are the answer to Indonesia's problem with terrorism, Ghazali is simultaneously realistic and hopeful.

"We will never be able to stop terrorism in Indonesia completely. But we can try to cut off the roots with schools like this."

THE MUSLIM CYBER ARMY AND THE VIRTUAL BATTLEFIELD

AINUR ROHMAH, AISYAH LLEWELLYN | 10 MAY 2018

The Muslim Cyber Army is a wide network operating online via social media platforms like Facebook, spreading anti-Jokowi content under the guise of defending Islam. New Naratif infiltrates an MCA group to get a glimpse of how they work.

It was 6am on 21 March 2018 when an account by the name of "Fathul Khoir Ham" asked members of the Muslim Cyber Army News (MCA News) Facebook group to attack an "intruder"—a possible supporter of the Indonesian president Joko "Jokowi" Widodo—Ham suspected was trying to spy on the MCA's activities.

"It's been a long time [since] we've had an intruder. Let the 'R' [report] button go wild," Ham said, including a link to the account. In the comment field Ham, an administrator of the MCA News group, wrote, "Go to the intruder's wall. Spam and report the post. "

He also gave a step-by-step tutorial on how to report an account to Facebook to get the website to shut it down. Dozens of MCA News members liked the post and replied to say they had done as instructed, although there were no follow-up comments on whether the account was suspended as a result of their actions.

Such is the modus operandi of the Muslim Cyber Army (MCA). MCA News, which boasts over 300,000 members, is only one of three Facebook groups under its umbrella: there's also the United Muslim Cyber Army (United MCA) and the Muslim Cyber Army 212 (MCA 212), with over 150,000 and 18,000 members respectively.

These three groups all claim to defend Islam and Muslim clerics and are populated with derogatory posts about the government, especially President Jokowi, who's often referred to by the name of meme characters "Dilan" and "Mukidi" (comedic figures who are backwards and easily bullied), or "Anything But Jokowi" (Asal Bukan Jokowi or ABJ).

Members are directed to act against particular online targets, with the goal of getting the accounts of their "enemies" shut down.

Apart from that, MCA has been accused of spreading fabricated content and hate speech to fan religious and ethnic divisions, as well as stoking fears over the resurgence of PKI (the former Indonesian Communist Party, banned in 1966), ethnic Chinese Indonesians and the LGBT community. *New Naratif* saw various posts that showed the group disseminate falsehoods about the persecution of Muslim clerics and post slanderous content about the president. The Indonesian police have also said the members were fraudulently reporting Facebook accounts and sending viruses to Jokowi supporters to damage the recipients' electronic devices.[1]

But the Facebook-reporting game works both ways. A day after Ham's post about "intruders", another administrator with the account name "Fauzul Putra Anam" announced to the group that Ham's account had been attacked and taken down. He pointed the finger at "tadpoles"—a reference to the rumour that Jokowi keeps tadpoles and frogs as pets at the presidential palace, and now used as a derogatory term for the president's supporters.

It all points to a troubling development in Indonesian political contestation, when battlegrounds exist both online and off, and not all players are clearly identifiable.

Enlisting in the Army

"In Indonesia, there has been significant concern about the so-called rise of '*berita hoax*' ('hoax news') in the aftermath of the 2017 Jakarta gubernatorial election," says Ross Tapsell, author of *Media Power in Indonesia: Oligarchs, Citizens and the Digital Revolution*. "As more and more Indonesians turn to social media for their daily news intake, political parties and interest groups have, unsurprisingly, attempted to influence people via these platforms". The Muslim Cyber Army is one such group.

While United MCA is an open group with public posts, it's a little tougher to join the ranks of MCA News and MCA 212. Prospective members must write the *shahada* (declaration of one's belief in Islam) and swear that they love Muslim clerics and *habaib* (the descendants of

1 https://www.theguardian.com/world/2018/mar/13/muslim-cyber-army-a-fake-news-operation-designed-to-bring-down-indonesias-leader

the Prophet Muhammad) before their request to join is approved by an administrator. Only then can one consider oneself a defender of the faith.

"If there are any members here who promote the presidents and vice presidents of political parties that support blasphemers or who support the dissolution of mass organisations, with all due respect please get out of here," Ham once wrote in a post. It was liked by nearly three thousand members.

In the MCA's book, "blasphemers" are political figures such as former Jakarta governor Basuki "Ahok" Tjahaja Purnama, who was sentenced in 2017 to two years' imprisonment for insulting Islam. Those who support the Government Regulation in Lieu of Law regarding the Dissolution of Mass Organisations (Peraturan Pemerintah Pengganti Undang-Undang or Perppu Ormas)—issued by Jokowi's administration in 2017 to prevent the spread of ideology contradicting the state ideology of Pancasila, a philosophical theory based on five moral principles such as the belief in one true God, and the 1945 Constitution—are also particularly reviled. Soon after the law was issued, the government dissolved the hard-line Muslim group Hizbut Tahrir Indonesia (HTI), a move that MCA members have interpreted as an attack. "Muslims were victimised by the Ahok case and the dissolution of mass organisations like HTI," Anam claimed in a post.

As Tapsell explains, the rise of groups on Facebook reflect deeper issues in Indonesia, such as a distrust of traditional news media and ongoing struggles with identity: "Citizens can be compelled by the opinions prevailing in their social media feeds to become divided on sectarian or other identity issues. Facebook is the central medium for this divisive discourse. Facebook bloggers…are a highly innovative new form of campaign communication practice…Their social media-centric strategies are perfect for citizens who spend more and more time on their mobile phones scrolling through social media sites."

Moving on despite the clampdown

New Naratif infiltrated the MCA News group for a week and found it operating as usual, with tens of thousands of posts in the past month alone, even though 14 members of the group had been arrested in late February 2018.[2]

---

2 https://www.washingtonpost.com/world/asia_pacific/indonesia-police-break-up-islamist-cyber-network-promoting-extremism/2018/03/01/ff575b00-1cd8-11e8-98f5-ceecfa8741b6_story.html

After the arrest, one of the group's administrators, "Muslimah Marifatullah", said that those arrested by the police were part of the 212 protests—the demonstrations on February 21, 2017, that demanded Ahok's imprisonment—and was quick to portray the MCA members as victims of a politically-motivated clampdown.

"They were fighting to get rid of the accounts of the blasphemers," said Marifatullah in a post on the MCA wall. "They are victims of regime slander. We must all be aware that the police are a political tool of the government, the police are not on the side of Muslims, especially the MCA."

In carrying out research for this article, *New Naratif* found countless posts, both from administrators and MCA News members, asking other members to attack "intruder" accounts, as well as pages by Jokowi's supporters or fan pages for Jokowi that had been labelled as "tadpole" and "deceiver" accounts. The rationale for this, according to Anam, is that "tadpole" accounts allow "blasphemers" to flourish and getting their accounts deleted prevents them from spreading ideology contrary to that of Muslim clerics. When approached, Anam confirmed that some of the individuals arrested in February 2018 were members known for attacking or reporting accounts of "blasphemers".

"Yes, they are 100% MCA members, but they were not leaders of the MCA or anything like that, the media and the police just exaggerated it. And they did not spread hoaxes—that's slander," Anam says.

From Anam's point of view, the police's actions reflect a clear political slant. "If the news is against the government, it's categorised as a hoax," says Anam, explaining that the Indonesian Law on Electronic Information and Transactions (UUITE) does not cover parties who report accounts to Facebook.

He points to some of the members behind pro-government accounts on Facebook even when they have allegedly harassed Muslim clerics, arguing that there's a double standard in response from the authorities. "Just try to join a group like Ahoker Followers, Poso Watch, Save Ahok and many more. Did the police arrest them? How many clerics and workers who are not pro-regime have been shamed, abused and had their photos edited?"

This is not strictly true however, and there have been a number of high profile cases across several different online groups where individuals have been arrested due to defamatory comments about religious leaders and political figures, in addition to the recent arrests of former MCA members.

MCA and the 2019 Presidential Election

Anam says members of MCA News came together in the beginning simply to defend Islam: "I myself joined MCA as I wanted to defend my religion because under this regime the law is selective." Although almost all the posts support particular figures and parties, he insists the group isn't affiliated to any of them.

Every post sent by members to the MCA News group must first be approved by an administrator, and almost all the topics of discussion and subsequent responses follow the same pattern. Over the course of the week that *New Naratif* followed the group, administrators and MCA News members regularly voiced support for the "Habib Rizieq Coalition", a group that allegedly supports firebrand Indonesian cleric Habib Rizieq, the leader of the Islamic Defenders Front (FPI) who wants Indonesia to adopt Shariah law across the country, and potentially one of Jokowi's opponents in the 2019 presidential election.

Despite their claim of being apolitical, an administrator for MCA News named "Mahsyar Oddy" announced that, for the 2019 presidential election, MCA News would only recommend candidates from the "four parties of Muslim advocates and clerics": namely the Great Indonesia Movement party (Gerindra), the National Mandate Party (PAN), the Prosperous Justice Party (PKS) and the Crescent Star Party (PBB). Anam told *New Naratif* that every administrator has the right to nominate certain political figures or groups for discussion, as long as that figure isn't Jokowi, a member of a party supporting "blasphemers", or someone from a party that supports the Perppu law.

The important role of administrators

Although the term "cyber Muslims" has existed for quite some time, Anam says the group really started to gain momentum after a series of actions defending Islam from 2016 to 2017 including mass demonstrations in the capital city of Jakarta which called for ex-Jakarta governor Ahok to be jailed for blasphemy. Its main role, as defined by its members, has been to eradicate supposedly blasphemous accounts, or "nasty accounts" that allegedly insult Muslim clerics.

But Hendardi, who like many Indonesians goes by one name and is the chairman of the human rights organisation Setara Institute, says the MCA network—with its hundreds of thousands of followers—spreads hoaxes and hate speech based on religious, racial, and inter-religious (SARA) content on social media on an even larger scale than other counterparts.

"MCA looks more ideological, has thousands of networks in different parts of Indonesia and therefore the destructive power of this group is greater than that of Saracen," he warns, referring to another hoax-sharing group that triggered police action in 2017.

Administrators have a huge amount of authority to filter incoming posts, but MCA News doesn't have a rigid organisation structure. Anam refuses to divulge the number of group administrators, but admits they are spread across a number of countries. "Many MCA administrators are based abroad," says Anam, whose Facebook profile says he lives in Bangkok. "[The other administrators] just look at how much time you spend taking care of the group and how strong your account is against an opponent's attack – that's all."

He also claims that administrators are unpaid: "If we got paid, maybe I'd already be rich, because I spend almost 15 hours or 18 hours just tapping away on my phone continuously." There is no suggestion, from speaking to MCA members and from posts in the MCA News Facebook group, that anyone is paid for their services as administrators. If they are, this has yet to be made public by any members of the group.

Anam refuses to reveal if he's using a fake or genuine account, but once suggested using an anonymous account when criticising the government. "Use genuine but anonymous accounts if you want to be vocal [about protesting against the government]. Remember, anonymous means freedom of speech," he wrote in the group on March 2, 2018.

Hendardi suspects that MCA's practice of spreading falsehoods and hate speech is underpinned by the political motivation to overthrow certain parties or the incumbent government. This, he says, not only endangers the integrity of political contests in Indonesia, but also causes conflict in society which undermines the unity of the nation.

There is no easy fix for this situation; dealing with such a wide network is a mammoth task. There's only so much a taskforce set up by the authorities can do; at the end of the day, it's an issue that will require many more organisations and individuals—from political parties to fact-checking groups to ordinary citizens—to step up.

THE MAKING OF A FEMALE ISIS BOMBER

FEBRIANA FIRDAUS | 04 JUN 2018

A conversation with Dian Yulia Novi, the first woman to be convicted for plotting a bomb attack in Indonesia, sheds light on the journey taken towards radicalisation and violence.

It was raining hard in Kelapa Dua in West Java that Tuesday afternoon one year ago, when I entered the gates of the Police Mobile Brigade Command headquarters prison (also known as Mako Brimob). She was waiting for me.

We were introduced—"this is Dian Yulia"—then led to a small room with a table and four chairs. She was wearing a niqab, grey gloves and a dark brown *gamis* (robe), a sombre outfit in stark contrast with the mood: relaxed, calm and cheerful.

"I have nausea," she said lightly in Bahasa Indonesia, holding a bottle of eucalyptus oil. She was two months pregnant.

Dian Yulia Novi was meant to be the first female suicide bomber for the Islamic State (ISIS) in Indonesia. She'd planned to detonate a bomb in a pressure cooker at the Indonesian presidential palace, but the scheme was foiled when the police raided her boarding house in Bekasi on the eastern border of Jakarta in December 2016.

While the prosecution pushed for a 10-year sentence, the East Jakarta District Court sentenced her to seven-and-a-half years in prison after she confessed. She was the first woman in Indonesia to be convicted for planning such an attack, and ended up in a small room in Mako Brimob with two female police officers assigned to guard her.

In May 2018, a year after I met Novi, a riot broke out at Mako Brimob, leading to a 36-hour hostage situation that left five police officers and one inmate dead. According to a police spokesperson, most of the officers had had their throats cut.¹ The riot, as well as bombings in Surabaya that took place within the same week, has been connected to Jamaah Ansharud Daulah, an Indonesian terror group that pledges allegiance to ISIS.²

Novi was in Mako Brimob with her six-month-old baby daughter during this incident. Media reports say she and her child have now been evacuated to another prison in central Java.³

Women and families carrying out attacks

Multiple deadly bombings in East Java followed the prison riot. On 13 May, one family of five targeted three churches—while the two teenage sons blew up the Santa Maria Catholic Church in Surabaya, the father drove a bomb-laden car to the Surabaya Centre Pentecostal Church. The mother, accompanied by her 12- and eight-year-old daughters, hit the Diponegoro Indonesian Christian Church. All this occurred within minutes of each other.

Later that night, another family died just outside Surabaya when their bomb exploded prematurely. Three children between the ages of 10 and 15 survived.

The next day, a third family attacked a police station, also in Surabaya. They'd used two motorcycles—the only survivor from the family was an eight-year-old girl who'd been wedged between her parents at the time.

The police have said that the families who attacked the churches and police headquarters had recently returned from Syria (these claims have been disputed by some of their neighbours).⁴ While Novi's plot had been unsuccessful, the attacks carried out by these mothers, bringing their daughters with them, mean that ISIS has officially unleashed the first female suicide bombers in Indonesia.

---

1 http://www.thejakartapost.com/news/2018/05/09/most-police-victims-of-mako-brimob-riot-had-throats-cut.html

2 http://www.thejakartapost.com/news/2018/05/14/what-is-jad-terror-group-behind-mako-brimob-riot-surabaya-bombings.html

3 https://news.okezone.com/read/2018/05/10/338/1896661/bayi-dan-ibu-napi-teroris-ikut-dievakuasi-ke-lapas-nusakambangan

4 http://www.bbc.com/news/world-asia-44101070; http://www.abc.net.au/radio/programs/worldtoday/neighbours-dispute-police-claims-about-surabaya-suicide-bombers/9758622

It's still not clear how ISIS recruits, indoctrinates and convinces women, children and even entire families to become suicide bombers. But my conversation with Novi sheds some light on how a journey of radicalisation unfolds.

Growing up and working abroad

Novi, an only child, grew up in Bandung, helping her parents with their shop in a traditional market. Like many other Indonesians, she joined a *mengaji*, a common study group for Indonesian children to learn about the Quran. She would stay home at night; her parents were conservatives and never permitted her to hang out with friends.

After graduating from high school, Novi worked in a textile factory, hanging out and shopping with friends in her free time. She later moved to Cirebon, West Java, but decided after several months to leave Indonesia to work as a migrant domestic worker.

She moved to Singapore in 2010 at the age of 23, where she worked in the home of a Chinese Christian teacher at a local high school, taking care of three young children; one of thousands of Indonesian women working in Singapore at the time. She was paid USD330 (IDR3 million) every month. She says she wasn't really happy in her job because it was difficult to get days off—a common complaint among migrant domestic workers in the wealthy city-state.

She decided to return home after one-and-a-half years, but took a new job in Taiwan after just a couple of months. She worked for an elderly couple who she called *Ama* (grandma) and *Yeye* (grandpa).

"My boss was Buddhist-Taiwanese, but *alhamdulillah*, they were tolerant," she said. Although Muslims are a minority in Taiwan, her employers were understanding and allowed her to wear the niqab. Although she'd started wearing the hijab before going to Singapore, it was only in Taiwan that she started getting more serious about covering her hair and face. "My boss was okay with it. They were quite tolerant. They said it's my own business."

The work was simple, but tough: Novi was responsible for cleaning the four-storey house in Taichung as well as cooking meals and caring for her 78-year-old employer. The work kept her busy, leaving her with no time to socialise with the sizeable migrant domestic worker community in the city. With few close friends and little opportunity to go out, she tended to stay home and spend her free time on social media platforms.

Learning about jihad online

It was during this time—scrolling through Facebook while working overseas—that Dian became aware of people talking about jihad, or holy war. She wasn't the only one; migrant domestic workers who find themselves isolated in a foreign country might be vulnerable to extremist recruiters or rhetoric online.

Between 2015 and 2017, for instance, Singapore repatriated nine allegedly radicalised migrant domestic workers.[5]

When approached by *New Naratif*, Nava Nuriyah, a researcher with the Institute for Policy Analysis and Conflict (IPAC), brings up a domestic migrant worker she'd interviewed in Singapore. The worker had described her life working abroad as an empty vacuous hole; she often watched Korean dramas until she got bored of them.

"She began to search for any [Islamic] reading [material] on the Internet. Most of the time Google would bring up Salafi content, and then it will lead the reader to VOA Islam," Nava says. The Salafi movement is a strictly orthodox, ultra-conservative branch of Sunni Islam, while VOA Islam is a counterfeit version of the US-funded media organisation Voice of America. VOA Islam deliberately publishes fabricated content and disinformation, tricking readers into thinking they are reading the actual VOA website.

Nava adds that, aside from Google, Facebook algorithms have also played a significant role in a providing links that connect migrant workers with online terrorist networks. "They want to find 'a religious friend' and the [Facebook] algorithm will directly suggest a friend; that's how these people live in their own bubble," she says.

Sometimes male jihadists also actively seek out targets via Facebook, using "online dating" to woo vulnerable women working as migrant workers and manipulate or "tame" them.

Novi started connecting with jihadists on Facebook. "At first, I was curious about these accounts on Facebook posting about jihad. I was 'stalking' them. Asking them, 'What's the hell is this? Why is this so weird?'" Novi recalled. At that time, she couldn't understand why people would want to sacrifice their lives and die as martyrs.

Despite her own experience of being a religious minority in Taiwan, Novi carried her own prejudices. She refused to accept the Shia Muslim minority in Indonesia: "Shias are not Muslim. No tolerance for them!"

---

5 https://www.todayonline.com/singapore/9-radicalised-domestic-workers-repatriated-2015

Tensions between Shia and Sunni sects[6] of the Muslim faith are long-standing and found all across the world. Although they share many fundamental beliefs, there are significant differences in theology, practice and doctrine. While the majority of the world's Muslims are Sunni, Shia Muslims form the majority in countries like Iran, Bahrain and Lebanon; much of the violence in the Middle East has been attributed to this sectarianism.[7]

Novi's rejection of Shia Muslims fit right in with ISIS ideology. The group, which gained global prominence in 2014, follows a fundamentalist doctrine of Sunni Islam.

Novi reached out to a number of individuals posting on Facebook about jihad. One, Fulana binti Fulan, eventually replied to her questions. She convinced Novi that she lived in Syria, and taught her about jihad. Fulana also explained about the different between al-Qaeda and ISIS.

"Al-Qaeda, in the past, they followed the Quran and *Sunnah* (the traditional custom and practice of Islam based on the teachings of the Prophet Muhammad), but lately, the leader seems to use jihad for politics. If they talk about politics, it means they're no longer fighting in the name of Allah," Novi said, mentioning the terrorist network's late leader, Osama bin Laden.

She also cited Jabhat al-Nusra, a jihadist organisation fighting against the Syrian government with the intention of establishing an Islamic state; following ISIS' scorn for both al-Qaeda and al-Nusra, she accused them of "joining" the United States of America and referred to them as "minions".

"Jihad is about fighting to uphold the religion of Allah without any other intentions, including for one's own business or one's group's interest," Novi explained.

A different Indonesia

Novi also took issue with Pancasila[8], the five principles that underpin the philosophy of the Indonesian state. She referred to Pancasila as a case of *shirk*, or the practice of polytheism or idolatry.

---

6 https://theconversation.com/what-is-the-shia-sunni-divide-78216

7 https://www.theguardian.com/world/2016/jan/04/sunni-shia-sectarianism-middle-east-islam

8 https://www.britannica.com/topic/Pancasila

"Why do have we to adhere to Pancasila and not Islam?" she demanded, arguing that following Pancasila was indication of a lack of trust in the Quran's law. She didn't understand why Indonesia, as the largest Muslim community in the world, did not adhere to Islam and the Quran as their basic principles.

It's a view also held by the hardline Islamist group Hizbut Tahrir Indonesia (HTI), disbanded by the Jokowi administration for conducting activities that contradicted Pancasila and the principle of a unitary Indonesian state—a move that attracted the ire of more strident voices online, such as the Muslim Cyber Army.[9]

Robertus Robert, a Pancasila expert from Universitas Negeri Jakarta said that the Pancasila had actually once been closer to Islamist desires: at one point in its drafting in 1945, the first principle was phrased as "*Ketuhanan dengan kewajiban menjalankan syariah Islam bagi pemeluk-pemeluknya* (Belief in Almighty God with the obligation for its Muslim adherents to follow Islamic law)".[10] It was included in the Jakarta Charter by the Muslim faction in the Investigating Committee for Preparatory Work for Independence (BPUPKI).

The clause on the obligation for Muslims to abide by Islamic law created a heated debate among members of BPUPKI. While nationalist leader Sukarno himself defended the clause, he changed his mind at the last minute. He and Mohammad Hatta held a meeting with a number of Islamic figures where Hatta argued for the removal of the clause on following Islamic law "[f]or the sake of the undivided unity of Indonesia."

The first principle was then revised to "*Ketuhanan yang Maha Esa* (Belief in One God)" after Indonesia's prominent leaders from different backgrounds—both Islamic and secular nationalists—agreed to compromise.

Apart from her scorn for the Pancasila, Novi laid out other beliefs picked up from ISIS: a Muslim, she said, is not a true adherent of Islam

---

9 http://www.thejakartapost.com/news/2017/07/19/govt-disbands-hti.html; https://newnaratif.com/journalism/muslim-cyber-army-virtual-battlefield/

10 https://books.google.co.id/books?id=gJC5DAAAQBAJ&pg=PA44&lpg=PA44&dq=%22 Ketuhanan+dengan+kewajiban+menjalankan+syariah+Islam+bagi+pemeluk-pemeluknya %22&source=bl&ots=4MZgg_yazM&sig=1ewdEtPNh7RyZKNzMUF2sD86OUQ&hl=en&sa= X&ved=0ahUKEwjMg56s4InbAhWBEpQKHXAjBMMQ6AEISDAD#v=onepage&q=% 22Ketuhanan%20dengan%20kewajiban%20menjalankan%20syariah%20Islam%20bagi% 20pemeluk-pemeluknya%22&f=false

if they follow a political leader such as a president. In ISIS' eyes, a leader is someone who rules under the administration of the Islamic State.

Individuals who idolise an *ulema* (a body of Muslim scholars with knowledge of sacred Islamic law and theology) seen as using the teachings of the Quran for their own business or political interests are also rejected by ISIS, Novi said. For example, she saw both the Indonesian Ulema Council, the country's top Muslim clerical body, and the Islamic Defenders Front, a far-right Sunni Islamist organisation, as political organisations that compromised far too much with Jokowi's administration. She angrily insisted that they were unworthy of respect.

For Novi, her country, although majority Muslim, was a long way away from the true Islamic nation she felt it should be.

Becoming a bomber

Novi had believed that she was fulfilling all the duties of a good Muslim: praying five times a day, fasting during Ramadan and reading the Quran. But after learning about jihad online, she decided that she wanted to go much further: she wanted to join the holy war.

Novi said her compulsion to join ISIS' crusade came from a sense of emptiness and incompletion as a Muslim: "Someday we will have to take responsibility for what we're doing now, from the moment we're born to the day we die. We are Muslims, but we haven't really applied ourselves as Muslims."

She'd even spoken to her parents about suicide bombing. "I said children in Syria have been suffering because of the war, don't you feel that your heart is broken to watch our brothers and sisters being treated like that? Where's our Muslim brotherhood?"

Her parents said, "But why does it have to be a suicide bomb? It's not allowed in our religion."

It's a question for which Novi does not seem to have a very clear answer. She told *New Naratif* that she had simply wanted to do something meaningful, at least once in her life.

For a year before her arrest, Novi learned about syariah Islam from Fulana over Facebook and applied it as much as possible in her everyday life; she said it strengthened her intention to participate in jihad.

She told another ISIS follower, Ummi Abza, about her plan. At that point, Abza was only a Facebook friend; she had never met this person before.

Novi then met Abza once and was introduced to Nur Solihin, who in turn had been recruited by Bahrun Naim, the most infamous Indonesian fighting with ISIS in Syria and Jamaah Ansharud Daulah's chief provocateur. Novi, who wanted to get married before being martyred, wed Solihin in Malang, East Java, without her parents' knowledge. They had never met in person or even swapped photographs before marrying; Solihin was also already married with three children.[11]

Both her new husband and Bahrun told her that she had to target the Indonesian president, Joko "Jokowi" Widodo. They said that he was an infidel, just like the President of the United States, Donald Trump. They pointed at Trump's executive order which blocked citizens of seven Muslim-majority countries from entering the United States for 90 days—highly criticised as a "Muslim ban"—as proof that the United States was anti-Islam.[12]

"There will be a war between Muslims and America (USA)," Novi declared.

"Jihad is fardhu ain"

Over the past two years, there has been a perceived rise in the participation of women in ISIS in Indonesia. For the first time in Indonesia's history of counter-terrorism work, in December 2016 the police arrested three women involved in planned bombings: Novi, Arida Putri Maharani and Tutin Sugiarti. This month, Puji Kuswati[13], who attacked the church in Surabaya with her daughters, and Puspita Sari[14], who died with her family when the bomb they were making went off prematurely in a flat in Sidoarjo, died as the first female ISIS militants in Indonesia.

"Yes, there is a difference between men and women in Islam. For example, in jihad, it is not mandatory for women [to participate]. But for now, jihad is *fardhu ain* (mandatory for all Muslims), like praying," Novi said. ISIS' view, as she understood it, was that every Muslim had to join the war.

---

11 https://www.channelnewsasia.com/news/asia/
    indonesian-would-be-suicide-bomber-worked-in-singapore-as-nanny--7640822

12 https://www.aclu.org/blog/immigrants-rights/muslim-ban-what-just-happened

13 https://www.straitstimes.com/asia/se-asia/
    indonesias-first-female-suicide-bomber-a-mum-of-4-0

14 https://coconuts.co/jakarta/news/
    police-believe-family-suspected-terrorists-behind-yet-another-explosion-sidoarjo-3-dead/

According to Novi, Indonesia's female brigade was inspired by the al-Khansaa Brigade, an all-female ISIS police brigade that keeps other women in line with the group's ideas of Islamic practice. When Raqqa was still an ISIS stronghold, the al-Khansaa Brigade were, essentially, the morality police, ensuring that women were fully covered in public and accompanied by male chaperones.

"It's not a so-called emancipation of the female jihadist," Novi said. Although the women of the al-Khansaa Brigade were trained, armed and reportedly paid, their operations were still about keeping women subservient to men.[15]

The same applied to the Indonesian brigade Novi joined; no matter how fervent the women's belief, the men were still the leaders. Nur Solihin, who has also been arrested and jailed, led her operation.

"In jihad, if it's needed then women can join," she explained. "But as long as the man can do the jihad, we'll prioritise them to do that." Despite the belief that participating in jihad is the duty of every Muslim, ISIS still emphasises the involvement of men over that of women.

That said, Novi asserted that men were more likely to dodge jihad duties: "Maybe because the [male] ISIS followers feel that they still want to enjoy their life with their wife and children. Maybe they are afraid."

Lingering questions

We spoke for two hours before she asked me to leave; it was time for her to pray.

I left feeling twitchy and restless. Indonesia has the largest Muslim population of any country in the world, and, while on the fringes, ISIS wields some influence here. I still couldn't quite comprehend why she had been so committed to kill and die for ISIS, and many questions remained: how many members are there in ISIS' female brigade? How many children will be sacrificed in the name of an Islamic State?

The recent bombings have been unprecedented in that they've been family efforts. Little is known about how family networks figure into the ISIS presence in Indonesia, although some efforts, like deradicalisation schools, are trying to address generational terrorism.[16]

---

15 https://www.independent.co.uk/news/world/middle-east/escaped-isis-wives-describe-
life-in-the-all-female-al-khansa-brigade-who-punish-women-with-40-lashes-10190317.html

16 https://newnaratif.com/journalism/deradicalisation-schools-the-answer-to-terrorism-
in-indonesia/

"The need for this knowledge is urgent," wrote Sidney Jones, director of the Institute for Policy Analysis of Conflict in Jakarta. "If three families can be involved in two days' worth of terrorist attacks in Surabaya, surely there are more ready to act."[17]

As terror attacks occur in Indonesia during this Ramadan season, the fear is that there might be many more like Novi out there.

---

17 https://www.lowyinstitute.org/the-interpreter/surabaya-and-isis-family

WALKING A TIGHTROPE ON RELIGION

MICHAEL MCLAUGHLIN | 16 AUG 2018

Who decides what is or isn't "heresy"? The Vietnamese government's reaction towards the World Mission Society Church of God highlights the complexity of a nominally atheist state's relationship with the faithful.

As you get off the boat at Phoenix Island in the heart of the Mekong Delta in Ben Tre, Vietnam, one of the first things you'll notice is an oddly shaped structure with nine blue-hued pillars. Colourful dragons wind their way up six-metre columns capped by large lotus-like domes. Made from broken ceramic dishes, they are one of the few remnants of the Coconut Kingdom religion, which, at its peak during the Vietnam War, was reported to have had nearly 4,000 followers.

The structure was once a floating pagoda constructed by the followers of Nguyen Tranh Nam, a French-educated crucifix-wearing engineer who was said[1] to have sustained himself solely on coconuts for three years. Known as the Coconut Monk, he ran unsuccessfully for election as President of South Vietnam in 1971.

After winning the war in 1975, the communist Vietnamese government sought to repress religion and religious practices in the reunified country. Groups like Coconut Kingdom were banned. But policy could not overcome reality in a country whose citizens have shown willingness to embrace a range of religious and spiritual practices.

Today, Vietnam is open for business: although technically still a communist country, its leaders have introduced reforms aimed at attracting investment and foster further economic growth. But opening up has other effects, and foreign money isn't the only thing flowing into Vietnam.

---

1 https://www.ozy.com/flashback/vietnams-cult-of-the-coconut-was-no-joke/65389

Various religious groups have jumped on the opportunity to make their presence felt in the nominally atheist country, sometimes placing the authorities in a conundrum. The Vietnamese government's recent reaction towards a church from Korea highlights their uneasy relationship with religions and cults.

The World Mission Society Church of God

The World Mission Society Church of God (WMS) is a Christian sect that emerged out of a schism within a church founded by South Korean minister Anh Sahng-hong. According to its website, WMS has established over 2,500 churches in around 175 countries.

It doesn't just recognise Anh as its founder; WMS believes that Anh is God himself. WMS' website refers[2] to Anh as "Second Coming Christ Anhsahnghong" and credits him with restoring "the truth of life". Followers also believe in a matriarchal God, whom they call "God the Mother[3]". As with their belief in Anh, this mother figure it not just an abstract deity, but an actual woman, Jang Gil-ja.

While WMS has received some recognition internationally for its charitable work—in 2016, a group of volunteers from WMS won[4] the Queen's Award for Voluntary Service in the United Kingdom—it has also been denounced[5] by ex-followers as a "doomsday cult" that "isolates its acolytes from their families and friends by controlling information and using brainwashing techniques."

According to a report[6] by *PEOPLE* in the United States, the church sought out people who were "more psychologically vulnerable", such as recently-returned army veterans. Former congregants also said that the church "worked to deliberately dissolve marriages between devoted members and their unconvinced partners", and pressured women to get abortions as they believed that bringing more children into the world was "pointless and selfish." While NBC also led its own investigation[7], the WMS faces no criminal charges in the U.S.

---

2 http://english.watv.org/intro/introduction.asp

3 https://www.youtube.com/watch?v=AnEByCPkjt4

4 https://www.gov.uk/government/uploads/system/uploads/attachment_data/file/527091/Queens-award-voluntary-service-winners-2016.csv/preview

5 https://people.com/celebrity/ex-followers-say-south-korean-church-is-mind-control-cult/

6 https://people.com/celebrity/ex-followers-say-south-korean-church-is-mind-control-cult/

7 https://www.youtube.com/watch?v=dvM8JvUn9CI

An uneasy relationship

WMS is far from the first outlandish religion (or cult) to emerge in Vietnam. In fact, the country has been home to a variety of spiritual practices, from major recognised faiths and traditional folk religions to outright bizarre beliefs.

Apart from the reign of "His Coconutship", some Vietnamese have also worshipped a turtle god, and, before 1975, promoted polygamy as part of their faith. The third-largest religion in Vietnam, *Cao Dai*, identifies Confucius, Muhammad and Victor Hugo—yes, the author of *Les Miserables* and *The Hunchback of Notre Dame*—as its holy prophets. In North Vietnam, a religion—with practices that involve fire, swords, liquor and showering worshippers with cash—known as *Dao Mau* or Mother Goddess worship[8], was banned until the early 2000s, but has since been recognised[9] by the United Nations Educational, Scientific and Cultural Organisation (UNESCO) on the Representative List of the Intangible Cultural Heritage of Humanity.

Unable to completely stem the tide, yet wary of any organisation that could challenge its power, Vietnam's communist government maintains a complicated relationship with religious groups. Although the Constitution officially recognises freedom of religion, the government exercises control[10] over religious practices. Laws include broadly-worded provisions that allow for the restriction of religious freedom, supposedly for national security reasons.

Christianity, in particular, is politically sensitive. 8.5% of Vietnamese have declared themselves as Christian; while the vast majority are Catholics, Protestantism is on the rise[11]. The strained relationship between Christianity and the government comes from the country's own history.

Following the 1954 Geneva Accords, which split Vietnam in two, hundreds of thousands of Vietnamese moved from the North to the South. This mass exodus was partly encouraged[12] by a propaganda

---

8 https://english.vov.vn/your-vietnam/the-unique-mother-goddess-worship-of-vietnam-344764.vov

9 https://ich.unesco.org/en/RL/practices-related-to-the-viet-beliefs-in-the-mother-goddesses-of-three-realms-01064

10 https://vn.usembassy.gov/international-religious-freedom-report-2016-vietnam/

11 https://www.iseas.edu.sg/images/pdf/ISEAS_Perspective_2017_34.pdf

12 https://books.google.cz/books?id=h0_MU8uU60cC&lpg=PA37&hl=cs&pg=PA45#v=onepage&q&f=false

campaign covertly engineered by the United States' Central Intelligence Agency (CIA), targeting the North's anti-communist Catholics. At that time, most of the country's Catholics lived in North Vietnam; entire Catholic communities packed up and fled South during the US-managed Operation Passage to Freedom. In the South, Catholic refugees were given preferential treatment under Prime Minister Ngo Dinh Diem, himself a member of the faith.

Christians were continually persecuted during and after the Vietnam War. Bishop Nguyen Van Thuan, Diem's nephew, was appointed Coadjutor Archbishop of Saigon less than a week before the end of the War in 1975; after the Communist government swept into Saigon, he spent thirteen years in Communist re-education camps, nine of them in solitary confinement. Various Christian sects also have long records of persecution; even after the government allowed Christian groups to fully return to the country in 2003, the tension persists.

Clamping down on WMS

As one of the newer Protestant sects in Vietnam—WMS is believed to have first gained a foothold in the northern port city of Hai Phong in 2016—WMS has attracted public attention after a number of YouTube videos featuring members of Hanoi's WMS chapter circulated online. One video shows a man proselytising on Hanoi college campus, exhorting other students[13] to abandon fake idols and prepare for Armageddon. Another video shows a young girl, apparently in a prayer-induced reverie, crying out for God to save her for nearly six minutes[14]. At one point in the video, a passerby with an umbrella tries to shield her from the rain; she pushes him away.

On 21 April 2018, Religious Affairs Committee Chairman Vu Chien Thang released a public statement warning citizens, especially students, to be aware of WMS. Thang stated that the group had been operating in Vietnam for close to two years without official recognition.

The committee chairman's announcement prompted the state-controlled mainstream media to begin lambasting WMS, publishing allegations made by former church members and accounts of individual experiences with the church.

---

13 https://www.youtube.com/watch?v=abeftiCxZds
14 https://www.youtube.com/watch?v=l0gd69MUtQ0

News videos circulating online show church services with veiled women, believers prostrating themselves in prayer, or even crawling on the ground as they claim to be filled with a spirit. Still others show purported followers smashing traditional Buddhist statues[15]. Relatives tell of losing loved ones to WMS control. Like some other religious organisations, WMS tells its followers to give 10% of their income to the church.

A Catholic, interviewed by *New Naratif* on condition of anonymity, pointed to Nguyen Van Hoa, one of the WMS founders in Ho Chi Minh City, as the individual "who forced my parents to return home and smash Jesus' photos, and remove our ancestor altar table. [Hoa] told them that our ancestors, or even my siblings and I, are all demons."

He is now a little estranged from his parents, and laments that he no longer sees them: "Now I can only call my father on the phone."

The media campaign reached its peak on 7 May when the mainstream newspaper *Tuoi Tre* reported that the government had labelled WMS as a "heresy" of "real Christianity"; the official statement claimed that WMS "did not conform to existing catechism." The authorities later seized WMS property and assets in Hanoi and Ho Chi Minh City. This is the first known case—since the 1981 consolidation of Buddhist organisations and the banning of the politically oriented Unified Buddhist Church of Vietnam[16]—of the Vietnamese government trying to completely wipe out a religious organisation.

The government's reference to catechism is key. A catechism is a church-manifested document delineating the faith's doctrines and principles. By taking it upon themselves to decide—in both official channels and the media—whether a religious group is or isn't conforming to catechism, the government is effectively dictating what the accepted "true word of God" is, and who is or isn't a Christian.

These moves highlight the control that the government can exercise over religious groups, particularly unregistered ones. "Members of unregistered Christian, Hoa Hao, Cao Dai, and other groups… face regular arrests and harassment from local and provincial authorities, and dozens of people are believed to be behind bars in connection with

---

15 https://www.youtube.com/watch?v=WoaVqrPsKpw

16 http://content.time.com/time/world/article/0,8599,1595721,00.html

their religious beliefs," says Freedom House in its 2018 *Freedom in the World* report on Vietnam[17].

Even registered groups can run into sticky situations. A 2013 Catholic Ecumenical News article reported[18] that "the situation in Vietnam in recent years for Catholics and other Christians has deteriorated." The Church, since at least 2012, has regularly aided Vietnamese activists and other convicted for political dissent. In 2014 and 2016, the Church held prayer vigils for land rights activist Can Thi Theu, days before her separate convictions and sentencing for dissent. Catholics claim to regularly face small, aggressive encounters with the police and other officials, and are prohibited from holding posts in the military, police or other "sensitive" government positions.

Despite this, many leaders of the Vietnamese Catholic Church say the congregation is growing. Father Joachim Hien, ordained in Vietnam in 1974 and now retired, told[19] *Catholic World Report* that the country's churches are "prosperous and packed". But there's still a red line that can't be crossed. Although Father Hien said that there's now more space for priests to criticise communism, he added, "just as long as they don't try to stir up any [organised] revolt"—a fairly expansive caveat in a country known[20] to brand activists as "reactionaries" and accuse them of attempting to overthrow the government.

Responses in Vietnam

The unequivocal response to WMS has people wondering about the government's motives, and whether this could mark another tightening of control over religion, especially Christianity. How do the authorities determine whether a religious sect conforms to "existing catechism"?

It's an issue that points to further questions over the process and criteria used to distinguish between legitimate worship and "heresy". Take, for instance, the Church of Jesus Christ of Latter Day Saints (LDS), which claims more than millions of followers globally.

---

17 https://freedomhouse.org/report/freedom-world/2018/vietnam

18 https://www.ecumenicalnews.com/article/vietnamese-catholics-fleeing-to-australia-to-avoid-persecution-22345

19 https://www.catholicworldreport.com/2016/12/05/catholic-vietnam-growing-despite-communist-oppression/

20 https://www.theguardian.com/world/2017/sep/26/vietnams-state-largest-crackdown-on-dissidents-years

The LDS Church, whose followers are called Mormons, was branded by critics as a cult in much of its early history. Leaders of fundamentalist Mormon offshoots have been indicted in the US in 2017 for organising sexual religious rituals with underage girls. But Vietnam's Government Committee for Religious Affairs granted the Mormons official status in June 2016; two years later, it claims that WMS' teachings is "heresy" and that it's breaking a loosely-worded prohibition on "unsanctioned religious activities."

Still, some practices are hard to defend, and there's a rational basis for government intervention if WMS was engaged in coercion and abuse in Vietnam. On the same day Hanoi seized WMS assets and detained Hoa, a state-run newspaper reported[21] that relatives of WMS adherents told police that that WMS worship includes drinking a "sacred liquid" with allegedly psychoactive properties. While the police did confiscate several bottles of liquid and vials from WMS properties, there has been no further public update on what the substances were. The police also confiscated hundreds of marijuana plants allegedly owned by one of the adherents; they claim that the "missionary" of WMS, Do Xuan Hieu, would "lure potential converts back home to take drugs."

But not everyone in Vietnam agrees with the clampdown. Pastor Le Minh Dat of the evangelical Vietnam Agape Outreach Church told the BBC[22] that the WMS should be viewed as a normal religion and that people "have the freedom to choose their faith in accordance with the law." He criticised the government for making claims about "heresy" or catechism, which he sees as being the church's territory.

The government's actions have also triggered alarm bells. Redemptorist priest Father Le Ngoc Thanh reported[23] to Catholic Press Agency Asianews.it that "he was afraid that the propaganda campaign against the World Mission Society Church of God was designed to create tensions between religious and non-religious people", and that the WMS crackdown is simply the Vietnamese government getting a feel for whether it could get away with grabbing assets, including prime land, from Christian groups.

21 http://www.doisongphapluat.com/tin-tuc/chat-la-cua-hoi-thanh-duc-chua-troi-me-la-chat-gi-a228805.html

22 https://www.bbc.com/vietnamese/vietnam-43890229

23 http://www.asianews.it/news-en/Authorities-seize-cult-assets-and-detain-cult-members-43834.html

Other Christian religious leaders have been more circumspect in their comments, preferring to draw a clear line between the WMS and their own practice. "I have nothing to do with them, I cannot comment on, nor evaluate their activities," says Father Tran Nguyen Duy Thang of the Catholic Church of God in Ho Chi Minh City.

Still, he added that—if allegations of WMS forcing members to abandon their loved ones are true—their actions were "not true of what our Catholics do, not exactly what is taught in the Bible to love, forgive and support."

When contacted, the Archdiocese in Hanoi declined to respond.

This matter is by no means confined to just Vietnam; many religious practices and beliefs around the world have been controversial or potentially illegal, prompting state intervention or judicial action. But Vietnam's tense relationship with religion, and Christianity in particular, provides a backdrop that makes the implications of such regulation more fraught than in other contexts.

No criminal charges have been filed against WMS or its leaders thus far. Nguyen Van Hoa has been publicly silent after a solitary interview[24] professing his innocence. The government has de-legitimised the WMS officially and socially; years' worth of content has been wiped from the Vietnamese WMS Facebook page[25], which suggests that the government has seized the page.

The Vietnamese government could be heading in a couple directions. The first matches its official justification for intervention: protecting the general welfare (albeit through autocratic methods) of the people in lieu of a proper legal framework on psychological coercion. The second is the one that's keeping some of the religious up at night: a fresh crackdown.

Perhaps these two possibilities aren't mutually exclusive; if a problematic sect like WMS is behaving badly in Vietnam, it could provide the government the excuse it needs to overturn the existing, shaky balance of religious freedom.

---

24 https://video.infonet.vn/thoi-su-24h/hoi-thanh-cua-duc-chua-troi-chinh-thuc-len-tieng-x6m94ko1.html

25 https://www.facebook.com/H%E1%BB%99i-Th%C3%A1nh-C%E1%BB%A7a-%C4%90%E1%BB%A9c-Ch%C3%BAa-Tr%E1%BB%9Di-774359376007813/

POLITICS TRUMPS HUMAN RIGHTS IN INDONESIA
AISYAH LLEWELLYN | 23 AUG 2018

Between Jokowi and Ma'ruf Amin, and Prabowo Subianto and Sandiaga Uno, human rights is likely to be left by the wayside in the 2019 Indonesian presidential election.

On 9 August 2018, the current President of Indonesia, Joko "Jokowi" Widodo announced his running mate for the presidential elections, due to be held in April 2019. It was Ma'ruf Amin, the 75-year-old chairman of Indonesia's top Muslim clerical body, the Indonesian Ulema Council (MUI) and "supreme leader" of Nahdlatul Ulama (NU), Indonesia's largest mass Muslim organisation.

Amin's name had been widely circulated several weeks before the announcement, but still came as a surprise to many. Human rights lawyers, activists and researchers were quick to condemn the choice; online commentators said they would only vote for "an empty ballot box", meaning boycott the elections altogether. Most of their ire focused on the fact that, while he may be one of the most influential Muslim figures in Indonesia, Amin has been linked to a string of unpopular decisions to clamp down on human rights issues and minority groups over the last 20 years.

"Amin's statements on LGBT rights and his support for the criminalisation of the LGBT community are unacceptable. It shows his inability to protect and respect human rights," Jakarta-based women's rights activist, Tunggal Pawestri tells *New Naratif.*

But in the face of an online firestorm, Jokowi, once the darling of the foreign media and often described as a "liberal" or even "progressive" president, remained unmoved. Speaking[1] to the press during his announcement, he tried to make a case for Amin. "Maybe there are

---

1 https://www.reuters.com/article/us-indonesia-politics/indonesian-president-picks-cleric-as-running-mate-for-election-idUSKBN1KU0JF?il=0

questions from the people all over Indonesia why Professor Dr Ma'ruf Amin was chosen," he said. "Because he is a wise religious figure [...] I think we complete each other, nationalistic and religious".

Jokowi: once a great new hope

Jokowi's often painted as a moderate politician and a breath of fresh air on the political scene in Indonesia. He was, after all, the first Indonesian president to have come from outside the ranks of the military, or the political and religious elite. He used to be a furniture salesman and was known for his humble style and clean governance when he was the mayor of Solo, a city in Central Java, from 2005 to 2012. His signature style back then, and when he was Governor of Jakarta from 2012 to 2014, was to regularly arrive unannounced at government offices to make sure that civil servants, notorious for playing hooky, were doing their jobs. In 2014, *Time Magazine*[2] put him on their cover, calling him "A New Hope" and "The New Face of Indonesian Democracy".

But Jokowi has come under fire during his presidency, following a string of clampdowns on human rights, including overturning an unofficial moratorium on the death penalty soon after assuming office, and ordering police to shoot drug dealers as part of his "war on drugs"[3]. As it turns out, "the new face of Indonesian democracy" is more about conservative politics than a progressive dream.

But the majority of Jokowi's more controversial policies are thought to have been an attempt to push back against critics from other political parties and religious groups who have accused him of being ineffectual and insufficiently "Indonesian" (by which they insinuate he's actually Chinese, and not really Muslim). He's had to weather accusations of Communist sympathies, with doctored pictures surfacing[4] of him purportedly attending a Communist rally. As Jokowi has pointed out, he wasn't even born at the time the pictures were meant to have been taken, but in Indonesia, a country where Communism is banned following anti-Communist purges in the 1960s that left millions of people dead, such wild claims have done damage to his reputation. He even

---

2 http://time.com/3511035/joko-widodo-indonesian-democracy/

3 https://thediplomat.com/2018/01/beware-indonesias-quiet-drug-war/

4 https://coconuts.co/jakarta/news/hoax-photo-alleging-jokowi-attended-speech-pki-leader-spreads-social-media-jokowi-wasnt-even-born-1955/

experienced a birther moment, similar to that of former US President Barack Obama, when it was alleged that he is part Chinese.

Now, seemingly to counter all of these allegations, Jokowi has chosen a running mate who's arguably one of the most religious men in Indonesia. And religion is a big selling point in elections in a country where 87% of the population is Muslim.

Having been accused of not being religious enough, Jokowi's trying to beat his naysayers at their own game. "He has simply done what his rivals have advocated in order to 'defeat' them electorally," says Ian Wilson, a lecturer in Indonesian politics and security studies and a research fellow at the Asia Research Centre, Murdoch University.

Many others agree that Jokowi likely selected Amin to curry favour with religious voters. According to Pawestri, "Choosing Amin is definitely showing us that Jokowi is lacking in confidence in dealing with and facing conservative groups. And this is also a sign of where this country is going to be brought in the future."

Jokowi's willingness to court conservative religious organisations to protect his presidency is a chilling strategy that doesn't bode well for a more tolerant and democratic Indonesia. As Wilson explains, "He's shown he's happy to sacrifice minorities and his friends to keep the MUI and Islamic hardliners on side. Amin, and some factions of the MUI, though maybe not all, will see this as their moment."

Politics and religion: the history of Ma'ruf Amin

Amin was born in Tangerang, a regency to the west of the Indonesian capital city of Jakarta, in 1943. Having attended Islamic boarding school and then studied Islamic philosophy at university, his career has always shuffled between religion and politics—two concepts forever entwined in Indonesia. He also served as an advisor to former presidents Abdurrahman Wahid (Gus Dur) and Susilo Bambang Yudhoyono (SBY). In 2015, he was elected as chairman of the MUI, having had senior positions within the organisation for years.

"If Jokowi and Amin are elected, it's going to bring a new and dangerous trajectory for the future of Indonesia," Indonesia researcher for Human Rights Watch, Andreas Harsono tells *New Naratif*. "Over the last 20 years Amin has used his influence and power to advocate for what he considers to be Islamic syariah law against gender and religious minorities in Indonesia."

The MUI, of which Amin is the head, is one of the main religious bodies in Indonesia. As Wilson explains, "It began as an organisation to co-opt ulama and provide a religious rubber stamp for state policy. Over the years it has faced challenges from an array of competing voices, but has managed to maintain its semi-state backed status and used it to pursue its own brand of social conservatism and illiberal politics."

The MUI is also responsible for issuing fatwa[5], non-legally binding but authoritative legal opinions and pronouncements on Islamic law. From 1999 to 2004, while also a member of the Indonesian parliament, Amin chaired the committee responsible for issuing fatwa. From 2004 to 2010 he was chairman of the National Sharia Committee within the MUI, before becoming its overall chairman in 2015.

Many of the fatwa overseen by Amin have sparked concern and conflict across Indonesia. In 2008, the MUI issued a fatwa supporting female genital mutilation (FGM) following a ban on the practice in Indonesia in 2006. In 2015, another fatwa was issued calling for same-sex acts to be punished by caning and the death penalty. In 2016, yet another fatwa was issued which branded the Gafatar religious community based in Kalimantan as "heretical". As recently as August 2018, it's been reported[6] that the MUI are investigating a religious group called the Jellyfish Kingdom in Banten Province outside Jakarta following complaints that the group were claiming that the Prophet Muhammad was a woman.

Such religious pronouncements have had a serious knock-on effect across the country. According to the Setara Institute[7], an organisation in Jakarta that compiles data on religious freedom, acts of religious intolerance rose from 236 in 2015 to 270 in 2016. "The MUI's fatwa [against religious minorities] has generated a hostile and dangerous atmosphere that's been used by right wing forces to attack and further marginalise progressive voices and movements," says Wilson.

It doesn't stop there.

---

5 https://www.hrw.org/news/2018/08/10/indonesia-vice-presidential-candidate-has-anti-rights-record

6 http://www.thejakartapost.com/news/2018/08/14/banten-sect-jellyfish-kingdom-ruffles-muis-feathers.html

7 https://www.hrw.org/news/2017/02/02/indonesias-religious-minorities-under-threat

Amin is also behind the formation of Forum Kerukunan Umat Beragama (FKUB)[8] or Regional Harmony Forums, a group of regional advisory bodies across Indonesia created when he was an advisor to SBY in 2006. The Regional Harmony Forums are meant to be responsible for approving the building or renovation of houses of worship, but are widely thought to be used as a cover to quell religious freedom.

Although the stated purpose of the Religious Harmony Forums is to foster harmony between majority and minority religions in Indonesia, the way they've been put together bolsters the needs of the majority. Part of the Religious Harmony Forums decree says that the structure of the bodies have to be proportional to the population of a particular area and "mirror the composition of religions". This means that, in a Muslim majority area, the majority of members must be Muslim.

If there's a dispute between majority and minority religions about the need to build a house of worship in a particular area, for example, the minority is always set up to lose the dispute. To that end, thousands of churches have been shuttered across Indonesia, including 1,056 under SBY, in addition to 33 Ahmadiyya mosques from 2005 to 2008, according to Harsono.

While also working with SBY, critics have pointed to Ma'ruf and the MUI's role in the erosion of the rights of minorities in other ways. "This included the introduction of the anti-pornography law and the increasing use of the blasphemy law, both of which served to further bolster the MUI's authority and influence," says Wilson.

The anti-pornography law has been used[9] to arrest and convict members of the LGBT community and the blasphemy law was used[10] in 2015 to convict Jokowi's former political ally, Basuki "Ahok" Tjahaja Purnama, who, as a Chinese Indonesian and a Christian, is a double minority. Ahok is currently serving a two-year sentence for blasphemy after it was deemed that comments he made on the campaign trail during the Jakarta gubernatorial election in 2017 insulted Islam. At the time, Amin and the MUI issued a strong statement which roundly condemned Ahok and was thought to be one of the driving forces behind his conviction.

---

8 https://www.hrw.org/news/2014/05/14/undoing-yudhoyonos-sectarian-legacy

9 https://www.hrw.org/news/2018/02/20/indonesias-anti-lgbt-drive-should-concern-all-asia

10 https://thediplomat.com/2017/08/the-toxic-impact-of-indonesias-abusive-blasphemy-law/

It says a great deal about the lengths that Jokowi is now willing to go to in order to secure a second term as president. Ahok ran as Jokowi's deputy during the 2012 gubernatorial elections in Jakarta, and took over from him as governor when he ascended to the presidency in 2014. Now, Jokowi has chosen the man who's widely seen as partly responsible for putting Ahok behind bars as his running mate.

Still, some are not surprised by the political game which is now afoot.

"Over the years Jokowi has drawn the MUI's leadership close as a protective strategy. This has been relatively easy for him considering his own conservatism but also comes at a cost. The greatest cost is being paid by those targeted such as Ahmadiyya, Shia Muslims and LGBT Indonesians," says Wilson.

Prabowo Subianto and Sandiaga Uno

Jokowi's controversial choice now presents a quandary for Indonesian voters. Jokowi and Amin will face off against former major general Prabowo Subianto and former deputy governor of Jakarta, Sandiaga Uno, whose human rights records aren't any more encouraging.

Prabowo, in particular, has long been considered[11] an egregious violator of human rights. He was once denied a visa[12] to the to the United States following allegations that he instigated riots during the fall of Suharto in May 1998 that left over 1,000 people dead. When serving in the army in Timor-Leste during the period when Indonesia occupied the country from 1975 to 1999, there were allegations that he oversaw the killings of local pro-independence fighters, with rumours abounding[13] that he sent the severed head of resistance fighter, Nicolau Lobato, to Suharto as a war trophy.

Prabowo was discharged from the military following accusations of abductions of pro-independence activists and sending in thugs to exacerbate civil unrest during the 1998 riots. Prabowo said that he was simply following orders in the abduction cases; he has never been tried for any alleged abuses.

Speaking in his own defence, Prabowo has always claimed that he's nothing like the man he's often painted to be. In a televised speech on

11 https://newnaratif.com/journalism/crisis-and-complicity/

12 https://www.reuters.com/article/us-indonesia-usa-prabowo/indonesian-election-presents-u-s-with-modi-style-visa-headache-idUSBREA4J12020140520

13 http://www.insideindonesia.org/prabowo-and-human-rights

local channel TV One, Prabowo pushed back hard against his critics. "I'm being created as someone who is anti-democracy. That I want authoritarian government. [That] I want to go back to the New Order," he said, shaking his fists for effect. "No, please be assured I'm a democrat. I believe in democracy. I was a soldier, I was a professional soldier, and I swore an oath to the Indonesian Constitution."

Some members of the audience guffawed. Others clapped.

A bleak future?

Some hope that Amin has become more moderate in his views. "Yes, he has a history of being a hardliner but in the past two-and-a-half years, he has not issued fatwas against groups like Ahmadiyahs and others," Ahmad Suaedy, a senior researcher at the Wahid Foundation, told Channel News Asia[14].

"Ma'ruf in the past two years is far more interested in redistributing wealth and eradicating poverty. I believe this is what he will sought to do as a vice president," he added.

But Amin's recent comments show that his position on issues like LGBT equality hasn't shifted. "We all agree that being LGBT is a violation. We must prevent it. It's a very bad thing," he said in an interview[15] this year. "How can men love men? It's a deviation. So those who are like that must be educated."

Whoever voters now choose, the presidential candidates and their vice presidential picks indicate a worrying trend towards more conservative politics in Indonesia generally. The choice of Amin in particular, as one of the main conservative Islamic figures in the country, now looks as if it may push Indonesia in a more conservative direction, where religion will dictate policy if he becomes vice president.

There are concerns that conservative religious organisations like MUI are now in the position to accrue more political power. "What's significant about Amin, beyond the focus upon him as an individual, is the further moving of the MUI to the centre of power. His mainstreaming of their brand of illiberal conservatism is nearing completion," says Wilson.

---

14 https://www.channelnewsasia.com/news/asia/indonesian-election-jokowi-running-mate-muslim-cleric-maruf-amin-10610028

15 https://www.rmol.co/read/2018/01/29/324521/Kiai-Ma%E2%80%99ruf-Amin:-LGBT-Itu-Memang-Haram,-Sudah-Seharusnya-Masuk-Delik-Pidana-

And while many potential voters may have been joking when they said they intend to vote for an empty ballot box, neither set of candidates in the April 2019 presidential election inspires much hope for a more democratic and tolerant Indonesia.

For people like Indonesian human rights lawyer, Veronica Koman, Jokowi is now showing his true colours, having failed to live up to the hype of many of his campaign promises to investigate historical human rights abuses in the country. "Jokowi has not fulfilled any of his presidential campaign [promises] on solving human rights violation cases. And he just chose someone [Amin] who is infamous for discrimination against groups like Ahmadiyya and the LGBT community. He had better not use human rights issues as his presidential campaign any more because it would contradict his choice of vice president," she says.

It's anyone's guess right now what the 2019 election results will be, but one thing is already certain: human rights will be left by the wayside come next April. As Koman says: "The future of human rights cases looks grim in Indonesia because we can't expect Prabowo—a human rights abuser himself—to be any better than Amin."

"HOW DO YOU INTERVIEW GOD?"

STANLEY WIDIANTO, AISYAH LLEWELLYN | 06 SEP 2018

A Chinese-Indonesian woman is just the latest casualty of Indonesia's opaque blasphemy law. But despite allegations that the law targets religious minorities, there appears to be little political will to change it.

It's a long drive to the city of Tanjung Balai in North Sumatra, Indonesia—almost five hours from the provincial capital of Medan, on winding roads past emerald green paddy fields and through palm oil and rubber plantations. The city is one of the main ports in North Sumatra, and connects both Malaysia and Singapore with Indonesia. Like many port cities, a large proportion of residents in Tanjung Balai make their living from the sea.

Meiliana, a Chinese-Indonesian and a Buddhist, was no exception. Having lived on Jalan Karya in Tanjung Balai for eight years, she owned a simple store selling salted fish with her husband, Atui. But in July 2016, Meiliana's life was thrown into disarray, and in August 2018 she was sentenced to one and a half years in prison for blasphemy by the Medan District Court.

How it all began

It started out almost as a throwaway comment.

In July 2016, Meiliana walked across the road from her small house on the sleepy street of Jalan Karya to buy breakfast buns from Kasini, a 51-year-old Javanese Muslim who owns a small shop selling sundries. It was something she did almost every morning.

Kasini and Meiliana weren't exactly friends, but they had a cordial relationship. At Eid-ul-Fitr, the end of the Muslim fasting month, Meiliana would bake cakes and take them to Kasini's house.

On that fateful morning, as Meiliana paid for her buns, she had a request for Kasini. "Can you tell *Wak* [grandfather] to turn down the volume of the mosque speakers? It's so loud it hurts my ears."

Kasini's father, 75-year-old Kasidik, has worked at the Al Ma'shum Mosque since 2007 as one of its caretakers. Five times a day, he walks the few feet to the mosque from the home he shares with Kasini and her children and puts a cassette in an old-fashioned tape player. The *azan* (prayer call) then rings out across Jalan Karya, reminding Muslims that it's time to pray.

Karsini didn't think much of Meiliana's comment, other than wondering why, having lived just ten paces away from the mosque for the last eight years, she was suddenly bothered by the sound of the *azan*.

"I did think, why is she saying this to me?" she tells *New Naratif.* But the mood was calm, and Kasini passed the request on to her father. He, in turn, told another caretaker, who then told the *imam* (the spiritual leader of the mosque).

That comment, first made over a breakfast bun, then started to take on a life of its own.

Just a few days later, Kasini and Kasidik noticed that the street outside Meiliana's home was suddenly clogged with cars and motorbikes. People started showing up at all times of the day and night, and they could hear shouting. At one point Kasini says she thought she heard Meiliana's eldest son exclaim, "We're all adults here! What's wrong with you?"

Word of Meiliana's comment about the mosque speakers had spread from a neighbour to her father, from a father to his co-workers, from the co-workers to more neighbours, and from the neighbours to social media. The message got distorted as it passed from one to another, and eventually people were saying that Meiliana had tried to stop the Islamic call to prayer and insulted Islam, violating Indonesia's infamous blasphemy law (Pasal 156A KUHP), which carries a maximum five-year prison sentence.

A few days later, Meiliana's husband Atui went to the mosque to publicly apologise for his wife's comments. Meiliana was either too scared or too stubborn to go with him. In the end, it hardly mattered; her husband's apology failed to insulate her against what happened next.

Prominent Islamic organisations, such as Front Umat Islam (FUI), successfully pressured[1] the police to file an official report. In 2017, the North Sumatra chapter of the Majelis Ulama Indonesia (MUI), one of the largest Muslim organisations in Indonesia, issued a *fatwa* (a non-legally binding but official pronouncement on Islamic law) against

---

1 https://tirto.id/rekayasa-kebencian-dalam-kasus-meiliana-di-tanjung-balai-cUEe

Meiliana. A mob proceeded to riot, pelting Meiliana's home with rocks and bottles. They then set fire to Buddhist temples in Tanjung Balai.

Kasini claims that Meiliana was originally taken into custody for "her own protection", as the authorities were worried she'd be lynched if she stayed at home. But instead of protecting her, they charged her with blasphemy.

According to one of Meiliana's lawyers, Ranto Sibarani, the court proceedings were chequered at best.

The prosecutors presented the *fatwa* and a written statement from a witness at the riot outside Meiliana's home as evidence. Sibarani claims it was mostly based on hearsay; no recordings of the original comment were provided. "They brought the mosque amplifiers as an item of evidence," Sibarani tells *New Naratif*. "The officials welcomed the rioters with open arms. The case was heavily influenced by an intervention from the masses."

A sense of disbelief over the legitimacy of Meiliana's case continues to loom large. "She did not commit blasphemy. What she did was offer a neighbourly complaint, and that is not an insult to Islam," Ismail Hasani, the research director at the rights advocacy group Setara Institute, told[2] *The Washington Post*. "More generally, we believe that the blasphemy law itself does more than anything else to limit freedom of religion in Indonesia."

Particular to Meiliana's case, there's also been a debate about the volume of the call to prayer, and whether a request to lower it qualifies as blasphemy. In 1978, Indonesia's Religious Affairs Ministry released[3] instructions on how to properly manage the volume made by a mosque amplifier, prioritising melody over loudness; Indonesia's current vice president, Jusuf Kalla, has also advised mosques in Indonesia to be mindful of the volume of their speakers, and dispatched[4] technicians to help fix faulty amplifiers.

Kasini says she feels "exhausted" by the case. She had to go to the police station countless times to give her testimony about Meiliana's comment, and once attended court in Medan to give evidence. She says that when she made her statement to the judge, Meiliana was not there

---

2 https://www.washingtonpost.com/world/2018/08/23/womans-blasphemy-conviction-indonesia-sparks-backlash-intensifies-concerns/?utm_term=.fc078e7194ad

3 https://tirto.id/pelantang-masjid-macam-apa-yang-ramah-bagi-telinga-cUKe

4 http://www.thejakartapost.com/news/2015/06/26/mosques-turning-down-volume.html

to hear the testimony against her, so the former neighbours didn't have to face each other.

When asked if she believes Meiliana committed blasphemy, Kasini shrugs her shoulders and looks confused. "I don't know anything about the blasphemy law, so I just leave it up to the judge. He must have known what he was doing," is all she will say.

Kasini isn't the only one who's exhausted.

Meiliana's story is one of fatigue for anyone who has tried to follow the trajectory of Indonesia's nebulous and opaque blasphemy law, and the myriad cases that have unfolded over the years, always following a similar pattern.

Here, the cycle continues: frivolous litigation favouring the offended and mobilised mob; a president's inability "to intervene in the legal process[5]"; an outpouring of signatures in an online petition[6]; political convenience.

The blasphemy law in Indonesia is built upon all of these things—this is the story of how it's wielded, how it unfolds, and how it (still) stands.

Indonesia's problem with blasphemy

The blasphemy law has its roots in the administration of Indonesia's first president, Sukarno. Signed into force by Sukarno in 1965, the law was originally meant[7] to "accommodate requests from Islamic organisations who wanted to stem the recognition of indigenous beliefs." It was later used as a way for President Suharto, the authoritarian second president of Indonesia, to prosecute anyone who dared to criticise his government.

Attempts to revoke the law have failed on more than one occasion. Indonesia's fourth president, Abdurrahman "Gus Dur" Wahid—who wrote an article in 1982 for *Tempo* magazine entitled "Tuhan Tidak Perlu Dibela (God Does Not Need to be Defended)"—was once involved in an unsuccessful petition to revoke the blasphemy law. In July 2018, a petition[8] launched by the Ahmadiyya Muslim community in Indonesia, who claimed that the law inhibits their religious freedom, was also rejected.

Anyone who stands accused of blasphemy in Indonesia also faces a tough legal battle with little chance of acquittal.

---

5 http://www.thejakartapost.com/news/2018/08/25/support-flows-in-for-meiliana.html

6 https://www.change.org/p/bebaskanmeliana-tegakkan-toleransi

7 https://tirto.id/asal-usul-delik-penistaan-agama-b49e

8 https://www.hrw.org/news/2011/06/27/faith-indonesia-still-unenlightened

"Since 2004, there hasn't been an appeal [in blasphemy cases] that has been granted by the court," Andreas Harsono, a researcher at Human Rights Watch, tells *New Naratif.* "Out of 89 cases [in Indonesia's sixth President Susilo Bambang Yudhoyono's administration], 125 [individuals] were convicted. And out of 20 cases, 22 [individuals] were convicted in President Joko Widodo's current administration."

One of the more recent blasphemy cases involved the erstwhile Jakarta governor, Basuki "Ahok" Tjahaja Purnama, who was sentenced to two years in prison under the blasphemy law. Accused of insulting Islam for having quoted the Quran while on the campaign trail during the 2017 Jakarta gubernatorial election, thousands of demonstrators took to the streets, calling for Ahok to be imprisoned.

Although the scale of Ahok's case was far greater, the patterns in Meiliana's case mirrored his.

A continuing streak of religious intolerance

At the very heart of Meiliana's case—and all of the other cases preceding it—is Indonesia's continuing streak of religious intolerance.

Tanjung Balai is known for having a sizeable Chinese-Indonesian population; Chinese traders, arriving by sea, started to pour into the area in the 1800s. According to official records, the city has just over 185,000 residents, 157,000 of whom are Muslim and 11,000 of whom are Buddhist. At times in the city's history, tensions between the different communities have flared.

In 2009, Tanjung Balai bore witness to the removal of a Mahayana Buddha statue. "The appearance of the Buddhist statue elicited a violent reaction from Islamic leaders. Wahhabi leaders under the United Islam Movement (GIB) organised rallies and protests in May and June last year, calling for the statue to be taken down. They argued that it tarnished the image of Tanjung Balai as a Muslim town," wrote Human Rights Watch in a report[9].

Following Meiliana's comments in 2016, a mob tore through the city and targeted several of its 16 Buddhist temples.

This outbreak of violence is now considered to be one of the worst examples of racially motivated mob "justice" that Indonesia has seen

---

9 https://www.hrw.org/news/2011/06/27/faith-indonesia-still-unenlightened

since 1998, when rioters attacked primarily Chinese-Indonesian communities in Medan, looting from shops and attacking local residents. The riots then swept[10] across the country, leaving 1,000 people dead.

Atu is the 68-year-old caretaker of the Tiau Hau Biao Buddhist Temple, which sits on the estuary of the Asahan River in Tanjung Balai. The air is heavy with the scent of drying fish, and fishermen sit in front of the temple and cast their nets in the shadow of its crimson roof.

Atu has worked as a caretaker of the temple for 10 years, since it was first built, and works from 5am to 8pm, seven days a week. His main duties include sweeping the floors and replenishing the incense. Back in 2016, he was at home when the temple was attacked in the middle of the night. When he arrived in the early hours of the morning, the building was still aflame.

"I don't know how much gasoline they brought with them, but they sure used up every single drop," he tells *New Naratif.* Atu, and local residents who had come to help, set up a crude pump system to funnel water from the river to quench the flames.

It took over an hour to put the fire out.

Once the flames subsided, Atu saw that the roof of the temple has been destroyed. The statues had been burned. The floor tiles smashed.

The restoration of the temple to its former glory took several months. According to Atu, the money promised by the government to help pay for it never materialised. Instead the refurbishment was made possible by donations from the local community.

19 perpetrators were eventually caught. According to news reports[11], "Eight were charged with looting, nine with malicious destruction of property and two with inciting violence". All were given sentences ranging from one to four months in jail. Despite having ransacked official houses of worship, none of the rioters were charged with blasphemy, because no one filed an official complaint against them—one of the stipulations for someone to be tried under the law.

Atu laughs dryly and shakes his head when asked about this. "Not fair, of course it's not fair. They should have got longer sentences."

He also says that the case appears to show a trend towards rising religious intolerance in Tanjung Balai. "We used to be more united, but

10 https://newnaratif.com/journalism/it-was-a-political-issue/

11 http://www.thejakartapost.com/news/2018/08/23/the-meiliana-case-how-a-noise-complaint-resulted-in-an-18-month-jail-sentence.html

now the different religious groups have started to split," he explains. "For years I went to sea as a fisherman and left my family at home. I never worried about them."

Now he can't forget the sight of his beloved temple burning in the morning light.

The attacks on temples in Tanjung Balai certainly appear to show worrying echoes of the race riots that traumatised the Chinese-Indonesian community in 1998.

Sirojuddin Abbas, a researcher at Saiful Mujani Research and Consulting (SMRC), says that Meiliana's case shows how the blasphemy law is being deployed to punish members from minority groups. "The target is always a member of the minority groups," he says. "That still is the thing that has not healed from our majority groups: their distrust. In a pluralistic town, for example, even if there's only a person who is not a Muslim, not having to hear excessive noise from a mosque speaker is still a human right."

Atu dismisses the idea that the people who attacked the temple were hired thugs, brought in to stir up racial unrest. In 1998, it was thought that members of the Indonesian military deliberately did just that to spark widespread riots and deflect attention away from the failings of the government, which led to the fall of President Suharto after 32 years in power. But, despite the fact that these attacks in Tanjung Balai seem to have been less tightly organised and politically motivated, it doesn't reassure Atu.

"I heard the rioters were mixed," he says. "Some outsiders. But they must have had someone on the inside. Someone from Tanjung Balai."

After news of the fire at the temple spread, Atu says local residents started visiting in droves to check out the damage. Buddhist festivals are held at the temple every January and October, and are popular events with the local community. Muslims also come to watch the colourful festivities.

Atu says he hopes for a bigger crowd than usual this coming October, due to the publicity that the blasphemy case has sparked, which has actually raised the temple's profile. He feels that a large, mixed crowd of spectators will be a good thing, and that local Muslims getting a taste of Buddhist culture which will help bolster relations between the different communities once more.

"But this year, the police will be guarding us," he adds.

The politics of blasphemy

Rising religious intolerance is one way of looking at Meiliana's case. But there are other lenses through which to examine this issue. One of them has to do with the question of whether religious intolerance is a mere manifestation of political expediency.

In April 2019, Indonesian voters will go to the polls to elect a president. As both candidates, current President Joko Widodo and former Major General Prabowo Subianto, look to curry favour with Muslim voters in a country where 87% of the population is Muslim, changing the blasphemy law could be a risky move that could cause a backlash from more conservative sections of the Islamic community.

As Savic Ali, an activist with the Jaringan Gusdurian network of progressive Muslims, says, "I think [Prabowo and Jokowi] won't make concessions with regards to the blasphemy law. Jokowi wants a safe position, as to not anger his Muslim voting base, and I think Prabowo does, too."

And it goes beyond just individual voters.

Ali continues to say that two of Indonesia's largest Muslim organisations, Nahdlatul Ulama (NU) and Muhammadiyah, won't allow for the possibility of the blasphemy law being completely revoked anytime soon, as both believe it to be an important tenet of Islamic law. Fast forward to the presidential elections in 2019, and it's likely that both Jokowi and Prabowo will be wary of alienating voters affiliated with either organisation—or indeed the organisations themselves, who hold significant political power in Indonesia.

Another warning sign that the blasphemy law is unlikely to be overturned or discarded anytime soon is the appointment Ma'ruf Amin as Jokowi's running mate in the race for the presidency. Amin, who is the chairman of the MUI and known for his conservative views on Islamic law, initially said[12] that he deplored the violent riots in Tanjung Balai following Meiliana's comment. But, this did not stop the North Sumatra chapter of the organisation issuing a *fatwa* against her in early 2017.

Amin has also thrown his support behind other high-profile blasphemy cases in the past, and wields significant political and judicial influence. "He plays the most important role in sending people to jail,

---

12 http://www.thejakartapost.com/news/2018/08/23/the-meiliana-case-how-a-noise-complaint-resulted-in-an-18-month-jail-sentence.html

like Ahok," says Harsono, in a reference to Amin's statement[13] against the former governor of Jakarta, widely thought to have been one of the driving forces behind his conviction.

Another example of the way politics and the blasphemy law are entwined is evident in Meiliana's case when you consider the collateral damage: her family. Sibarani tells *New Naratif* that Meiliana's son is still "afraid of the sight of a crowd" after the riots outside his home. Jokowi has said that he can't intervene in legal cases or in Meiliana's appeal, but there are those who think that he could show goodwill in other ways.

"He needs to say something about the need for Meiliana's family to be, say, socially and psychologically rehabilitated," says Abbas.

A few words from the president could perhaps go a long way in helping Meiliana's four children to heal—still, he has remained silent, presumably so as not to offend any members of his conservative fanbase.

Yet again it seems, politics has turned the blasphemy law into a matter of convenience for those jostling for power. This refusal of politicians in Indonesia to engage in discussions about the blasphemy law has serious implications, and muddies the waters about its essential premise.

While outright revocation may not be on the cards, in its current form the law is porous and easily abused. Not everything can or should fall under the umbrella term "blasphemy", and one of the main criticisms of the current version of the law is that it's overly broad, encompassing a range of other issues like hate speech.

Ali says that, for serious situations that could be construed as blasphemous in nature, like urinating on a Bible, for example, there needs to be a revision to the law instead of an outright repeal. But for other cases, such as a complaint about the volume of a mosque speaker, the law needs to be clear about what the term "blasphemy" actually means. "Several points of the law need to be amended so that it can't be a catch-all law," he says.

As it currently stands, the only thing that's clear is that the core meaning of "blasphemy"—and what it should encompass—is something that's confused and confusing in Indonesia. And the lack of political will to even discuss potential changes to the law means that the absurdity of the very concept of blasphemy still remains in the shadows.

---

13 http://www.thejakartapost.com/news/2018/08/09/who-is-maruf-amin-jokowis-running-mate.html

After all, were there people *rightly* convicted according to the blasphemy law in Indonesia?

For people like Harsono, this question goes right to the heart of the issue. "Of course there weren't. How do you interview God?", he says.

Hope for a change to the law?

Politicians might not want to rock the boat, but there might be a glimmer of hope on the horizon.

Since her sentencing, Meiliana has had some support from surprising allies.

As well as a Change.org petition with over 202,000 signatures, members of both Muhammadiyah and NU have criticised[14] Meiliana's sentencing—although not the blasphemy law itself, other than to say that it was incorrectly implemented in this case. Still, "both of these statements are unprecedented," says Harsono. On Twitter, Indonesia's religious affairs minister, Lukman Hakim Saifuddin, offered[15] his services as Meiliana's key witness if needed.

Though conceding that the situation is "bleak" and that electoral prospects are likely to get in the way of either presidential hopeful wanting to fully embrace reform, Abbas says that public support for Meiliana gives him cause for optimism.

Sibarani tells *New Naratif* that Meiliana's counsel plan to file an appeal. This will add yet another chapter to her story, and could have repercussions across Indonesia if it's successful. "If it goes through, we hope that it can be a legal breakthrough," he says.

Until then, Meiliana's former home remains shuttered.

A neighbour tells *New Naratif* that Meiliana's husband was forced to move. Several members of the Chinese community from Jalan Karya asked him to relocate, as they were scared that they too would be the victims of reprisals and violence—tarred with the same brush of being "anti-Islam". The neighbour also says that the couple had to give up their salted fish business on Jalan Asahan as they lost their permit to operate in the building as a result of the outcry surrounding the case. It's unclear who gave the order for this to happen.

---

14 http://www.thejakartapost.com/news/2018/08/22/nu-muhammadiyah-criticize-meiliana-blasphemy-verdict.html

15 https://twitter.com/lukmansaifuddin/status/1032594467138756609

Atui has now moved to the city of Medan to be closer to Meiliana in prison, and is trying to build a new life.

When asked how she feels about this, Kasini looks pained. She wasn't the one who made the original comment about the mosque speakers, but if she hadn't passed on Meiliana's request to her father, then perhaps none of this would ever have happened.

Does she think that Meiliana truly committed blasphemy and got the punishment she deserved?

Kasini looks lost for words. "Well… why did she buy a house so close to a mosque?" she says. "And why did she live here for eight years without any problems? Even if we had turned down the volume, she would still have heard the sound of the *azan*."

Pressed again, and asked if this was fair and if she feels responsible for Meiliana's fate, Kasini's chin starts to tremble and her eyes fill with tears. She looks completely overwhelmed by the firestorm this case has caused—and which has consumed her life for over two years.

She insists she was just the messenger, when she passed on the words that ended with a woman in jail and a family torn apart.

Finally she looks up from the floor.

"If I'd known this was going to happen…" she says, her voice breaking, "then maybe I wouldn't have said anything at all."

POLITICS AND POWER

THE DUTERTE PLAYBOOK

SOL IGLESIAS | 09 SEP 2017

The "War on Drugs" waged over a year now by Philippine president Rodrigo Duterte is not about addressing drug crime at all. It's the use of violence for political control and it's happened before—in Davao City.

S ince assumption of the Presidency on June 30, 2016, Rodrigo Duterte's "War on Drugs" may have killed as many as 12,000 people.[1] He won the 2016 Philippine presidential election on May 9 explicitly promising to kill millions of criminals, and urging people to kill drug addicts, and has consistently argued that the violence is necessary for his "War on Drugs", to prevent the Philippines from becoming a narco-state.

One simple graph shows the impact of Duterte's actions. All the Presidential administrations in the post-Marcos democratic period have significantly lower levels of documented counter-insurgency related combat deaths, extrajudicial killings and lethal shootings by police. However, there is a huge spike in the first year of the current administration based on even the most conservative estimate of lethal police shootings from the Philippine National Police, specifically of drug personalities, from July 1, 2016 to June 13, 2017.

The only problem is, Duterte's lying. It's not about drugs. He has framed and deployed violence throughout his terms as Mayor of Davao City, almost unbroken from 1988 to 2016, and as president in the same exact way. The "War on Drugs" is nothing more than a figleaf for his real goal: political control. He's still using the same playbook from when he was Davao City's mayor, ruling through fear as vigilante death squads killed a hundred people a year. The worst part? We're all falling for it.

---

1 Jodesz Gavilan, "CHR: Death Toll in Drug War Higher Than What Gov't Suggests," *Rappler* (2017), https://www.rappler.com/nation/179222-chr-number-drug-war-victims.

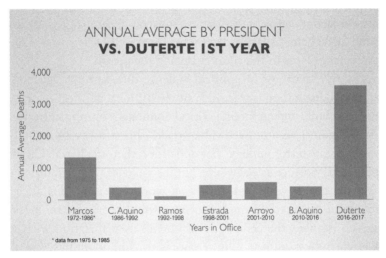

Figure 1: State Violence Estimates since 1972 Martial Law under Marcos (Source: Author's compilation from the Uppsala Conflict Data Program, the Philippine Human Development Report 2005, Ibon Foundation, Karapatan, US State Department Human Rights Reports, Amnesty International, Rappler, Kreuzer (2016), Kessler (1989))

Blame the Victim: How Duterte Used Political Violence in Davao City

Duterte's use of a violent, anti-crime campaign as a pretext for total control is repeat of his tactics as mayor of Davao City. Until winning the presidency last year, since 1988 Duterte was re-elected every three years as mayor, pausing only to serve in Congress (1998-2001) and as his daughter's vice mayor from (2010-2013) due to legal limits on consecutive terms.

Political violence in Davao City initially seems puzzling. In other Philippine cities, political violence follows a predictable pattern. Violence tended to intensify in the months leading to the filing of election candidacies in October and shortly after the May polls, every three years from 2001. The pattern of electoral violence is tied in with processes of building and defending political dynasties. If you can't persuade, you use violence. Either way, you ensure your candidates can run unopposed.

However, in Davao City, elections did not produce patterns of bloody rivalry that can be seen elsewhere. In and of itself, that is not remarkable. Davao is the third most populous city in the Philippines; election related conflicts may have been peacefully resolved at the ballot box rather than through violence. Moreover, Davao City does not fit a national pattern of attacks against activists in a counter-insurgency campaign that peaked around 2006 before sharply declining. Yet the city was also one of the most violent places in the country during the period.

Why were patterns of political violence different for Davao City? The crucial distinction is that, in Davao City, local political actors used violence to build and maintain political dominance by mimicking casual violence against an atomized urban poor. This strategy concealed but amplified state terror under a "law and order" rhetoric. Davao City thus experienced violence as elsewhere, but the violence was used differently.

Yet the city government's effective monopolization of both legitimate and illegitimate forms of violence would not have been possible, however, without the central government's own flirtation with state violence. Understanding this difference is also important towards understanding how then Mayor Duterte utilizes violence at a national level as President Duterte.

I'll break down these three points in the following sections. Warning: they are, by necessity, data heavy. Feel free to skip to the ending.

The puzzle of the "safest" city in the Philippines

In the last two decades, Davao City gained a reputation for being an oasis of stability in conflict-ridden Mindanao, the stage on which protracted Muslim *Moro* and communist insurgencies continue to play. Some even considered it the safest city in the country and the locale received the Philippine presidential award for being the "child-friendliest" city three times.[2] Yet the highest number of violent incidents occur in the Davao region, with Davao City alone making up 45% of the cases in its region and 14% of violence overall (See Figure 2). How do we explain this puzzle?

To answer this, I spent much of 2016 digging through data from Commission on Human Rights (CHR) records, daily newspaper archives and NGO reports. I studied cases related to political activities e.g. elections, activism, involving officials or state security forces (military, police, paramilitaries, state-sponsored vigilantes), consisting mostly of killings or attempted killings. I focused on five regions in the Philippines from January 1, 2001 to June 30, 2016: Northern Luzon, Central Luzon, Eastern and Western Visayas, and Davao, where Davao City is located.

2 "Davao City Ranks as 9th Safest in the World," *Philippine Daily Inquirer* (2015), http://newsinfo.inquirer.net/690252/davao-city-ranks-as-9th-safest-in-the-world.

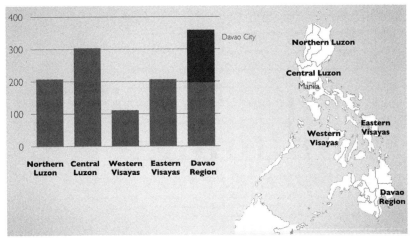

Figure 2: Cases of Political Violence by Region, 2001 to 2016 (Source: author's data)

Some general trends can be seen across all the regions:
- Violence generally peaks around 2006, supporting the assertion among activists, academics and other practitioners that a campaign of state terror, "Operation Plan *Bantay Laya*" (OBL, or Operation Freedom Watch), was waged following an exposé that then-president Arroyo may have committed electoral fraud in 2004 (See Figure 3). For example, the periods where the military was active in Central Luzon and Eastern Visayas show pronounced levels of violence, particularly against left-wing activists.[3] Activists, community organizers, journalists and other "enemies of the state" found themselves on military "Orders of Battle", secret military documents that allegedly listed targets in order of priority for elimination.[4]

---

3 "Who's Afraid of General Palparan?," *Philippine Daily Inquirer*, October 19 2005.

4 Norman Bordadora, "Left Groups in Orders of Battle, Say Papers," ibid., June 20 2006. See also "Oplan Bantay Laya: The Us-Arroyo Campaign of Terror and Counterinsurgency in the Philippines," in *Fourth of a Series on State Terror and Human Rights in the Philippines* (Quezon City: Ibon Foundation, Inc., 2010).

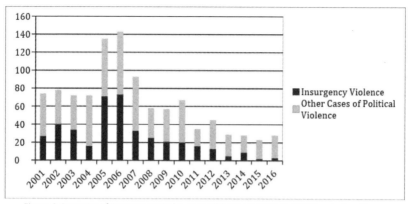

Figure 3: Patterns of Insurgency Violence in All Regions, 2001 to 2016 (excluding Davao City) (Source: author's data)

- Military presence also tended to coincide with instances of "casual violence"— essentially, disproportionate use of violence without any specified, strategic purpose. For example, in 2005 in Nueva Ecija, a soldier stationed in the area shot and killed a resident over the latter's having "blinded" the soldier with his headlights.[5]
- While some elections were more violent than others, violence tended to intensify in the months leading to the filing of candidacies in October and shortly after the May polls, every three years from 2001 (See Figure 4).
- Assassinations followed a distinct *modus operandi*: gunmen riding tandem on a motorcycle or a lone gunman making the hit in broad daylight. While some cases were brought before the ombudsman or before the courts (especially those that had victimized mayors, judges, lawyers and activists), the violence was commonly committed with impunity. The police and military's casual excesses contributed to a pervasive acceptance: people were resigned to state forces' virtual freedom from accountability.

---

5 Regional Director Jasmin Navarro-Regino, "CHR Resolution Case No.: III-C-06-2810 Re:Antonio R. Alarcon, Jr for Violation of Art. 3 UDHR and Art. 6 ICCPR," (Commission on Human Rights, October 3, 2006).

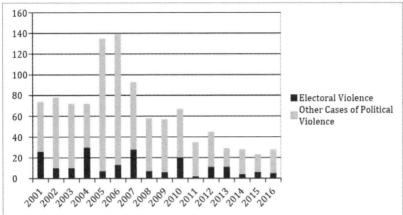

Figure 4: Patterns of Electoral Violence in All Regions, 2001 to 2016 (excluding Davao City), 2001 to 2016. Election Years: 2001, 2004, 2007, 2010, 2013, and 2016. (Source: author's data)

In Davao City, however, the variations in political violence were very different compared to the national pattern and other regions (See Figure 5). Davao City only had a couple of cases of election-related violence within the 15-year period, including one of a village chair from a neighboring town who just happened to be assassinated in the city.[6]

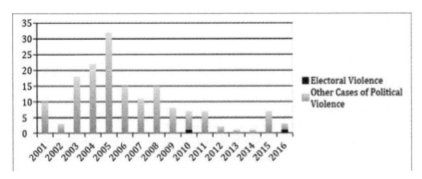

Figure 5: Patterns of Electoral Violence in Davao City, 2001 to 2016. Election Years: 2001, 2004, 2007, 2010, 2013, and 2016. (Source: author's data)

Neither is it insurgency-related violence. The number of cases was quite small compared to the rest of Davao region and generally restricted to

---

6 In May, Altavista village chair Edison Alisoso was killed and tribal chieftain Emelito Angga wounded in an attack scant days before the election. Inquirer Bureaus, "Security Beefed up in Provinces for Polls," *Philippine Daily Inquirer*, May 9 2016.

outlying rural areas; moreover, unlike other regions, such cases clustered around 2008 rather than 2006 (See Figure 6). For instance, the secretary-general of the peasant union *Kilusang Magbubukid ng Pilipinas* (KMP) Celso Pojas was gunned down due to his advocacy of farmers' rights.[7] Leftists had been killed by the military nationwide since 2001; but no leftist leader had been killed in Davao City until Pojas in 2008.[8]

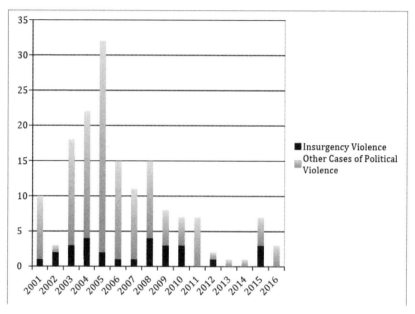

Figure 6: Patterns of Insurgency Violence in Davao City, 2001 to 2016. (Source: author's data)

What sets Davao City apart is the sheer commonness of violence against unaffiliated civilians: individuals who were non-combatants, who had no evident ties to any political faction nor any history of activism. About a third of all violence against such unaffiliated civilians (32%) among the regions in this study occurred in Davao City and 76% of the victims of violence in Davao City were unaffiliated civilians (see Table 1).

---

7 Regional Director Alberto Sipaco, "CHR Resolution Case No.: XI-2008-3041dc Re: Death of Celso Pojas," (Commission on Human Rights, November 10, 2008).

8 Jeffrey Tupas and Dennis Santos, "Davao Farmer Leader Gunned Down," *Philippine Daily Inquirer*, May 16 2008.

Type	N Luzon	C Luzon	W Visayas	E Visayas	Davao (region)	Davao City
Activists	23	62	14	35	21	7
Civilians	26	70	37	64	64	121
Journalists	8	9	7	2	8	2
Insurgents	16	53	10	20	22	6
Local Officials	104	80	19	49	41	9
Military	17	11	12	28	32	7
Police	10	12	1	8	14	3
Private armed groups	4	5	0	1	1	2
Unknown	0	2	0	1	1	2
Total 1,183	208	304	100	208	204	159

Table 1: Targets of Political Violence in All Regions, 2001 to 2016 (Source: author's data)

The reality of the "murder capital" of the Philippines

Davao City has a history of violence. Until the late 80s, many armed paramilitary groups operated there and it was the NPA's laboratory for urban warfare.[9] While the NPA's "sparrow" units initially eliminated abusive policemen, soldiers and common criminals, its terror tactics against civilians precipitated the anti-communist, paramilitary *Alsa Masa* movement. This conflict fueled violence in Davao for decades.[10] From 1988 – 2002, Rodrigo Duterte claimed to have reduced the *per capita* crime rate to one of the country's lowest, declaring that he transformed the former "murder capital" into one of the most peaceful cities in the Philippines.[11] But we know that's not true. We also know that

9 F.A. Mediansky, "The New People's Army: A Nation-Wide Insurgency in the Philippines," *Contemporary Southeast Asia* 8, no. 1 (1986).

10 Oude Breuil, Brenda Carina, and Ralph Rozema, "Fatal Imaginations: Death Squads in Davao City and Medellin Compared," *Crime, Law and Social Change* 52, no. 4 (2009): 415. See also Sheila Coronel, "I Will Kill All the Drug Lords: The Making of Rodrigo Duterte," *The Atlantic* (2016), https://www.theatlantic.com/international/archive/2016/09/rodrigo-duterte-philippines-manila-drugs-davao/500756/.

11 Breuil, Carina, and Rozema, 415.

there was very little insurgency-related violence after this period. So what accounts for the shift? A new play on violence for political control.

In the course of his tenure, Duterte gained the moniker "The Punisher" or "Dirty Harry" due to his association with vigilante killings attributed to the mysterious Davao Death Squad (DDS) or DDS.[12] The DDS can be linked to as high as 1,424 killings in Davao City from 1998 to 2015. These estimates by Coalition Against Summary Executions, a local NGO, show a rapid acceleration from 2001 onwards, peaking in 2008 with about 180 dead.[13] Moreover, the violence tended to occur in intense "spates" of killings, with multiple vigilante killings in one day over the course of a few days or spread out over a month. In my study, I found around seven such spates of killings attributed to DDS vigilantes were documented.[14] Not all of them were linked to the DDS: for example, a series of lethal police shootings of alleged drug and robbery criminals in April, August and October 2015 were punctuated by Duterte's public pronouncements against drug criminals.[15]

Fully formed by 1997, the DDS reportedly consisted of former insurgents, paramilitary members and, in some cases, former targets. The hitmen allegedly had handlers among the police and village officials.[16] In earlier years, Duterte used to read lists of criminals on the radio, and within a certain period of time, sometimes as brief as a day or two, some of those on the list would be killed by unidentified gunmen on motorcycles. The lists came from anti-narcotics crime bureaus of the police and intelligence gathered by village officials, but the DDS also

12 See, for instance, Phil Zabriskie, "The Punisher," *Time Asia*, June 24 2002.

13 Coalition Against Summary Execution, "Data on Summary Executions in Davao City Based on News Clippings from Davao Sunstar, Sunstar Super Balita, Mindanao Times and Brigada Editors from 19 August 1998 to December 2015," (Davao City2015). Unpublished.

14 Seven periods of heightened killings after a lull of a month or more occurred during the following: September to November, 2001; May to July, 2003; February 2004; June to August 2004; December 2004 to January 2005; Mar to April 2006; August 2009.

15 See for instance Germelina Lacorte and Allan Nawal, "'They Would Have Lost Their Heads'," *Philippine Daily Inquirer*, July 18 2015. Allan Nawal, "Davao Drug Suspect Dead after Duterte Ultimatum," ibid., October 30. Karlos Manlupig, "Duterte Justice: Robbery, Slay Suspect Dead," ibid., August 21. See also Dennis Santos, "2nd Crime Suspect Dead on Heels of Duterte Ultimatum " ibid., November 1.

16 "You Can Die Any Time: Death Squad Killings in Mindanao," (New York: Human Rights Watch, 2009), 49-50.

began targeting newly-released convicts from prison, individuals with cases pending against them or with a criminal record.[17] In many cases, the targets or their families would learn directly from village officials or through word of mouth that they were "on the list," prior to the attacks.[18]

Over time, however, motives for some killings became less clear— police would claim that victims were *known* criminals but CHR investigators would be unable to find any evidence to substantiate the claim.[19] In time, the myth of the DDS became self-referential. For example, in January 2005, Coca-Cola bottling plant worker Hilario Ortega was shot dead; according to the CHR, police authorities believed that the motive was a personal grudge, noting that Ortega was a "good person" and had no criminal record, "and could not be a victim of 'summary execution' that frequently transpires in this city." [20]

The targeting of political rivals was rare. Perhaps the most prominent hit attributed to the Davao Death Squad was that of local *Radio Ukay* broadcaster Juan "Jun" Pala. Pala would frequently lambast Duterte and his "reign of terror" in Davao City on the airwaves.[21] Pala survived assassination attempts in 2001 and April 2003, amid public accusations

---

17 Anthony Allada, "Death Squad Killings," *Philippine Daily Inquirer*, May 17 2003. For example, the 2005 killing of Roberto Gonzales, whom police identified as a member of the *Akyat Bahay* house burglary gang with a criminal record for illegal drugs and robbery. The CHR also noted the similarity of his case to prior DDS killings and that Gonzales's death may have been one of six such killings that day. Regional Director Alberto Sipaco, "CHR Resolution Case No.: XI-05-2400dc Re: Death of Intong Gonzales Alias "Pasmo" Tn: Roberto Gonzales," (Commission on Human Rights, September 28, 2006).

18 References to being "on the list" featured in almost half of the Davao City cases that Human Rights Watch had investigated. See "You Can Die Any Time: Death Squad Killings in Mindanao," 29-46.

19 For example, the case of Jorie Pacana, allegedly a member of the *Simpleng Grupo* gang in Bankerohan and involved in snatching, extortion and robbery; however, the CHR found no corroborating evidence to substantiate the allegations. "CHR Resolution Case No.: XI-2008-3017dc Re: Case of Pacana, Jorie," (Commission on Human Rights, July 7, 2008).

20 "CHR Resolution Case No.: XI-05-2397dc Re: Death of Hilario C. Ortega," (Commission on Human Rights, November 8, 2006).

21 ABS-CBN News, "Lookback: The Assassination of Jun Pala," *ABS-CBN News* (2017), http://news.abs-cbn.com/focus/02/24/17/lookback-the-assassination-of-jun-pala.

between him and Duterte for the blame.[22] However, on February 20, 2017, former Davao City senior police officer Arthur Lascañas recanted his earlier testimony at the Senate, affirming instead that the Davao Death Squad existed and, as a longtime and trusted member, he personally witnessed Duterte's direct involvement.[23] Lascañas furthermore confessed that he himself had been tasked to organize the attempt on Pala's life and that after Pala was finally killed on the third try on September 6, 2003, Duterte paid him and his crew PhP 3 million.[24]

During a Davao City council session held three days after Pala's assassination, a local councilor decried the unabated summary executions and accused the mayor of turning the city back into the murder capital of the Philippines. Duterte reportedly quipped in response: "By all means let's kill all the criminals and be the murder capital of the country."[25]

In other words, overt state violence in Davao City disappeared. But in its place was unfettered anti-crime vigilantism, likely to have been orchestrated with the local police. Davao City is, was, and continues to be a violent place. Duterte was responsible for over a thousand dead in Davao City's streets, without suffering any consequences. Why?

22 Ayan Mellejor and Anthony Allada, "Anti-Red Leader Wounded in Ambush," *Philippine Daily Inquirer*, August 1 2001. Ayan Mellejor, "Duterte Dares Pala to Confront Him on Slay Try," ibid., May 6 2003. Regional Director Alberto Sipaco, "CHR Resolution Case No.: XI-2008-3019 Do Re: Death of Elvis Española," (Commission on Human Rights, July 10, 2008).

23 Arturo Bariquit Lascañas, "Affidavit," (February 19, 2017). Lascañas's testimony corroborated statements of self-confessed DDS hitman Edgar Matobato at the aforementioned Senate hearing in September 2016. Dharel Placido, "NUJP Wants Probe into Death of Duterte Critic," *ABS-CBN News* (2017), http://news.abs-cbn.com/news/02/22/17/nujp-wants-probe-into-death-of-duterte-critic.

24 Audrey Morallo, "Lascañas: Duterte Behind Killing of Jun Pala," *The Philippine Star* (2017), http://www.philstar.com/headlines/2017/02/20/1674120/lascanas-duterte-behind-killing-jun-pala.

25 Dennis Santos and Anthony Allada, "Witness Absence Making Vigilante Killings Hard to Solve, Says CHR Exec," *Philippine Daily Inquirer*, September 29 2003.

Strategies for Success

Five strategies ensured the success of Duterte's violent gambit for political control.

First, the violence was selective, not indiscriminate: this personalized the threat and strengthened the ability of the local state agents to control dense sections of the urban populace.[26] Similar to the military's orders of battle, lists of drug criminals were an effective a tarring brush—anyone could be tainted. No documentary evidence of the lists has surfaced so far, yet local knowledge of the lists has been a definitive feature. However, unlike the activists targeted in political violence elsewhere, the DDS targets in Davao City were mostly unaffiliated with little means to seek redress.

Second, as with elections and counter-insurgency campaigns, there were definable periods of high and low intensity over time. The spates of violence intensified the sense of the threat and the immediacy of local power. However, unlike the regularity of election cycles or the concentration of military campaigns around 2006, it is far more difficult to infer immediate explanations for the timing of these spates—that requires further research and evidence. What is clear is that the violence followed a locally-oriented logic, perhaps known only to Duterte and close associates, independent of external or national exigencies.

Third, the absence of overt election-related violence and marginal incidence of violence related to insurgency-counterinsurgency suggests that Duterte had an effective monopoly over both legitimate and illegitimate use of violence in the territory. Two episodes dramatize this point further. On July 28, 2002, Mohammad Bahnari Ampatuan, the 18-year old son of Mayor Datu Ampatuan and grandson of Maguindanao governor Andal Ampatuan, shot and killed a man named Carlo Asistido. Duterte consequently issued a shoot to kill order against bodyguards of prominent families bearing arms into the city.[27] In March 2010, the bodies of the anti-communist campaigners of former general Jovito Palparan's political party *Bantay*, Donald Caigas and Juliana Noquera, were found after the pair were abducted from a local supermarket on

---

26 On the theory of selective violence, see Stathis Kalyvas, *The Logic of Violence in Civil War* (Cambridge: Cambridge University Press, 2006).

27 Anthony Allada, Ayan Mellejor, and Dennis Santos, "Scion of Political Family Shoots Dead Davao Resident," *Philippine Daily Inquirer*, August 1 2002.

March 24.[28] When accused of orchestrating the abduction-killings, Duterte scoffed at the claim saying "What will I gain? People will only sympathize with the party-list group."[29] The first case suggests ways in which private armed groups common to local politics were kept at bay; the second highlights the antagonistic relationship Duterte had with military elites.[30]

Fourth, unlike any other region or city in this study, political violence in Davao City combined the appearance of casual violence, as a variant of police excessiveness, with the purpose and resources of state violence. This was the strategy for control. In large part, Duterte was so effective because he avoided overt political repression that would have courted backfire from well-organized NGOs and political parties. Instead, he made an oblique attack on an acceptable "foe": crime. In this manner, a "social cleansing" allowed elites to accommodate death squads as an effective solution, in a way protecting the perpetrators of these killings as they made the city otherwise *safe*.[31]

Fifth, and finally, Duterte's success also came from his ability to form alliances with national politicians. In 2002, then-president Arroyo threw her political weight behind Duterte and appointed him to head a national consultative taskforce on kidnapping and illegal drugs, endorsing

28 Regional Director Alberto Sipaco, "CHR Resolution Case No.: XI-2010-0151dc Re: Case of Donald Caigas and Juliana Noquera," (Commission on Human Rights, May 20, 2011).

29 Jeffrey Tupas and Dennis Santos, "2 Palparan Campaigners Found Dead," *Philippine Daily Inquirer*, April 6 2010.

30 Incidentally, these two stories also feature infamous men accused of mass murder: the late Ampatuan, Sr., who had been charged for masterminding the Maguindanao massacre in 2009 but died before the trials concluded. Palparan was known as the *Berdugo* or the butcher, is currently being tried for the forced disappearance of student-activists Karen Empeño and Sherlyn Cadapan; human rights groups hold him responsible for the worst of the anti-activist assassinations under Oplan *Bantay Laya*. See Carolyn Arguillas, "Maguindanao: The Long Shadow of the Ampatuans," in *Democracy at Gunpoint: Election-Related Violence in the Philippines*, ed. Yvonne Chua and Luz Rimban (Quezon City: Vera Files Inc., 2011). Also see "Oplan Bantay Laya: The Us-Arroyo Campaign of Terror and Counterinsurgency in the Philippines."

31 Breuil, Carina, and Rozema, 422.

his methods in no uncertain terms.[32] In June 2003, Arroyo launched a national anti-drugs campaign[33]; one of the early spates of DDS killing occurred from May to July that year. Moreover, the estimated DDS killings rise sharply that year from 29 in 2001, the death toll begins to average at about 119 per year until 2005 and continues at similar levels until 2013.[34] Arroyo and Duterte fell out toward the end of her presidency,[35] but he managed to ensure his political succession in Davao City and, restricted by his term limits, successfully ran as his daughter Sarah Duterte's running mate. The city government's effective monopolization of both legitimate and illegitimate forms of violence would not have been possible, however, without the larger climate of permissiveness during the Arroyo presidency.

Taking the Playbook to the National Level

Just like other local bosses, Duterte sought to maintain his hold on power and seed a political dynasty that would immunize him from retribution. By his final term as Davao City mayor, he made a first foray into national politics and was successful in his bid for no less than the presidency. His first seven months in office have clearly shown a strong imprint from his strategies and tactics at the local level. As in Davao City, state violence against the urban poor conceals itself through the guise of vigilantism and police excess. All the while, Duterte has made known that all power concentrated in his hands yet he manages to escape official accountability.

As before, his government deploys violence for political control, not against illegal drugs; the rhetoric on drugs is but a fig leaf. The president has mobilized the country's security apparatus to bring state power to bear on the population. Because suspicion is based on lists of offenders

---

32 TJ Burgonio and Dona Pazzibugan, "Move over Dirty Harry, Duterte's Here," *Philippine Daily Inquirer*, July 10 2002. Dona Pazzibugan, R. Nazareno, and R. Ponte, "Duterte's Tough Stance Rubs Off on GMA," ibid., July 13.

33 Anthony Allada, "Pushers Fear Davao Death Squad, Surrender," ibid., July 4 2003.

34 Calculations based on 1998 to 2001 data from Coalition Against Summary Execution.

35 In 2009, Arroyo appoints Duterte's rival, Prospero Nograles, to replace him on a regional peace and order council and allows the Commission on Human Rights to investigate the DDS killings. Jeffrey Tupas, "Duterte Gives up City Police Control, Quits Napolcom Post," *Philippine Daily Inquirer*, April 1 2009. Christian Esguerra and Leila Salaverria, "Palace Backs CHR Probe," ibid., March 31.

that come from neighborhood and village officials, the threat of violence is personal. With the nightly killings, people are habituated to an excessive use of state force and supposed vigilantism, living in a state of fear. At the top, the efficacy of a purported anti-drugs campaign has been effective in neutralizing opposition. Most notably, Duterte and his allies tarred his most vocal critic in the senate, Leila de Lima, with the same brush of suspected drug-related crime. They have a history, after all: as CHR chair, De Lima investigated the Davao Death Squad in 2009.

Duterte's purported anti-crime campaign must thus be understood alongside the regime's attempts to consolidate political control. Building directly on his long experience in Davao City, he has learnt from Arroyo's example not to launch a frontal assault on Philippine democracy but instead attack its vulnerable flank: crime and corruption. As with right-wing populists elsewhere, Duterte plays on fear and instability to enhance his political power. His strategies for political control in Davao City are key to understanding the on-going violence in the Philippines.

References

ABS-CBN News. "Lookback: The Assassination of Jun Pala." *ABS-CBN News* (2017). Published electronically February 22. http://news.abs-cbn.com/focus/02/24/17/lookback-the-assassination-of-jun-pala.

Alberto Sipaco, Regional Director. "CHR Resolution Case No.: XI-05-2397dc Re: Death of Hilario C. Ortega." Commission on Human Rights, November 8, 2006.

———. "CHR Resolution Case No.: XI-05-2400dc Re: Death of Intong Gonzales Alias "Pasmo" Tn: Roberto Gonzales." Commission on Human Rights, September 28, 2006.

———. "CHR Resolution Case No.: XI-2008-3017dc Re: Case of Pacana, Jorie." Commission on Human Rights, July 7, 2008.

———. "CHR Resolution Case No.: XI-2008-3019 Do Re: Death of Elvis Española." Commission on Human Rights, July 10, 2008.

———. "CHR Resolution Case No.: XI-2008-3041dc Re: Death of Celso Pojas." Commission on Human Rights, November 10, 2008.

———. "CHR Resolution Case No.: XI-2010-0151dc Re: Case of Donald Caigas and Juliana Noquera." Commission on Human Rights, May 20, 2011.

Allada, Anthony. "Death Squad Killings." *Philippine Daily Inquirer*, May 17 2003.

———. "Pushers Fear Davao Death Squad, Surrender." *Philippine Daily Inquirer*, July 4 2003.

Allada, Anthony, Ayan Mellejor, and Dennis Santos. "Scion of Political Family Shoots Dead Davao Resident." *Philippine Daily Inquirer*, August 1 2002.

Arguillas, Carolyn. "Maguindanao: The Long Shadow of the Ampatuans." In *Democracy at Gunpoint: Election-Related Violence in the Philippines*, edited by Yvonne Chua and Luz Rimban. Quezon City: Vera Files Inc., 2011.

Bordadora, Norman. "Left Groups in Orders of Battle, Say Papers." *Philippine Daily Inquirer*, June 20 2006.

Breuil, Oude, Brenda Carina, and Ralph Rozema. "Fatal Imaginations: Death Squads in Davao City and Medellin Compared." *Crime, Law and Social Change* 52, no. 4 (2009): 405-24.

Burgonio, TJ, and Dona Pazzibugan. "Move over Dirty Harry, Duterte's Here." *Philippine Daily Inquirer*, July 10 2002.

Coalition Against Summary Execution. "Data on Summary Executions in Davao City Based on News Clippings from Davao Sunstar, Sunstar Super Balita, Mindanao Times and Brigada Editors from 19 August 1998 to December 2015." Davao City, 2015.

Coronel, Sheila. "I Will Kill All the Drug Lords: The Making of Rodrigo Duterte." *The Atlantic* (2016). Published electronically September 20, 2016. https://www.theatlantic.com/international/archive/2016/09/rodrigo-duterte-philippines-manila-drugs-davao/500756/.

"Davao City Ranks as 9th Safest in the World." *Philippine Daily Inquirer* (2015). Published electronically May 9. http://newsinfo.inquirer.net/690252/davao-city-ranks-as-9th-safest-in-the-world.

Esguerra, Christian, and Leila Salaverria. "Palace Backs CHR Probe." *Philippine Daily Inquirer*, March 31 2009.

Gavilan, Jodesz. "CHR: Death Toll in Drug War Higher Than What Gov't Suggests." *Rappler* (2017). Published electronically August 19, 2017. https://www.rappler.com/nation/179222-chr-number-drug-war-victims.

Inquirer Bureaus. "Security Beefed up in Provinces for Polls." *Philippine Daily Inquirer*, May 9 2016.

Jasmin Navarro-Regino, Regional Director. "CHR Resolution Case No.: III-C-06-2810 Re:Antonio R. Alarcon, Jr for Violation of Art. 3 UDHR and Art. 6 ICCPR." Commission on Human Rights, October 3, 2006.

Kalyvas, Stathis. *The Logic of Violence in Civil War.* Cambridge: Cambridge University Press, 2006.

Kessler, Richard. *Rebellion and Repression in the Philippines.* New Haven: Yale University Press, 1989.

Kreuzer, Peter. "'If They Resist, Kill Them All': Police Vigilantism in the Philippines." Frankfurt: Peace Research Institute Frankfurt, 2016.

Lacorte, Germelina, and Allan Nawal. "'They Would Have Lost Their Heads'." *Philippine Daily Inquirer*, July 18 2015.

Lascañas, Arturo Bariquit. "Affidavit." February 19, 2017.

Manlupig, Karlos. "Duterte Justice: Robbery, Slay Suspect Dead." *Philippine Daily Inquirer*, August 21 2015.

Mediansky, F.A. "The New People's Army: A Nation-Wide Insurgency in the Philippines." *Contemporary Southeast Asia* 8, no. 1 (1986): 1-17.

Mellejor, Ayan. "Duterte Dares Pala to Confront Him on Slay Try." *Philippine Daily Inquirer*, May 6 2003.

Mellejor, Ayan, and Anthony Allada. "Anti-Red Leader Wounded in Ambush." *Philippine Daily Inquirer*, August 1 2001.

Morallo, Audrey. "Lascañas: Duterte Behind Killing of Jun Pala." *The Philippine Star* (2017). Published electronically February 20. http://www.philstar.com/headlines/2017/02/20/1674120/lascanas-duterte-behind-killing-jun-pala.

Nawal, Allan. "Davao Drug Suspect Dead after Duterte Ultimatum." *Philippine Daily Inquirer*, October 30 2015.

"Oplan Bantay Laya: The Us-Arroyo Campaign of Terror and Counterinsurgency in the Philippines." In *Fourth of a Series on State Terror and Human Rights in the Philippines*. Quezon City: Ibon Foundation, Inc., 2010.

Pazzibugan, Dona, R. Nazareno, and R. Ponte. "Duterte's Tough Stance Rubs Off on GMA." *Philippine Daily Inquirer*, July 13 2002.

Placido, Dharel. "NUJP Wants Probe into Death of Duterte Critic." *ABS-CBN News* (2017). Published electronically February 22. http://news.abs-cbn.com/news/02/22/17/nujp-wants-probe-into-death-of-duterte-critic.

Santos, Dennis. "2nd Crime Suspect Dead on Heels of Duterte Ultimatum " *Philippine Daily Inquirer*, November 1 2015.

Santos, Dennis, and Anthony Allada. "Witness Absence Making Vigilante Killings Hard to Solve, Says CHR Exec." *Philippine Daily Inquirer*, September 29 2003.

Tupas, Jeffrey. "Duterte Gives up City Police Control, Quits Napolcom Post." *Philippine Daily Inquirer*, April 1 2009.

Tupas, Jeffrey, and Dennis Santos. "2 Palparan Campaigners Found Dead." *Philippine Daily Inquirer*, April 6 2010.

———. "Davao Farmer Leader Gunned Down." *Philippine Daily Inquirer*, May 16 2008.

"Who's Afraid of General Palparan?". *Philippine Daily Inquirer*, October 19 2005.

"You Can Die Any Time: Death Squad Killings in Mindanao." New York: Human Rights Watch, 2009.

Zabriskie, Phil. "The Punisher." *Time Asia*, June 24 2002.

THE POLITICAL APATHY OF VIETNAMESE YOUTH

YEN DUONG | 01 DEC 2017

In the age of Trump, refugees and social media, many young Vietnamese speak of a disconnect with the rest of the world, while others eagerly embrace radical change.

Duong agrees to catch up at a café in the centre of Hanoi on a humid Thursday evening. It's one of her favourite places to hang out in the weekends' one of thousands of cafés that have sprouted up across the Vietnamese capital, where idleness and a lack of public space have created unlikely business opportunities. Her week-days, though, are more like Groundhog Day. She works a nine-to-five job at a big university, and there's little variation in her daily routine: commuting to work, returning home, sleeping, rinse and repeat.

She sat an exam earlier in the day for entry into the civil service. The stakes are high: a job in the public sector is akin to an iron rice bowl, a promise of job security for the rest of one's professional life. But Duong doesn't seem too bothered; she knows she'll pass.

The 2016 Governance and Public Administration Performance Index confirmed that nepotism and corruption within Vietnam's public sector is "a systemic problem"; personal connections and bribes are essential for those who wish to pursue careers in the civil service.

Such entrance exams are seen more as a formality than a challenge for young Vietnamese like Duong. Wealth, higher education, con-nections and career stability: these are the things that largely define Vietnam's new middle class, and Duong, born into a privileged family, has them all. Her decision to become a civil servant is similar to her reason for working in the university: she couldn't think of easier, faster or better alternatives.

Such privilege can easily breed apathy. "When everything is already laid out for you, you don't really think about what tomorrow will hold," Duong says. "It's just going to be the same thing."

Apathy is a disease

According to a 2015 estimate by the United Nations, half the population of Vietnam is under the age of 30, which means millennials have the potential to be a considerable force for change in the country. The Communist Youth Union, the country's largest youth organisation, actively reaches out to Vietnamese youth to spread the message of the Communist Party of Vietnam (CPV). But youth leaders are finding it increasingly difficult to connect with a generation comfortable with the Internet, Facebook, and smartphones—and all the distractions now at their fingertips.

Experts say that campaigns to enlist young people in public activities tend to be too rigid to engage or motivate. Despite various efforts designed to mobilise them, Vietnamese millennials still generally appear to be politically apathetic.

In 2015, Towards Transparency—a non-profit consultancy and official national contact for the global civil society organisation Transparency International—interviewed 1,110 Vietnamese between the ages of 15 and 30 for the Vietnam Youth Integrity Survey.[1] They found that 74% of respondents had very little or no information on anti-corruption initiatives, and 45% of educated youths held the opinion that reporting corrupt behaviour was futile. They're worrying findings, especially considering Vietnam's fairly low ranking in Transparency International's Corruption Perceptions Index 2016.[2]

This apathy and ignorance goes beyond the issue of corruption: research suggests that young middle-class Vietnamese show greater interest in consumption, leisure activities, maintenance and achievement of social status than in politics.

This was explained in the paper "Professional Middle Class Youth in Post-Reform Vietnam: Identity, Continuity and Change"[3] as the result

---

1 https://towardstransparency.vn/vietnam-youth-integrity-survey-2014

2 https://www.transparency.org/news/feature/corruption_perceptions_index_2016

3 https://www.cambridge.org/core/journals/modern-asian-studies/article/professional-middle-class-youth-in-post-reform-vietnam-identity-continuity-and-change/618A20218B9678E0D372562B34747703

of a confluence between the middle class' relationship to the state and global capitalism. The middle-class Vietnamese who rose following economic reforms in the latter half of the 1980s in many ways resemble the middle class in many other countries, particularly in areas like an orientation to consumption and harbouring aspirations for personal and career development, but also have close ties to the Vietnamese state. With their privilege and material advantages connected to the political status quo, young middle-class Vietnamese tend to exhibit the characteristics of other middle-class youth without a corresponding sense of political identity or participation.

Duong admits that she has no idea about the political structure in Vietnam, nor about any of the country's leaders. For her, voting for local councillors is little more than an exercise in randomly choosing between one unfamiliar face and another.

She also says she doesn't care about rampant corruption, local land disputes, important events such as the recent Asia-Pacific Economic Cooperation summit, or even international issues such as Donald Trump's polarising presidency (she's heard of his name but doesn't know what he's been up to).

"Why would I have to care anyway?" she asks. "Once you have the privilege of not having to think, you just don't."

It's not just her, either; Duong says her colleagues at the university—many of whom are training to become full-time professors—are the same. "We're aware of the headlines if they show up on Facebook or on the news, but they're simply subjects of gossip at work. Those issues quickly leave your head when there's something else to talk about… Plus, there are many other distractions."

Protesting via Facebook

Hoang Duc Minh was only 18 when he became the programme director of a project to raise awareness of climate change. He later founded Wake it Up, a startup aiming to empower through social activities. Minh's recently been involved in a campaign that helped save 6,700 trees in Hanoi by mobilising hundreds to march down the streets in protest.

"Participating in social activities is not only an interest, but also an opportunity for me to develop my personal skill sets," Minh says. "The important thing is to find voices that are loud enough to start doing something together."

The public outrage and movement to protect those 6,700 trees marked a significant change in Vietnamese civic participation, demonstrating the potential impact of public mobilisation via social media.

Like in many other countries, social media platforms like Facebook have gained traction in Vietnam as millennials' main source of information. According to Reuters, Vietnam's 52 million active accounts makes it one of Facebook's top ten countries. The social network's popularity has proven to be so instrumental in contributing to social change that the Ministry of Information and Communications earlier this year requested Facebook, Google and YouTube to remove and block content deemed "toxic" by the state. Google partly complied by blocking 1,500 out of the over 2,000 YouTube videos the government wanted removed.

Like Wake it Up, many social initiatives started by NGOs such as Live and Learn, ISEE and Viet Pride reach out to millennials via Facebook. The rise of social media has provided a platform for young people with a desire to be heard, filling the vacuum left by the lack of officially-sanctioned spaces.

Responses also differ based on the cause. Some, like environmental issues and LGBTQ equality, have gained traction in Vietnam. Other issues—corruption, gender, minorities' rights, freedom of speech—have not yet received as much visibility; a sign that some issues are considered more political, and therefore more sensitive, than others. But the risk of virtualising activism, even for more "palatable" causes, is the inadvertent cultivation of "slacktivism", reducing political and social movements to heavily-marketed online media events.

Bui Tra My, a young media and culture teacher at The Olympia Schools in Hanoi, has written several research papers on youth participation in social media. She believes that social networks have changed the way young people think about participation; shows of online solidarity might often be mistaken for substantive action. "You can type an online signature on petitiononline.com and feel assured that you have fulfilled your civic responsibility. And it's also super-easy to just click and join groups and networks on Facebook," she says.

"But caring about social and political affairs is not a responsibility, it's a demand," she adds. "And actions only take place when people are made aware that such problems can have a direct impact on them."

A generation caught in transition

There are many reasons why Vietnamese youths are not engaging with politics. Tri Phuong is a researcher from Yale University who studies youth culture and youth participation on social media in Vietnam, and says that the current education system has failed to fulfil the need of young people to express themselves or encourage them to actively participate in civic activities. While young people might be aware of social problems, many lack the motivation to seek solutions as they feel excluded from decision-making processes.

"Young people rise up when they feel their rights are denied," he says. "That's clearly happened in certain parts of the world, such as the Occupy Movement or the Arab Spring, but in those contexts, there was either heavy repression or young people felt disenfranchised from the social system. They became politicised because they felt angry and they had no other options."

"In Vietnam, I think as long as young people have other options to distract themselves, it provides a pressure release from politics," he adds. "Vietnamese youth don't participate in politics simply because it's not meaningful to their lives."

Duong, Minh and My come from roughly the same age group, with very similar profiles: all three are young, urban, and educated. But their differing attitudes towards society reveals the many complex layers within Vietnam's new middle class.

"I was born during a period of economic transition, witnessing the ups and downs of social organisation, the reinvention of many values and the influence of many cultural currents on my generation," says My. "Being caught in such changes makes me feel an urge to know more, and to research social developments."

Minh, the activist, is optimistic about his generation's contribution to society. "Over the past seven years, there have been major changes among the youth," he says. "I still think that urban youths play a fundamental role in social activism in Vietnam. In our national context, when you consider the quality of education, as well as the economic and political conditions, it's not difficult to understand why young people spend less time on social issues and more on personal distractions."

"The job of social activists is comparable to that of a salesperson," he adds. "You need to be able to sell [your cause] so that people feel inspired to fulfil their civic responsibility. You can't just expect society to be better off by itself, or for young people to be more active on their own."

Back in the café, Duong says she has never heard of the movement to save the 6,700 trees, or any other similar social activities. "I don't really trust Facebook activism because there are so many fake events created as clickbait."

She falls silent when asked about her dream job. "I feel desensitised to everything," she says. "There are times when I think about quitting my job because I'm going to be a teacher, and that'll definitely influence my students. But I've been brought up being dependent on my overprotective parents, and I just don't think I have enough courage to change."

MYANMAR'S FAILED PEACE PROCESS
BRENNAN O'CONNOR | 10 JUL 2018

The third Union Peace Conference takes place from 11–16 July 2018. But with ongoing conflicts around the country—and a history of dialogues leading nowhere—things don't look good for Myanmar's peace process.

It's time to admit it: Myanmar's bumpy journey towards peace and reconciliation with its many ethnic groups hasn't merely fallen off track; it's completely derailed. Over the years, conflict and displacement has marred both sides of Myanmar's borders and other areas—from the currently high-profile Rohingya crisis to the ongoing conflicts in places like Kachin State. In recent months, it's only getting worse.

The Union Peace Conference—a venue for the government, military and many of the ethnic armed organisations to talk about the country's progress towards peace—was supposed to happen every six months. After being delayed at least three times (the last sitting took place over a year ago) the third session will happen from 11–16 July in the capital city of Naypyidaw.

Ongoing conflict
Under the country's 2008 Constitution[1], it's the army's commander-in-chief, Min Aung Hlaing, who steers the direction of the peace process and many other matters of national importance. Even though Aung San Suu Kyi, the leader of the National League for Democracy (NLD), won a landslide victory in the 2015 election, her government doesn't control the military.

The Constitution allows the army, also known as the Tatmadaw, to appoint leading officials for key ministries—Home, Defence, and Border—and control 25% of the parliamentary seats. As the Constitution

---

1 https://www.economist.com/the-economist-explains/2014/03/04/what-is-wrong-with-myanmars-constitution

can't be amended without the consent of over 75% of parliamentarians and over 50% of votes at a national referendum, it's impossible to make changes that fall outside of the Tatmadaw's interests.

Despite a stated desire to move towards peace, the Tatmadaw is still locked in violent conflict or repression in various parts of the country.

Most high-profile, of course, is the brutal clampdown on the Rohingya in Rakhine State on the country's western coast. About 713,000 Rohingya—seen by many as Bengali interlopers, even though they have lived in the country for generations—have been expelled or pushed out of Rakhine State; they remain in squalid camps in Bangladesh during the monsoon season.

In Kachin State in the north of the country, the Tatmadaw has been pummeling[2] the Kachin Independence Army (KIA) in resource-rich Tanai Township with fighter jets and assault helicopters bought from Russia[3] and China, according to KIA personnel on the ground. KIA soldiers have reported that drones were sent in to sniff out their mountain locations before the jets were sent in. With many gold and amber mines, the area is an important source of revenue for both the military and the KIA.

Over 100,000 Kachin civilians have remained displaced from fighting that first started in 2011. About 10,000 civilians have been displaced by fighting in recent months; many are still trapped inside the conflict zone. The Tatmadaw initially refused a rescue mission, but relented after Kachin groups lobbied the state government. Over a thousand people, many of them internally displaced persons (IDPs) caught in the jungle, were rescued[4].

Fighting between the state military and various ethnic armed groups is ongoing in northern Shan State, southern Chin State and northern Rakhine State. Villagers were recently also displaced in Karen State[5] as the Tatmadaw locked horns with the Karen National Liberation Army (KNLA) after entering its area to upgrade a military road abandoned since the 2012 ceasefire.

---

2 http://www.atimes.com/article/a-vision-for-war-without-end-in-myanmar/

3 https://frontiermyanmar.net/en/myanmar-to-buy-russian-fighter-jets-in-deal-worth-more-than-200m

4 https://www.irrawaddy.com/news/last-group-awng-lawt-villagers-rescued-forest.html

5 https://newnaratif.com/journalism/displaced-karen-state/

Attempts at peace

After the previous quasi-civilian government initiated a series of sweeping democratic reforms beginning in 2011, many of the country's ethnic armed groups signed ceasefire agreements with the government and military. The hope was that such ceasefires would provide the opportunity for long-desired political dialogue with the Tatmadaw and the government.

It didn't happen. Instead, leaders were offered business concessions such as licenses to import car parts. It was a move that appeared intended to distract from calls for dialogue on more autonomy by the groups and the development of a federalist Union. In some cases, it worked.

A few years later, the civilian government under President Thein Sein came up with yet another "peace-making" scheme: the Nationwide Ceasefire Agreement (NCA). But because there were limitations on which groups could join—some groups, such as the Arakan Army and the Ta'ang National Liberation Army were excluded—the NCA was perceived as a way to divide and rule, breaking up loose alliances among the ethnic armed groups.

Before coming to power, Suu Kyi told the ethnic armed groups that there was no urgency to the agreement; she urged them to take as much time as they needed to consider the NCA before signing it. Once the NLD won the election, though, she began to press the groups into joining.

David Scott Mathieson, an independent analyst based in Yangon, says Suu Kyi was never really sincere in taking the necessary steps to building peace: "Suu Kyi, in opposition, pretended to be a genuine peace builder, which is why she urged the [ethnic armed organisations] not to sign until she had installed a more democratic government."

"But on gaining power, she talked peace as a priority and then failed to articulate a credible plan, barely met with ethnic leaders or their counties, and very soon her approach to peace was one in synchronicity with the military: capitulate and sign, with no negotiation or concessions. That isn't durable peace, its a recipe for division, and has resulted in expanding conflict."

Only eight out of the 15 groups invited signed the NCA in 2015. (Two other groups became signatories this year.) Most of these signatories are fairly minor players in the numerous conflicts—apart from the Restoration Council of Shan State/Shan State Army (RCSS/SSA) and the Karen National Union (KNU), most of the signatories only maintain small armies, if any all. In contrast, more powerful groups like the United Wa State Army and the KIA that were invited have chosen not to be included in the agreement.

Playing one side against the other?

Suspicions that the Tatmadaw might be striking alliances with some groups over others has also proven to be an obstacle to peace- and trust-building. Less than two months after the NCA signing ceremony fighting broke out[6] between signatory RCSS/SSA and non-signatory Ta'ang National Liberation Army (TNLA) as the former sent troops from its southern base to areas close to TNLA positions.

Although the RCSS/SSA's chairman denied that the state military had approved its move, he failed to explain how they had managed to deploy several hundred soldiers across a distance of over 300 kilometres along a route with multiple Tatamadaw checkpoints without authorisation or tactical support. During a trip to the frontline in 2016, TNLA leaders have also told this reporter that they have occasionally fought against a combined force of RCSS/SSA and Tatmadaw troops.

But such alliances can also be short-lived amid the complex landscape of shifting allegiances and priorities. If the RCSS/SSA had a cosy relationship with the Tatamadaw, it might be a thing of the past—on top of fighting with the TNLA, the group has started having sporadic clashes with the state military themselves. They were also forced to end a series of public consultations, organised in preparation for the Union Peace Conference, after the Tatmadaw stormed its meetings "fully armed with war weapons as if to seize an enemy stronghold" according to an RCSS/SSA statement[7].

Money and international interests

Leaders from the KNU's military arm, the Karen National Liberation Army (KNLA) have threatened[8] to boycott peace talks after the government stalled on political negotiations promised under the NCA. It's unclear at the time of publication if these KNLA leaders will be joining the third sitting of peace talks.

---

6 https://frontiermyanmar.net/en/the-war-in-the-hills

7 https://www.burmalink.org/restoration-council-shan-state-statement-national-political-dialogue-shan-nationalities/

8 https://www.irrawaddy.com/news/burma/knla-says-wont-attend-third-session-panglong-peace-conference.html

It wouldn't be the first time political wrangling has come to naught. Control of the land and abundant resources in contested areas has always been the driving force behind the numerous conflicts in Myanmar since (and before) the country's independence from the British in 1948. Ceasefire agreements between various ethnic armed organisations and the Myanmar government—even when under the previous military regime—have been repeatedly signed and broken as promises of political dialogue gave way to more instant economic gratification; instead of continuing talks, the government sold off land and natural resources to both local and overseas business interests.

The jade industry in Kachin State, for instance, is the "significant driver of Myanmar's most intractable armed conflict", says a report[9] by international NGO Global Witness. A year-long investigation by the London-based group put the total value of jade mines in Myanmar—most of which are located in Kachin State—at US$31 billion in 2014.

International players, including countries that claim to be supportive of Myanmar's peace process, have also been implicated. Norway, for example, has invested in the Middle Yeywa dam project in central Shan State. In 2016, the Shan Human Rights Foundation, the Shan Sapawa Environment Organisation and the Shan State Farmers' Network issued an open letter[10] addressed to Aung San Suu Kyi, urging her to suspend the dam project. The groups criticised a pre-feasibility study done by SN Power, a Norwegian state-owned company.

"The study makes no mention at all of the ongoing conflict in Shan State, and how the project may impact or be impacted by this conflict," they wrote, adding that "the issue of natural resources is a key driver of the ethnic conflict, with ethnic forces fighting to resist unitary government control over resources in their areas, and with increased Burma Army militarisation around resource extraction projects."

Jan Cederwall, SN Power's Myanmar country director, took a different view. "Some people are saying we shouldn't go to Shan State until there is peace, but the way we see it is that if you let the difference in development between Shan and neighboring States become too great it

---

9 https://www.globalwitness.org/en/campaigns/oil-gas-and-mining/myanmarjade/

10 http://www.shanhumanrights.org/eng/index.

php/294-to-daw-aung-san-suu-kyi-state-counsellor-and-foreign-minister-naypyidaw will only add to the social tension," he told[11] the *Norway Asian Business Review* in 2016.

The Middle Yeywa Dam is not the only big-ticket project in Myanmar that has fuelled violence. The Myitsone Dam in Kachin State was a contributing factor that ended a seventeen-year ceasefire between the Tatmadaw and the KIA's political arm, the Kachin Independence Organisation (KIO) in 2011. The dam project was suspended later that year after facing widespread opposition across the country. The planned Hatgyi Dam in Karen State—backed by investment from Myanmar, China and Thailand—has also triggered fighting between the Tatmadaw and small Karen armed groups. The clash, which took place in in late 2016, caused the displacement of about 10,000 people, many of whom have still not been able to return home. China is also involved in other projects, such as a special economic zone and deep sea being developed in Kyaukphyu in central Rakhine State.

Stumbling blocks to peace

Sincere reconciliation efforts are necessary to push Myanmar's reforms forward. Yet the Tatmadaw has demonstrated a consistent disregard for the terms of ceasefire agreements that it itself has signed. By launching offensives against both NCA signatories and non-signatories in areas where large-scale energy projects have been planned, expanding military bases and roads in contested areas and obstructing public consultations, the state military has undermined efforts by its own government to move towards a lasting peace.

11 https://www.pressreader.com/norway/norway-asia-business-review/
20161025/282127816018554

CRISIS AND COMPLICITY
AISYAH LLEWELLYN | 21 JUL 2018

A newly released cache of American documents highlights how military ties between the US and Indonesia influenced the American response to the economic crisis in Indonesia.

In 1997, Indonesia was problematic by anyone's standards. It had invaded, and still occupied, East Timor (also known as Timor-Leste), was plagued by allegations of state-sponsored kidnappings of pro-reform activists, and faced a monetary meltdown due to the Asian Financial Crisis. After a 1991 massacre by the Indonesian army in East Timor that left over 270 people dead, the Congress of the United States of America cut off the country from the US' International Military and Education Training (IMET) programme.

Despite this disastrous human rights record and a series of financial blunders that led Indonesia to seek a bailout from the International Monetary Fund (IMF) in October 1997, the United States was more than happy to back the beleaguered nation—it supported Indonesia's IMF request and approved an additional USD3 billion line of credit.

Now, a newly released cache of US State Department files—some of which have been classified for 20 years—shines a light on the US-Indonesian relationship of that period: from the close relationship between US President Bill Clinton and President Muhammad Suharto, to the unravelling of the United States' connection to, and complicity in, Indonesia's human rights abuses.

They also show that, while the Clinton administration publicly denounced human rights violations in Indonesia, it was also in possession of a swathe of documentation that linked key figures from the Indonesian military and government—who the United States had cultivated and continually engaged with for years—to horrific allegations of abuse and repression.

"I say not only as the President of the United States but as a friend that I think you will have an incredible legacy when you complete your work," Clinton once gushed[1] to Suharto during a meeting at the November 1997 Asia-Pacific Economic Cooperation (APEC) Summit in Vancouver—the same meeting in which he had weakly tried to discuss the kidnappings and the Indonesian occupation of East Timor.

From the US to Indonesia: military training and hardware

The United States military had, for years, courted the Indonesian government in an effort to sell military training and equipment. In 2001, *World Policy* published a special report[2] outlining the flow of weapons and training:

> "The United States transferred USD328 million in weapons and spare parts and almost USD100 million in commercial weapons exports to the Jakarta regime in the last decade. Military training has also been significant during this period—the Defense Department allocated more than USD7.5 million in International Military Education and Training program (IMET) funding for Indonesian soldiers."

But Congress stopped IMET funding to Indonesia in 1992 following a bloodbath in East Timor, during which armed soldiers shot 271 people at a funeral in Santa Cruz Cemetery. Indonesia had invaded East Timor in 1975, and only withdrew in 1999.

In 1993, Congress made the ban official with the Foreign Operations Appropriations Act. The United States was no longer meant to offer military assistance to the Indonesians. But the declassified documents tell a different story; one tied up with the Southeast Asian economic meltdown that hit Indonesia hard.

The declassified documents

The newly released documents, many of which are cables and emails from the US embassy in Jakarta to the US capital Washington DC, reveal how, throughout the 1997 Asian Financial Crisis, the Americans continued to cultivate high-profile figures in the Indonesian army, including Major General Prabowo Subianto—a current presidential hopeful who

---

1 https://nsarchive2.gwu.edu//

  dc.html?doc=4616936-Document-03-White-House-Memorandum-of

2 https://worldpolicy.org/indonesia-at-the-crossroads-u-s-weapons-sales-and-military-

  training/#weapons

was alleged to have ordered the kidnappings of pro-reform activists in Indonesia from 1996 to 1998. They also demonstrate how the military relationship between the Indonesians and the Americans informed much of the United States' attitude to the financial crisis and the escalating violence it caused across Indonesia.

The cache also includes transcripts of conversations between Clinton and Suharto, highlighting the sympathetic attitude that the former had for his Indonesian counterpart. This position coloured the United States' support of Indonesia and encouraged the Clinton administration to turn a blind eye to well-documented patterns of abuse by the Indonesian military, even as their president panhandled for financial bailouts on Suharto's behalf. The bailouts would total over USD43 billion by the end of the crisis in 1999.

Many of the cables and emails in the cache were written by J. Stapleton Roy. As the US Ambassador to Indonesia from 1996 to 1999, he was one of the key players closest to the action. His duties at the US embassy in Jakarta included sending frequent reports on the political, economic and social situation in Indonesia, based on information gleaned from local news reports, embassy sources and his own analysis. For months, Roy monitored the financial crisis as it began to devour Indonesia and fed his thoughts back to Capitol Hill in Washington DC.

The start of the financial crisis

If Roy had any inkling that Indonesia would be forever changed in the six months following 10 October 1997, he didn't mention it in his report[3] to Madeleine Albright, then-US Secretary of State, updating her on Indonesia's IMF bailout request:

> "In conversations on October 9, the Jakarta-based representative of both the World Bank and the IMF told the ambassador that the intent was to provide Indonesia an IMF Assistance package large enough to restore market confidence without, ideally, having to be used."

This, as it turned out, was painfully optimistic.

---

3 https://newnaratif.com/wp-content/uploads/2018/06/Early-Readout-on-Indonesias-Approach-to-the-IMF-ilovepdf-compressed.pdf

The Asian Financial Crisis first took hold in Thailand at the start of July 1997. The Thai government had accrued huge amounts of debt from abroad and made the disastrous decision to float the baht, hoping that it would cause export revenues to pick up. The plan failed, and the crisis spread across Southeast Asia as investors pulled out and abandoned Asian currencies in droves. Many of these states had at one time been dubbed the "Asian Economic Miracle Countries[4]"; it was a swift and spectacular fall from grace.

Although many analysts predicted that Thailand would bear the brunt of the crisis, it ultimately wasn't the country that suffered the most. The Indonesian rupiah began to depreciate from August 1997, losing 30% of its value by October 1997.

Private companies in Indonesia that had been borrowing extensively from abroad—taking on short-term loans for long-term projects—were left saddled with debt as the rupiah destabilised. Indonesia was also being buffeted by other issues: a drought brought on by El Niño; forest fires which caused widespread haze and health problems; a lack of imported products like baby formula; and panic buying and hoarding of basic necessities like oil and rice. By the time the market stabilised in 1998, Indonesia had experienced not only economic near-collapse, but also social and political unrest that caused the government to unravel.

On 29 October 1997, though, Suharto was still full of bluster during a speech[5] at a youth gathering in Pasuruan, East Java. "We are different from Thailand," he boasted. "Thailand's economy had already collapsed when they invited the IMF to come help… We are different. Indonesia already has a programme, so come take a look, IMF experts…"

"A friend on whom Indonesia can count in the crunch"

Roy, however, was more prosaic. His reports chart how quickly the financial crisis ravaged Indonesia and shines a light on the response from the United States. On 23 October 1997, he reported back[6] to

---

4 https://www.indonesia-investments.com/culture/economy/asian-financial-crisis/item246?

5 https://newnaratif.com/wp-content/uploads/2018/06/IMF-Negotiations-on-Track_
    compressed.pdf

6 https://newnaratif.com/wp-content/uploads/2018/06/Scenesetter-for-the-Deputy-
    Secretary_s-Visit-to-Indonesia_compressed.pdf

Washington in preparation for East Asian and Pacific Affairs (EAP) Assistant Secretary Stanley Roth's trip to Indonesia:

> *"On the eve of your visit, Indonesia together with its ASEAN neighbors is facing a time of troubles more severe than any in Suharto's long period of rule. Your visit is well-timed to convey a clear signal that the US remains committed to a strong bilateral relationship."*

This relationship was important to the Americans. US funding for military education and training (IMET) had largely been cut off by Congress, and diplomatic accord had been in short supply in previous months. But, Roy assured Roth, "[t]he US-Indonesian relationship has turned a corner since mid-summer."

The Americans had been rattled by Suharto's decision to withdraw from a deal to buy F-16 fighter jets, choosing to purchase Sukhoi 30s from Russia instead. "President Suharto personally directed the switch... when he felt congressional critics were having too strong an influence over our approach to Indonesia," explained Roy, referring to Congress' enactment of the Foreign Operations Appropriations Act and in-fighting on Capitol Hill about whether to go ahead with the F-16 sale.

While Roy remained optimistic, he admitted that "the relationship still needs work. Visits by senior US military leaders... have shored up our security ties but the prolonged absence of IMET training or military sales is weakening the links between our two military establishments."

He suggested other ways to boost morale: "Our responsiveness to the region's financial troubles will have an enormous impact on our credibility as a friend on whom Indonesia can count in the crunch." The Americans also knew that both the Chinese and the Russians were offering Indonesia "dazzling deals for sophisticated weaponry, and exploiting the Indonesian perception that we are an unreliable source of military equipment".

They were keen to smooth things over and win favour once more.

IMET had long been a source of contention for both Indonesia and the US. After Congress initially cut off IMET funding to Indonesia in 1992, it again tried to stop all military training in 1995, voicing concerns that it was being used in East Timor to kidnap, torture and imprison pro-independence activists.

Congress' efforts were unsuccessful; a concession was made to allow E-IMET, or Expanded-International Military Education and Training, instead. E-IMET claimed[7] to be an "'educational program' briefing officers on issues of human rights, military justice and civilian control of the military."

But in March 1997, the House Foreign Operations Appropriations Subcommittee heard that the Pentagon had gone ahead with military training exercises in Indonesia in 1996 without notification, and thus limited Indonesia's access to E-IMET as well.

That was meant to be the end of the joint military relationship.

Despite the fact that Congress was opposed to the sale of military training and equipment to Indonesia, some state departments saw it as an important factor in bilateral relations. As reflected in the cache of documents, multiple state officials repeatedly peddled the claim that such exchanges were designed to impart "exposure to our society and values" and give the United States influence in the region to quell unrest if needed.

In reality, the US had been "the largest supplier of weapons and military training to Indonesia"[8] until 1992; the ongoing relationship was much less about imparting human rights and democratic values than it was about economic and political incentives.

It wasn't a relationship the Americans were prepared to lose.

The IMF bailout

On 14 October 1997, the US embassy in Jakarta received a copy of a report[9] prepared by the US Treasury Department. The report detailed a number of different loan options, in addition to the IMF bailout, for the United States to consider. Although the report noted that a medium-term loan would carry "significant political risk", it pointed out such a move would "provide the strongest possible signal of US support."

In the end, the United States chose to approve a USD3 billion line of credit to Indonesia and threw its support behind the IMF bailout package. Indonesia signed[10] an arrangement for USD10 billion from

---

7 http://www.insideindonesia.org/indonesia-us-military-ties

8 https://worldpolicy.org/indonesia-at-the-crossroads-u-s-weapons-sales-and-military-training/#weapons

9 https://newnaratif.com/wp-content/uploads/2018/06/Options-for-US-Financial-Support-for-Indonesia-ilovepdf-compressed.pdf

10 https://www.imf.org/external/np/exr/ib/2000/062300.htm

the IMF in November 1997 and another USD1.4 billion in July 1998. It also received USD8 billion from multilateral institutions and another USD18 billion from bilateral donors.

But all was not well on Capitol Hill. On 4 November 1997, Congress member Bernie Sanders sent a letter of complaint[11] to Robert E. Rubin, the Secretary of the Treasury. The letter referenced the 1994 Frank/Sanders Amendment—which Sanders had drafted—which required the US Treasury to make decisions that supported workers' rights around the globe through their votes at institutions like the IMF.

Sanders wrote:

"Since this provision was first enacted in 1994, I have been deeply disappointed that its implementation and enforcement have been essentially ignored. Nevertheless, the financial relief package for Indonesia, an egregious violator of worker rights by anybody's standards, now being negotiated and finalised at the IMF and World Bank presents anew a fresh opportunity for you to uphold the dictates of US law."

The letter also called out the Indonesian military:

"As a matter of government policy, the Government of Indonesia continues to systematically deny freedom of association and the right to organise independent trade unions and bargain collectively to Indonesian workers. This brutal suppression of internationally recognised worker rights is routinely enforced with the iron fist of the Indonesian armed forces."

This was swiftly followed on 6 November 1997 by another letter, signed by five more members of Congress: Barney Frank, Patrick Kennedy, Joseph Kennedy, Tony Hall and Nancy Pelosi. The letter expressed "serious concerns" about the IMF and World Bank loans, as well as the US' USD3 billion commitment.

The letter raised another issue: "Indonesian rule in East Timor is one of the most oppressive and brutal we have seen." The letter urged the Treasury to withdraw support for the IMF bailout package and the credit from the US.

---

11 https://newnaratif.com/wp-content/uploads/2018/06/Letters-from-Sanders-Pelosi-and-Rubin_compressed.pdf

The letter's assessment of the Indonesian government was also scathing: "They are not accepting this assistance as a favor to us. They are doing it because it is even more in their self-interest than in ours."

On 9 December 1997, Rubin replied: "The United States and the international community have a strong interest in restoring market confidence in Asia and heading off contagion to other financial markets. In addition, emerging economies, including those of Southeast Asia, account for a significant share of total US exports."

The export market coloured pretty much every decision made by the Clinton administration regarding Indonesia. This focus also explained the "friendship" (Clinton's word) between Clinton and Suharto, which began in earnest in 1996. Before that, while still on the presidential campaign trail, Clinton had been vocal about human rights abuses in East Timor and his administration had supported a UN resolution in 1993 criticising the Indonesian government after the 1991 attack at Santa Cruz Cemetery.

But Clinton's tune changed soon enough after assuming office. He'd realised the potential for American companies to make money in Indonesia—regularly touted as one of the big emerging markets in Southeast Asia. If Clinton wanted a way in, he needed to curry favour with one man. "American firms want access to the Indonesian market, but President Suharto *is* the Indonesian market," said an article, "Clinton and Indonesia"[12], in 1996.

"The 'driving dynamic' behind US policy, one senior official told the *Washington Post,* has been the desire 'not to totally screw up the trade relationship' while keeping up demands for a better human rights performance. In practice, that means Clinton and his advisers 'raise' human rights issues whenever they meet with Suharto and his ministers," it continued.

But this was all pretty toothless. The Clinton administration, at best, sent mixed messages to the Indonesian government; on the one hand chiding Suharto for human rights abuses, and on the other pushing for a larger stake in the Indonesian market. At its worst, the US government had clearly prioritised getting a piece of Indonesia's emerging economy over the well-being of Indonesian activists and the people of East Timor.

In the end it was, as always, all about the money.

---

12 https://www.weeklystandard.com/robert-kagan/clinton-and-indonesia

Raising human rights abuses

On the same day the five Congress members sent their letter to Rubin, East Asian and Pacific Affairs (EAP) Assistant Secretary Stanley Roth was in a Jakarta meeting[13] with Indonesian Special Forces Commander, Major General Prabowo Subianto.

Roth touched on the special relationship between the United States and Indonesia, and mentioned the USD3 billion support money that the US had contributed to the IMF bailout package. Then talk turned towards military matters.

Prabowo wanted "to buy US military training through foreign military sales (FMS)," Roy wrote of the meeting. "He wants to send Special Forces officers overseas to be exposed to Western values, standards of accountability and professionalism."

Prabowo also had a complaint: "'somebody', he claimed, in the State Department or the Pentagon has stopped his request for FMS training." Roth promised to follow up and check the current status of plans by the Indonesian government to buy more military training from the Americans using FMS, under which purchases of military hardware would be accompanied by training for personnel. It was a way to work around the restrictions on both IMET and E-IMET.

According to the cable, written by Roy and cleared by Roth, no one at the meeting—including the Deputy Chief of Mission in Jakarta and Defense Attaché Colonel Don McFetridge—made any reference to human rights abuses by the Indonesian military either in East Timor or elsewhere.

Five months later, in April 1998, Roy reported on a luncheon[14] between US staff delegates and Indonesian pro-reform activists regarding the "disappearances" that had been a feature of the Suharto government since 1996. For years, pro-reform activists, NGO workers and opposition figures had been vanishing—accused of wanting to overthrow the government, they were allegedly kidnapped and intimidated into silence. Some were never heard from again. "Many interlocutors believed Major General Prabowo to be behind the disappearances," Roy noted in his report, without going into detail.

---

13 https://newnaratif.com/wp-content/uploads/2018/06/ASSISTANT-SECRETARY-ROTH_S-MEETING-WITH-ilovepdf-compressed.pdf

14 https://newnaratif.com/wp-content/uploads/2018/06/STAFFDELS-VISIT-WITH-PRO-REFORM-ACTIVISTS-ilovepdf-compressed.pdf

On 24 November 1997 Clinton and Suharto met at the APEC summit in Vancouver. It was the last APEC meeting that Suharto would ever attend. The Indonesian president was tired, having flown to Vancouver via South Africa, and the meeting was tense. While pledging his support to the Indonesian president, Clinton raised[15] the ongoing human rights abuses in East Timor and the clampdown on pro-reform individuals. These issues, Clinton said, were hurting Suharto's image abroad, and could jeopardise support from the IMF and foreign investors.

Suharto was dismissive: "Those who commit offences or defy the people entrusted to uphold the constitution and those who violate the constitution will be brought to court to face the rule of law. This is what Indonesia has been doing for years and outsiders do not understand. Thank you."

"End of conversation," reads the next line on the meeting transcript.

The IMF's stipulations

Suharto's unwillingness to discuss or rein in oppressive actions was not Clinton's only problem.

On 8 January 1998, he called[16] Suharto from Air Force One. While at great pains to remind Suharto of their close relationship, Clinton also knew the Indonesian president hadn't been implementing the reforms required by the IMF as part of the bailout package deal. "I have long valued our friendship, and I just wanted to talk to you personally," he said.

The deal included a 50-point reform plan and items such as ending public subsidies and quashing Suharto's system of patronage. [16] banks owned by Suharto's cronies were closed down… only for some of them to later reopen under new names. Clinton described it as having "a huge influence on the psychology of investors" in the United States.

Still, failure to implement the IMF reforms and get the country back on a sound financial footing was not enough for the United States to withdraw their support. Clinton went on to explain other ways to deal with the crisis, including keeping interest rates high—an idea that didn't appeal to Suharto. He ended with another moment of bonhomie:

15 https://newnaratif.com/wp-content/uploads/2018/06/Meeting-with-ASEAN-Leaders-compressed.pdf

16 https://newnaratif.com/wp-content/uploads/2018/06/Telcon-with-President-Suharto-January-ilovepdf-compressed.pdf

"I also intend to release a statement in the next few minutes reiterating the importance of the relationship between our countries and to make it absolutely clear that we support you and that we will stand with you throughout these difficult times."

But the United States was coming under more and more pressure to justify its support of Indonesia, particularly as it hadn't offered similar financial assistance to Thailand. On 12 January 1998, a document[17] was circulated to all Asian and Pacific posts with press guidelines. It provided a glimpse of the media scrutiny that the United States was dealing with.

"Aren't critics at least partially right when they allege that these IMF programs are bailing out investors and corrupt governments?" read one anticipated question.

"If these efforts were directed at bailing out investors, we would not spend a penny on them," was the tart suggested response.

On 15 January 1998 Clinton called[18] Suharto once more, this time from the Oval Office. He'd sent Deputy Treasury Secretary Larry Summers to Indonesia to meet with the beleaguered president, who had also been visited by Deputy Managing Director of the IMF, Stanley Fischer, and Managing Director Michel Camdessus.

"I am glad to hear your voice," cooed Clinton, before Suharto launched into a spirited explanation of how he'd set up a Council of National Economic and Financial Resilience to better manage the implementation of the stipulations made by the IMF. He'd also signed a letter of intent promising to make good on the reform measures in the IMF package and appeal to overseas investors who were rapidly losing confidence in the Indonesian government's handling of the crisis.

Clinton was charmed: "First of all, I think the agreement is good, but I am most encouraged by the explanation of how it will be implemented... I will release a statement saying you called me and that I welcomed these steps, and I am encouraged by them."

This peace of mind was not to last.

The documents show that, less than a month later, the United States was once again rattled by Suharto's increasingly erratic response to the

17 https://newnaratif.com/wp-content/uploads/2018/06/1998-Press-Guidances-for-the-EAP-Region_compressed.pdf

18 https://newnaratif.com/wp-content/uploads/2018/06/Telcon-with-President-Suharto-15-January-1998.compressed.pdf

crisis. On 13 February 1998 Clinton called[19] Suharto again; he'd heard that Suharto had a wild plan to implement a currency board—which takes the power of managing the exchange rate away from the central bank by pegging it to a fixed rate with a foreign currency—and wanted to warn against it.

"I wanted to stay in touch and am calling now because I am concerned about the financial situation," said Clinton. "If markets go after the board, it could create a run that seriously depletes Indonesia's reserves and complicates the efforts of the IMF and the international community to provide support."

Suharto seemed, if not reluctant to accept advice, at least out of his depth. "If the currency board is not introduced, what is the alternative?" he asked. "How do we stop the rupiah's fall? I appeal to you to approach the G-7 and ask them to pay attention to the situation in Indonesia."

Clinton agreed.

Letting the cat out of the bag

By now, things weren't looking good—not just in Jakarta, but also in Washington DC.

On 16 March 1998, an American reporter in Jakarta held a press conference to publicise allegations about previously undisclosed US-Indonesia joint training programmes, which coincided with the release of a cache of Pentagon documents by Congressional allies of the East Timor Action Network (ETAN).

Both the reporter and the documents alleged that the Pentagon had sold military training to Indonesia behind Congress' back, and not just in 1996. They said that the US army had been training Indonesian soldiers since 1992 via something called the Joint Combined Exchange Training (J-CET) programme—an attempt to circumvent the ban on IMET.

"Indonesian troops were trained in air assault, urban warfare, and psychological operations *thirty-six times* between 1992 and 1997 without congressional knowledge or approval," said *World Policy*'s special report[20].

It was also alleged that many of the J-CET training exercises had involved Kopassus, Indonesia's elite counter-insurgency unit that also

---

19 https://newnaratif.com/wp-content/uploads/2018/06/Telcon-with-President-Suharto-13-February.compressed.pdf

20 https://worldpolicy.org/indonesia-at-the-crossroads-u-s-weapons-sales-and-military-training/#weapons

operated in East Timor and which was "accused of carrying out torture, disappearance and extra-judicial killings[21]".

This training, while not illegal, "clearly violated Congressional intent", wrote[22] Kurt Biddle, Washington coordinator for the Indonesia Human Rights Network, in 2007.

On 28 March 1998, a cable[23], signed off by Albright, was sent from Washington DC to the US embassy in Jakarta, noting tensions between Congress and the wider administration:

"We are getting vibes from the Hill, indicating that Congress is greatly displeased with the administration's response to the J-CET training issue. We may see fallout in the form of a congressional restriction on all joint training/exercises with the Indonesian military."

By April, demonstrations were taking place across Indonesian university campuses. Students were losing patience with the lack of financial stability; to make matters worse, people were still going missing, only to turn up months later claiming that they'd been kidnapped and tortured by the Indonesian military—who, it was now apparent, had received undisclosed training from the Americans.

Not only had the US administration been selling military training to Indonesia—which, while legal, had been done without informing Congress—but it had also agreed to a loan of USD3 billion to assuage Indonesia's financial woes, and Clinton had released statement after statement in support of Suharto. It was now clear that they'd continued to do this even in the face of all the human rights violations laid at the Suharto administration's door.

On 6 April 1998 Roth requested a meeting[24] at the US State Department with the Indonesian Ambassador to the United States, Dorodjatun Kuntjoro-Jakti. Roth said he hoped that Indonesia would reach another agreement with the IMF for more bailout money before

21 https://worldpolicy.org/indonesia-at-the-crossroads-u-s-weapons-sales-and-military-training/#weapons

22 https://worldpolicy.org/indonesia-at-the-crossroads-u-s-weapons-sales-and-military-training/#weapons

23 https://newnaratif.com/wp-content/uploads/2018/06/Official-Informal-PIMBS-to-Jakarta_compressed.pdf

24 https://newnaratif.com/wp-content/uploads/2018/06/AS-ROTH_S-APRIL-6-MEETING-WITH-AMB.-DORODJATUN_compressed.pdf

15 April 1998, but added that the Clinton administration and Congress had concerns about potential plans by the Indonesian government to stop on-campus demonstrations, the detentions of hundreds of peaceful demonstrators, and the continued disappearances of activists.

Despite this, Roth also said that, "The USC [US Congress] appreciates the military's restraint to date in dealing with protests, the allowance of on-campus demonstrations so far, and the decrease in anti-Sino Indonesian violence," all of which he called "positive developments".

Even though Suharto had wilfully ignored most of the IMF's stipulations over the previous months, the IMF, supported by the United States, signed a third agreement with Indonesia in April 1998 and poured another tranche of money into the country, on the understanding that Suharto would work on restructuring the banking system and implement bankruptcy laws.

Rumblings in Washington

As Indonesia continued to struggle with the social and economic fallout, the issue of kidnappings and disappearances was becoming a real headache for the United States.

Of all the documents in the newly declassified cache, one of the most explosive was sent by Roy on 7 May 1998—it had been classified for 20 years. In a cable[25], sent with a priority notice to Washington DC, Roy detailed how the US embassy in Indonesia solicited sources, including student activists, to inform on where those kidnapped were being held and who was responsible.

The document doesn't explain what brought on the sudden desire for this information; the problem had existed since 1996, and was hardly a new mystery. It seems possible that the embassy was under newly applied pressure from Washington DC to find out if there was a provable link between Kopassus—the elite force within the Indonesian army that carried out special operations for the government—and human rights abuses, and if they were using skills learned through J-CET to kidnap and torture pro-reform individuals.

The names of the sources that the embassy solicited are redacted, but the report is clear: "A leader of a mass student organisation told Poloff

25 https://nsarchive2.gwu.edu//

dc.html?doc=4616943-Document-10-Telegram-002579-from-US-Embassy

[Political Officer] that he was informed by a Kopassus source that the disappearances were carried out by 'Group Four' of Kopassus…"

Even more devastatingly for the Americans, the report continues, "Disappearances were ordered by Prabowo, who was following an order from President Suharto."

The cable then goes on to list one of the potential locations where the victims were taken, described as "[t]he old 'Kopassus team 81 anti-terrorist unit' facility located off the old road to Bogor [a city south of Jakarta]."

While previous reports sent by Roy to Washington DC detailed rumours about Prabowo and the military's involvement in the kidnappings, this document is the clearest sign that the Americans now had a firm idea of who was responsible for the human rights abuses: Suharto, who had had months of financial and bilateral support from the United States and the IMF; Prabowo who had been hosted by a cheerful Roth back in November to discuss military sales; and Kopassus, who had been trained by the US military without Congress' knowledge.

The next day, 8 May 1998, the Pentagon sent a memo[26] that stuck stubbornly to its narrative:

"Continued contact with the Indonesian military can serve US national security interests and contribute to our efforts to urge ABRI [The Indonesian Armed Forces] and other Indonesian authorities to exercise restraint".

The memo did, however, try to put some space between the United States and the Indonesian actions:

"However, in the current situation in Indonesia, careful policy-level review of individual activities is necessary. Accordingly, effective immediately, and until further notice, all US military activities in Indonesia will require prior approval by the Under Secretary of Defense for Policy".

The J-CET activities were put on ice.

---

26 https://newnaratif.com/wp-content/uploads/2018/06/Military-Activities-in-Indonesia_compressed.pdf

The fall of Suharto

Regardless of this decision by the Pentagon, Suharto still had the IMF's money and continued to ignore the stipulations in the bailout package. As part of a new set of reforms, the IMF gave Suharto until October 1998 to gradually decrease fuel subsidies; in May 1998, he slashed them in one fell swoop.

It turned out to be a fatal mistake. Violent riots erupted and Indonesian security forces from the army and the police started shooting protesters, including four students at Trisakti University in Jakarta on 12 May 1998.

Roth had also spoken too soon about the "decrease in anti-Sino Indonesian violence". In May 1998, student protests against the government that began in Medan became a flashpoint[27] for anti-Chinese violence that spread across the country.

The wheels had come off the US-Indonesia relationship: by this point, the J-CET programme had been suspended and an upcoming US-Indonesian joint military exercise had been cancelled. Congress was in uproar, and had forced the Department of Defense Assistant Secretary, Franklin D. Kramer, to testify in front of the Senate Foreign Relations Committee; Indonesia was consumed by rioting against the Suharto government; and the security forces were rapidly losing control, shooting demonstrators and displaying none of the "restraint" that Roth had previously praised, and that the Pentagon had insisted would come out of continued engagement.

Just six months after he confidently welcomed the IMF to "come take a look" at Indonesia, Suharto called a press conference on 21 May 1998 to announce his resignation.

His 32 year rule of Indonesia was over; Clinton would have to find a new friend.

* We thank Brad Simpson and his team at the National Security Archive for facilitating access to the declassified documents. Their briefing book[28] can be found here.

---

27 https://newnaratif.com/journalism/it-was-a-political-issue/

28 https://nsarchive.gwu.edu/briefing-book/indonesia/2018-07-24/
    us-promoted-close-ties-indonesian-military-suhartos-rule-came-end

RESTORING THE PEOPLE'S "THIRD VOTE"
KENNETH CHENG | 02 AUG 2018

Local elections were a crucial part of Malaya's political landscape before being abolished in 1965. Reviving local democracy will increase democratic accountability, transparency and clarity in the political system.

The dictum "All politics are local" was coined by former Speaker of the United States House of Representatives Tip O'Neill to emphasise that politics, at its core, is about engaging and solving the mundane concerns of citizens. Subsidiarity, meanwhile, is a principle of social organisation that holds that social and political issues should be dealt with at the most immediate (or local) level that is consistent with their resolution. It is presently best known as a general principle of European Union law. If problems should be solved at the local level, and all politics are local, then the people solving your local problems should be local politicians. In other words, the best way for governments to address their citizens' problems is via local democracy: citizens should elect the local representatives who are responsible for solving their local mundane problems. For Malaysians, however, local democracy has not existed since the abrupt suspension of local elections in 1965. But has this been for better or for worse?

From local elections to local selections

The earliest local council elections in Malaysia were held on 5 and 20 December 1857 in Georgetown, Penang, and Fort of Malacca. These local elections were imperfect from any modern perspective. They had a limited franchise—voters had to own properties and required to pay an annual assessment rate of 25 rupees—and high barriers of entry for candidates.[1] However, it would be a mistake to judge these local elections

---

1 Nahapan, A. (1970). *Report of the Royal Commission of Enquiry to Investigate into the Workings of Local Authorities in West Malaysia.* Kuala Lumpur: Jabatan Cetak Kerajaan, p.13.

by who it excluded rather than what it symbolised. The principle of having elected representatives in the local decision-making process, and ensuring local councils should have an elected majority, are important principles enshrined in these elections, which predated Malaya's independence by almost exactly 100 years. Unfortunately, these elections were abolished in 1913.[2] There are no clear reasons for the abolishment of these elections, but the probable explanation lies in how the drastic increase in immigration had transformed municipal centres. By the early 1900s, the majority of the population in urban areas comprised immigrants from Indonesia, China, and India, but the British did not want to enfranchise them. Yet they could hardly have representative local elections if the vast majority of residents were not enfranchised. Better, then, to simply and quietly do away with elected council.[3]

lengthy process

After World War 2, the British brought back local elections in 1951 with the aim of familiarising Malayans with the rigmarole of elective processes and procedures, and therefore easing the path to independence for Malaya at that time. Page 1 of the *Report on the Introduction of Elections in the Municipality of George Town, Penang, 1953* reads:

> The introduction of the modern type of democratic election, based on adult suffrage, has been made more carefully. It starts with local government and will, in due course, work outward and upward to Settlement, State, and Federal Councils. The transition from bureaucratic Local Government to a popularly elected Municipal Council has among its by-products the popularising of the idea of registration, the training of registration and polling staff, and the holding of the first democratic elections in the Federation of Malaya.[4]

The Kuala Lumpur Municipal Elections in 1952 played a crucial factor in establishing the Alliance – the political coalition which negotiated the transition of power from British rule to independence. The origins of the Alliance could be traced from the hastily established political cooperation set up by the Selangor state branch of Malayan Chinese Association (MCA) and the Kuala Lumpur branch of the United Malays

2 Ibid., p.14-15.

3 Ibid.

4 Rabushka, A. (1970). The Manipulation of Ethnic Politics in Malaya. Polity, 2(3), 349.

National Organization (UMNO) during 1952. The informal 'alliance' was initially formed to combat the threat posed by the multi-ethnic Independence of Malaya Party (IMP) led by Dato' Onn Jaafar. It proved successful when it captured nine out of 12 municipal seats in the Kuala Lumpur election.[5] From this alliance, the Alliance was formed, with the inclusion of Malayan Indian Congress (MIC) in 1954. Their landslide victory in the 1955 Federal Elections (51 out of 52 seats) helped convinced the British that the state was in firm hands, and paved the way towards the nation's independence in 1957.

In 1963, the Federation of Malaya merged with Singapore, North Borneo, and Sarawak to form Malaysia. President of Sukarno accused the new state of being a neo-colonial British invention to perpetuate British colonial rule in the region, and declared a "Konfrontasi" (confrontation). For this reason, Malaysia's nationwide local elections (due by 1965) were suspended by the federal government . Then Prime Minister Tunku Abdul Rahman assured the public that these measures were only temporary and promised that the suspension would be lifted "the moment peace is declared".[6]

At the same time, the Royal Commission of Enquiry on Local Authorities was set up by the federal government in June 1965, headed by the former Senator Athi Nahappan, to study the workings of local authorities in Malaysia. Subsequently, a report was produced in 1968 and published in 1970. It called upon the government to reaffirm the principle of having elective representations in local government. However, the suspension remained in force even after the return of peaceful relations between Indonesia and Malaysia. Local elections were officially abolished and replaced by a system of appointed local councillors in 1976.

Suspension and Abolition

Konfrontasi was blamed for the suspension of local elections in 1965, but in 1964 there was a peaceful General Election of much greater complexity and magnitude than local elections, held during the height of Konfrontasi. Also, even before the general suspension of 1965, individual councils had been taken over by state governments. Thus, this

---

5 Stubbs, R. (1979). The United Malays National Organization, the Malayan Chinese Association, and the Early Years of the Malayan Emergency, 1948–1955. Journal Of Southeast Asian Studies, 10(01), 82.

6 "Off: All local elections". The Straits Times, 2 March 1965, 1.

justification for suspending local elections is at best incomplete and at worst, disingenuous.

The Alliance's poor performance in local elections was probably the main reason why local elections were suspended. At the national level, Malaya's 2nd General Election in 1959 was a major shock to the Alliance, especially after its overwhelming victory of 1955.[7] In 1959, the Alliance only garnered 51.5% of the popular vote (down 30.2% from 1955) and lost 30 seats after only losing one in 1955. Most surprisingly, it lost control in Terengganu and Kelantan at the state level.[8]

At the local level, state capitals such as Penang and Ipoh were constantly under the control of opposition parties and the Alliance even suffered a humiliating defeat when it lost all 8 seats it contested in municipal elections in Penang at 1956.[9] Popular support for the Alliance was on the wane across the country, and local councils controlled by the opposition formed local training grounds for opposition politicians while hindering the Alliance's ability to implement their policies with minimal opposition and consolidate their support.

Against this backdrop of diminishing support, the federal capital, Kuala Lumpur, was the first to have its local elections suspended and placed under direct control of the federal government by the passing of The Federal Capital Act, 1960. The act effectively put an end to local elections in Kuala Lumpur and replaced the elected council with an appointed commissioner and advisory board. This was perceived as the federal government's first attempt to cripple the autonomy of local government.[10] Other city councils such as Seremban, Georgetown, Malacca, Johor Bahru, and Batu Pahat soon followed, with the state assuming control over the cities' local government.[11]

The federal government alleged corrupt practices and mismanagement to justify taking control of local government and suspending elections. These were the official reasons given in the takeover of the local town councils of Seremban, Johor Bahru, Georgetown, and Malacca. In the

---

7 Norris, M. (1980). Local government in peninsular Malaysia. Farnborough, Eng.: Gower, p.23.

8 Smith, T. (1960). The Malayan Elections of 1959. Pacific Affairs, 33(1), 38-47

9 Ibid.

10 Wong, C., Chin, J., & Othman, N. (2010). Malaysia – towards a topology of an electoral one-party state. Democratization, 17(5), 941.

11 Norris, M. (1980). Local government in peninsular Malaysia. Farnborough, Eng.: Gower, p.23.

case of Seremban, the Commission of Enquiry for Seremban did find that there had been maladministration and malpractices perpetrated by local councillors.[12] However, the Seremban corruption case was the only officially-proven case of local corruption pertaining to the abolition of elective councils.[13] The cases of alleged malpractices of other councils were either inconclusive or not pursued by relevant authorities.

It was also argued that local elective councils were inefficient in terms of their provision of local service and financial management.[14] A number of councils, including Malacca Municipality and rural district councils in Penang, Malacca, and Kelantan, were in dire financial situations.[15] However, these were exceptions; what was more common was that local councils and state/federal governments disagreed on policies. For example, conflicts between the council and federal government in George Town (Penang's capital)—where disputes ranged from the council's refusal to decorate the city on national day to supplying water to a squatter settlement that the state had condemned and was about to abolish[16]—embarrassed the administration of Penang. The first major project of the Kelantan State Economic Development Corporation was delayed for many months in its own capital by the Kota Bahru city council.[17] Abolishing elective local councils and replacing it with an appointed system was a crude but effective way of liberating federal and state governments from local councils resistant to their vision of national development, regardless of whether local councils genuinely had important or relevant concerns.

---

12 Nahapan, A. (1970). Report of the Royal Commission of Enquiry to Investigate into the Workings of Local Authorities in West Malaysia. Kuala Lumpur: Jabatan Cetak Kerajaan, p.27.

13 Tennant, P. (1973). The Decline of Elective Local Government in Malaysia. Asian Survey, 13(4), pp.362.

14 Tennant, P. (1973). The Decline of Elective Local Government in Malaysia. Asian Survey, 13(4), pp.363

15 Ibid., 364

16 Norris, M. (1980). Local government in peninsular Malaysia. Farnborough, Eng.: Gower, p.24.

17 Tennant, P. (1973). The Decline of Elective Local Government in Malaysia. Asian Survey, 13(4), pp.362.

From these series of events, we could infer that the Alliance had a strong preference for centralisation of power[18] and was sceptical towards local democracy.[19] It seemed that the Alliance at that time was distrustful towards the idea of local elective councils and perceived them as an obstacle towards their control and dominance over a nascent Malaya then.

Are Appointees Better?

Under the replacement system (which continues to be used today), local government representatives in Malaysia such as Presidents (Yang Dipertua), Mayors (Datuk Bandar), and local councillors (Ahli Majlis) are appointed by the state government. List II of the Ninth Schedule of the Federal Constitution states that the state government would have control over the functioning and workings of local government, including local elections. Ideally, an appointment system would lead to higher calibre of councillors as, unlike elected councillors, appointed councillors would be above partisan politics, able to make decisions independent from party politics, and selected from a broader pool of talented individuals that included those not interested in participating in electoral politics.

The issue of party politics in elective councils was anticipated and comprehensively discussed in the Chapters 7 - 8 of the *Report of the Royal Commission of Enquiry.* According to the *Report,*

> The system in the Federal Capital has brought about complete harmony between the Federal Government and the Municipality of the Federal Capital. This was only possible by the **abolition of an elective council** and substituting therefore a nominative board. This transformation has effectively introduced a climate of deliberations based on merits of matters. On the other hand, it has eliminated irresponsible and irrelevant electoral promises, party bias in deliberations and decisions in council, opposition for opposition's sake with little or no regard for the interests of the ratepayers, and other inherent psychological phenomena,

18 Wong, C., Chin, J., & Othman, N. (2010). Malaysia – towards a topology of an electoral one-party state. Democratization, 17(5), 941.

19 Tennant, P. (1973). The Decline of Elective Local Government in Malaysia. Asian Survey, 13(4), pp.363

> e.g. political antics normally associated with party politics in an elected council.[20]

Thus, the idea of replacing the elected council with an appointed one was conceived with the design of eliminating partisan politics from the local council – but it did not achieve this purpose. Instead, the system perpetuated a 'winner-takes-all' mentality, where the party/coalition that controlled the state government, *de facto* gained the right to appoint all the local councillors in its local government. Hence, the appointment of officials by elected politicians means that party politics still heavily influences the local councillors. An instructive comparison might be the system in the USA, where leading government officials are appointed by the elected President. This has not led to non-partisan, non-political appointees.

In this way, party politics will always be inextricably linked to a local government regardless of whether it functions with an elective representations or appointment system. Governments have the difficult decisions of distributing resources and picking winners. It is inherently political, whether officials are appointed, elected on a non-party basis, or elected on a party-basis.

Rather, a better way of framing the issue is about accountability, transparency, and clarity to citizens and taxpayers. The appointment system obfuscates the lines of accountability of officials. More importantly, it currently lacks a mechanism to compel appointed councillors to be held answerable or accountable to the constituents they are supposed to serve. As they are not elected and are answerable to politicians above them, they have little incentive to make themselves known to their constituents. It is no surprise that most Malaysians generally have no idea who their local councillors are. As a result of that, the elected Member of Parliament (MP) and State Assemblyman (ADUN) becomes the person that voters approach when they encounter problems in their residential areas such as illegal dumping of rubbish or clogged drains, which are outside their area of responsibility.

According to calculations made by the Commonwealth Local Government Forum (a global local government organisation which brings together local authorities, their national associations and the ministries responsible for local government in the member countries

20 Nahapan, A. (1970). Report of the Royal Commission of Enquiry to Investigate into the Workings of Local Authorities in West Malaysia. Kuala Lumpur: Jabatan Cetak Kerajaan, p.98.

of the Commonwealth), the total expenditure by local governments in Malaysia is estimated to be around RM10,687 million in 2017.[21] Local councillors should be held accountable for the local government's expenditure but the current appointment system with its diminished checks and balances are unable to properly regulate or monitor the spending of the local government.

The lack of accountability and transparency within the local government has also gave rise to instances of political patronage, whereby the granting of infrastructure projects and business licences are rewarded to political affiliated individuals. One recent example is a police report lodged against Mohd Noorhisyam Abdul Karim of Parti Pribumi Bersatu Malaysia (a party of the current governing Pakatan Harapan coalition) accusing him of benefitting from misusing his political connections to secure 80 bazaar lots from Kuala Lumpur City Hall (KLCH).[22] Noorhisyam allegedly secured licenses of 80 bazaar lots from KLCH and subsequently rented them out at exorbitant prices. If there had been local elections in Kuala Lumpur, the procurement process for business licences would be made more accountable, transparent, and subject to scrutiny by the public. The MP of Bukit Bintang, Fong Kui Lun (Democratic Action Party, also part of Pakatan Harapan), admitted that local elections in Kuala Lumpur could have averted the scandal of this nature and provided more accountability and transparency in Kuala Lumpur City Hall.[23]

Local democracy is an integral part of Malaysia

Nahappan's report argued that fully (or almost fully) elected local councils played a critical role in connecting Malaysia's rural villages to the fledging democratic state in the 1950s. Malaysia's rural villages and new villages were generally out of administrative reach and vulnerable to the communist insurgency. However, providing them with local councils enabled them to exercise the rights of democracy in managing their civic affairs. Introducing the concept of self-determination through democracy, he argued, enabled villagers to see the "virtue of

---

21 http://www.clgf.org.uk/default/assets/File/Country_profiles/Malaysia.pdf

22 https://www.thestar.com.my/news/nation/2018/06/16/
   pribumi-lodges-police-report-over-ramadan-bazaar-allegations/

23 https://www.edgeprop.my/content/1396007/
   local-polls-can-check-problems-ramadan-bazaar-controversy

democracy as a way of corporate life", building their connection to the broader Malayan nation-state Therefore, it argued, local democracy had a deep-rooted influence on the early political culture of Malaya, before they were abolished in 1965.

Regardless of whether his characterisation of local democracy is correct, there are undoubtedly many success stories of elective town councils which possessed exemplary records for managing local affairs and were democratically popular. Ipoh Municipality (Perak), for example, was time and again being praised for its efficient management and its innovative development, making important contributions in the provision of markets, abattoirs, low-cost housing, and parks.[24] Nahappan's report states that:

> What is important to be recorded here is that with the correct mutual appreciation of each other's roles, powers and duties of two unequal authorities under two different political parties can function side by side with understanding and goodwill. The credit must go to both the Perak State Government and the Municipality of Ipoh.

This short chapter of local democracy in Ipoh proves that local elective government in Malaysia can flourish as long as it was given the opportunity and both sides acted in good faith for the benefit of the people.

Undoubtedly that there were defects within the functioning of local elective governments in Malaya, but democratic principles should be preserved and prioritised, and systems improved upon rather than discarded instantly at the first sign of trouble. If political partisanship had indeed caused inter-governmental conflicts and encumbered the development of the country, the natural remedy of the situation should be building consensus and/or ameliorating the divisions. If the solution to conflict lies on abolishing elective representations of the lower tier of government, it follows then that state governments which are governed by the opposition should also naturally suffer a similar fate and have its elective representations abolished by the federal government in the future – and indeed, all lower divisions should be replaced by appointed officials. The logical but farcical implications of such conclusions become very clear.

---

24 Norris, M. (1980). Local government in peninsular Malaysia. Farnborough, Eng.: Gower, p.25.

At the heart of this argument lies the incorrect notion that democracy and efficiency are mutually exclusive beliefs which cannot usefully coexist. The contestation between two ideals in the local government has led to Malaysia abandoning the former in pursuit of the latter but through his report, Athi Nahappan made it abundantly clear that:

> Efficiency, though highly desirable in itself, should be made an indivisible part of a democratic process rather than be divorced from it. Democracy with efficiency is always more desirable and better than efficiency without democracy. In the journey towards attaining an efficient democracy, we should not allow the difficult terrain of the journey to discourage or divert us from striving to reach the goal.[25]

In recent years, there has been recent talks of reviving local elections, more commonly known as restoring the 'third vote' back to Malaysians (after federal and state elections as the 'first' and 'second vote', respectively). In 2014, the then-opposition led Penang state government challenged the constitutionality of abolishing local elections.[26] The federal court ultimately ruled against the state government. Since then, there has been a lack of political will and interest from both sides of political aisle to push for the revival of local elections.

Nevertheless, there remain grounds to feel optimistic over the prospect of local elections in Malaysia. The historic 14th General Election that led to a change of government for the first time in Malaysia has obviously expanded the scope of reviving local elections. Newly elected member of parliament Maria Chin Abdullah has vowed to call for a Royal Commission of Inquiry on bringing back local elections.[27] On the level of federal government, newly appointed Minister of Housing and Local Government Zuraida Kamaruddin has also promised that there will be a detailed study on the reimplementation of local elections in three

---

25 Nahapan, A. (1970). Report of the Royal Commission of Enquiry to Investigate into the Workings of Local Authorities in West Malaysia. Kuala Lumpur: Jabatan Cetak Kerajaan, p.102.

26 https://www.thestar.com.my/news/nation/2014/08/15/no-to-penang-local-govt-elections-federal-court-rules-that-state-government-has-no-jurisdiction-over/

27 https://www.thestar.com.my/news/nation/2018/04/26/former-bersih-chief-maria-chin-unveils-manifesto/

years.[28] The history and practice of local elections and local democracy are deeply embedded in Malaya, and it remains to be seen whether there will be a revival of local elections in Malaysia. Democracy in Malaysia has taken a giant leap forward when the principle of peaceful transition of power through elections was faithfully adhered to. However the progress of local democracy in Malaysia remains stagnant. Malaysians are still awaiting its long forgotten 'third vote' to have a local government that is by the people, for the people, and of the people.

---

28 https://www.nst.com.my/news/nation/2018/05/373449/
local-council-election-can-be-held-three-years-nsttv

MALAYSIA'S WATERSHED ELECTION

A SYMBOL OF FREE SPEECH IN MALAYSIA

SHARMILLA GANESAN | 26 MAR 2018

Political cartoonist Zunar has been a long-time critic of the Malaysian government and a target of oppression, but says he has the responsibility to keep using his talents to push for regime change and a better Malaysia.

Malaysian cartoonist Zulkiflee SM Anwar Ulhaque was only 17 when his first cartoon was banned; he had criticised a teacher in his school magazine for what he saw as a failure in fulfilling her duty. He could not have realised it then, but the incident portended his future.

Zunar, as he is better known these days, is now 56 years old, and is Malaysia's best-known—some would say only—political cartoonist, one who's fiercely critical of people in power who fail to uphold their duties.

Sitting in his office in the heart of Kuala Lumpur, Zunar's light-hearted speech and gentle demeanour belie the firebrand activist persona he's known for. Easily given to broad smiles, he breaks out in infectious peals of laughter when something particularly tickles him, such as when he gleefully opens a list of recent movie titles on his computer; he's adapted each one into puns based on Malaysian politics. Among the ones that have made it into his comics are "Sapuman: Man of Steal" ("sapu" means "to sweep" and can also refer to stealing) and "Steal Wars: The Teruk One" ("teruk" means "terrible").

"Laughter is the best protest for Malaysia," he says. "People are scared of the government, of losing their jobs, their scholarships. If you tell them to join a demonstration, they don't want to go. But if you say, come and laugh at our PM, they will. And of course, his wife as well, they laugh even more at her."

"This is the way I approach people. And nobody can say anything because there's no law against laughing. They can go against me, but they cannot stop you."

A target of oppression

Zunar is not speaking hypothetically—his cartoons have led to repeated persecution from the Malaysian government. On top of numerous raids, seizures, and bans of his books, Zunar is currently facing trial for nine charges under the Sedition Act, which could see him imprisoned for more than 40 years. He has also been placed under a travel ban since 2016; he's challenging this in court.

For the past two decades, Zunar has been a critic of Malaysia's government, run by the Barisan Nasional coalition party since the country's independence in 1957. While initially starting off in print media, his work really began making an impact with the rise of the Internet and social media, which enabled quick dissemination and easy sharing.

While five of his books have been banned, his cartoons remain widely shared online, often shared several thousand times on various social media platforms. His refusal to back down despite frequent attempts at censure by the government has also turned him into an icon of sorts, one of many prominent voices calling for a change in government.

Bitingly satirical, Zunar's cartoons push the boundaries in Malaysia, where free speech is often limited by the government through various means, including keeping a tight leash on traditional media outlets and enacting laws to criminalise peaceful speech and assembly. He usually engages with current political issues, using a combination of broad caricatures and specific cues to create cartoons that are immediately recognisable to the Malaysian public. His cartoons are also known for being rich in detail, with clues and allusions to specific people or ongoing scandals placed within many of his panels.

Putting the spotlight on Najib and Rosmah

He has increasingly turned his pen on Malaysia's Prime Minister Najib Razak and his wife Rosmah Mansor in recent years, focusing on what he sees as corruption and a failure of governance.

Since coming into power in 2009, Najib has had to contend with a surge of support for opposition parties, including his party's losing of the two-third majority in parliament. An extremely close race in the 2013 elections renewed questions about his leadership.

Things came to a head in 2015 when news of the 1MDB corruption scandal broke in the *Wall Street Journal*. The newspaper alleged that MYR2.6 billion (USD700 million) had been diverted from 1Malaysia Development Berhad (1MDB), a state investment fund, into Najib's personal bank account. Najib has denied any misconduct, but investigations related to the scandal are being conducted by various authorities around the world, including the United States' Department of Justice.

Najib's government has also overseen a steady tightening of control, with dissidents being pressured into silence by, among others, the Sedition Act—a colonial-era piece of legislation that criminalises speech with "seditious tendency", such as statements that create hatred or disaffection against the government, or incites hostility between Malaysia's different races. Meanwhile, critics within his own party—including former deputy prime minister Muhyiddin Yassin—have been sacked and replaced with more amenable candidates.

For Zunar, 1MDB and stories that swirl around it—allegations of Najib and Rosmah's lavish lifestyles, the luxury items purchased, connections with Hollywood—provided an opportunity to hone in on specific details and depict corruption in a way that's easily understood by all levels of readers, particularly as Malaysia continues to grapple with an uncertain economy.

It's notable that he skewers Rosmah almost as frequently as he does Najib, often positioning her as the one pulling the strings behind the scenes. Frequent jabs are also made at her supposed extravagant tastes, and her disconnect with the concerns of the common man.

He says, however, that he avoids getting personal, focusing instead on her role when it comes to politics.

"It is an open secret that she's the one in control; this is what happened with Imelda Marcos. When I choose my subject, this is what I think. If it's in their own home, we don't mind. But not when it comes to the management of the country. And for a cartoonist, she is very cartoonable. She keeps saying what she wants, without thinking!"

Cartoons for all Malaysians

"I always want my cartoons to reach from the highest to the lowest of Malaysia, from A to Z," Zunar says. "To do that, I need to understand what people want, what's in their hearts. In terms of subject, object, presentation, visual language. I want everybody to understand, but I will never sacrifice my commentary, my thoughts, my stand."

With an election looming in Malaysia this year, Zunar has increased his efforts, putting out a cartoon a day. His interests are not mainly commercial; instead, he sees his work as more of a public service. He offers his work copyright-free so they can be freely distributed.

"[M]y cartoons are free of copyright until we have a regime change. For me, my talent is not a gift, but a responsibility," he says.

Producing work that's both humourous and accessible is no small feat: each cartoon takes between eight to 10 hours to create, and involves an extensive amount of reading and research To maintain this level of productivity, Zunar holds to a strict schedule: his day starts at 6am, and he draws till lunchtime at noon. After lunch, time is set aside for reading and research. He then gives himself a break by listening to music or watching television. Dinner is at 6pm, bedtime at 10pm. He admits he's a creature of habit and doesn't like complicating his life with activities that distract him.

"I don't like numbers, I don't like giving or asking for directions, I don't like looking for parking spaces, I don't like queuing up. These things bother me. Because my mind is working all the time, and these things interrupt me," he says.

A born cartoonist

Born to a Malay-Muslim family in the state of Kedah in the northwest of Peninsular Malaysia, Zunar has been drawing cartoons since as far back as he can remember—his first published cartoon was at the age of 12, in a children's magazine called *Bambino*.

"It's something that came naturally. In school, I drew cartoons in my exercise books, on the school wall... and my teachers would become angry!"

Despite his natural talent, he recalls that cartooning was not viewed as a viable career choice: "I never studied art. In fact, until university, I took science. Parents in the 1970s, if you tell them you want to study art and become a cartoonist, they will say, how are you going to make a living?"

Entirely self-taught, he cites American editorial cartoonists as a defining inspiration, particularly Thomas Nast, who's often considered the "Father of the American Cartoon". Zunar recalls being so desperate to learn more about editorial cartooning that he stole a copy of *Time* magazine while in his early 20s.

"They had four pages of editorial cartoons! I couldn't afford the magazine at that time, so I had to steal it. I stole for good, I'd like to think," he says.

He quit university after one year and took on various odd jobs before joining a hospital as a lab technician. By then, he had a regular cartoon column with *Gila-Gila*, a humour magazine geared towards teenagers. He decided to take the plunge to become a full-time cartoonist around 1986, but felt that something was lacking.

"Even back when I was 17, I had started thinking that cartoons aren't just simple jokes. We need to put our mind, a message into it. When I joined *Gila-Gila* full time, I tried to do this, but the audience was not right," he says.

Wanting to focus on political cartooning, Zunar joined the *Berita Harian* newspaper in the early 1990s, where he had a regular column. He had his first real taste of controversy in 1992 when one of his cartoons—a commentary on the frequency of crashes by Nuri helicopters—earned the ire of the Ministry of Defence. He was suspended from his job for a week.

Zunar stayed on at *Berita Harian* for about four more years but left in 1996 dejected by the censorship his work faced within the organisation. But Malaysia's tightly controlled media landscape meant that the situation was no different elsewhere. After failing to publish in other Malaysian newspapers, Zunar decided to stop cartooning, taking on freelance work such as illustrating or teaching for the next two years to make a living.

1998's Reformasi

Zunar's turning point came almost at the same time as Malaysia's: during the Reformasi movement of 1998. When then-Prime Minister Mahathir Mohamad sacked and eventually jailed his deputy Anwar Ibrahim, a huge national movement against the Barisan Nasional government was sparked, leading to a wave of demonstrations and rallies. (Anwar has since gone on to become one of the leaders of the opposition coalition, now known as Pakatan Harapan.)

As an expression of solidarity, Zunar began printing and distributing his cartoons at rallies held outside Anwar's home and the courthouse. Encouraged by a friend, Zunar submitted some of his work to *Harakah*, a newspaper published by the opposition Pan-Malaysian Islamic Party, which was enjoying a surge of popularity as an alternative to mainstream media outlets. Zunar began publishing his cartoons regularly in *Harakah* from 1999 onwards.

"People started talking about me, I didn't expect that. I started hearing people say, 'Eh, what did Zunar say today?' This is what an artist needs," he says. "Maybe before that, I was at the wrong time, wrong place. But now, it was like I found the last missing piece of my puzzle. I got the freedom to do what I wanted to do, and that can bring out the best in you."

More opportunities followed as Zunar's popularity grew, including the publication of a series of books and a stint at online alternative news portal *Malaysiakini*. It was also around that time that run-ins with the authorities became more frequent, including seizure of his books and the raiding of printers who published his work.

Looking ahead

Zunar has since been honoured with, among others, the Human Rights Watch Hellman/Hammett Award, the International Press Freedom Award, and the Cartooning for Peace Award. Late last year, the United Nations also requested that all sedition charges against Zunar be dropped and the travel ban lifted, but the Malaysian government has remained unmoved thus far.

"I don't want to think about these charges now," says Zunar. "What is the biggest enemy of the artist? It's not the government or the law, it's self-censorship. And I want to avoid this by not thinking about what happens next; I want to concentrate on what I've got to do."

For now, that's got to do with the upcoming general election, which has been surrounded by no small amount of drama in the last few months—most controversially, Pakatan Harapan has aligned itself with the 92-year-old Mahathir, selecting him as their prime ministerial candidate in a bid to oust Najib. To those who hold Mahathir responsible for shaping Barisan Nasional into what it has become today, this is a difficult turn of events.

When asked his thoughts on the opposition's decision, Zunar—who has been pointed in his criticism of Mahathir—immediately grabs a sheet of paper and pen. He rapidly sketches out a football field with uneven goalposts; a representation of how Barisan Nasional plays politics.

"I support Pakatan Harapan one hundred percent," he says. "Because our election is not about changing a government, it's about changing a regime. Reform is what I want. I am only one part of this movement. We need writers, artists, activists, to all move in the same direction. We need a political party. And this is not about the individual. Whoever who moves in this direction now, I will accept them. Even if it is Mahathir."

"We need numbers now. All our institutions are gone. There's corruption. Our education system is failing. And nothing can be done. For changing the regime for a better Malaysia, I take this stand."

But what does the ideal Malaysia look like? His answer is immediate.

"Five important institutions much be overhauled: the judiciary, the police, the Malaysian Anti-Corruption Commission, the attorney-general's office, and the media. They must be professional and go through Parliament, not the PM. If you do that, it will create public monitoring. Then we can create a good government."

His job as a cartoonist in Malaysia, he asserts, is unlike those in Europe or the United States. "There, their job is to criticise the government of the day. But here, we want to change a regime. So when Pakatan Harapan comes into power, I will become a cartoonist who criticises the government of the day."

HOW MALAYSIA'S ELECTION IS BEING RIGGED

OOI KOK HIN | 19 MAR 2018

The unconstitutional and illegal redelineation of Malaysia's constituencies will create an extremely unfair election and result in a Parliament that is unrepresentative of Malaysia's people.

Malaysia's ongoing redelineation exercise is unconstitutional and will create a Parliament that is extremely unrepresentative of Malaysia's people, no matter who wins, because it is severely flawed in two main ways: it either creates *malapportionment*, which is the manipulation of electorate size where one person's votes become worth up to 3-4 times the votes of another person in a different constituency; or causes *gerrymandering*, which is the manipulation of electorate composition to the advantage of one party; or both. Schedule 13 of Malaysia's Constitution specifically prohibits malapportionment and gerrymandering of electoral boundaries, making the redelineation exercise unconstitutional. Furthermore, the Election Commission (EC) has broken the law by illegally redrawing the electoral boundaries *before* the electoral redelineation process had even started, and by illegally breaking up polling districts. This article explains in detail exactly how and why the redelineation exercise is unconstitutional and illegal.[1]

Background: Redelineation and Constitutionality

The General Election (Malaysia's 14th since independence, or GE14) must take place by August 2018. It is likely that new electoral boundaries will be used in the impending General Election. The EC started a

---

1 This essay is based on the collective research effort of Penang Institute in collaboration with Bersih 2.0 and Delineation Action & Research Team (DART). The project team is led by Dr Wong Chin Huat and assisted by Yeong Pey Jung, Nidhal Rawa, Kenneth Cheng, Dr Toh Kin Woon, and the author.

delineation review on 15 September 2016, and submitted its final report to Prime Minister Najib Razak on 9 March 2018. This process was rushed and controversial– the Selangor state government filed a legal challenge in October 2016 seeking to nullify the EC's notice of redelineation, arguing that it violated the Federal Constitution in drawing new electoral boundaries.

Najib will likely table it in Parliament in the March-April session. The redelineation proposal covers both federal and state and requires the approval of just 50% of Parliament, 111 votes, to be passed.

Several commentaries have criticised the redelineation as guilty of ethnic gerrymandering. Focusing on ethnic imbalance, however, not only unnecessarily limits our understanding of the redelineation process, it distracts from the real damage of the redelineation process by using race as a smokescreen. Looking at this issue through race suggests that there may be winners and losers from this process; in reality, all Malaysians are losers if this redelineation exercise is allowed to proceed unchallenged.

In the election, voters cast two votes: one for representation at the state level (state assembly) and one at the federal level (Parliament). The state constituencies are nested within a larger federal constituency, so it is typical for 3-5 state constituencies to exist within one federal constituency.

Malaysia practices a first-past-the-post system where a simple majority is decisive. No representation is allocated to the losing party no matter whether they get 49.9% or 9.9% of the vote. This creates vote-seat disproportionality at the constituency level, where 49.9% of voters may be against the winner and yet have no representation. This effect is then magnified significantly across constituencies. This was painfully evident in the previous election (GE13, 2013) where the Barisan Nasional coalition barely squeaked back into power. The opposition won 50.87% of the vote, but thanks to shamelessly biased gerrymandering of the constituencies, the Barisan Nasional's 47.37% was sufficient to win 133 out of 222 seats (59.9%) in Parliament.[2] As a result, the Parliament was not representative of the people. This disparity between votes obtained versus seats won means that many voters are under-represented or their votes are worth less. It violates a fundamental principle of equality and equal representation (or the "one man, one vote" principle).

---

2 Khoo Boo Teik ed. "13th General Election in Malaysia: Issues, Outcomes and Implications." IDE-JETRO, 2013.

Demographic shifts, development, and migration change the characteristics of constituencies over time. The Federal Constitution's Article 113 thus provides for a redelineation exercise, to be done at least eight years after the previous exercise. The exercise is designed to scrutinise the current population of each constituency and rebalance them, in accordance with principles laid out in the Constitution, aiming for "approximately equal" apportionment and to avoid "vote-seat disproportionality across parties" so that the ballot value of each voter can be equal across all political parties, preserving the principle of "one man, one vote".[3]

The process begins with the EC informing the Prime Minister and Parliament and publishing a notice of the 1st Recommendations for redelineation through gazette and newspapers. After a period for feedback, objections, and inquiries, the EC will revise their proposed redelineation and publicise a 2nd Recommendations. Another round of objections and inquiries ensue, after which the EC submits a final report to the Prime Minister to be presented in Parliament. After approval by Parliament, it will be presented to the King, who will proclaim an order effective upon the dissolution of the current Parliament.

> Article 113(2) of the Malaysian Constitution: "The Election Commission shall, from time to time, as they deem necessary, review the division of the Federation and the States into constituencies and recommend such changes therein as they may think necessary in order **to comply with the provisions contained in the Thirteenth Schedule**".

Thirteen Schedule of the Constitution details the provisions for a redelineation exercise to be carried out by the EC. In particular, clause 2 states:

The following principles shall as far as possible be taken into account in dividing any unit of review into constituencies pursuant to the provisions of Articles 116 and 117 –

a. while having regard to the desirability of giving all electors reasonably convenient opportunities of going to the polls, constituencies ought to be delimited so that they do not cross State boundaries and regard ought to be had to the inconvenience

---

3 Wong Chin Huat et all. "An Analysis on the Constitutional Compliance of the Election Commission's 1st and 2nd Recommendations (September 15, 2016 and March 8, 2017) for the State of Perak." Penang Institute, 2017.

of State constituencies crossing the boundaries of federal constituencies;

b. regard ought to be to the administrative facilities available within the constituencies for the establishment of the necessary registration and polling machines;

c. the number of electors within each constituency in a State ought to be approximately equal except that, having regard to the greater difficulty of reaching electors in the country districts and the other disadvantages facing rural constituencies, a measure of weightage for area ought to be given to such constituencies;

d. regard ought to be had to the inconveniences attendant on alterations of constituencies, and to the maintenance of local ties.

If any of the above principles are not followed–for example, instances of constitutional non-compliance are left uncorrected without due justification, or worse, instances of constitutional non-compliance are aggravated by the changes proposed–then the redelineation exercise would be unconstitutional.

Malapportionment: your votes are not equal

2. The following principles shall as far as possible be taken into account in dividing any unit of review into constituencies pursuant to the provisions of Articles 116 and 117 – […]

(c) the number of electors within each constituency in a State ought to be approximately equal except that, having regard to the greater difficulty of reaching electors in the country districts and the other disadvantages facing rural constituencies, a measure of weightage for area ought to be given to such constituencies;

– Clause 2(c) of the Thirteenth Schedule of the Malaysian Constitution

Malapportionment is a manipulation of electorate *size*, which not only violates the moral democratic principle of "one man one vote" but also violates the constitutional principle spelled out in Thirteenth Schedule 2(c) which states that, "the number of electors within each constituency in a State ought to **be approximately equal**" (with one exception for rural constituencies – see below).

The typical example used to showcase the violation of this "equal apportionment" rule is the comparison between the electorate size of two federal constituencies: Kapar's 146,317 voters and Putrajaya's 17,627 voters. But the two federal constituencies do not reside in the same state and Putrajaya, being a separate unit of administration, is an exceptional case. A stronger case can be made by comparing malapportionment of constituencies in the same state (intra-state malapportionment), in particular because the Thirteenth Schedule 2(c) specifically mentions that the number of electors *within each constituency in a State* ought to be approximately equal.

With that in mind, let's take a look at Penang, which is comprised entirely of urban constituencies (examining Penang enables us to make comparisons without the rural weightage clause exemption, which we address in further detail in a separate section below):

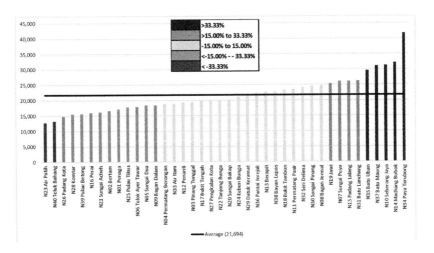

Figure 1: Intra-state malapportionment in the state of Penang. The deviation, in percent, from the average size of the state constituencies (21,694 voters) is denoted by the colour.

Severely under-represented constituencies (those with an excessively large electorate, coloured in red) and severely over-represented constituencies (excessively small electorate, coloured in dark green) would have been outright unconstitutional if not for the two constitutional amendments in 1962 and 1973. Prior to the first amendment in 1962, the permissible range of deviation from the state average was capped at 15%. The 1962 amendment increased the range of permissible deviation from 15% to 33.33%. The cap was entirely removed in the 1973 amendment.

With the removal of quantified criteria, the deviation has skyrocketed from a maximum of 33.33% up to 92.25% (N34 Paya Terubong in Penang) and above. In peninsular Malaysia, the worst case of intra-state malapportionment (by deviation from the state average) is in Johor: 121.66% (N48 Skudai). This is a clear violation of the principle of "approximately equal" apportionment.

In Penang, intra-state malapportionment can be most clearly seen by comparing the largest state constituency, N34 Paya Terubong, and the smallest, N23 Air Putih, which are neighbouring and both urban. Paya Terubong has 41,707 voters, which is more than three times the size of Air Putih's 12,752 voters. N34 Paya Terubong exceeded the average electorate size in Penang (21,694 voters) by 92.25%. Such extreme deviation cannot be justified as "approximately equal".

Another way of thinking about intra-state malapportionment is to calculate by the ratio of the largest constituency to the smallest constituency in the same state. In Selangor, the ratio is 3.94, which means that a vote in the smallest federal constituency (P092 Sabak Bernam) has nearly four times the value of a vote in the largest federal constituency (P109 Kapar) in that same state. In other words, if you vote in P109 Kapar, your vote is worth merely a quarter of a vote compared to a voter in P092 Sabak Bernam.

STATE	2003 Redelineation	2013 Election	2017 Proposed Redelineation
Selangor	3.29	3.86	3.94
Perak	3.22	3.47	3.43
Johor	3.12	2.83	3.17
Pahang	2.25	2.87	2.93
Kedah	2.71	2.54	2.70
Malacca	2.16	2.16	2.44
Kelantan	2.69	2.45	2.42
Sabah	2.43	2.16	2.22
Negeri Sembilan	2.18	2.28	2.18
Penang	1.71	1.65	1.68
Wilayah Persekutuan	1.45	1.65	1.45
Terengganu	1.61	1.49	1.45
Perlis	1.16	1.22	1.20

Table 1: Ratio between largest and smallest federal constituencies in various Malaysian states.

In no fewer than nine states, the ratio of the largest to the smallest federal constituency is more than two. The worst culprits are Selangor, Perak, and Johor. In Perak and Johor, a vote in the smallest federal constituency in each state has *three times* the value of a vote in the largest federal constituency.

This is a clear violation of the constitutional provision that "the number of electors within each constituency in a State ought to be approximately equal". While it is possible to argue that the ratio between the largest and smallest federal constituencies in Perlis (1.20 – see Table 1 above) is within acceptable limits of "approximately equal", the same can't be said when the population of the largest constituency is more than three times the size of the smallest constituency in Johor (3.17), Perak (3.43), and Selangor (3.94).

The Rural Weightage Clause

Approximately equal apportionment is the rule, but one exception is allowed on the basis of area (land mass) where rural disadvantages are a necessary additional condition. Section 2(c) in the Thirteenth Schedule says,

> "...having regard to the greater difficulty of reaching electors in the country districts and the other disadvantages facing rural constituencies, a measure of weightage for area ought to be given to such constituencies,"

Since rural areas are harder to access and their population spread out across a large area, a rural constituency may cover a significantly larger area than an urban constituency in order to have the same number of voters as the urban constituency. However, at some point the constituency may simply get too big to be practical – hence, the rural weightage clause, which grants this exception to permit such a constituency to have fewer voters. The EC, however, has (mis)interpreted this as "rural weightage"—that rural constituencies should have fewer voters in proportion to urban constituencies, merely because they are rural constituencies, thus giving rural votes greater weight.

This clause pertaining to rural districts has been repeatedly used to justify electoral malpractice. If this rule was applied properly, we should expect all constituencies to have approximately the same number of voters, with the exception of the largest rural constituencies, which would have slightly fewer voters. In other words, the only constituencies that rural weightage should be applied to are the absolute largest constituencies. In practice, there is minimal correlation between landmass and electorate size – rural weightage is applied to rural constituencies regardless of size.[4] Some of these constituencies are very small. In Table 2 below, which lists four rural constituencies in Selangor, P094 Hulu Selangor and P113 Sepang have the largest land area amongst the four and yet they have electorate sizes that fall perfectly within the acceptable limits (coloured in yellow; less than 15% deviation from the state average). Yet in the same state, we also see the much smaller P093 Sungai Besar and P092 Sabak Bernam (the state's smallest). If we combined P093 Sungai Besar and P092 Sabak Bernam, we would have a single constituency with 79,959 voters, which would be approximately 85% of the state average but in an area still only 55% the size of P094 Hulu Selangor. There is no basis, therefore, for P092 and P093 to be separate constituencies.

FEDERAL CONSTITUENCIES	Landmass (km²)	Electorate	As Percentage of Average
P094 Hulu Selangor	1,718.40	86,599	91.67%
P113 Sepang	791.34	85,395	90.39%
P093 Sungai Besar	609.26	42,833	45.34%
P092 Sabak Bernam	335.08	37,126	39.30%

Table 2: Comparison of four rural constituencies in Selangor.

This misapplication of rural weightage can also be seen in state constituencies. In Table 3, the three state constituencies of N06 Kuala Kubu Baharu, N05 Ulu Bernam, and N07 Batang Kali, are the largest in Selangor (by land area). If the third largest, N07 Batang Kali, could have an electorate 5% larger than the state average, there is no justification for any of the smaller constituencies to be eligible for rural area weightage. N01 Sungai Air Tawar (the state's smallest constituency) simply cannot be eligible for rural weightage and have less than half the electorate of N07 Batang Kali when the latter has more than twice its landmass.[5]

4 Wong, Chin Huat. "The Election Commission's 2nd Recommendations on Delimitation of Federal and State Constituencies in the State of Selangor (January 15, 2018): A Case of Non-Compliance with Article 113(2) of the Federal Constitution." 2018.

5 Ibid.

RANKING BY AREA	STATE CONSTITUENCIES	Landmass (km²)	Electorate	As Percentage of Average
1	N06 Kuala Kubu Baharu	665.39	26,707	71.96%
2	N05 Ulu Bernam	573.86	20,920	56.37%
3	N07 Batang Kali	479.15	38,972	105.01%
4	N03 Sungai Panjang	367.85	26,725	72.01%
5	N54 Tanjong Sepat	292.68	22,026	59.35%
6	N55 Dengkil	289.32	39,380	106.11%
7	N04 Sekinchan	241.41	16,108	43.40%
8	N56 Sungai Pelek	209.34	23,989	64.64%
9	N01 Sungai Air Tawar	178.75	15,033	40.51%
10	N02 Sabak	156.33	22,093	59.53%

Table 3: Comparison of state constituencies in Selangor by land area.

Likewise, while the rural clause justifies an exception for some rural areas, it does not justify the *under*-representation of urban areas. Thus, Section 2(c) cannot be used to justify excessively large constituencies— of which there are many. Referring back to Figure 2, the excessively large constituencies in Penang (coloured in red—N35 Batu Uban, N37 Batu Maung, N10 Seberang Jaya, N14 Machang Bubok, and N34 Paya Terubong) all deviated from the state average by more than 33.33%. The clause is meant to ensure representation for rural voters and may make exception for a rural constituency small in electorate size but does not justify excessively large urban constituencies. Doing so is amounting to reducing representation for the voters in those areas.

Gerrymandering: manipulation of electorate composition and severance of local ties

2. The following principles shall as far as possible be taken into account in dividing any unit of review into constituencies pursuant to the provisions of Articles 116 and 117 – [...]

(d) regard ought to be had to the inconveniences attendant on alterations of constituencies, and to the maintenance of local ties.

– Clause 2(d) of the Thirteenth Schedule of the Malaysian Constitution

Gerrymandering is a manipulation of electorate *composition* to the advantage of one party. By deliberately arranging the constituency to advantage one party, gerrymandering enables politicians to choose their voters rather than the other way around. This is particularly effective in "First Past The Post" systems, because (as noted above) of the "winner-take-all" nature of the system. The gerrymander only has to redistrict a small number of voters in order to win a seat; do this a few times and you produce a massive swing in the number of seats won. Because the changes can be very small, but the gain from cheating very high, it is very lucrative for parties and politicians to engage in it.

The Constitution's Thirteenth Schedule 2(d) provides safeguards against gerrymandering by specifying that "regard ought to be had to the inconveniences attendant on alterations of constituencies, and to the *maintenance of local ties*." Put simply, a constituency should represent an actual community of common interests, and not an arbitrary collection of citizens.

"Inconveniences" arising from the alteration of constituencies (including those arising specifically from the severing of local ties) can be grouped into three types:

- Type 1: Constituencies unnecessarily cutting across local authority areas, causing municipalities or districts to be fragmented.
- Type 2: Electoral boundaries cutting through and breaking up local communities or neighbourhoods.
- Type 3: Constituencies combining communities with few ties and few common interests.

All three types of gerrymandering fail to adhere to the constitutional stipulation that electoral constituency should as far as possible maintain local ties.

Gerrymandering Type 1 involves constituencies that cross several local authority areas (local council, or Pihak Berkuasa Tempatan, PBT). The map below demonstrates cross-local authority areas in Johor that are constitutionally non-compliant with 2(d) in Thirteenth Schedule of the constitution. State constituencies cut across multiple local authorities' jurisdiction (represented by the colours).

Map 1: State constituencies (represented by the lines) in Johor state which cut across multiple local authority areas (represented by the colours).

In the example above, the state constituency N41 Puteri Wangsa (centre in the map) in the state of Johor incorporates sections of three separate local authorities: Majlis Perbandaran Kulai (Kulai Municipal Council, in red), Majlis Perbandaran Johor Bahru Tengah (Johor Bahru Tengah Municipal Council, in green), and Majlis Bandaraya Johor Bahru (Johor Bahru City Council, in blue).

Constituencies that cut across two or more local authority areas create unnecessary complications that inconvenience both the voters and elected representatives. The voters in the same local authority area are likely to share common interests and live in the same neighbourhood, and form a logical single constituency. A constituency that cuts across multiple local authorities represents an arbitrary combination of communities with distinct interests, and forces the elected representative for the constituency to work with multiple local authorities to solve problems.

Gerrymandering Type 2 involves breaking up communities/neighbourhoods that share common interests and background.

Neighbourhoods are cut up in oddly shaped boundaries and voters living in the same residential area find themselves voting in separate constituencies. To pick one example, the neighbourhoods between the constituencies of N44 Larkin and N45 Stulang (Map 2) found themselves partitioned by a zig-zag boundary drawn by the EC.

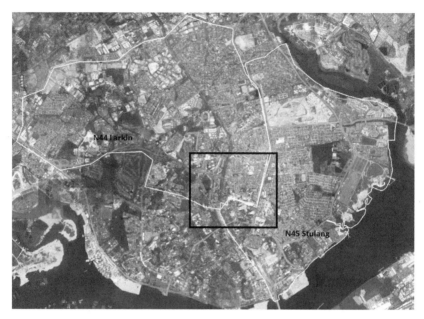

Map 2: Boundary between two state constituencies in Johor state.

Zooming into the highlighted area, Map 3 shows the boundary should have been drawn as a straight line down the highway (Lebuhraya Tebrau). But instead, the EC draws a sharp turn into Jalan Dato Abdullah Tahir, then again at Jalan Dato Sulaiman, creating a zig-zag separating Taman Abad from their neighbouring communities.

Map 3: Closeup of the boundary between two state constituencies in Johor state showing divided communities.

If the EC had drawn the boundary down the highway, the Taman Abad, Yahya Awal, and Wadi Hana communities on the left side of Lebuhraya Tebrau would be grouped into the same constituency, while the Taman Maju Jaya communities on the right side of the highway would be grouped into another constituency. The current proposal puts neighbourhoods on the same side of the highway in two different constituencies, and neighbourhoods on different sides of the highway in one constituency.

Map 4: Arbitrary partitioning of townships of Banting and Jenjarom between three state constituencies.

Another example can be found in Map 4 above. The townships of Bant ing and Jenjarom are arbitrarily partitioned in zig-zag style between N51 Sijangkang, N52 Banting (now renamed Teluk Datuk) and N53 Morib. The arbitrary zig-zags appear to be motivated by gerrymandering. The deliberate movement of voters saw N52 Banting receiving 5,760 elec tors from N53 Morib and 4,804 electors from N51 Sijangkang, who are mostly Chinese and expected to be pro-opposition while 7,365 electors – mostly Malays and expected to be supportive of the ruling regime – are

transferred from N52 Banting to N51 Sijangkang.[6] While three constituencies were previously won by the opposition, these changes result in
the packing of N52 Banting into a super-stronghold for the opposition
party Democratic Action Party (DAP) and cracking of N51 Sijangkang
and N53 Morib to make them more winnable for the United Malays
National Organisation (UMNO).

Gerrymandering Type 3 involves arbitrary grouping of communities
which have minimal common interests into one constituency.

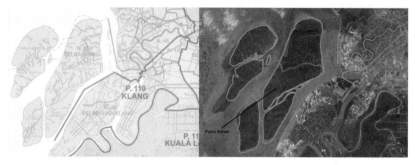

Map 5: Misallocation of Pulau Ketam into N45 Selat Klang instead of N46 Pelabuhan
Klang.

A clear example is Pulau Ketam (highlighted areas in Map 5) in the state
of Selangor. Grouping the Pulau Ketam community with the urban strip
(into N45 Selat Klang) has had serious implications for the electors in
real life. As Pulau Ketam islanders make up only 13% of the state constituency, they complain being neglected by the elected representative
who naturally focuses her energy on the 87% majority on the mainland
which has no social or economic ties and few common interests with
the islanders. This negligence is magnified at the federal level as the
4,770 electors on the islands constitute an even tinier minority, just 3%
in P109 Kapar (146,317 electors), the nation's largest constituency in
terms of number of voters.

The Pulau Ketam community should have been incorporated into
N46 Pelabuhan Klang as its economic and social activities are closely
tied to the maritime township of Port Klang and by extension the

---

6 Wong, Chin Huat. "The Election Commission's 2nd Recommendations on Delimitation of
    Federal and State Constituencies in the State of Selangor (January 15, 2018): A Case of
    Non-Compliance with Article 113(2) of the Federal Constitution." 2018.

Klang town. The EC's failure in making such an intuitive correction preserves non-compliance with the Constitution, defying the purpose of a delimitation review under Article 113(2).

Hidden hands: Exclusion from redelineation and illegal changes

In many cases, extreme malapportionment and gerrymandering of constituencies already exists, and yet is not corrected as the constituencies are excluded from the redelineation exercise i.e. when no changes are proposed. In the current redelineation exercise, not all constituencies will have their boundaries redrawn. Many constituencies have been excluded and will be left untouched.

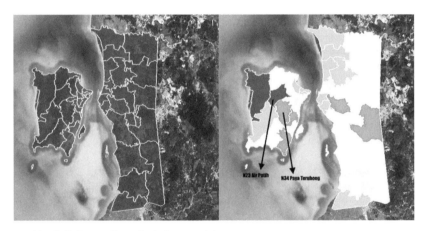

Map 6: State constituencies in Penang state.

On the left, Map 6 shows the state constituencies in Penang which are entirely excluded from the redelineation exercise. No justification for their exclusion has been provided. On the right, Map 6 shows the levels of malapportionment in the same state (the colour-scheme being identical as Figure 2). Given the severity of intra-state malapportionment in Penang, there is no reason why these constituencies should be excluded.

There are two severely over-represented state constituencies (dark green in colour) and five severely under-represented constituencies (red in colour). Their exclusion from the redelineation exercise is baffling because the existing malapportionment is severe. The Election Commission is failing to perform its duty, as mandated by the Constitution, to redelineate to correct extreme malapportionment.

Logically, N34 Paya Terubong (red, centre of Penang Island) should have ceded some of its voters to N23 Air Putih (dark green, directly on top of N34 Paya Terubong). Since the former is excessively large, the latter excessively small, and they are next to each other, it is a straightforward change. This failure to correct an obvious violation of the constitutional principle laid out in the Thirteenth Schedule is unconstitutional. The Election Commission fails its duty by excluding these constituencies from the redelineation review.

This is not an exception. The exclusion of constituencies is widespread. At least 96 federal constituencies and 246 state constituencies are excluded from the redelineation proposed by the EC, thus sustaining pre-existing malapportionment and gerrymandering and defeating the purpose of the redelineation exercise.

STATE	FEDERAL CONSTITUENCIES				STATE CONSTITUENCIES			
	EXCLUDED	REVERSED	INCLUDED	TOTAL	EXCLUDED	REVERSED	INCLUDED	TOTAL
Perlis	100%	0%	0%	100%	100%	0%	0%	100%
Kedah	66.67%	0%	33.33%	100%	63.89%	0%	36.11%	100%
Kelantan	42.86%	7.14%	50%	100%	33.33%	20%	46.67%	100%
Terengganu	37.5%	37.5%	25%	100%	34.38%	40.63%	25%	100%
Penang	100%	0%	0%	100%	100%	0%	0%	100%
Perak	41.67%	12.5%	45.83%	100%	40.68%	10.17%	49.15%	100%
Pahang	71.43%	28.57%	0%	100%	69.05%	19.05%	11.9%	100%
Selangor	22.73%	54.55%	22.73%	100%	17.86%	55.36%	26.79%	100%
Kuala Lumpur	0%	18.18%	81.82%	100%				
Negeri Sembilan	50%	25%	25%	100%	61.11%	0%	38.89%	100%
Malacca	50%	33.33%	16.67%	100%	32.14%	21.43%	46.43%	100%
Johor	42.31%	3.85%	53.85%	100%	26.79%	17.86%	55.36%	100%
Sabah	72%	16%	12%	100%	45.21%	9.59%	45.21%	100%

Table 4: Exclusion of constituencies up to 2nd Recommendations. "Excluded" refers to the constituencies that are excluded from the redelineation exercise (no changes proposed), "Reversed" refers to constituencies with changes proposed in the 1st Recommendations but reversed in the 2nd Recommendations (changes are cancelled, so ultimately no changes proposed), and "Included" refers to constituencies which are included in the redelineation exercise.

The exclusion viewed in terms of actual number of voters that are moved is even more dramatic. In the state of Selangor, despite significant malapportionment and gerrymandering in the existing constituency boundaries, only about 2% of voters will actually be moved in the redelineation proposal.[7]

	PARLIAMENTARY	STATE
Affected Constituencies	5	15
Total Constituencies	22	56
% of Consituencies	**22.73%**	**26.79%**
Affected Electors	3,962	36,433
Total Electorate	2,078,311	2,078,311
% of Electorate	**0.19%**	**1.75%**

Table 5: Number of voters that are actually moved in the state of Selangor after the 2nd Recommendations proposed by the Election Commission.

But does the EC really not change the boundaries of these excluded constituencies? Shockingly, unconstitutional pre-delineation changes (changes which are not part of the redelineation exercise) are also being made to polling district and electoral boundaries!

N37 BATU MAUNG

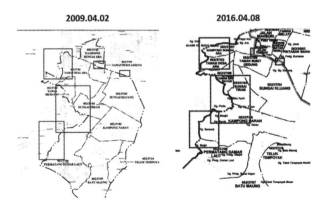

Map 7: Boundaries of N37 Batu Maung state constituency in Penang state.

7 Wong Chin Huat. "Why 98pct of S'gor voters untouched by redelineation?". Malaysiakini. 28 February 2018.

Map 7 shows that the boundaries of a state constituency in Penang, N37 Batu Maung. The boundaries are demonstrably different between the years 2009 and 2016, despite the Election Commission's exclusion of N37 Batu Maung from the redelineation exercise. The only explanation is that the changes were discreetly made by the EC *prior* to the commencement of the redelineation exercise. An estimated 96% of Federal Constituencies in Perak, 77% in Johor, and 69% in Penang are affected.[8] These pre-delineation changes effectively render the redelineation exercise meaningless as most changes were introduced before redelineation. More importantly, because they are not done in accordance with the procedure for changing electoral boundaries spelled out in the constitution, any pre-delineation exercise changes are therefore unconstitutional and illegal.

Another sneaky change made by the EC is the breakup of polling districts. This was done during the redelineation exercise but is no less illegal. The Election Commission is empowered to alter the division of a constituency into polling districts under the Election Act 1958. The Election Commission may *move* polling districts into different constituencies, but they do not have the power to *divide* one polling district into two polling districts scattered across two constituencies. Additionally, the EC must use the same electoral roll throughout the redelineation process. By altering polling district in the delineation process, the EC has directly violated Section 3 of the Thirteenth Schedule which reads, "For the purposes of this part, the number of electors *shall be taken to be as shown on the current electoral rolls*".

N. 24 TANJUNG DUMPIL	1. Muhibbah	3,431
	2. Pasir Putih	3,774
	3. Lok Kawi	4,574
	4. Taman Pantai Lok Kawi	1,291
		13,070

Figure 3: Polling district Lok Kawi in September 2016 when the EC publicized the 1st Recommendations.

8 Wong, Chin Huat. "Unconstitutional Pre-redelineation Changes Exposed". Briefing for diplomatic community. 6th July 2017.

N.24 TANJUNG KERAMAT	1.	Muhibbah	3,431
	2.	Pasir Putih	3,774
	3.	Lok Kawi	3,550
	4.	Taman Pantai Lok Kawi	1,291
			12,046

Figure 4: Polling district Lok Kawi in March 2017 when the EC publicized the 2nd Recommendations.

In Sabah, the number of voters in the polling district named Lok Kawi under the state constituency N24 Tanjung Keramat (previously named N24 Tanjung Dumpil) is noticeably different. It was split from 4,574 voters into 3,550. The difference (1,024) was transferred to another state constituency, N23 Petagas. In N23, two polling districts (Sailan and Putatan) were renamed and reconfigured with the additional 1,024 voters from N24 to become three new polling districts. This is procedurally wrong but also has real consequences for the voters. The original 4,574 voters would not know which constituency they would be in (one of the 3,550 who stay put, or one of the 1,024 who were moved) because there are no new polling district maps to inform them—new polling district maps are normally issued alongside new electoral rolls. In any event, the EC must use the same electoral roll throughout the entire redelineation exercise. When they break up a polling district, they have altered the electoral roll, thereby making the redelineation exercise unconstitutional as per Section 3 of the Thirteenth Schedule.

Conclusion: Demand reforms to the electoral system

The redelineation proposed by the EC severely violates the provisions contained in the Thirteenth Schedule of Malaysia's Constitution. Consequently, the entire redelineation exercise is unconstitutional. Worst, the outcome of GE14 will certainly not be genuinely representative of the Malaysian people.

As things stand, the legal avenues to challenge the redelineation exercise have almost been exhausted. Multiple legal challenges by the Selangor state government, Penang state government, and members of the public have been unsuccessful.[9] Activists and a former senior judge expressed disappointment over the Federal Court's ruling.[10] The EC rushed to submit the final recommendation to the Prime Minister, who will table it in Parliament very soon.

Electoral watchdog Bersih 2.0 has called for a Royal Commission of Inquiry (RCI) on the electoral system.[11] The RCI can investigate and propose reforms to the electoral system, promote vote-seat proportionality and political inclusion of all communities and segments in Malaysia, and reform the Election Commission. *delay by being evasive*

The ruling Barisan Nasional has stonewalled Bersih 2.0's demand for free and fair election. The best hope for implementing this RCI is the opposition coalition, Pakatan Harapan, led by former Prime Minister Mahathir Mohamad. The coalition's recently launched election manifesto is promising, with institutional reforms on the cards, but stopped short of pledging electoral reform and local election.

With recent court decisions rendering objections to the proposed redelineation all but moot now, existing malapportionment and gerrymandering will not be corrected. It will be at least eight more years till the next redelineation exercise. If the next incoming government is serious in cleaning up malapportionment and gerrymandering, proper diagnosis of and reforms to the electoral system are necessary. The RCI, which can be immediately convened, is a big step forward to that direction.

Good, honest governance requires genuine accountability from our elected politicians. Accountability requires free and fair elections. Free and fair elections can only happen in the absence of malapportionment and gerrymandering, with redelineation carried out in accordance with the constitution and in obedience with the law. For reforms to happen, it is paramount for the Malaysian people and interest groups to demand electoral system reforms and exert influence on politicians to act and put electoral system reform on their agenda.

9 See for example, http://www.freemalaysiatoday.com/category/nation/2018/03/09/selangor-govt-once-again-fails-in-challenge-against-ec/and http://www.themalaymailonline.com/malaysia/article/ec-federal-courts-decision-proves-redelineation-exercise-constitutional.

10 http://www.freemalaysiatoday.com/category/nation/2018/02/20/ex-judge-court-not-using-power-it-has-over-ec/

11 http://www.themalaymailonline.com/malaysia/article/bersih-2.0-political-parties-must-push-for-rci-on-poll-reforms

"I NO LONGER LOOK BACK"

JULES RAHMAN ONG | 01 MAY 2018

Often perceived as little more than a seat–warmer for her husband Anwar Ibrahim, the male–dominated Malaysian political scene tends to overlook Wan Azizah Wan Ismail as an accomplished politician in her own right.

Wan Azizah Wan Ismail arrives late for our appointment; it'd been a strenuous day in Parliament debating against a crucial motion on electoral redelineation. She apologises, but still makes sure not to miss her afternoon Asar prayer. Immaculately dressed in a neat light-coloured headscarf and baju kurung, Wan Azizah is a perfect picture of Muslim piety, modesty and moderation.

The good doctor has sandwiched our appointment between her parliamentary duties as Leader of the Opposition to object to a motion hastily pushed through by the ruling party—a common occurrence in Malaysian politics—visiting her husband, former opposition leader Anwar Ibrahim. He's currently in jail on a sodomy charge that many believe was politically motivated to prevent him from contesting in the coming elections. The authorities have said that Anwar will be released from prison on 8 June 2018.[1]

On the day of our meeting, Anwar's recuperating in hospital from a shoulder operation; a blessing in disguise, as the hospitalisation allows him daily family visits instead of the once-a-month permitted prison visit, separated by a thick pane of glass with no physical contact, that the family has endured since 2015. The pleasure is visible on his wife's face.

But there's bad news, too. That afternoon, the highly-criticised motion on electoral redelineation[2] was bulldozed through with a simple majority. Many see the redrawing of the boundaries as a case of blatant

---

1 https://www.straitstimes.com/asia/se-asia/
malaysian-opposition-leader-anwar-ibrahim-to-be-released-on-june-8

2 https://newnaratif.com/research/malaysias-election-rigged/

gerrymandering to benefit the incumbent coalition, Barisan Nasional, in the coming elections to be held on 9 May.

"It's to be expected… But it still hits me hard when it happens, that our country's democracy has come to this. This erosion of democracy," Wan Azizah laments.

Ignoring the way in which different ethnic communities live in close proximity in Malaysia, the electoral boundaries had been redrawn in such a way that the ethnic Malays are almost neatly divided from the ethnic Chinese populace, possibly based on an assumption that Malays are more likely to support the Malay-dominant government while the Chinese lean towards the opposition. It relegates opposition constituents to super large constituencies—in some places, these constituencies are 10 times larger, in terms of the number of voters, than pro-Barisan areas. It's an oft-used strategy to exploit the weakness inherent in a first-past-the-post electoral system, ignoring the popular vote in favour of representation in Parliament.

"This is among many of the ways Barisan puts us at a disadvantage. But it has never been so blatant," says Wan Azizah. Fellow opposition veteran leader Lim Kit Siang of the Democratic Action Party was suspended from Parliament following a heated debate during which he questioned the embargoing of the motion until the eleventh hour, thus losing another critical vote.

The skewed playing field

The United Malays National Organisation, more commonly known as UMNO, has ruled Malaysia with its coalition partners under the umbrella name of Barisan Nasional since the country gained independence from the British in 1957, making it the world's longest-ruling coalition. Its unbeatable record is thanks to a combination of strict controls over the media and civil liberties, elections plagued by allegations of vote-rigging and corruption and compromised public institutions. According to the Freedom House's Freedom in the World report, Malaysia is described as only "partly free", with an aggregate score of 45 out of 100.

In the last few years, the government under Prime Minister Najib Razak has been embroiled in a massive corruption scandal described by US Attorney General Jeff Sessions as "kleptocracy at its worst." Sessions revealed that nearly half of all the corruption proceeds seized by the US government is related to 1Malaysia Development Berhad (1MDB), a government investment fund spearheaded by Najib. Funds raised by 1MDB and guaranteed by the Malaysian government have allegedly been used to finance lavish spending sprees ranging from expensive artworks, jewelries, real estate, a luxury yacht and two Hollywood movies. Red Granite Pictures—whose CEO Riza Aziz is Najib's stepson—agreed in March to make a forfeiture payment of USD60 million to resolve legal action taken in relation to its role in the 1MDB scandal.[3]

With such a high-profile scandal hogging headlines, Najib is doing all he can to maintain power. According to some observers, this election is nothing more than a desperate bid for a third term to avoid potential arrest.

The electoral redelineation isn't the only piece of legislation that Najib's government has hurriedly bulldozed through Parliament. The Anti-Fake News Bill was passed in early April, just a week after it was first tabled. It was then gazetted as the Anti-Fake News Act on 11 April, ensuring that it'll be in effect during the election campaigning period. The broadly-worded law gives the government the power to determine what is or isn't "fake news", triggering fears that the law will be used to muzzle opponents and silent dissent.

But despite such unequal grounds of contest, Wan Azizah still believes that change is at hand. "I am optimistic. I have to be. Anwar's incorrigible optimism has rubbed off me," she says. "We never expected Congress in India and Golkar in Indonesia to fall. I never thought they [would] fall, but they did. So give us time for change. The PM [Najib Razak] has an expiry date."

A baptism of fire

Time is something Wan Azizah is accustomed to. She was thrust into the political limelight twenty years ago when Anwar Ibrahim was sacked as Deputy Prime Minister and jailed on a corruption charge relating to sodomy which many believed was politically motivated. Anwar's political differences with then-Prime Minister Dr Mahathir Mohamad had come to a head during the Asian financial crisis in 1998.

Anwar was arrested at his home in the night of 20 September 1998. It was an overly dramatic display of force: balaclava-clad special forces stormed the family home, pointing automatic machine guns at unarmed

3 https://www.thestar.com.my/news/nation/2018/03/07/
wolf-of-wall-street-producer-to-pay-us60mil-in-1mdb-case/

civilians consisting of Wan Azizah, their children, relatives, friends and supporters.

That night still haunts her and had a lasting effect on her youngest daughter, Nurul Hana, who was only five at the time. Wan Azizah recounts the traumatic events in her memoirs: "They stormed our house during Isya [night time prayers] pointing their sub-machine guns. It was so tense, uncalled for and inhumane. There were children, relatives and our supporters at that time. My husband, father of my children, was dragged [out] in a humiliating and frightening way in front of his children."[4]

During the six years Anwar Ibrahim was imprisoned, Wan Azizah, who never had any political ambitions, stepped up to lead the fledgling Reformasi movement started by her husband. The movement later evolved into the only viable opposition coalition to challenge Malaysia's one-party system. Her strength, she says, was derived from her personal tragedy and her faith in God.

"I steeled my heart, strengthened my spirit. Because I know, if I fail, my children will fail. Perhaps, my husband will not make it. Only my prayers and surrender to Allah with the effort I put in," she wrote in the memoirs published on her blog.

Anwar Ibrahim has spent a total of nine years in jail and is regarded as a prisoner of conscience by Amnesty International. The personal anguish suffered by Wan Azizah and her family was transformed into a movement to free Anwar, giving ammunition to the Reformasi movement to fight against the tyranny of Mahathir Mohamad, Malaysia's longest-serving Prime Minister.

Today, the efforts of Wan Azizah and her supporters have undergone a subtle transformation, coalescing into a movement for justice to free the country from a system of governance that breeds corruption, symbolised by Prime Minister Najib Razak. But a greater change has occurred, one widely described as a potential game-changer as Malaysia heads to the polls.

The Mahathir drama

A controversial leader, Mahathir was credited as the architect of Malaysia's economic power. Among his local detractors, he was known as "Mahafiraun" (The Great Pharoah) and "Mahazalim" (The Great

Evil One)—in short, a dictator with no tolerance for dissent. Now, in a tale of karmic retribution, the 92-year old, horrified by Najib's alleged corruption, has come out of retirement to contest in the 14th general election against not just the party that brought him to power, but against the man he hand-picked to be prime minister. And he's doing it in Wan Azizah's Parti Keadilan Rakyat (PKR) colours.

Campaign posters of Wan Azizah and Mahathir, both medical doctors-turned-politicians, standing side-by-side leading the opposition coalition Pakatan Harapan (Alliance of Hope) in a bid to oust Najib Razak is a sight to behold, and a great irony not lost on both supporters and detractors.

"Can a leopard change its spots?" asked *The Economist* after Mahathir's appearance in court as Anwar stood trial for another sodomy charge. The two men shook hands. It had been 18 years since they'd last met; back then, Mahathir had been the prime minister and Anwar the out-of-favour former deputy prime minister facing his first sodomy charge.

I ask Wan Azizah if she's really able to forgive the man who had caused so much pain to her family. "He came to us. Mahathir. We did not seek him out," she replies. "It was hard for many, some are victims of Mahathir. But Anwar thinks more of the future. He doesn't hold any grudge. That is his strength."

It was because of her husband that she was able to forgive the former prime minister. "It was difficult for us initially. Me and my children were more wary of his move," admits Wan Azizah. But she overcame that personal grudge because she believes that Mahathir has had "time to experience what we went through." And the people—the *rakyat*— and the future of the country should come before her own personal feelings, she says.

The ice melted when Mahathir's wife, Siti Hasmah, paid a visit. Meeting after 18 years was an emotional experience for the two women; turning a strategic public relations event into a genuine reconciliation. The tearful meeting became a hot topic for the Malaysian electorate, garnering thousands of 'likes' on social media.

That public portrayal, as well as its response, points to a difference in framing when it comes to gender and politics: while men are occupied with forging strategic partnerships, women are shown to connect for heart-to-heart gatherings. Such a depiction obscures the fact that

Wan Azizah is not just a politician's spouse, but a prominent figure in Malaysian politics in her own right.

Despite having led the opposition for many years, Wan Azizah has stepped aside to field Mahathir as the candidate for the premiership, while she stands as deputy. In the event of a Pakatan Harapan triumph, the plan is to seek a royal pardon for Anwar Ibrahim; Mahathir will then vacate his seat for his former deputy. Wan Azizah's non-committal when asked if she's ready to be the first female prime minister of Malaysia, should the occasion arise: "Perhaps Malaysia is not ready for a woman prime minister, but a deputy, yes."

Early years

The potential to be the first female deputy prime minister of Malaysia didn't figure into Wan Azizah's aspirations growing up. Born in Singapore in 1952, Wan Azizah received her early education in a convent school in Alor Setar. She went on to study medicine at the Royal College of Surgeons in Ireland, where, in 1978, she became the first Malay to be awarded the MacNaughton-Jones Gold Medal—an award endowed by Irish otologist, gynaecologist and ophthalmologistHenry MacNaughton-Jones for the student who scores the highest marks in obstetrics and gynaecology in his or her qualifying year. She went on to serve as a government doctor for 14 years.

Wan Azizah credits her father as her inspiration to serve in public hospitals: "We were raised with the message that life is to be shared with the people, and to contribute as much as we can [with] society. This was the principle that was cultivated in me and my siblings."

Her father, who had served for 30 years as a government intelligence operative, initially opposed her choice of husband, regarding Anwar Ibrahim as a "troublemaker" student activist who had spent time in jail for demonstrating against rural poverty. She married him anyway; at that time, none of them could have known of the rollercoaster ride that was to come.

Unwillingly thrust into the rough and tumble of political life, the mother of six has since been a politician longer than she's been a doctor. "I was a good doctor," she says. "But I would say I have done rather well as a politician, I have no regrets."

Kak Wan the Politician

Despite her stellar academic background and long years in politics, many people still see Wan Azizah as a seat-warmer for her husband. Even her campaign for justice has always been linked to justice for Anwar. It's obscured her position as a politician in her own right, relegating her political achievements to merely being Anwar's wife and representative, holding the fort in his absence.

Some observers say she isn't outspoken enough to make an impression. "She appears to be always in the shadow of Anwar. She is not vocal. We don't hear her much, her personal statement or her principles and vision. Does she always wait for the party statement?" says Dr Ruhana Padzil, a gender and politics lecturer at the University of Malaya.

Politics in Asia has long been seen as a masculine vocation; many of the female Asian political leaders have inherited the legacy from powerful male family members. Wan Azizah is no different in this respect, but it's still hard to compare her to the likes of Corazon Aquino, Benazir Bhutto or Aung San Suu Kyi, who have fired the imagination of their people.

"Corazon was also a housewife," Ruhana points out, adding it didn't stop the Filipina from making her voice heard and leading the People Power Revolution to topple the dictator Ferdinand Marcos.

But while one can argue that leaders are molded by circumstances, realpolitik is often seen as aggressive and masculine. How can a woman navigate these gender traps and still be seen as a politician in her own right? Will she always be judged by whether she's too masculine or too feminine, rather than be measured by her own abilities? Do women need to be attached to their husbands or fathers in order to be recognised in politics?

These are questions that needs to be asked and in answering them, Wan Azizah's "failure" to live up to the model of an aggressive or dominant politician is perhaps as much a critique of the masculine political culture she belongs to.

"Dr Wan Azizah has a subtleness as a person in which I find positive in order to bring new dimension in the culture of doing and engaging in politics. I wish she can do more to bring a more nurturing and sustaining culture of politics as the leader of opposition," says a social political observer who asked to remain anonymous.

"Perhaps men need to explore this side more, so this too may change the culture of politics. I believe this is what politics is about, creating and engaging in politics," she adds.

To her credit, Wan Azizah has an excellent election record, be it a parliamentary seat or a state seat. She stood as a candidate in the Permatang Pauh constituency in the 1999, 2004, 2008 and 2013 general elections—she won every time. She voluntarily stepped down from the seat in July 2008 to trigger a by-election so that her husband could contest the seat, in a bid to return to parliament. She returned to contest the seat in 2015 after her husband was forced to relinquish the seat after his second sodomy conviction, winning it by over 8,800 votes.

Despite criticism of her perceived passivity, Wan Azizah has participated in every facet of political life as a party leader and a member of Parliament. She's spoken at the local and international level, campaigning and rallying the people, being active in Parliamentary debates and attending to her constituents. She has also been the Vice-Chair of the Malaysian Parliamentary Caucus for Democracy in Myanmar and a member of the ASEAN Inter-Parliamentary Myanmar Caucus. And she's achieved all this without stooping to the mudslinging that's common in Malaysian politics.

Wan Azizah has also led her party through some challenging times, particularly in the run up to this year's elections. Amid speculations of competing factions breaking out within the party over the candidate list just weeks away from the elections, Wan Azizah told reporters: "There is only one camp, my camp."[5] As an politician better known for comments about consensus and cooperation, the assertion of "my camp" was an uncharacteristically strong position—and provided a meatier soundbite for the press.

Holding the party together over the last two decades—neutralising internal power struggles and fending off competitors to maintain the top post for her husband—is perhaps the best demonstration of Wan Azizah's strength and ability.

"Yes, politics is masculine. But there are many ways to skin a cat. I don't have to shout. I don't have that oratory skill, I wished I had. But [the party sees] me as a mother figure. Everything we do is by consensus and they accept me," she says. She often credits the respect, support and consensus of her party members and coalition partners for her successes.

---

5 https://www.thestar.com.my/news/nation/2018/04/24/
wan-azizah-there-is-only-one-camp-in-pkr-my-camp/

Her image as a steadfast wife and motherly figure can sometimes also act as a coat of armour, shielding her from the concocted scandals or serious political attacks suffered by other opposition politicians. It's a protective perception that perhaps also extends to her daughter, Nurul Izzah, vice-president of PKR.

When Nurul Izzah was arrested for sedition for questioning the judiciary over Anwar's conviction during a 2015 speech in Parliament, many Malaysians were outraged by what they regarded as a low blow.[6] Even some UMNO members expressed their displeasure. Nurul Izzah was released after a night at a police lock-up.

"In the same way, if anyone tries to hurt Wan Azizah, Malaysians will rise up. She is too nice to be harmed," opines Dr Ruhana.

As a politician, Wan Azizah is less divisive than her husband, appealing to the ordinary men and women on the street. Known by her supporters as Kak Wan (Sister Wan), she has won admirers among the citizenry for her humbleness and gentleness. Snapshots of her grocery shopping in Tesco or taking public transport are often shared on social media, comparing her humility with the excesses of the prime minister's wife, who often flaunts pricey Birkin handbags, expensive jewellery and extravagant holidays abroad, even while her husband is embroiled in a major corruption scandal.

Women in politics

Interestingly, Wan Azizah has never been seen as a vocal proponent for women in politics. Almost treated as the token woman leader in Malaysian politics, her presence in the scene is never played up as anything special. Despite her husband's seemingly never-ending controversy, she herself appears to have largely avoided sensational headlines, attracting neither effusive praise nor vitriolic animosity. After twenty years in opposition politics, she's still widely seen as a gentle, motherly figure.

But one of her coalition's election promises aligns with a feminist struggle to recognise housework—often assumed to fall under a woman's responsibility in the household—as legitimate work. It's the first time in Malaysian history that any election manifesto contains a promise to provide housewives with social security under the Employer Providence Fund (EPF) system. Under this proposal, husbands will contribute 2% of their earnings into their wives' EPF accounts, while the federal

6 https://www.thestar.com.my/news/nation/2015/03/16/nurul-izzah-arrested-sedition-act/

government contributes RM50 (USD16.50) a month. It's based on the principle that homemakers should be compensated for their work—and therefore not left financially vulnerable in their old age— but some husbands are already grumbling. As one male Barisan minister asked: "So does it mean wives are working for their husbands?"

"We are offering this scheme in our manifesto as we see many cases of single mothers having to fend for their children after their husbands left the family," Wan Azizah explains in one of her campaign speeches. She herself was left with six children to fend for when Anwar was dragged to jail. Wan Azizah and Siti Hasmah, Mahathir's wife, are now campaigning to get Malaysian women to vote—an effort that hasn't garnered major media attention.

Wan Azizah might not be able to match her husband's oratory skills, or project herself as a political firebrand, but she's upheld the vision of a progressive multi-racial, multi-religious society based on religious moderation. She's also been a role model to her eldest daughter, Nurul Izzah, herself a prominent figure in Malaysian politics.

"I learned patience from her. She is very simple and heartfelt," says Nurul Izzah. "Being sincere is a rare commodity nowadays. They [party members, but also average Malaysians] see her as a figurehead, she cares about the right thing. The usual politician could be blasé and a turn off to others. So I think that could be part of her strength."

Not just a politician's wife

Wan Azizah has made no secret of the fact that everything she's done in politics has been for her husband's sake. But in doing it for Anwar, she's convinced that she's also doing it for the good of the nation, she writes in her memoirs.

"My fate is that I have a husband who is involved in everything that is called politics. As a Muslim wife, I strive to be an exemplary wife and a good mother," she writes in her memoirs. "I have gifted my whole body and soul to my husband for his struggle without regrets. Because I realise his struggle is not for himself, nor only for our family. It is clear, ever since I met him to this moment, his struggle was for the people and the country. That philosophy of his has never changed."

But she also makes clear that this outlook—the drive to be a devoted Muslim wife and mother—should not be mistaken for passivity or submission: "As days go on, I no longer look back for even a second. I realised that I am no longer an opthamologist, and I am aware I am not a wife to a husband who has a ministerial post. And I am not only a mother to my children. I am now a politician who brings the ideology of universal justice that so it may be celebrated [in] this land."

In many ways, it's astonishing that Wan Azizah has lasted as long as she has in the ruthless arena that is Malaysian politics—one need only look at her family's experience to see how difficult it can be to challenge the powerful. And she hasn't simply clung on; she's also led a fledgling movement to become the strongest challenge to the political status quo in Malaysia's independent history. Only time will tell if she succeeds in her mission.

A MAHATHIR EFFECT?

PATRICK BEECH | 07 MAY 2018

As 9 May approaches, the Barisan Nasional government is faced with the possibility of being uprooted by their own former leader, Mahathir Mohamad. But can Mahathir (and his new image as Malaysia's grandfatherly champion) actually drive BN out of Putrajaya?

For once in 61 years of ruling Malaysia, the incumbent coalition Barisan Nasional (BN) is feeling the fear. And the threat is coming from an unlikely source: their own former strongman.

A larger-than-life figure in Malaysian politics, Mahathir Mohamad, now 92, has emerged from retirement and entered the fray once more. In 2017, he registered a new political party, Parti Pribumi Bersatu Malaysia (PPBM), adding it to the opposition Pakatan Harapan coalition. Years ago, no one could have predicted such a turnaround. Now, BN, shrouded in allegations of corruption and abuse of power, quakes in anticipation of going head-to-head with their former leader at the polls on 9 May 2018.

A veteran's ability... and about face

A former die-hard member of the United Malays National Organisation (UMNO)—the largest party in the BN coalition—Mahathir has a political career spanning over seven decades, two of which were spent as the Malaysian prime minister. A master strategist when it came to elections, he's well-versed in every trick of the trade, and had continued to play a role in Malaysian politics even after he stepped down from the premiership in 2003. In fact, he was very much involved in current Prime Minister Najib Razak's rise to power.

Back then, Mahathir had been confident in Najib's leadership qualities, believing that his protege was well-suited to continue the policies and programmes implemented during Mahathir's own tenure. But expectation turned to disappointment and horror as Najib got entangled in a web of corruption scandals, namely related to state investment fund 1Malaysia Development Berhad (1MDB).

Mahathir has now joined forces with his former enemies in an attempt to overthrow Najib; an astonishing crossing of the aisle that's been met with a range of reactions running the gamut from jubilation to disbelief and scepticism. Mahathir has, unsurprisingly, been ridiculed by his former comrades in BN for throwing his lot in with Anwar, a former deputy he'd previously fallen out with. Anwar is currently in prison following his second sodomy conviction—his first conviction is widely believed to also have been politically motivated… with Mahathir himself pulling the strings.

There have also been serious doubts over the sincerity of Mahathir's political comeback; it was rumoured that he's only doing it to ensure the political future of his son, Mukhriz Mahathir, the former Chief Minister of Kedah. Frustration at the opposition's willingness to join hands with their former nemesis led to an online campaign—#UndiRosak, meaning "spoil your vote"—urging people to spoil their votes in protest of the lack of meaningful political change.[1]

Despite this, Mahathir is still seen as a game-changer as polling day approaches.

Memories of better days

There were also allegations of abuse and corruption during Mahathir's tenure as prime minister, but many Malaysians, especially those above the age of 40, might think back on those years as the "good old days" compared to where Malaysia is now.

During Mahathir's tenure, Malaysia grew from a near developing country status to the world's 13th largest economy. When Mahathir became prime minister in 1981, the country's gross national income per capita was at USD1,930; by the time he stepped down in 2003, it had increased to USD4,160.[2]

Things have not been as rosy in recent years under Najib's administration. Although the gross national income per capita had continued to rise after Mahathir's premiership, it dropped sharply from USD11,010 in 2014 to USD9,860 in 2016. The 1MDB scandal has been blamed as a contributing factor to the Malaysian ringgit's drop in value.

While Mahathir waived personal income tax for Malaysian wage-earners during the economic downturn of 1997–1998, the Najib

1 https://newnaratif.com/journalism/whats-young-voters-malaysia/

2 https://data.worldbank.org/indicator/NY.GNP.PCAP.CD?locations=MY&view=chart

administration has triggered unhappiness by imposing additional taxes—like the highly-controversial Goods and Services Tax—and cutting back on subsidies for necessities like fuel at a time when citizens are already struggling with the cost of living.

Furthermore, none of the allegations of misbehaviour in the Mahathir years approached the scale of the 1MDB scandal that has engulfed Najib. Siti Hasmah, Mathahir's wife, has also been favourably compared to the deeply unpopular Rosman Mansor, wife of the current premier.

Mahathir isn't the only former UMNO leader to have switched sides: he's strongly backed by Muhyiddin Yassin and Shafie Apdal, the former deputy president and vice-president of UMNO respectively. Together, this trio have boosted an opposition, giving it a strong chance of toppling the BN regime.

An image makeover

But the fact remains that Mahathir was not a democratic leader during his time in power. While prime minister, he had eroded democratic processes, cracked down on political opponents and imposed constraints on the press. Certain segments of the Malaysian electorate have thus found it difficult to embrace him as the country's champion for regime change. Aware of this scepticism, the opposition has been quick to emphasise that Mahathir is not the dictator he once was.

According Nurul Izzah, vice-president of Parti Keadilan Rakyat (PKR), Mahathir is a changed man, with a totally different style of politics from his time in UMNO. "We have put the past behind us. Our objective is the same now... to work together for the betterment of the people," she says. "The people are suffering with the increasing costs of living, while the GST is just too much to bear for most. The government is riddled with scandals and allegations of abuse. This is why we need all the help we can get to put things right."

"[F]or the man on the street, Najib cannot be an option anymore. The people are suffering and the country is so deep in debt. We never had any of this during Mahathir's time," argues PKR vice-president Xavier Jayakumar. "He may have had an iron grip on BN, but what is important is that the people never suffered during his time. Mahathir could have just been quiet and enjoyed his retirement, but he is back for the sake of the people and country."

The narrative is further backed up by heartwarming collaterals, such as a recent short film in which Mahathir chats to young Malay children about his decision to get involved in politics once more in his old age.

"I am already old. I am past 90. I don't have much time left. But within my means, I will try my very best to work together with all my friends to rebuild our nation—Malaysia," he tells the two young characters. It's as significant makeover of his public image: once the uncompromising strongman, now the grandfatherly champion of the nation.

Regime change?

A recent survey by the Selangor-based think tank Institut Darul Ehsan found that 61% of 4,920 respondents chose Mahathir as their preferred candidate for prime minister in the upcoming 14th general election, while 39% felt that Najib should remain in the top job.

But even with a heavyweight like Mahathir on board, wresting power from the incumbent will not be easy. Some still believe that Malaysia will be better off under BN. "Najib has done his fair share for the country. And besides, chances for a Pakatan Harapan victory are slim, considering there will no longer be straight fights in most constituencies and voter sentiment would work to the advantage of BN," says Sivamurugan Pandian, a professor of political sociology at the Universiti Sains Malaysia.

Political analyst Jeniri Amir shares these sentiments, adding that voter perception and opinion of the government has steadily improved because of BN's commitment to solving bread-and-butter problems like housing, education, employment and the cost of living.

"Despite the presence of Mahathir, I strongly believe Najib will lead the BN to a comfortable win this time. Compared with the last few years, the BN and Najib are now in a more solid position to be re-elected," he says.

According to Datuk Seri Ti Lian Ker, spokesman for the MCA, the main factor behind the upcoming election will be the Malay voters from rural areas, usually seen as long-time BN supporters. "This is in fact the main reason why Mahathir was roped in. The opposition are hoping for a Malay tsunami from these voters. However, even if there is such a thing, it would strongly favour PAS [the Malaysian Islamic Party] and not Pakatan Harapan. We, in the BN are confident the Malay rural voters will not be taken in by Mahathir," he says.

282 New Naratif: The First Year

Despite this professed confidence, the incumbent is still resorting to all kinds of tactics to counter any potential "Mahathir effect". Despite widespread criticism, the redelineation of the electoral boundaries was pushed through Parliament, heavily skewing the playing field.[3] The introduction of the Anti-Fake News Act—bulldozed through Parliament in a week—has also been seen as an attempt by the ruling coalition to maintain control of the narrative and disincentive dissent.

Giving out gifts and stacks of money during elections is nothing new for the BN and despite the clampdown on news, numerous videos showing BN leaders openly handing out money to voters have gone viral online.[4] In the last few weeks, Najib and his deputy Ahmad Zahid Hamidi have announced a host of goodies, including pay rises, housing and promotions for civil servants, the police and armed forces.

In some constituencies, opposition candidates have been told that their billboards will have to be taken down and the image of Mahathir—Pakatan Harapan's candidate for prime minister—removed, in accordance with new rules[5] regarding election campaign materials. The opposition candidate in Ayer Hitam had to watch on 30 April as officers from the Election Commission cut Mahathir's image out of his billboard[6], leaving a gaping hole in the middle of the massive banner. *Malaysiakini* also reported that an opposition billboard in Seremban had been taken down, pending the removal of Mahathir's image.

The coalition might continue insisting that it's not afraid of Mahathir, but it seems as if they're leaving nothing to chance. Zaid Ibrahim, a former cabinet minister, doesn't mince his words; he says Najib is the worst-ever UMNO president and prime minister the country has ever seen. "The only thing he will be remembered for is being the prime minister who had billions of ringgit in his account. He is afraid to be honest and admit that UMNO has lost the Malay support and is in fact afraid to face PPBM," he says.

---

3 https://newnaratif.com/research/malaysias-election-rigged/

4 http://www.sarawakreport.org/2018/02/bns-shame-handing-out-money-without-a-blush/

5 https://www.nst.com.my/news/politics/2018/04/361383/
ec-announces-additional-requirements-over-election-campaign-materials

6 https://www.malaysiakini.com/news/422280#.WubRcPz8tjw.facebook

Waiting on the swing

According to a senior leader from Umno, fence-sitters will play a significant role in determining the outcome of this fierce political battle. He claims that in 2013, 11.05 million people voted—approximately 85% of all registered voters. "This year, we have more than 14 million voters and if 15% of them are fence-sitters, then this could be the group that actually determines the outcome. This group usually waits for the last minute before making a decision and could swing either way," he says.

"We do not expect any miracles from Dr Mahathir. What we know for sure is that he is sincere in his cause and wants to make a change for the better. He, along with Muhyiddin and the others have made a significant change and based on the large turnouts at our ceramahs, we believe our chances are good," says PKR president Wan Azizah Wan Ismail.

For Malaysians frustrated by the increasing costs of living and other issues like immigration, crime and employment, Mahathir—who led Malaysia at a time of economic growth—is perceived as a beacon of hope. "Dr Mahathir is no angel… but he does offer us new hope," says Imran Bakhtiar, a voter from the Pagoh constituency. "Many of us are suffering and are fed up hearing of the abuse and scandals linked to Najib. It is surely a time for change and that is what Pakatan Harapan offers us."

MALAYSIANS PREPARE TO #PULANGMENGUNDI

JEAMME CHIA, DEBORAH AUGUSTIN | 08 MAY 2018

A mid-week vote for Malaysia's 14th general election prompted an outcry as critics accused the ruling coalition of trying to impact voter turnout. But Malaysians have stepped up to organise a nation-wide "homegoing", pooling money and resources to get out the vote.

When Malaysia's Election Commission announced that polling day would be on 9 May, a Wednesday, the criticism was swift and fierce. A weekday vote, though unusual, is not unprecedented in the country, but the decision was nonetheless alleged to be a move to impact voter turnout and skew the playing field in favour of the ruling coalition Barisan Nasional (BN). Even though the day has since been declared a public holiday, a mid-week vote still presents a logistical headache for the multitudes of Malaysians living and working outside their hometowns.

It's estimated that 400,000 Malaysians live in Singapore, with 250,000 Malaysians commuting daily between the two countries; one million Kelantanese work outside the state and 150,000 East Malaysians live in Peninsular Malaysia.[1] According to Malaysian election regulations, these voters are not allowed to cast postal votes; that option is reserved for Malaysians residing further abroad. (Overseas Malaysians, though, are now worried they won't be able to cast their ballots in time.)[2]

Shortly after the Election Commission's announcement, the cost of flights from Singapore or the Peninsular Malaysia's urbanised west coast to smaller towns and rural areas within the Peninsular or in East

---

1 https://www.channelnewsasia.com/news/commentary/
   malaysia-voting-day-may-impact-over-a-million-voters-10131718

2 https://www.straitstimes.com/asia/se-asia/
   malaysia-election-malaysians-abroad-fret-over-whether-their-postal-votes-can-reach-on

Malaysia began to climb in response to demand. By 11 April, signs declaring "*Semua tiket untuk May 8 dan 9 sudah habis* (All tickets for May 8 and 9 sold out)" were posted at all inter-city railway ticket booths in KL Sentral.

The rapidly rising cost of transport options bothered 27-year-old Sarah[*3], who lives in Kuala Lumpur but votes in Miri, Sarawak. Although all major carriers began offering fixed prices[4] after public criticism, she pointed out that for many Sarawakians, the travel cost "doesn't end at flight tickets—there's the transportation to and from airport and also accommodation", especially if they no longer have family in their hometown. Many Malaysians could be prevented from exercising their right to vote simply for reasons of cost and access to reasonable options.

The political impact

The fight in Malaysia's 14th general election is a tough one. Prime Minister Najib Razak is still neck-deep in allegations of corruption, particularly in relation to the 1Malaysia Development Berhad scandal. The rising cost of living has also triggered anxiety and unhappiness among the populace. On top of this, the emergence of Mahathir Mohamad—Malaysia's former premier who's had an outsized influence on its political scene—from retirement to stand against his former party has introduced variables that's making BN nervous.[5]

The declaration of a mid-week polling day was seen as an attempt by BN to skew the race in its favour; commentators expect the return of rural voters from urban areas—such as Klang Valley, Penang, and Singapore—to bolster the opposition Pakatan Harapan's (PH) chances.[6] Such voters are expected to be more likely influenced by the opposition-leaning sentiment in the cities than the local party politics of their homes states; making it more difficult for them to cast their ballot could give BN another advantage over their opponents.

---

3 Names have been changed to protect the interviewees' privacy

4 https://www.nst.com.my/news/nation/2018/04/356588/
  ge14-airasia-offers-special-fixed-fares-may-8-and-9

5 https://newnaratif.com/journalism/a-mahathir-effect/

6 http://www.malaysiandigest.com/frontpage/282-main-tile/728669-what-analysts-say-
  about-bn-chances-to-sway-urban-voters-their-way-come-ge14.html

Crowdsourcing trips home

As Malaysians scrambled to find transportation home, the hashtags #CarpoolGE14 and #PulangMengundi (Return to Vote) started trending on Twitter. Those in need of both financial and logistical aid used the hashtag to crowdfund flights and share transport. The need for sponsors, particularly for flights to and from East Malaysia, soon overwhelmed the informal match-ups taking place on Twitter.

Several other initiatives sprung up to meet demand. Among them was the website PulangMengundi.com, founded by five volunteers.[7] The easy-to-use website emphasises that it's not about disbursing funds, but providing a neutral platform for people to connect. Andrew Loh, its strategy lead, says they are focused on "creating a Malaysian culture of voting, not helping someone to win."

Focused on Twitter, #UndiRabu (Wednesday Vote)—also founded by volunteers—started collecting donations from the public to distribute to those in need. The group had an initial target of MYR50,000, but raised MYR65,000 just 24 hours after launch. They stopped collecting funds two weeks later; total donations had reached about MYR195,000. The fund has given more than 800 voters—many of whom are university students voting for the first time—the opportunity to return home to vote.

"We provide assistance to recipients regardless of political belief," says #UndiRabu's Elida Bustaman. "What this fund endorses is the constitutional right of every Malaysian to vote."

The impact of such a push by ordinary Malaysians to get out the vote is tangible, especially for first-time voters. This election is 23-year-old Ella's* first time voting in her hometown in Sarawak; she considers voting the "unspoken duty of each Malaysian... [it] doesn't matter for which party." As a fresh graduate, the costs of a round trip from Kuala Lumpur to Kuching—which hovered around RM600 shortly after the announcement of the polling date—was beyond her means. She turned to Twitter, and subsequently PulangMengundi.com, for help, and received funding through donors.

"For once I really felt that sense of oneness among Malaysians," she says. "Strangers who were helping each other purely for the sake of humanity."

Other voters have different motivations. 28-year-old Jas*, who lives in Kuala Lumpur but votes in Penang, believes that many voters have

---

7 http://www.pulangmengundi.com; http://says.com/my/news/a-team-of-malaysians-have-set-up-this-website-to-help-you-pulangmengundi

been motivated to return home to vote in reaction to what's been perceived as a "blatant attempt to rig the election." These attempts include the introduction of the Anti-Fake News Act, the highly-criticised electoral redelineation efforts and new electoral rules relating to the use of campaign materials, which she believes "has made some people even more determined to return to vote or encourage others to do the same."

The foundation upon which #PulangMengundi rests

#PulangMengundi has not occurred in a vacuum; the path to this grassroots effort has been paved by a growing engagement with electoral reform in Malaysia. Since 2007, Bersih, a movement for free and fair elections, has organised street protests that have drawn increasing numbers of participants in a country where peaceful protests are often shut down with excessive force. Malaysians who support Bersih's demands cut across race and class barriers, and also extends to the diaspora.

It also isn't the first time a campaign to get people home to vote has been launched; *Jom Balik Undi* (Let's Go Home To Vote) was launched during the last general election in 2013 amid scepticism over a newly instated overseas voting process.

Unlike #PulangMengundi, Jom Balik Undi did not offer voters financial assistance; instead, it encouraged Malaysians residing overseas to fly home to vote. Individual groups of voters self-organised to fund travel costs. By the close of polls during the 2013 election, Jom Balik Undi helped approximately 240 voters to return to Peninsular Malaysia and Borneo from across the world. Hundreds more crossed the Singapore-Malaysia border by public transport and carpools to reach their polling stations, some up to 800km away, in the northern states of Kelantan and Terengganu. While 2013's efforts emphasised the importance of exercising one's right to vote, #PulangMengundi has built on it by going beyond encouragement to broad-base facilitation, providing Malaysians with simple platforms to crowdfund and organise.

As for working with the rest of civil society, the people behind #PulangMengundi have been transparent about their collaborations with established Malaysian civil society organisations. PulangMengundi. com's website lists the different organisations they are working with, most notably the KL Selangor Chinese Assembly Hall (KLSCAH), which has been active in various socio-political issues in the country.

KLSCAH's team runs UndiRabu.com, complementing PulangMengundi.com by crowdfunding to help defray travel costs.

According to their website, they've raised MYR180,934, but their organising has gone beyond just pooling money. The group has also organised 50 buses of 40 seats each, traversing Peninsular Malaysia on 8 and 9 May to get people where they need to be.[8] Arrangements have also been made to help people with disabilities get to polling stations.[9]

"[These efforts show] that ordinary Malaysians can start their own initiative and new ideas without depending on political parties," says Lee Wai Hong, chairman of KLSCAH's youth section. "In some extent, this is also a part of civil empowerment and awareness."

But it's not just the "old-timers" that are leading the movement; while some of PulangMengundi.com's founders had previously been involved in civil society activities, Loh says that, for the others, it's their "first time doing something actively". Nonetheless, he says that all of them are, "avid followers [and] observers of Malaysia's political and socio-economic developments."

Although the platform is focused on empowerment instead of partisan mobilisation, Andrew admits the difficulties of remaining neutral, by "steering a fine line between [creating] impact, publicity, and being a target." It's a mission that's been complicated by the cut-and-thrust of politics on social media.

A boost for the opposition?

Whether on Twitter or otherwise, #PulangMengundi has stayed largely non-partisan, with the focus on getting people home to vote regardless of their political inclinations. Yet it's expected that urban Malaysians returning en masse to their more rural constituencies would be a greater benefit to PH than BN. It's perhaps for this reason that the #PulangMengundi hashtag has now become the target of pro-BN Twitter bots, flooding streams with spam and pro-BN imagery as part of an ongoing social media campaign that has attracted the attention of researchers.[10]

Reactions to the Twitter bots range from incredulity to caution. Although some are afraid of personal attacks, Loh believes the existence of the bots means they're doing something right, and that attempts by cybertroopers to flood the hashtag will only "make Malaysians more

8 https://balik.undirabu.com/free-bus/

9 https://balik.undirabu.com/orang-kurang-upaya/

10 https://www.reuters.com/article/us-malaysia-election-socialmedia/ahead-of-malaysian-polls-bots-flood-twitter-with-pro-government-messages-idUSKBN1HR2AQ

angry." On the other hand, Bustaman says that #UndiRabu has had "minimal encounters with bots", adding that "[the bots] did not affect our operations nor people's confidence in what we were doing." Overall, both PulangMengundi.com and #UndiRabu have not dignified the bots with responses.

It's too early to tell what impact #PulangMengundi will have on the election, or whether it will feed into more long-term political organising in Malaysia; not all the founders are continuing their initiatives post-Polling Day. PulangMengundi.com has publicly committed to delete all data 14 days after the election to protect the privacy of the people who used the site.

However, the direct action and mutual aid that thousands of Malaysians have participated in and benefited from through #PulangMengundi has uncovered the untapped potential of Malaysians to organise towards tangible short-term goals. There have been many political campaigns and efforts in Malaysia that have fizzled out, but #PulangMengundi could provide a blueprint for building sustainable civic engagement.

For Terence Gomez, a professor in the Department Of Administrative Studies and Politics at Universiti Malaya, #PulangMengundi is unprecedented: "We have never seen this kind of civil society engagement before, where a small group of people are mounting a serious campaign to overcome the challenges faced by voters."

He's also quick to point out the distinction between NGO action and individual efforts; #PulangMengundi differs from other civil society movements like Reformasi and Bersih in that it is "not an organised form of civil society; it was not initiated by an NGO, but by individuals; groups of people coming together to take action against the attempt to reduce voter turnout." The response to the movement, he says, is a possible indication of "the impact civil society can have in ensuring significant turnout during [the election]."

Francis Loh, a former politics professor at Universiti Sains Malaysia, views initiatives like #PulangMengundi and #UndiRabu as part of a wider trend of civic engagement among Malaysians, especially younger citizens. Malaysian youth, he says, "have been a critical part of the political ferment that has been occuring in Malaysia these past decades, especially since Reformasi [in 1997–1998]." He feels that the future for Malaysian civil society is bright if this kind of civic engagement continues, with the next generation "playing an important bridging role in bringing together the non-formal and formal realms of politics."

SKETCHES OF GE14: A TALE OF THREE CERAMAHS

CHARIS LOKE | 07 MAY 2018

Malaysian artist Charis Loke hits the ground during the 14th general election to capture the sights of a nation going to the polls.

The Barisan Nasional is the longest ruling coalition in the world, having governed Malaysia since its independence in 1957. But it's not invincible: in 2008, it failed for the first time since 1969 to win a two-thirds majority in Parliament, and in 2013 lost the popular vote, maintaining a parliamentary majority amid allegations of electoral fraud and gerrymandering.

In 2015, the Islamist party PAS split from the opposition coalition Pakatan Rakyat due to disagreements over their desire to implement sharia law in the country. The opposition rebranded as Pakatan Harapan, and is fielding Mahathir Mohamad[1], Malaysia's former prime minister, as its prime ministerial candidate, making this election one to watch.

2 May 2018: Pakatan Harapan Mega Ceramah in Han Chiang School Field (8pm)

It's Wednesday night—the country goes to the polls a week from now—and my housemate and I have decide to make the trip to Jalan Masjid Negeri to attend what will be my first election *ceramah* (rally speech). Since we live in Penang, which has been governed by the opposition coalition since the 2008 elections, we're sure that we'll see a large turnout for Pakatan Harapan.

We arrive early and walk around Han Chiang College's large compound. Stalls filled with T-shirts and vuvuzelas are set up along the perimeter of the field as well as outside the college gates.

"I've been selling merchandise since 2013," one of the vendors tells me as I draw him. He's bedecked in his own wares: headband, badges, shirt, name tags and the like.

---

1 https://newnaratif.com/journalism/a-mahathir-effect/

"Do you think Pakatan Harapan will win this time around?" I ask.

He looks off into the distance at the *ceramah* stage. "Yes, I'm sure of it. This time they aren't Pakatan Rakyat anymore—they're Pakatan Harapan."

The crowd is loud and jubilant; vuvuzelas blare as speakers take their turns on stage. Drone shots show that a few thousand people are present despite it being a weekday night. Jagdeep Singh Deo, the chairman for Housing and Town & Country Planning Committee and N29–Datok Keramat candidate, details the differences between the federal and state governments' low-income housing schemes. R. S. N. Rayer, the P50–Jelutong candidate, draws raucous applause and cheers when he speaks. Some candidates deliver parts of their speech in Hokkien.

"I'm here to see Lim Guan Eng," a teacher says. "I haven't heard him speak in person before."

Wanting to make an early escape, we leave at around ten o'clock. There are at least 50 people seated on their motorcycles outside the college fences, listening to the speeches. I see later on Facebook Live that the Chief Minister of Penang, Lim Guan Eng, and his father, DAP veteran Lim Kit Siang, have arrived from the other Mega Ceramah in Juru on the mainland. Thumbs-up and happy reactions float non-stop past the mostly positive comments on the livestream.

People are pretty confident that Pakatan Harapan will retain Penang. But anything's possible in Malaysia.

From left: a lady wears an Ubah Bird hat; a vendor; a man takes a phone call in the middle of the field.

4 May 2018: Pakatan Harapan *Ceramah* in Seremban 2 (8pm)

Two days later, I'm back in my hometown, Seremban. A flyer for the Pakatan candidate has already made its way into my mailbox.

Barisan Nasional retained their hold on the state of Negeri Sembilan in the previous election, winning 22 out of 36 state seats and five out of eight parliamentary seats. Pakatan Harapan are openly gunning to win 19 state seats this time, which would give them the majority in the state house.

It's harder to find information on both BN and PH *ceramah* taking place in Seremban; few candidates post in advance about where they'll be making appearances. After dinner I make my way to Seremban 2 for a Pakatan *ceramah*, where I'm pleased to see five women speakers on the poster—a much greater ratio of women to men compared to Penang, although not all of them are candidates.

There are a thousand or more people clustered in front of a stage set up on the road between two rows of shophouses in Seremban 2. It's quickly apparent that this crowd is markedly different from the one in Penang; for one, they're mostly seated on white plastic chairs, only a handful of them are waving flags, and there aren't any Ubah Bird (a mascot for the opposition Democratic Action Party) hats to be seen. They're also less likely to break out into shouts or cheers. But they listen attentively to the speeches.

A band is called onstage to lead the crowd in singing two Pakatan Harapan songs; volunteers distribute printed lyrics. The crowd waves flags and their mobile phones, lighting up the street.

Pakatan Harapan candidates for state seats make an appearance. Interestingly, they speak a wider variety of languages combined than the Penang speakers—between them, there are portions of speeches delivered in Malay, English, Cantonese, Mandarin and Tamil.

From left: a man listens while seated on his motorcycle; one of the speakers onstage; two men watch from the edge of the crowd.

5 May 2018: Pakatan Harapan Ceramah in Seremban Jaya (8pm)

The next day, I try (and fail) to find information online about nearby BN *ceramah*. So I head to yet another PH event, this time a few kilometres from my family home. The crowd looks to be larger than last night's—at least 1200 people gather around a stage set up in front of the Democratic Action Party office in Seremban Jaya. A handful of enterprising stalls are doing brisk business selling drinks and snacks. The incumbent Member of Parliament for P130–Rasah, Loke Siew Fook, makes a brief appearance before rushing off to another *ceramah* elsewhere in the state. "Help us to take control of Negeri Sembilan this time!" he exhorts the crowd, who cheer in response. The organiser makes full use of the large screen onstage to show videos of the new Rasah candidate, Cha Kee Chin, in his law firm's office as well as in Putrajaya, the seat of the federal government.

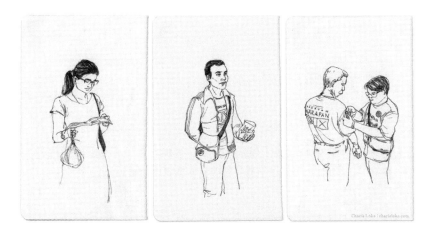

From left: a lady peruses leaflets containing the candidates' manifestos; a man snacks while listening to speeches; a younger man helps attach a button badge to the sleeve of an older attendee.

SKETCHES OF GE14: A LITTLE NIGHT MUSIC

CHARIS LOKE | 08 MAY 2018

Malaysian artist Charis Loke hits the ground during the 14th general election to capture the sights of a nation going to the polls.

6 May 2018: Barisan Nasional 'Konsert Gegar Indian Malaysia Superstar' in Thivy Jaya (8pm)

On Sunday I finally manage to find a poster for a Barisan Nasional event that'll take place in Taman Thivy Jaya, a residential area I used to pass on my way to school every day.

Loud Bollywood music is playing from the speakers; this is, after all, a "Konsert Gegar Indian Malaysian Superstar". Most of the concertgoers are Indian families from the residential area. There are a handful of older Chinese women and men but almost no Malays.

The Malaysian Chinese Association (MCA) candidate for my state constituency dances on stage with one of the featured singers for the night.

About 150 people are sitting on red plastic chairs, fanning themselves with plastic fans printed with photos of candidates, or milling around outside the tent. The emcee exhorts the crowd to applaud during every speech; the candidates plead for a chance to serve as their representatives.

The phrases "undilah dengan waras (vote with a sound mind)" and "keharmonian negara (harmony of the nation)" are used more than once, but almost no mention of policy or economy is made. After each speech, there's singing or dancing.

It's hard to miss the mountain bike on stage—one of many lucky draw prizes for the night—even though it's frequently wreathed in smoke from a fog machine. At one point, large containers of free mee hoon and warm tea are carried out from a van; people line up to grab a bite.

Finally, the MCA candidate for the parliamentary seat of Rasah takes the stage. He condemns a recent social media post by an opposition candidate as divisive, and tells the audience to continue voting Barisan National for national harmony. There's some clapping from the crowd. The loudest clapping comes from party members dressed in blue who are sitting up front.

From left: a child holds a goodie bag after performing a dance with her classmates; youth chat on their motorcycles nearby; members of the audience watch the performances.

Shortly after his speech, he's surrounded by a group of roughly ten to fifteen young adults who ask to speak to him.

"What are they talking about?" I ask two teens hovering on the edge of the circle.

"They're asking him what Barisan Nasional plans to do about inequality in Malaysia," one of them says.

The candidate is joined by his colleagues from MCA and MIC, who take turns explaining issues like the Goods and Services Tax (GST), which both Pakatan Harapan and the Malaysian Islamic Party (PAS) have pledged to abolish. It's hard to make out what he's saying over the pulsing beat of dance music and the singers' voices. It strikes me that this conversation is happening under a street lamp beside a drain instead of on stage, under the spotlight.

7 May 2018: Pakatan Harapan Ceramah in Oakland, 8pm

From left: a speaker commands the crowd's attention; people wave mobile phone flashlights for a photo op.

"Is Hannah Yeoh here?" an older lady asks. It's 9pm but people are still streaming into the street in Oakland Commercial Centre where tonight's Pakatan Harapan ceramah is taking place.

"We're here to see Hannah Yeoh," her husband reiterates.

"Has Karpal Singh's son spoken yet?" another auntie asks me in Cantonese.

Tonight's crowd—1700 at least—is the largest I've seen in Seremban so far, in no small part because well- known Pakatan figures like Tony

Pua and Gobind Singh Deo are slated to speak. Rapidly switching between Malay and Mandarin, Tony talks about the increase in both expenditure and reserves for the state of Selangor, which is under Pakatan governance. Both he and the incumbent Member of Parliament for this area, Loke Siew Fook, receive raucous applause when they speak. The crowd cheers when the latter announces that a few miles away in Paroi, Azmin Ali, the Selangor Chief Minister, is speaking to a Malay crowd that numbers in the thousands. (It turns out that Hannah is with him; several people are watching the livestream of that event on their phones.)

"Gobind is on his way here from Nilai," Loke announces. "Please be patient". The emcee gets the crowd to sing along to a Pakatan Harapan song, This Is The Time. The music video flashes on the large screen behind him. An upbeat tune plays as Mahatir Mohamad, dressed in a grey suit, hands a red puzzle piece to a young girl.

"I don't understand what's going on," one Indian lady says to another.

"The majority of the crowd here is Chinese, that's why they're playing the Mandarin version," her friend replies.

Since both the audio and subtitles are in Mandarin, I don't understand the song either. (The official version is in Malay—during the Seremban 2 ceramah[1] on 4 May, the organisers handed out lyric sheets with Malay and English lyrics to the crowd).

A deep-seated worry of mine bubbles to the surface: that the ceramah tonight has been overwhelmingly targeted towards a Mandarin- or Cantonese-speaking Chinese audience, and that this will be taken as a sign that Pakatan only cares about Chinese voters. I've seen countless comments on social media along the lines of "don't vote for this candidate—he's Chinese"; memes with "[Chinese-led Democratic Action Party] inside" superimposed within the eye that the opposition coalition has adopted as their logo; Photoshopped images of politicians with "UNDI PKR + UNDI KOMUNIS (Vote PKR + Vote Communists)".

Running events in specific ways to cater for a specific ethnic group isn't a new thing—the same has been done in Barisan campaigning for decades. Barisan's main component parties in Peninsular Malaysia are unabashedly mono-racial: the United Malays National Organisation, Malaysian Chinese Association, Malaysian Indian Congress. Last night's Bollywood affair was an awkward, contrived meeting between MCA candidates and Indian constituents.

---

1 https://newnaratif.com/comic/ge14sketches-tale-three-ceramahs/

The candidates take to the stage again after the song. "Our saudara Gobind Singh will not be able to make it tonight," one of them announces, and there's an audible groan from the crowd. "He is on his way back to Seri Serdang—I apologise, I truly apologise. I know many of you came tonight to hear him. He agreed to speak here even before nomination day. But I would ask of you—if you can, please head over to Taman Ampangan now to show your support. The Chief Minister of Selangor, Azmin Ali, is there..."

And the crowd disperses as This Is The Time plays over the loud-speakers, this time in Malay.

From left: a Pakatan Harapan volunteer sports the PKR 'eye' flag on his cheek; two ceramah-goers await Gobind Singh Deo's arrival; a man listens to the speeches.

SKETCHES OF GE14: POLLING DAY

CHARIS LOKE | 09 MAY 2018

Views of Malaysia on Polling Day, seen through an artist's pen.

9am: The sun is already out in full force as people stream into the polling station, SJK(C) Sin Hua.

9:30am: There's some confusion over how to line up outside the class-rooms for each *saluran* (channel); a police officer calmly directs voters. It's really stuffy—the temperature feels like 36°C, according to weather. com—but the fans in the corridors aren't turned on.

"Eh can you plug that in and on it?" a man asks the ladies standing next to some power outlets. Everyone watches the fans in anticipation but they don't whirr to life.

"Sorry bro!" someone else calls across the corridor.

10:10am: Most people are watching videos on their mobile phones or texting their friends in other polling stations. Any available chair or surface that can be sat on is immediately filled.

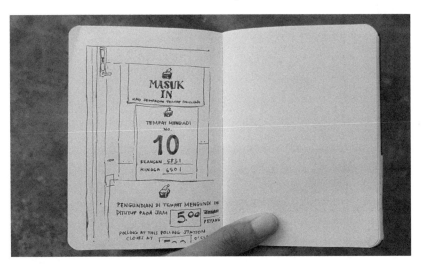

10:35am: I'm almost at the door of the classroom where my *saluran* (channel) is voting.

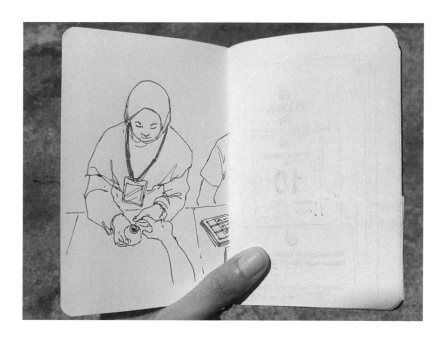

10:40am: The first clerk checks my name and identity card number against the register. The second clerk dips my finger into the well of indelible ink, after which the third clerk uses a ruler to tear off both state and parliamentary ballots from a book, which he folds into a quarter before handing it to me.

"No photographs allowed inside," I hear people reminding each other. Everyone sobers up as they approach the classroom, identity cards in hand.

10:43am: There's one blue ballpoint pen in the voting booth and nothing else, apart from instructions on how to mark the ballot. The order of the candidates' parties differs on the state and parliamentary ballot, so I have to read the papers twice to be absolutely sure who I'm voting for.

10:45am: Both ballot boxes are already quite full for this channel. Another clerk uses a wooden ruler to push the existing ballot papers in.

10:50am: Everybody takes indelible ink finger selfies when they exit the polling station.

11:25am: Although the huge crowd waiting at the *barong* agents in the school assembly ground has cleared up—there were conflicting instructions as to whether voters needed to line up to receive a slip with their number, or go straight to their *saluran*—there are still long lines of people waiting in the heat.

"Can we wear shorts?", asks a young man.

"Yes, there's no dress code," someone tells him.

"But they turned away an uncle who was wearing shorts—look!" He pulls up a Facebook post on his phone. One of my friends has also sent me a WhatsApp message about a similar incident. The Election Commission clarified earlier that there's no dress code, despite circulating reports to the contrary, but most of the voters in line are wearing long pants to be safe.

12pm: The temperature feels like 41°C now. An ice cream seller waits patiently outside the school gates.

4:05pm: After the oppressive heat, there's a brief shower. It lasts for twenty minutes before the sun comes out again. There are still around twenty or so people strolling in to vote.

"We had to wait quite a bit," exclaim two sisters as they walk out of the school gates. "Almost half an hour!"

"I've heard that people waited three to four hours in Kuala Lumpur," I tell them.

"Yah, that's terrible! Seremban is still not too bad. Pretty smooth here."

4:25pm: Barisan National volunteers are still manning their tent near the polling station.

4:35pm: Further up the road, the Pakatan Harapan volunteers sit in their tent.

Voters are still trickling into the polling station.

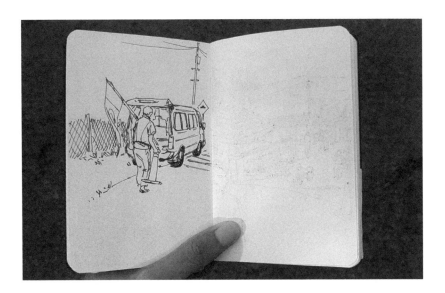

4:55pm: One of the PH volunteers begins to pack up their traffic cones and flags. Any voters who've arrived in the past half an hour have come out of the polling station, having made it in time to vote.

There are conflicting reports as to directives given by the head of the Election Commission; some news outlets report him saying that voters will still be allowed to cast votes as long as they are within the polling station compounds by 5pm. Others quote him as saying that 5pm is the cutoff point, regardless of whether voters are in the compound or not.

5:00pm: The police officer on duty shuts the gate to the school, marking the end of the voting period. It's been a relatively smooth process here in Seremban.

Now the counting of votes begins, and the long wait for the results.

A LONG ROAD TO CHANGE

KATHARINE EE | 28 MAY 2018

The "tsunami rakyat" that brought Malaysia its first ever change in government was built on long years of hard work by the country's civil society. There's no time for them to rest on their laurels, but activists say they've already experienced great change on a personal level.

After the 2013 election, self-declared "Non-Governmental Individual" Hishamuddin Rais—who also goes by the pen name Isham—told his friends it would be four decades before Malaysia would see a change in government. Five years later, the country has proved him wrong.

The veteran activist with a seat in the former opposition coalition's campaign "war room" says the Pakatan Harapan victory was the result of a "perfect storm" of events—from the corruption allegations swirling around former prime minister Najib Razak, to the decision to hold the poll on a Wednesday, and the opposition parties' willingness to stand behind a single party logo.

But mostly, he says, it was down to the coalition agreeing to rally behind one man'92-year-old Mahathir Mohamad, the bête noire of both Malaysia's opposition and the country's pro-democracy activists during his 22 years in power.

"It's actually the Mahathir factor," Isham explains about the Pakatan victory over tea one night in Kuala Lumpur. "Whoever tries to deny this has no idea what politics is all about."

The filmmaker and writer says it was he who proposed Mahathir chair the coalition, recognising that the elder statesman would appeal beyond the opposition's traditional urban strongholds. Having been arrested about 16 times, Isham says he's well aware of how unlikely such a rapprochement sounds. "Shocking!" he laughs, and takes another mouthful of tea.

The early days

Isham started out as an activist in the 1970s—first as secretary-general of the union at University of Malaya and then as president-elect. As in many other parts of the world, students in Malaysia were becoming more politically aware, but when they joined forces with rubber tappers to protest against poverty, the government cracked down.

Isham escaped through the jungle of northern Malaysia, and stayed away for 20 years.

When he did return home, he found a country in the midst of a Mahathir-engineered economic boom. Those willing to talk about democracy, human rights and corruption had shrunk to a small, tight-knit community.

"The general population was not so interested," recalls human rights activist Masjaliza Hamzah, who started her career as a journalist. "People were playing the stock market, making lots of money. It was the heyday for that kind of capitalism."

Newcomers were treated with suspicion, and many feared they were being followed or watched so it was difficult to win the trust of the few activists there were. The Internal Security Act allowed for detention without trial and Mahathir had shown he was not afraid to use it against his critics, notably in the 1987 crackdown known as Operation Lalang when more than 100 people were detained. Newspapers were also closed down; a blow to independent and critical reporting in the country.

"It was only in 1998 with the high profile targeting of Anwar Ibrahim, the public sharing of events on television that more people came to understand that if that could happen to him [Anwar]—someone in such a high position—it could happen to them," Masjaliza says.

The Reformasi movement

Anwar—then the Finance Minister, Deputy Prime Minister, and the man Mahathir had been grooming as his successor—was sacked as the Asian Financial Crisis brought Malaysia's economy to its knees. But Mahathir didn't just fire Anwar; he also sought to destroy his political career by accusing his younger rival of corruption and sodomy—a crime in Malaysia.

Malaysians of all backgrounds poured onto the streets of Kuala Lumpur, calling for Anwar's release and democratic reform. Masjaliza was among them. So was Isham. "Mahathir accused me of being the *dalang* (mastermind)," Isham says, able to smile now that he and Mahathir are on the same side. In 2001, he was arrested under the ISA and spent more than two years in detention.

Even though Anwar was eventually convicted and jailed, the urge for reform remained, and ordinary people had the feeling, perhaps for the first time, that change was possible.

"We can place the credit at the feet of 20 years of reformasi; no question," argues Kean Wong, Contributing Editor for the Australian National University's New Mandala blog, who covered both the 1998 protests and the recent election. "The seeds of Reformasi and what came before—Ops Lalang, the industrialisation boom that created a middle class that had a dream about Malaysia as something other than putting food on the table. Reformasi popularised and expanded that."

The more relaxed leadership of Abdullah Badawi, the man who took over from Mahathir when he eventually retired in 2003, further loosened the reins. Protests became a more regular feature of Malaysian life, despite the continued existence of laws designed to deter public gatherings and rallies. According to academic Bridget Welsh in her book, *Awakening: the Abdullah Badawi Years in Malaysia*, there were around 20 protests involving more than 100 people in 2003—the year Abdullah came to power—but nearly three times that many in 2011.

"The Reformasi movement brought the issue of reform into the public arena," Welsh, now an associate professor at John Cabot University in Rome, told *New Naratif* in an email. "All the victors of elections since 1999 have been couched as 'reformers', even Abdullah in 2004, and Najib in 2013. Mahathir (also) adopted the reform mantle. Second, there was opposition cooperation and learning. This was a long process of learning how to make compromises and strategic alliances, which was evident in the tie between Mahathir and his critics from the 1980s. And third, Bersih. This was the movement that extended the reform movement into society at large."

Bersih

Bersih's cause was simple: free and fair elections. At its first rally in 2007, tens of thousands of people took to the streets of Kuala Lumpur clad in the group's distinctive yellow shirts, only for the police to break up the crowd with tear gas and water cannon. But the police response, and government efforts to restrict assembles and even ban yellow shirts, didn't stop people coming out again and again. If anything, the more the authorities tried to crack down, the more determined people became.

Maria Chin Abdullah, having joined the movement from the beginning, took over as Bersih chair in 2013. The veteran women's rights activist, whose late husband went into exile with Isham in the 1970s, has endured tear gas, court battles and nearly two weeks of solitary confinement in a darkened cell under the Security Offences (Special Measures) Act, or SOSMA, in her battle for a better Malaysia. Now, having stepped down from Bersih, she's the newly-elected MP—independent, but under the Pakatan umbrella—for Petaling Jaya, a suburban town near the Malaysian capital.

Given the difficulties of mounting any meaningful challenge in a system where the media is controlled, and key institutions—including the electoral commission—are under the prime minister's department, the members of civil society pressing for democratic reform "never dreamed" the government would actually change, she says.

"A really long road"

Chin is mindful of the challenge of overhauling a political system tailored to the needs of a coalition that had run the country in one form or another since independence. At a weekend forum, she encourages Malaysians to get involved in their democracy. "People must always be engaged," she tells the audience. "We have done the first part, changing the government. The second part is the harder one. That is bringing democracy to Malaysia. That is a really long road."

Isham agrees, batting away any notion that the ideals for which activists have fought for so long will quickly come to pass. "That is too romantic," he says. Indeed, while many think of NGOs as progressive organisations pushing for democracy, Malaysia has also had groups that resist change. They still call themselves NGOs, but many suspect they are actually linked to the parties that have just lost power.

For Isham, the first test of the new government will be the repeal of the draconian laws that remain on the statute books, including the Anti-Fake News Act, SOSMA, the Peaceful Assembly Act and the Sedition Act, a relic of colonial rule that Najib promised to repeal, but kept. The new Home Minister, Muhyiddin Yassin, has committed to reviewing such laws.[1]

---

1 https://www.malaymail.com/s/1633675/muhyiddin-home-ministry-to-review-seven-unsuitable-national-security-laws#.WwPUtd0U0vw.twitter

Nik Nazmi Nik Ahmad, who watched Reformasi unfold as a high school student and has just been elected to parliament for Pakatan, says the new administration is committed to implementing its manifesto pledges. "(Civil society) will give us some time to implement our promises," he says. "But if we fall short then I can see them going back against us, and I think that's what they should do. If it's more of the same then they will definitely be our staunchest critics."

The Pakatan government has moved quickly to fulfil some of its promises: announcing the end of the much-hated Goods and Services Tax (GST) from next month, and launching investigations into the scandals that swirled around Najib and his administration, including the billions thought to have gone missing from 1Malaysia Development Berhad (1MDB).

But for many Malaysians, the biggest change has already taken place. As the results came in and it became clear that Pakatan was going to win, journalists abandoned their usual caution to report what they were really seeing, and ordinary citizens took to social media to express their delight at the outcome—and disgust for the previous administration.

It was as if people suddenly got a new lease of life. The day after the election, for the first time in a long time, Isham felt free.

"I no longer needed to look from my balcony to see whether there was a police car waiting for me," he says. "I no longer had to peer through the door to check whether there was someone waiting for me. On a very personal level that was the change for me."

ECONOMIC MIGRATION AND FORCED MIGRATION

PHOTOS OF THE ROHINGYA CRISIS: THE WORLD NEEDS TO SEE THEM

AISYAH LLEWELLYN | 29 MAR 2018

Mohammad Noyeem tells us why he will talk to anyone about the ongoing Rohingya crisis in Myanmar, and why he wants the media to publish the violent photos in his possession.

By Mohammad Noyeem, as told to Aisyah Llewellyn before he was resettled in the US

WARNING: Some photos within the article might be graphic and distressing.

My family and friends in Burma and Bangladesh always send me pictures of what's happening there. Sometimes I recognise the people in the photographs – they are my old neighbours. I'm from Shilkali (Chinkali) in Rathedaung Township and the situation is horrific. Now it has been burned to the ground and no one lives there anymore. I faced genocide in Burma. Monks used to stop the Rohingya on the road so they couldn't go to school. Then they made us do manual labour for no money or food. I left in 2015 to travel to Indonesia when I was 15 but until today there is no good news for the Rohingya. The situation is not moving on at all. That's why I want the media to publish the pictures I have on my phone.

I'm one of seven siblings and now my father, mother, brothers and sisters are in Balukhali Refugee Camp in Bangladesh. My father told me it's important to show the situation to the world. It's dire and the Rohingya are the most persecuted people in the world. My family always pushes me to share our story with anyone who wants to listen.

Most of the pictures I have on my phone come from my village of Shilkali. But many people outside Burma don't know the story of my village which is why it's absolutely important that they are published. I want the world to see what they did to us there. My family were still in Shilkali on August 25, 2017 when the Burmese military, security forces and Rakhine people secretly planned to attack our village. At exactly one o'clock in the morning when people were sleeping in their homes, they surrounded the village and started firing rocket launchers directly into the houses. People were running away as fast as they could. But many people couldn't get out of their homes in time because they were sleeping. They died instantly inside their houses. Not everyone who came outside survived because they were shot when they tried to run. Many old people and children died because they couldn't run fast enough. Around 150 people died that day, mostly women, old people and children as they were shot or perished inside their burning homes.

(Teguh Harahap)

My father told me that the military targeted old people like the village chiefs because they were the ones who spoke some English. They knew that if they escaped they would be able to tell the world about the situation in Shilkali so they killed them first because they had more education. But now we have pictures we can also show them to people even if we can't explain everything to them if we don't speak English well. They tried to take the phones of many people in the village and they killed people who took pictures because they want to lie about what happened there. So now if we have pictures we will give them to anyone who asks us. As many as you want.

The people in Shilkali who survived, and my family, ran into the nearby jungle and stayed there for five days without food or shelter. They didn't have anything to eat so after five days they came back to the village to get burnt rice. They saw that around eighty people had been slaughtered in a field. They purposely targeted people to kill them by shooting at them directly. Around 800 homes were burned that same day. Many people in the jungle were injured with multiple bullet wounds but no medicine was available so they died without treatment. My family travelled twelve days across the mountains to escape the brutal killing until they reached the Bangladesh border. My father told me they ate leaves and drank rain water to stay alive. Whenever I look at the pictures he sent me I remember the horror in Shilkali. I can't forget it.

My family are uneducated and they can't speak English. When I first arrived in Indonesia in 2015, I didn't even know the English alphabet. But I was able to study English every day and I can describe things that others in Burma and Bangladesh can't. My family and friends know this so they asked me to speak for them. Now I will speak to anyone. Whoever wants to hear about the genocide and ethnic cleansing in Burma. I will send them all the pictures I have.

The problem is that the Burmese government want to shut this down. They have denied citizenship for the Rohingya for years and now they are doing everything else. Their plan is to eliminate the Rohingya from Burma. They call us Bengali and say it's not our country. Our villages have been surrounded and attacked for years. From 2012 we couldn't go out or travel around Burma easily. So for a long time we couldn't tell our story and no one knew what was happening to us. Now people have escaped and we can finally tell the world. And now we have pictures.

I'm safe in Indonesia and I'm being resettled in Portland in the United States where I can study. I feel happy and lucky about that and I hope that one day my family can come and join me in the United States. Because of my situation of course I feel it is my job to share information about my brothers and sisters in Burma with the world. I feel I have a great responsibility. As Rohingya we must describe our detailed history to everyone.

(Teguh Harahap)

In my dreams I want to study journalism and politics. I used to want to be a doctor but now I want to be a journalist so that I can write articles about the Rohingya. It is not just about what's happening today. This genocide has been going on for years but it hasn't been stopped. The world doesn't have any good information about the Rohingya and the Burmese government lie about us all the time and say that there is no ethnic cleansing in Burma. But the pictures we have don't lie.

The pictures my family and friends have sent me from Shilkali are horrifically shocking but it's right that people need to know about them. If there are no pictures of the suffering of the Rohingya then it's a problem. It's good that we have pictures that show what is happening. We don't see journalists as bad for the Rohingya, instead we venerate them for trying to help. We will describe the situation in Burma to anyone who wants to know, even our friends who don't work for the media so they know the true story.

There are not many ways to tell our story if we don't speak to some media. I use Facebook, Twitter and Instagram to write about what is happening in Burma and also put the pictures my family and friends send me. There is not much I can do. But many other Rohingya can't speak English well so they can't do this. I talk to journalists and told my story to UNHCR when they processed my refugee application for resettlement in the United States. When the American government spoke to me they asked me if I killed anyone in Burma or if I beat people. They didn't understand the situation and asked me if it was about religion or ethnic cleansing. But I am not scared to answer those questions. This is about genocide.

It's difficult to hear that people don't want to look at pictures of the Rohingya because they are upset. I don't understand why they don't want to see them. People should look even if the pictures are horrific and dire. I hear stories about what is happening every day from my family but pictures are better than reading about it. People can understand more easily. I think news articles about the Rohingya are better if they also have pictures. I feel sad if people think that the pictures are not real. Now there are pictures all over the internet about the Rohingya so you can see we are not lying. If you type in 'Rohingya Genocide' on Google now there are so many pictures of the things that the Burmese military and Rakhine people did to us. So that's a very good thing.

If people look at the pictures then maybe someone will stop what is happening in Burma. Then it will become peaceful again and I can go back.

PHOTOS OF THE ROHINGYA CRISIS: A SERIES OF DILEMMAS

AISYAH LLEWELLYN | 29 MAR 2018

When a Rohingya refugee in Indonesia approached us with graphic photos from Rakhine State, we were faced with the dilemma of how to handle them. Our North Sumatra editor reflects on the issues we grappled with.

WARNING: Some photos within the article might be graphic and distressing.

Mohammad Noyeem, a Rohingya refugee, looks at a picture that appears to show a Myanmar police officer photographing a bloated corpse in a rice paddy. Asked if the man is wearing an official police uniform and if he recognises the victim, the 18-year-old pushes the phone away and says, "I can't." He's been looking at photographs of corpses and identifying them for over an hour.

For three years, Noyeem lived in a refugee camp in Medan, Indonesia, where *New Naratif* interviewed him. He has since moved to the United States to be resettled in Portland. He escaped the violence in Rakhine State in Myanmar when he was just 15 years old and has pictures on his phone that were sent to him by his brother-in-law, Samsualom, who fled to Malaysia five years ago. Samsualom has since been meticulously compiling pictures sent to him by friends and family in Rakhine. Noyeem also has pictures from his father and other friends in refugee camps in Bangladesh. The photographs are almost inconceivably violent, but Noyeem and the other refugees at the Hotel Beraspati in Medan would like them to be published by the foreign media.

"We are not lying, the world needs to see this," is a regular refrain.

But the publication of such images presents a series of dilemmas for journalists, even if the refugees themselves urge us to do so.

The pictures that Noyeem and the other refugees have on their phones are graphic and shocking in their brutality. They show bloodied corpses lying in ditches and victims with gratuitous knife wounds, including severed heads. Several pictures show women being burned over an open fire. Others show dead babies lying in pits or being burned on sheets of corrugated metal with a fire beneath them. There are images of women who've been mutilated and who appear to have been raped. Some of the people in the pictures look like they have gunshot wounds. Noyeem's phone is a gallery of horror.

How violent is too violent?

To publish, or not? It's a moral dilemma for editors who have to make the call. As Roger Tooth, head of photography at *The Guardian*, says in a piece written in 2014 after the onslaught in Gaza and the MH17 crash over Ukraine: "If you had died a violent and unjust death, wouldn't you want the world to know all the details surrounding that death? On the other hand, in showing those images, are we perhaps feeding a propaganda machine and fuelling more conflict?"

[Publishing graphic images can be gratuitous, employed as sensationalist clickbait for views. Not only do such moves fail to help, they heap another layer of exploitation on to already-persecuted individuals, turning the dead and wounded into objects of fascination to satisfy an audiences' morbid curiosity.

And if the photographs are so graphic that people can't bring themselves to look at them, then journalists are doing themselves and their subjects no favours. If people stop reading an article because they are distressed by the accompanying photographs, then we would have failed in our goal of telling an important story in front of the largest number of people possible.

So how far is too far when it comes to violent images, and how much can we expect the public to conceivably handle? In the book *War Porn*, photographer Christoph Bangert confronts the question: "How can we refuse to acknowledge a mere representation—a picture—of a horrific event, while other people are forced to live through the horrific event itself?"[1]]

It's a fair point, but the images on Noyeem's phone would challenge even the most stoic of photography editors. In the cases of the women

---

1 http://time.com/3705884/why-violent-news-images-matter/

and children in particular, many are them of naked or mutilated. While their violent deaths deserve to be documented, their dignity in death should also be preserved. It's tough to know where to draw the line.

A photograph appears to show a police officer photographing a corpse in rice paddy.
(Teguh Harahap)

For wire agency Agence France Presse (AFP), it's about what's necessary to convey a sense of what's happening on the ground: "The goal is not to shock or sensationalize, but to inform. And that means to show, within certain limits, the impact of the conflict on people who live in rebel zones or regime-controlled areas. Not to do so would amount to taking away the victims' humanity".

Problems with verification

The fact that many of the photographs coming out of Rakhine are unverified (and extremely difficult to verify) adds another layer of complexity and moral ambiguity to the issue of publication. Almost all the pictures provided by the refugees at the Hotel Beraspati look like they've been taken using a mobile phone, often from a distance. A quick search also finds some of these photographs online, published on blogs and social media pages. Many Rohingya are snapping pictures on a mobile phone rather than using a camera, then uploading them to the internet immediately where they take on a life of their own. For many journalists, verifying such photographs is almost impossible, although some news agencies have other measures in place.

One news agency at the forefront of photograph verification is Agence France Presse (AFP), which uses a network of local stringers or 'citizen journalists' to take photographs in places like Syria.[2] To verify photographs, they check the metadata of the image and cross reference this with information from Google Maps to identify local landmarks. AFP is one of the few news agencies in the world with sophisticated software and a photo lab in Paris that can authenticate photographs. The majority of smaller newsrooms simply don't have the resources to do this.

Noyeem identifies these women as housewives from Shilkali. (Teguh Harahap)

When Noyeem looks at the photographs that his brother-in-law sent from Malaysia and his father and siblings sent from Bangladesh, he says he recognises places around his hometown of Shilkali, particularly the areas by the river. He recognises some of the people in them. One photo shows three women lying dead in the mud, and Noyeem says his brother-in-law told him they were housewives, although he can't remember their

2 https://correspondent.afp.com/behind-afps-syria-coverage

names. In another photo, he identifies a man who appears to have had his lower legs hacked off; Noyeem says he was a fisherman who lived at the other end of Shilkali so he didn't know him well.

Out of all the pictures, Noyeem positively identifies only one person by name; an older man he says was called Antamia is lying dead on the ground, covered in blood. Noyeem says he was around 60 years old and had worked as one of the village chiefs, providing guidance to the youngsters in Shilkali. Noyeem thinks he had been deliberately targeted for being someone in a position of authority in the village. He recounts all this matter-of-factly, but when asked how he feels he shakes his head and says, "Sad. A kind man."

Noyeem identifies this man as Antamia and says he was one of the village elders. (Teguh Harahap)

But it's not enough that one source claims to know the people in the pictures and says that they are from Shilkali. Noyeem provides names of people who sent him the pictures, like his brother-in-law Samsualom and his friend Rayullah who's now in Bangladesh. But they're still only unknown entities at the end of a mobile phone. It isn't clear who took the photographs, who owns the copyright or if they've been doctored in some way. And while there's no suggestion that Noyeem isn't telling the truth, journalists face other problems when recording testimonies.

Scepticism and responsibility

Journalists like *The New York Times*' Hannah Beech have written about their experience reporting from Rohingya refugee camps in Bangladesh. "Within an hour, I had a notebook filled with the kind of quotes that pull at heartstrings. Little of it was true," she wrote.[3]

As Beech explains, the reasons why Rohingya refugees sometimes don't tell the full truth are varied. Some might believe that it's in their interests to make their story sound as shocking and interesting as possible, so journalists would be inclined to print it and get the world to pay attention to the crisis. Refugees may also be struggling with trauma that makes it difficult to recall details with accuracy. It's the reason why some victims of violent situations, such as robbery, fail to remember the faces of their attackers or make mistakes about times and dates. It's understandable that the severe repression and violence that Rohingya refugees have suffered will take its toll.

As Beech explains, publishing something that later turns out to be untrue can have dire consequences: "[…] false narratives devalue the genuine horrors—murder, rape and mass burnings of villages—that have been inflicted upon the Rohingya by Myanmar's security forces. And such embellished tales only buttress the Myanmar government's contention that what is happening in Rakhine State is not ethnic cleansing, as the international community suggests, but trickery by foreign invaders."[4]

Even the best of intentions might end up being counter-productive. Beech's own article was criticised for playing straight into the hands of the Myanmar authorities; commentators questioned her decision to single out particular individuals, the veracity of their accounts, and the whole point of her article. That some refugee stories might be false should, after all, not come as a surprise to journalists, who deal with unreliable sources all the time—and not just among refugees, but also businesspeople, public relations executives, politicians or government representatives.[5]

That one journalist's attempt to try to convey the complexity of her reporting experience ended up being used by the authorities to discredit and undermine an already-marginalised community just demonstrates how carefully the media should tread in handling such a fraught situation.

---

3 https://www.nytimes.com/2018/02/01/world/asia/rohingya-myanmar-camps.html

4 https://www.nytimes.com/2017/09/11/world/asia/myanmar-rohingya-ethnic-cleansing.html

5 http://www.rohingyablogger.com/2018/02/hannah-beech-journos-power-without.html

Our decision

New Naratif spent some time discussing, as a team, how to respond to Noyeem's request that we publish the photos in his possession. We talked about all the issues mentioned above, taking into particular consideration our capacity, as a small start-up with very limited manpower and funding, to verify the photos. We knew that it would be problematic to publish such graphic images, but also felt that we couldn't turn away from Noyeem's plea for help.

In the end, we've decided to publish the photographs that Noyeem showed us the way we first saw them: on his phone. We've also asked Noyeem to explain why he believes so strongly in the publication of these photos; he gave his account shortly before he left for the United States, and it has been reproduced with minimal edits.[6] It was important to us that Noyeem be portrayed as more than just a victim, but as an individual with agency who speaks for himself.

There are no perfect answers or easy solutions for journalists faced with reporting on complicated issues involving some of the worst suffering on the planet. As Fred Ritchin, *co-director of the Photography & Human Rights program at the Tisch School of the Arts in New York*, says, "There is no calculus to determine the most effective way to show horror."

---

6 https://newnaratif.com/journalism/photos-rohingya-crisis-world-needs-see/

A CREATIVE OUTLET FOR "INVISIBLE" HANDS

SARA MOULTON | 12 JUL 2018

Migrant workers are often seen as "transient" and separate from everyone else in Singapore. But literary activities like poetry workshops are helping to break down barriers and reduce segregation.

*Still in the same world, we belong to different spheres
You on that side and me on this:
we can do nothing but remember each other
The memories of you and me hang like posters*

These lines from *Pocket 2* by Zakir Hossain Khokan won the 2014 Migrant Worker Poetry Competition. The idea came to him one evening while on a bus back to his dormitory. He missed his wife. "The bleak and gloomy sky made me miss her voice, her warmth, and her touch all the more," he says. He thought back to the time he attended Bangladesh's national book fair with his wife, passing by the florists of Shahbag as the rickshaws went by. The nostalgia made him pick up a pen and start writing.

The Migrant Worker Poetry Competition

Three years after Zakir's win, the 2017 Migrant Worker Poetry Competition, held in the polished environs of the auditorium in Singapore's National Gallery, was attended by a fairly even split of migrant workers and Singaporeans, Permanent Residents (PRs) and expatriates. It was a welcome sight; an opportunity, as seen by founder and coordinator Shivaji Das, to change the public perception of migrant workers in the city-state.

Das has noticed a change in attitude among the workers from when the competition first begun in 2014. At first, he noticed a sense of wonder among the poets that people were interested in listening to their work. "Many of the contestants asked to take a photo with an audience member," he says.

The poets don't do this so much anymore; now, they are the stars of the show, performing for an appreciative audience. They own the stage and recite poetry with admirable gravitas.

Migrant workers—distinguished by terminology from the more privileged "expatriates"—travel to Singapore from nearby developing countries like the Philippines, Indonesia, India and Bangladesh. As of December 2017, Singapore is home to 246,800 migrant domestic workers and 284,900 migrant construction workers. Collectively, these men and women number over half a million; a significant proportion for a country whose total population is about 5.5 million. Often referred to as "unskilled workers", they can be subjected to infantilising treatment as employers confiscate mobile phones and passports or control the amount of time off they have from work.

This sentiment is echoed in Rolinda Onates Espanola's poem, *My Story*, which won the 2016 Migrant Worker Poetry Competition. In the poem, the speaker says:

> Not allowed handphone not allowed to bathe everyday even brushing teeth too
> Can't talk to anybody not even to my fellow Filipino
> Worst to my disgrace, noodles and slices of bread is my only sustenance
> With conviction, give my strength and endurance

For this entry, Espanola had been inspired by accounts of maltreatment of domestic workers, such as the high-profile case of Thelma Gawidan, whose employers were convicted and jailed in 2017[1] for starving her. Gawidan had lost 20kg over a 15-month period, losing about 40% of her body mass. She was required to seek permission before drinking water, and was banned from using the bathroom in the house—she had to use the visitor's toilets in the condominium complex.

The myth of being "unskilled"

A common myth is that these workers, coming as they do from nations with limited opportunities, are lucky to have the chance to work in a thriving metropolis like Singapore. Such a mindset contributes to

---

1 https://www.todayonline.com/singapore/singaporean-couple-sentenced-starving-their-domestic-helper

discussion of migrant workers are little more than units of labour; it's common to see comments online about how they're in Singapore only "to work", as if aspects of life can be separated into such silos.

But the migrant worker poets' performances challenge these stereotypes and biases. "The feedback from the audience [at the beginning was that] they didn't know the migrant worker poets could be so talented. Then the audience members gain a greater appreciation for the difficulties that these poets face in their day-to-day life," Das says.

Much of the poetry revolves around the experience of migrant workers in Singapore; the homesickness, the longing for children and parents left behind, the challenges that they face in a new land. Watching these performances give audience members an insight into their lives and prompt them to take a more compassionate view.

Espanola used to avoid some conversations, especially if she thought there would be hurtful comments made about migrant workers. Since participating in the competition, though, she's discovered that "young Singaporeans are a loving and humane people. Singapore gives us a platform where we can showcase our talents. Now, society is more aware of us [migrants], and that we are not just workers. We are human, we have talent."

Who *isn't* in the audience is as important as who's there. While Das estimates that 20% of the poetry competition's audience are newcomers, they tend to be young and outgoing, with experience of travelling or living overseas. The challenge is in reaching the heartland and Singaporeans aged 50 and above.

Connection and community

Singapore is an attractive destination for migrants hoping to support families back home, but some arrive to find the city a much less hospitable place than they'd hoped for. There have been many stories about the mistreatment—from arriving in Singapore with debt equivalent to several months' salary, to living in less than ideal conditions, to being restricted to when one can talk to friends and family, to not being accepted or integrated into the community.

Feelings of isolation—compounded by stressors like financial struggles, longer working hours, and less time to connect with loved ones—are bad for mental health. A survey[2] by the Humanitarian Organisation for Migration Economics (HOME) found "an overall elevated level of mental stress" in migrant domestic workers, affected by factors such as a perceptions related to integration, privacy and dignity. Of all the 91 respondents surveyed, 47% said they didn't feel integrated into the family they work for, leaving them feeling isolated and vulnerable in a strange city.

A similar sense of loneliness and alienation can affect the men, too. Zakir first arrived in Singapore in 2003, and searched for a poetry community where it would exist in his native Bangladesh: in the newspaper.

"Outside of my work hours, I was curious to know more about Singapore, especially its literature and poetry. So, for four months I bought *The Straits Times* hoping to find poems inside the pages," he says. "In Bangladesh, there are always poems published in books and in newspapers, but I could not find poems in any of the Singapore newspapers, no matter how hard I searched."

Zakir had left his job as a freelance journalist in Dhaka to become a construction supervisor in Singapore. He eventually found like-minded individuals at *Amrakajona*, a poetry interest group. *Amrakajona* means "we are" in Bengali.

"After a tiring six-day work week, we would gather together on Sundays to exchange insights and share our latest creative works with one another," he says. "Immersing myself in Bengali poetry alleviated fatigue and homesickness. Sharing this interest with fellow members also made me feel that I was not alone."

Activities like poetry workshops and creative writing classes provide migrant workers with community and companionship, as well as opportunities to express themselves in a country where people might not always listen. These workshops also expose migrant workers from different communities to each other. Eli Nur Fadilah, a domestic worker from Indonesia, says that attending a poetry workshop changed how she felt about Bangladeshi migrant workers because "at first, I was very scared of them because I had heard bad stories. But after I got to know them, I don't feel scared."

---

2 https://static1.squarespace.com/static/5a12725612abd96b9c737354/t/5a1fe5610d9297c2
b97526ff/1512039798091/Report_Home-sweet-home_work-life-and-well-being-of-foreign-
domestic-workers-in-Singapore.pdf

Removing barriers

Although Singapore is often seen as a melting pot, segregation exists when it comes to these low-income workers. While domestic workers reside in their place of work, construction workers live in dormitories, often sited away from the rest of the Singaporean population. Conditions have been reported to be quite dire, with one construction company recently fined[3] for housing 60 migrant workers in a rat-infested dormitory.

It's a physical manifestation of mindsets that constantly frame migrant workers as the Other, distinct and separate from everyone else living and working in the city-state. But as the migrant worker poets grow in prominence in the city, the lines are slowly, finally, beginning to blur.

The workers have been prolific and enthusiastic, collaborating on poetry anthologies that have raised their profile. In 2016, local publisher Ethos Books published the poems of Md Mukul Hossine in a volume entitled *Me, Migrant*[4]. Migrant worker poets have also been featured[5] during the Singapore Writers Festival.

Events like Carnival of Poetry[6], which brings together Singaporean and migrant worker poets, continue to take down barriers—in such gatherings, there is no "them" or "us", only wordsmiths.

"Migrant worker poets are involved in events throughout the week, and every week there are poetry events where migrant worker poets and Singaporean poets perform on the same stage," Das explains, although he notes that these interactions are mainly happening in the artistic community, and not yet within the wider community.

"For other poets, either Singaporean or those who do not belong to the migrant worker poetry community, the doors of Carnival of Poetry are open to them. We believe poetry has no barrier, border, or subgroup," Zakir says.

Other events, like Human Library SG, where individuals volunteer as "Books" to tell their stories to interested "Readers", also provide migrant workers with platforms to meet Singaporeans.

"Being a book in the Human Library helps me learn a lot, especially about the younger generation in Singapore. They are compassionate

3 https://www.straitstimes.com/singapore/manpower/
  construction-firm-charged-for-housing-60-foreign-workers-in-rat-infested
4 https://www.ethosbooks.com.sg/products/me-migrant
5 https://www.facebook.com/events/2048044582091854/
6 https://www.facebook.com/carnivalofpoetry/

and through sharing my experiences, hopefully someday when they employee a foreign domestic worker, they will have empathy for their helper," Espanola says.

Privileges and rights

Although these are all promising schemes, it's worth noting that the poets who participate in writing groups and competitions are the fortunate ones. Their ability to be present at these events means that they have time off work, with employers who are either supportive or not overly strict. For many other workers in Singaporean homes or in dormitories across the island, these opportunities for community, connection and talent cultivation have become luxuries.

Winning better institutional protections, entitlements and rights for migrant workers is a long-term goal for the country's migrant rights groups. But smaller, grassroots efforts to reach out to migrant workers still exist.

Zakir started the "One Bag, One Book" project to encourage migrant workers to read more. It's a simple idea: get the workers to adopt the habit of carrying a book in their bag wherever they go, and they'll read at least one book a year. He's really put his money where his mouth is: while back in Bangladesh, he purchased 250 books with his own money to give out once back in Singapore. He also sometimes receives English books from donors to include in the project.

"Since these books are in the migrant worker's mother tongue, reading connects him to his home country. It also serves as a leisure activity to relieve stress and increase productivity at work," Zakir explains.

Whether reading or writing poetry, what it comes down to is a very human need for connection, the ability to step into someone else's shoes. But what's also important is the willingness to listen—only then can the connection be complete.

UNDOCUMENTED IN THAILAND

LEONIE KIJEWSKI | 27 AUG 2018

Thailand recently launched a crackdown on undocumented workers in an effort to combat trafficking, but the lack of a victim-centric approach means that new measures are likely making things worse for vulnerable migrant workers.

O ver the past year, 20-year-old Malai has been living in constant fear. She moves from construction site to construction site in Nonthaburi province, just north of the Thai capital Bangkok, as her assignments change. She came to the Kingdom from rural province in northwest Cambodia as a teenager with her family.

"I don't have a proper employer, no legitimate documents, and I don't know where I'll go next. I am afraid I'll get deported," she says.

Thailand passed a royal decree mid-2017 to impose hefty fines on undocumented workers and their employers, as well as brokers. While the proposed fines for workers initially ranged up to almost USD3,000 and included five years' imprisonment, this provision has been scrapped in an amendment.

Instead, workers now face fines of up to USD1,500 and theirs employers up to USD3,000 per worker. Repeat offenders face imprisonment of up to one year and a fine of up to USD6,000 per worker, as well as a ban from hiring migrant workers for three years.

The law was initially set to be enforced at the end of July last year. Following protests over the heavy penalties and the proposed speed of implementation by migrant rights advocates and employers, the government granted a grace period until December, and extended it until the end of June this year. During this grace period, undocumented migrants were expected to register with the authorities.

Undocumented Cambodians in Thailand

It technically costs USD100 to apply for a passport in Cambodia, but applicants often report having to pay more. Until this year, it was also only possible to apply for a passport in the capital, so Cambodians in rural provinces would have to find the means to travel to Phnom Penh. Although the government has said it will open new passport centres in other provinces, progress on this has been unclear thus far.

Malai couldn't afford the lengthy and costly process to obtain a passport and migrated to Thailand undocumented when she was 10 years old. She's not alone: rights groups estimate that about 750,000 undocumented Cambodian workers lived in Thailand before the crackdown began in July. According to Cambodia's Ministry of Labour, more than a million Cambodians—both registered and unregistered—lived in Thailand last year. This makes Cambodians the second largest group of migrants in Thailand, after the Burmese.

But the numbers provided by the two different governments contradict each other: while Thai authorities reported[1] that 350,840 Cambodian workers were properly registered by the end of June this year, Cambodian authorities had earlier claimed that all Cambodians, bar a few, had registered.

For THB300 (about USD9) a day, Malai starts work at 7am and only finishes about 8pm. "Sometimes I live on the worksite with other people," she says. "We need to avoid the authorities. We're very fearful."

The past year has revealed problems with the process of getting documented. First, migrants without passports had to go to the Cambodian embassy to apply for passports in Thailand itself—an exception the Cambodian government made for this situation. Then one would have to get Thai documents, but there were only a few centres at which you could register, requiring migrants to travel long distances. The centres were so overrun that some migrants, including children, told *New Naratif* that they had to sleep in the centres to wait their turn. Rights groups reported corruption in the foreign embassies and centres, making the process even more costly.

As a result, thousands of Cambodians, Burmese and Laotians chose to flee across the borders to return home, instead of remaining in Thailand at the risk of getting caught. Repatriation was not without difficulties: migrants complained about being extorted by the authorities on both sides of the border.

---

1 https://www.bangkokpost.com/news/general/1495782/cops-crack-down-on-illegal-migrants

Not seeing any way to make a living in Cambodia, Malai has decided to stay in Thailand for now despite the risks.

She also doesn't see any way to get documented. "I heard that I need to have a decent amount of money to obtain a passport, and I'm afraid the embassy officials will blame me, maybe deport me back to Cambodia," she says. "I hope they won't arrest me… I will try to stay as long as I can."

This fear of arrests has been a reality for many Cambodians over the past month. When the deadline to register expired, Thailand launched a crackdown on irregular migrants, deporting at least a thousand Cambodians within a few days at the beginning of July.

Paying to become legal

Maryann Bylander, a professor at Lewis & Clark College and an expert on migration in the Global South, says the new laws triggered unintended consequences. "I'd say that the main impact of the new law is that workers are paying exorbitant amounts of money to become legal—often taking on debts in order to do so," she tells *New Naratif* in an email.

A conversation Bylander had with a Burmese worker illustrates this issue. "The main impact of the new law is to reduce our savings, because every time we have to process a document we have to pay. And the process changes frequently, so we pay frequently," he told her.

Chonticha Tangworamongkon, a project manager at Human Rights and Development Foundation in Thailand, says costs associated with registering, or even renewing documents, means that many migrant workers borrow money from their employers. They then pay it off as they work. "This can be conducive to debt bondage, a form of human trafficking," she points out.

According to the United Nations Special Rapporteur on Contemporary Slavery Urmila Bhoola's 2016 report[2], debt bondage is one of the four practices similar to slavery or forms of servitude addressed in the UN's Convention on the Abolition of Slavery and can be classified as forced labour, or even slavery.

"Migrant workers often become trapped in situations of bondage by borrowing money at exorbitant interest rates to pay recruitment fees or

2 https://www.ohchr.org/en/NewsEvents/Pages/DisplayNews.aspx?NewsID=20504&
    LangID=E

by taking an advance payment from intermediaries to secure work in the country of destination," she writes. "Once migrants arrive in the country of destination they are often forced to work in harsh conditions to pay back debt they have accrued."

In Thailand, the report states, many migrant workers from Cambodia, Laos, and Myanmar were "lured to work on fishing boats free of charge and once they start working are charged for the costs of recruitment and the travel expenses, with high interest rates."

Is this fighting trafficking, or counter-productive?

In an effort to curb human trafficking, the Thai government has not only launched a campaign against undocumented migrants, but also embarked on stricter law enforcement against traffickers over the past year. These moves have pushed its status in the US State Department's Trafficking in Persons 2018 report[3] from Tier 2 Watchlist up to Tier 2.

"The government demonstrated increasing efforts by prosecuting and convicting more traffickers, and decreasing prosecution time for trafficking cases through the use of specialised anti-trafficking law enforcement divisions," the report says.

But while more traffickers were convicted in 2017, the report states that fewer victims have been identified in the same period: the government identified 445 victims of trafficking in 2017, versus 824 in 2016. For labour trafficking, the difference is even starker: 119 were reported last year, compared to 489 in 2016.

This, the report writes, has raised concerns among NGOs and experts that victims were left "vulnerable to penalisation and re-trafficking." Tougher enforcement has not necessarily translated to better protection of victims.

Another drawback of the new law, says Bylander, are that some clauses actually make migrants more vulnerable. "In some cases, the law is also creating exactly what it seeks to eliminate," she says.

She explains that the easiest way to finance passports and work visas is for employers to pay for them first, then confiscate the workers' documents until the debt is paid. The practice of holding documents, she says, has "increased significantly" due to the new law.

Chonticha says that although the confiscation of documents is illegal under the decree, the stricter law enforcement has pushed more employers

3 https://www.state.gov/j/tip/rls/tiprpt/2018/index.htm

to breach this provision. "This is because the number of workers with documents [is] possibly far lower than the actual demand of workers for Thailand's economy. So workers with proper documents are precious to the employers," she says.

The only way left for employers to hire new migrant workers in a documented way would be to go through the Memorandum of Understanding process—which can take months and cost several hundred dollars through the use of brokers—between Cambodia and Thailand. This increases the employers' fear of losing migrant workers, Chonticha says. Employers therefore rather confiscate documents and risk a fine than risk losing their employees and face a labour shortage.

Moreover, the new law requires workers to register under specific employers and jobs, making them more vulnerable to deportation should they perform other work than indicated.

And while the new law has put many hurdles in migrant workers' way over the past year, Bylander says it's not clear whether they've reaped any benefits: "While we might assume that when migrants gain legal status, their wages would increase, I haven't seen any evidence that this is true."

The lucky ones

Some migrants, however, have been luckier. 30-year-old Chheng Chhang has been working in a cake shop in Chonburi province since 2011. He's been successfully registered, obtaining his documents in April with his employer's help.

Like Malai, he doesn't earn much: just THB250 per day (about USD7.50). He says the cost of food and accommodation has increased over this past year—but at least it's still enough to pay off his family's debts back home. And it's better than back in Cambodia's Kampong Cham, where he'd been a farmer. "I didn't earn enough to survive," he says. "It was very stressful. We did not eat enough."

Although he hasn't been directly affected by the crackdown, he's seen its effects. "My friends [started] leaving as soon as they heard of the rumor of a crackdown," he says. "Some of my extended [family was] arrested while they were crossing the border [to apply for documents in Cambodia]... Now they are traumatised; they have no interest to come back."

Leng Len contributed reporting to this article.

ENVIRONMENTAL AND HUMAN HEALTH

MYANMAR'S RUBY TRADE

JOSHUA CARROLL | 18 JAN 2018

*Precious gems could be an opportunity to earn one's fortune, or bring trag-
edy to miners toiling in unforgiving circumstances. Can the industry pivot
towards more ethical practices?*

Before he became a well-heeled gems trader, Maung Gyi toiled in
the ruby mines of Myanmar's Mogok valley for twenty years. He
risked landslides and falling rocks as he sifted through the earth
in search of the valley's famed pigeon blood-coloured gems, considered
the world's finest. But it wasn't until a chance encounter with a prospector one beer-fuelled evening about five years ago that he struck it rich.

The prospector, an acquaintance, charged into the simple bar where
he had been drinking with friends and declared he had found an unex-
plored patch of land that looked rich in deposits. He was assembling a
group to go digging that very night, he said: who wanted in?

Maung Gyi offered to invest 100,000 kyats (about USD100) in tools
and other essentials for the ragtag enterprise. Others agreed to dig in
exchange for a cut of any profits. Even the lady who owned the bar
chipped in a little money, the equivalent of a couple rounds of drinks.

The group arrived at the prospect around midnight and began digging
a vertical shaft mine. This unlicensed, off-the-cuff operation was illegal,
and even though a black market thrived thanks to corrupt local officials,
it was best to work under cover of darkness. The crew, intoxicated off
the thrill of the gamble they were taking, worked through the night.

The next morning, their gamble paid off in spectacular fashion;
shortly after sunrise they struck a 113-carat stone. It was so valuable
that the bar owner recouped thousands of dollars. The gem made the
crew more than USD800,000 and Maung Gyi's cut of the profits was
worth about USD100,000, he said.

"Things got a lot better for me after that," says the 43-year-old as we
sip masala tea at a restaurant in downtown Yangon, where he now enjoys
a comfortable life buying and selling precious stones. On a tree-lined
street nearby, gem traders perch on the curb bartering over trinkets. One

man peers through a loupe as he inspects a small lump of jade before bursting into laughter, apparently unimpressed by its quality.

Those in Myanmar's precious gems market navigate a realm of extremes that would be familiar to many in resource-rich yet economically dysfunctional nations. Vast wealth sits below the earth while extreme poverty blights those living on top of it.

"In Mogok, a man can struggle to feed his family in the morning and be rich in the evening," says Lakshmann Neopane, another gems trader who spent much of his youth grinding away in Mogok's mines before becoming a businessman. He wears a large blue sapphire on his right ring finger; he bought it in the town, a couple hundred kilometres north of Mandalay, Myanmar's second city.

A controversial trade

Few miners get as lucky as Maung Gyi and Neopane. The majority continue to toil in harsh, dangerous conditions for low pay while the Burmese military and its cronies enjoy the bulk of the profits, maintaining a tight grip on the industry despite economic reforms that began in 2011.

Myanmar reportedly produces more than 80% of the world's rubies, but thanks to decades of isolation under the former junta and restrictions on access for foreigners to mining areas like Mogok, the trade remains opaque and mired in controversy. A decision by the US to lift sanctions on Myanmar's jade and rubies in late 2016 drew criticism from rights campaigners, but industry figures argued it was an opportunity for new buyers to push up standards.

There might be some validity to the calls for reinstating sanctions. For traders like Neopane, the arrival of new foreign buyers has so far had minimal impact. He has dealt with a small number of American buyers since the end of sanctions, but overall, he says, medium-sized businesses weren't affected by the US ban because military figures and cronies, as well as buyers from China and India, continued to buy gems from Mogok as a way to store their wealth off-the-books. But the ban did make it more difficult for top elites to sell their gems onwards, he says.

If this assessment holds true, it strengthens the calls of boycott campaigners. "US sanctions didn't hit Mogok people," says Neopane, "but they did hit the cronies."

Myanmar's new government, led by Aung San Suu Kyi, has been vocal about its desire to reform the sector. After a landslide in the jade mining area of Hpakant in Kachin state that killed well over a hundred people in late 2015, her newly-elected administration vowed to tighten safety standards. The following year, officials announced a freeze on all new mining licenses until reforms were in place. They also kicked off a public consultation on mining, with meetings held recently in Myitkyina, Kachin's capital, and Mogok.

Civil society groups and watchdogs say these moves are encouraging, and until recently the debate over the lifted sanctions had fizzled out. But the brutal crackdown against Rohingya Muslims in Rakhine state since last August has reignited anger at those in the precious gems industry helping to line the military's pockets.

Profit and responsibility

Luxury jeweller Cartier announced last month that it would stop buying gems from Myanmar after it was targeted in a campaign accusing it of profiting from "genocide gems". The US-based International Campaign for the Rohingya is now pushing for the same from Bulgari, which sells necklaces and earrings that include sapphires, rubies and jade from Myanmar.

Meanwhile, tucked away in a small, brightly-lit store next to an artisan restaurant in Yangon's downtown, one start-up jewellery business is aiming to prove that more good can come from engaging with the gems industry than shunning it.

The gems on sale at Mia Ruby, which opened a year ago, are "responsibly sourced," says Amber Cernov, the store's Australian co-founder. That means the business aims to avoid doing any deals that might lead to money ending up in military pockets, she explains. The rubies glistening in glass cabinets here are all sourced from a family-run mine in Mogok that, as far as she can tell, has no ties to the generals.

Cernov says she has made it clear to this supplier that her business has a policy of not trading with any military mines, "and they know that that is absolutely my standard". The family enterprise operates under a joint venture with the Ministry of Natural Resources, which was formed when the new civilian government merged the mining and environment ministries after coming to power in 2015.

But it is impossible to be certain that the military doesn't benefit somewhere along the supply chain. "As with everything in the gems trade, it is really about trusting the commitments made by the family that we buy off," says Cernov. Her supplier's conduct so far looks promising, she adds. "In some instances… we cannot source the gems that we need, as the family will say they can only find that size, quality or quantity from military-linked sources."

Merely avoiding military enterprises, though, is not enough to bring the industry up to an acceptable standard. "I don't say we're ethical," Cernov adds. "I say we're responsible, in that we're trying to operate the best we can within the restraints of the current environment."

For example, the miners working for her supplier are "from what I can tell… actually paid relatively well in terms of their contribution, but whether that fully complies with the labour law is still questionable."

Cernov argues that being in the industry and pushing suppliers to up standards will help things improve faster. Mia Ruby regularly raises the issue of "workplace health and safety standards" with its supplier, she says. "However, this is not something that we have the capacity as a small new business to police ourselves."

She adds, "I think there are still a lot of issues there in terms of working conditions. Occupational health and safety… is not a culture that has been embraced here in Myanmar full stop, so that's certainly an issue."

Paul Donowitz, campaign leader for Myanmar at natural resource watchdog Global Witness, says: "Companies interested in sourcing rubies in a high-risk context such as Myanmar should be taking steps to ensure that they are engaging in responsible trade. This means putting in place measures to assess potential risks to human rights and other harmful impacts in the ruby supply chain."

Dangerous conditions

Maung Gyi is keenly aware of the treacherous conditions mine workers face in Mogok. When he was in his early twenties, his younger brother was killed while operating a hand-powered pulley to lift an enormous lump of rock out of a quarry. "People even blamed him and said 'he should have been more careful, he knew that it was risky'," Maung Gyi says.

"Every worker has to risk their life," adds Neopane. He plucks a deep-fried onion pakora ball from the table and holds it between his thumb and forefinger. "If a rock just this size falls down a mine shaft and hits you, it can kill you," he says.

Sometimes shaft mines are dug too close to one another, he adds, and the earth between them gives way and collapses. In deeper mines, where there isn't enough oxygen, some have suffocated. He estimates that between 10 and 20 people die every year in Mogok in such accidents.

For things to change, "Myanmar's ruby industry needs to open up and bring in strong checks against corruption and abuse," says Donowitz. "This is essential to assure responsible companies that they can engage in the trade without contributing to harms."

BACKED BY BANKS, VIETNAM EMBRACES DIRTY COAL

MICHAEL TATARSKI | 22 MAR 2018

A controversial coal-fired power plant in Vietnam, backed by international financing, is emblematic of the country's environmentally destructive stance on energy generation.

A petition calling on several major Singaporean banks to end their funding of thermal power plants in developing nations like Vietnam and Indonesia has shed light on the complex, transnational nature of financing for such projects.

The open letter, released last month and signed by 14 environmental groups from around the world—including Greenpeace and Friends of the Earth—singles out DBS, OCBC and UOB for "falling critically behind, not only failing to deliver policy and practical responses to climate change, but instead becoming an increasing part of the problem through the continued multi-billion dollar financing of coal-fired power stations and related infrastructure."[1]

A close look at one such power plant in Vietnam, the Nghi Son 2, reveals that Singaporean banks are not alone in this activity. According to Market Forces, an affiliate of Friends of the Earth Australia which analyses the financing of development projects, funding will not only come from the above-mentioned Singaporean banks, but also the UK's Standard Chartered, the Korea Export-Import Bank, the Japan Bank for International Cooperation and several Japanese commercial banks: Mizuho Financial Group, the Bank of Tokyo-Mitsubishi UFJ (MUFG) and the Sumitomo Mitsui Banking Corporation (SMBC). Financing for this USD2.5 billion coal-fired plant, to be located in Thanh Hoa

---

1 http://www.greenpeace.org/seasia/PageFiles/807917/Open%20letter%20calling%20on%20 DBS,%20OCBC%20and%20UOB%20to%20take%20action%20on%20climate%20change. pdf

Province just north of central Vietnam, is expected to be finalised by the end of this month.

Unwinding the finances behind a blockbuster project like Nghi Son 2 isn't easy, but Julien Vincent, executive director of Market Forces, explains how such funding is generally structured.

"Like most other deals in the region it is led by government-backed institutions like the Korea Export-Import Bank, and in the case of Nghi Son 2 it's largely Korean and Japanese," he shares. "The way it generally works is they come in and provide a large bunch of loaning interest and long-term credit, and they can do that because there's some sort of national interest imperative."

The involvement of these state-linked organisations signals that a project is safe enough for commercial banks to enter the equation and provide further financing. Since funding for Nghi Son 2 has not yet been confirmed, it is unclear exactly how much each bank is set to contribute. But the fact that they're involved at all is worrying, as the power plant would breach some of their own regulations.

The environmental cost

Several independent analyses of Nghi Son 2's Environment Impact Assessment (EIA) have concluded that the project would be disastrous for the local environment. Market Forces estimates that the plant would create twice as much CO_2 for every unit of generated power in comparison to the average thermal facility in Vietnam.

A report titled "Comments on the Environmental Impact Assessment (EIA) of Nghi Son 2 Thermal Power Plant" by the Hanoi-based Green Innovation and Development Centre (GreenID) points out numerous red flags.[2] For example, the plant is just one part of the planned Nghi Son Power Centre, which would include two other coal-fired plants. The EIA, which runs 375 pages and is only in Vietnamese, fails to take one of these other facilities into account, and therefore doesn't present the cumulative impact.[3]

These power plants will also be located within the huge Nghi Son Economic Zone, home to other industrial sites such as steel and petrochemical refining plants, ship yards and consumer goods export facilities. The EIA excludes these factors when accounting for overall emissions.

---

2 http://en.greenidvietnam.org.vn/view-document/5aaa28f45cd7e8d038169432

3 https://www.jbic.go.jp/ja/business-areas/environment/projects/pdf/60385_2.pdf

Nghi Son 2's impact of local fisheries is also a matter of concern given its coastal location, and GreenID found problems here as well. While the plant's EIA claims that there'll be no impact on aquatic species, GreenID points out that the report "does not have [a] record of fisheries species prior to the construction of the plant, so it does not assess the level of reaction of each species to the change of environment, so there is no bases of evaluation."

The NGO's studies of ecosystems around four other thermal power plants with similar capacities elsewhere in Vietnam found that fisheries have been decimated. According to their report, fishermen have had to quit fishing in certain areas, while fish farms have had to be relocated away from contaminated water.

Finally, GreenID found that the people living around the Nghi Son 2 site have not been consulted. Therefore, "local people hardly know impacts of the projects in advance. It is only after the plant is constructed and operated that they get to know. That's why there are many complaints filed by local people afterwards."

Standards on climate change and energy
DBS and Standard Chartered have borne the brunt of the criticism over Nghi Son 2 financing and how it relates to their corporate environmental policies.

DBS released a new policy on sustainability commitments in January this year. One section states: "DBS will stop financing new greenfield coal-fired power generation projects in OECD/developed markets. In developing countries, DBS will change its focus to more efficient technologies."[4]

The fact that their explicit commitment to end funding for coal-fired power plants applies only to developed countries hasn't been received well in places like Vietnam. "We see that as a double standard," says Tuong Nguyen, program manager at CHANGE Vietnam, one of the signatories of the petition. "It's unfair for people in Vietnam because that means we don't deserve clean air like people in developed countries."

Tuong and her organisation have taken direct aim at DBS in a separate online petition addressed to Peter Seah, DBS' chairman, and

---

4 https://www.dbs.com/newsroom/DBS_shares_sustainability_commitments_addressing_

climate_change

Piyush Gupta, the bank's CEO. The letter refers to Nghi Son 2, as well as three other coal-fired power plants that DBS is considering funding in Vietnam.[5]

DBS did not respond to request for comment for this article.

Meanwhile, *The Straits Times* recently reported[6] that Standard Chartered is reconsidering its potential support for Nghi Son 2 since technical analysis of the project's Environmental Impact Assessment has revealed that the completed plant would breach the bank's own publicly-stated position on climate change and energy.[7]

Standard Chartered's statement on the issue says that the bank "[w]ill not provide debt or equity to new coal-fired power plants which do not achieve a long-run emissions intensity of below 830g/CO2/kWh." The measurement refers to the amount (in grams) of carbon dioxide per kilowatt-hour of energy production. Lauri Myllyvirta, Greenpeace's Beijing-based coal and air pollution expert, estimates that Nghi Son 2 would have an average emissions intensity of 890-900g/CO2/kWh, well above the bank's limit.

In response to questions based on this analysis, a Standard Chartered spokesperson said: "For a potential coal project, we will work with an independent consultant to review the project's potential impact on the environment and have the consultant report objectively on its projected long-term emissions. Upon getting the consultant's report, if the findings fall short of our standards, our approach is to first work with the client to try to ensure the project can be aligned with our standards, and if this is not possible, we can and would decline participation. In the case of Nghi Son 2, it is still under review."

But DBS and Standard Chartered aren't the only banks running the risk of breaching their own commitments. Like Standard Chartered, Mizuho, MUFG and SMBC are also members of the Equator Principles. Members of this group, which includes 92 global financial institutions,

---

5 https://www.change.org/p/k%C3%BD-t%C3%AAn-k%C3%AAu-g%E1%BB%8Di-ng%C3%A2n-h%C3%A0ng-dbs-ng%C6%B0ng-%C4%91E1%BA%A7u-t%C6%B0-v%C3%A0o-nhi%E1%BB%87t-%C4%91i%E1%BB%87n-than-g%C3%A2y-%C3%B4-nhi%E1%BB%85m-t%E1%BA%A1i-vi%E1%BB%87t-nam

6 http://www.straitstimes.com/business/banking/singapore-banks-under-scrutiny-over-coal-lending

7 https://av.sc.com/corp-en/Climate-Change-and-Energy.pdf

commit to more rigorous standards for project financing and environmental policies.

Bernadette Maheandiran, research and legal analyst at Market Forces, believes their potential participation in Nghi Son 2 goes against the Equator Principles, as members of the group are required to look into other power sources such as natural gas or renewable energy before throwing their support behind coal. "They need to say that these alternatives are not plausible, and they didn't do that in this case," Maheandiran explains. "So the fact that these banks are jumping on board is in violation of something that they've signed up to."

Requests for comment were sent to all the banks concerned in this story, but OCBC was the only other financial institution to respond.

According to Koh Ching Ching, head of group corporate communications, "OCBC has a responsible financing framework and policies that assess environment, social and governance (ESG) risks of the projects and their impact on the environment. In the financing of energy projects, beyond the evaluation of the credit worthiness, we review their Environmental Impact Assessment (EIA) reports and perform enhanced due diligence on the operational aspects of the customers' business activities. Our responsible financing policies are strengthened over time. Environment sustainability is a journey. We seek to positively influence our customers' behaviours by engaging them in adopting appropriate sustainable practices."

What Nghi Son 2 tells us about Vietnam's energy policy

This controversial power plant is emblematic of Vietnam's energy production strategy over the next decade, a period during which electricity consumption is expected to triple. While many countries around the world are focused on phasing out coal-fired plants, Vietnam is going in the opposite direction.

According to the government's long-term master plan on power and energy generation, which was approved in March of 2016, the country's share of power created by thermal plants will increase in coming years.

The plan forecasts that coal-fired thermal power will account for 49.3% of all electricity produced in Vietnam by 2020 before rising to 55% by 2025 and dipping to 53.2% by 2030. By that point, the power sector will be consuming almost 130 million tons of coal per year.

Vietnam's leadership had once planned to enter the nuclear energy sector, with Russian and Japanese firms agreeing to help build plants on the south-central coast. However, this policy was abandoned in late 2016 due to the cost of the proposed facilities. Hydroelectric, wind and solar production is expected to rise by 2030 as well, but coal will still provide the majority of Vietnam's energy for the foreseeable future.[8]

Tuong of CHANGE Vietnam believes the battle over Nghi Son 2 is just one step in a broader fight against this policy direction. "Vietnam has great potential for developing renewable energy, and we're not saying we should stop all coal power plants that are in operation," she explains. "But we want to stress that we need to stop investing into new coal power plants."

She's been disappointed by the tepid response from locals and media outlets alike. "We've done media training and briefings to provide information on this issue to Vietnamese journalists… but the topic of coal power plants is very sensitive, so it's hard to do that," she says. "Even organising a petition in Vietnam is something that we are not officially allowed to do, to ask the government to stop doing something."

The petition directed towards DBS, which was launched on 6 March, had garnered 713 signatures as of the time of writing. CHANGE is aiming for 2,000 signatures by 22 March.

"We need local voices in this case," Tuong says. "Otherwise the banks will think the local people didn't react to this information, so they won't do anything."

---

8 http://www.world-nuclear.org/information-library/country-profiles/countries-t-z/vietnam.
aspx

METHANOL POISONING: A SILENT EPIDEMIC
AISYAH LLEWELLYN | 04 MAY 2018

Occasional reports of tourist deaths draw sporadic attention to the danger-ous consumption of poisonous bootleg alcohol in Indonesia, but methanol poisoning is a constant, silent killer across the archipelago.

Indra[1] had a hangover. He'd been drinking bootleg whisky until the early hours of the morning and now felt decidedly unwell. Rolling over on the thin mattress in his shared room in Medan, North Sumatra, he opened his eyes and looked for his roommate Roby. Peering through a thick fog, he rubbed his eyes and noticed his vision was blurry. "I could barely lift my head off the mattress. It felt like I had a brick lodged in the back of my skull. The pain was excruciating, not like a normal headache at all," he says.

As he tried to get up, Indra heard coughing. Even though his eyes couldn't focus properly, he was able to make out Roby slumped in the doorway. His friend was covered in blood; Indra initially thought he'd been stabbed. When Robby started coughing again, Indra saw that he was vomiting blood which had soaked through his white vest. Neither man knew it at the time, but they were both in the grips of methanol poisoning.

A silent killer
From March to April 2018, Indonesia experienced its worst ever spate of methanol poisoning incidents[2] in West Java, Jakarta, and Papua, leaving more than 100 people dead and over 160 in hospital after drink-ing bootleg alcohol containing fatal amounts of methanol. It's caused a renewed wave of interest in methanol poisoning, but this has been a silent killer in Indonesia for years. It's difficult to get serious figures on

---

1 Name has been changed at the interviewee's request.

2 http://www.abc.net.au/news/2018-04-10/indonesia-bootleg-alcohol-kills-82-people/
9639332

the number of people who die of methanol poisoning every year, largely because it's often misdiagnosed or attributed to something else, such as bleeding in the brain. A report by the Centre for Indonesian Policy Studies (CIPS) provides an indication: "Nationwide, 487 people died from illegal alcohol poisoning between 2013 and 2016—a 226% increase over figures from 2008 to 2012."[3]

Methanol, which is colourless and odourless, is a by-product produced during the fermentation process of making alcohol. Just 30 ml of methanol—about a shot glass' worth—can kill you. It's meant to burn off naturally when alcohol is being distilled, but a mistake made during this process may leave it present in the final product. Looking to cut costs and speed up production targets, Indonesian home breweries and black market alcohol factories sometimes fail to sufficiently heat the alcohol—or eschew the heating process completely—leaving the deadly methanol behind.

Reports of methanol being deliberately added to poison consumers are extremely rare, if they happen at all; it's far more likely to be a case of human error. To make things worse, some illegal brewers deliberately mix spirits with rubbing alcohol and other products like mosquito repellent, rat poison or shoe polish to make the alcohol stronger and give it hallucinogenic properties. This in turn confuses the issue of straight methanol poisoning versus those who have been poisoned by other illicit substances.

When humans ingest methanol, it metabolises into formaldehyde. "It's like your body is being embalmed from the inside out," Lanang Suartana Putra, a doctor at Sanglah Hospital in Bali, told the press in 2016.

Methanol poisoning is not a widely understood issue, so many drinkers don't know they've been poisoned until it's too late. Because it can't be detected in drinks through taste or smell, many people think they're just suffering from a hangover. The initial symptoms do closely resemble a night of heavy drinking: headaches, stomach cramps, nausea, loss of appetite and sensitivity to light. One key sign of methanol poisoning is blurred vision as the methanol attacks the central nervous system. Methanol poisoning also happens fast: within 12–24 hours of

---

3 https://www.vice.com/en_au/article/aeyznp/indonesia-banned-beer-in-mini-markets-to-protect-the-youth-its-having-the-opposite-effect

consuming tainted alcohol, many drinkers may be asleep, hungover or still drunk when they start to feel unwell. It's essential that consumers get medical treatment as soon as possible, but methanol poisoning is often misdiagnosed—with dire consequences.

Misdiagnosis

There are various reasons for misdiagnosis. Indonesia is the most populous Muslim nation on earth and has always had a contentious relationship with alcohol. Although alcoholic drinks are available legally across most of the archipelago, alcohol is prohibited in Islam, so poisoning victims who visit hospitals in Indonesia may be judged, refused treatment or misdiagnosed by medical staff unfamiliar with methanol poisoning. In rural areas in Indonesia, deaths are sometimes blamed on demons or as righteous punishment for drinking alcohol in the first place.

When Indra saw his friend vomiting blood, he managed to get up off the floor, put him in a pedicab and take him to a local hospital. Once there, however, the hospital staff diagnosed Roby with alcohol poisoning—a common misdiagnosis—and hooked him up to an intravenous drip. Indra says that when it started to take effect, Roby began screaming and tried to rip the needle out of his hand. "It was as if the medication was reacting with the methanol in his bloodstream," says Indra. "He said his veins were on fire."

When the treatment didn't work the hospital finally—hours after he'd been poisoned—agreed to perform dialysis on Roby, the only treatment for advanced methanol poisoning. It ultimately saved his life. But the delay left Roby with severe side effects. When *New Naratif* spoke to him about the incident, he says he remembers little of that night other than waking up in hospital after the dialysis. He struggles with severe memory loss nowadays and can barely remember the questions he's been asked, losing the thread halfway through his answers. Indra also says that Robby suffers from delusions; he keeps claiming that he's getting married soon, even though he's housebound and has been married for years.

Indonesia's alcohol problems

Indonesia is not the only country in Southeast Asia that has a problem with methanol poisoning; Thailand and Vietnam have also had cases of people being poisoned by bootleg liquor. But Indonesia does have some unique alcohol-related issues that have led to the rise in methanol poisoning deaths across the country.

One such issue is an alcohol tax of 150%, meaning that imported spirits are prohibitively expensive for many Indonesians—the average starting salary of a university graduate is around IDR3 million (USD225) per month. But it's not just about less affluent Indonesians; everyone, from students to holidaymakers, wants to buy alcohol as cheaply as possible. If a bar is going to sell a vodka and coke for IDR15,000 (USD1.80), something widely advertised outside drinking establishments in Bali, it needs to keep costs down by using locally brewed illicit alcohol rather than genuine imported spirits.

Even if you can afford it, there's another problem with accessing legal alcohol in Indonesia. A law enacted in 2015 made the sale of alcohol illegal in mini-markets across Indonesia (with the exception of Bali), a policy introduced by then-trade minister Rachmat Gobel, who declared that alcohol was to blame for moral corruption engulfing Indonesian youths. All the new law has done, however, is make it more difficult to buy alcohol, a consequence highlighted by critics of the bill from the beginning. The bill was also opposed by former Jakarta Governor, Basuki "Ahok" Tjahaja Purnama, who said that "the ban could encourage the illegal sale of alcoholic beverages in the city".[4]

The rise of bottle shops

Purnama was right; many Indonesians, unable to purchase alcoholic drinks in mini-markets, have turned to unlicensed "bottle shops" which usually sell fake alcohol or moonshine like the whisky that Indra and Roby drank. The alcohol sold in these shops is not properly regulated and there's no way of knowing what it contains. According to CIPS, the ban on prohibiting the sale of alcohol in mini-markets has had a negative impact and "[…] research in six Indonesian cities confirmed that, instead of curbing the desire for intoxication, prohibition facilitates the growth of black markets, a case especially evident in areas with partial prohibition that limits the distribution of alcohol to particular zones." In other words, prohibition doesn't work—it just drives the market underground, sometimes with lethal consequences for consumers.

4 http://jakartaglobe.id/news/indonesian-ban-sale-alcohol-minimarkets-takes-effect/

When *New Naratif* interviewed Indra about the bottle shop where he purchased the whisky that almost killed him and Roby, he brought up an allegedly widespread practice that's endangering the lives of drinkers. Indra identifies the bottle shop in Medan only as "Warung X"—the owner refused to speak on record, referring us instead to Indra, who self-identifies as a "loyal customer", as his spokesperson.

Indra's been buying bottles of liquor from Warung X since 2004 and explains how they buy and test their alcohol: "When a sales representative comes from one of the local factories, the shop asks loyal customers like me to act as testers." It's an amazing revelation. According to Indra, the bottle shop, and many others like it in Medan, uses "loyal customers", in return for free drinks, to sample new batches of alcohol to see if they're poisoned.

But what if a bottle of alcohol contains methanol? "If it has methanol in it then, yeah, you die," replies Indra, laughing uproariously and slapping his thigh. "But look at me, I'm still alive." He says he sometimes feels unwell when sampling new batches of alcohol in the shop; if that happens, he always stops drinking immediately. Still, such a method of using customers as tasters of unlicensed or home-brewed alcohol is highly risky.

When *New Naratif* approached five different bottle shops in Medan, none of the owners would speak on record about exactly where and how they obtain their alcohol or allow us to take photographs, despite claiming that they were selling alcohol legally from licensed local factories.

Lifesaving campaigns

Over the years, the Indonesian government response to the epidemic of methanol poisoning has been virtually non-existent. Banning the sale of alcohol in mini-markets has had the opposite effect when it comes to keeping consumers safe, and it's been left to other groups to pick up the slack. One such group is LIAM—Lifesaving Initiatives About Methanol—Charitable Fund, an Australian charity founded by Lhani Davies following the death of her son Liam Davies at the age of just 19.[5]

Liam drank vodka and lime mixes at Rudy's Bar on Gili Trawangan in Lombok on New Year's Eve, 2012. The drinks that he thought contained imported vodka were actually locally brewed *arak*, a kind of fermented

---

5 http://liamcharity.com/

liquor, which contained lethal amounts of methanol. Liam suffered a seizure on his way to hospital in Lombok, where he was misdiagnosed with a brain bleed before being flown back to Australia where it was tragically too late to save his life.

New Naratif spoke with Davies, who lives in Perth, to find out what the charity has been doing since it was set up in 2013 to warn people about the dangers of methanol poisoning. Davies explains that they've just finished a training session in the city of Yogyakarta, teaching doctors and local hospitals about the international standards and protocols of using ethanol as a blocker for methanol poisoning. For many in the medical field in Indonesia, this is one of the most difficult things to get to grips with, as the treatment for methanol poisoning is actually to introduce more alcohol, in the form of ethanol, to slow the process of methanol attacking the body and buy time for a patient to reach a hospital where dialysis can be performed.

LIAM Charitable Fund has now run training sessions across Indonesia in cities like Yogyakarta and Makassar as well as the island of Lombok. In Bali alone, the charity has trained 80 local hospitals and clinics on how to administer ethanol blockers to patients presenting with methanol poisoning symptoms. Davies says that Dinas Kesehatan, the Indonesian Health Authority, has been extremely supportive of the training sessions, but it still hasn't all been plain sailing. In a recent training session, 16% of doctors said they would not treat patients using ethanol blockers and Davies has had reports of patients attending hospitals in Lombok only to be refused treatment for any symptoms related to alcohol—and by extension methanol poisoning—for religious reasons.

I ask Davies whether she's surprised by the recent spate of deaths across Indonesia. "No. It's like a ticking time bomb and it doesn't affect the rich," she says. "They can just get duty-free or pay for a cocktail using imported alcohol. It's always the people at the bottom who are going to be affected."

There is also resistance to campaigns against methanol poisoning both at home and abroad: "We get accused of 'Bali bashing' when we talk about methanol poisoning. But we're not telling people not to go to Bali or not to drink when they're there. All we want to do is give people information so that they can make informed choices" says Davies. This includes recommending that consumers in Indonesia stick to beer or drink duty-free spirits that they have brought with them.

Davies wishes there was more media coverage of both local and international cases. Methanol poisoning in Indonesia is usually only reported when a Western holidaymaker is involved and it's deemed newsworthy. Although there have been tourist deaths in Bali, Lombok, and North Sumatra, the recent spate of poisonings this year—half of which are thought to have come from a single contaminated batch of alcohol—resulted in deaths across Java and Papua Province. Methanol poisoning isn't just about backpackers partying cheaply; it's a country-wide issue that affects everyone.

Davies also wishes more cases of "near misses" were in the news; she cites a recent case in Bali where a backpacker was successfully treated for methanol poisoning but didn't want to speak out for fear they would be blamed for drinking cheap alcohol. But such reticence has the inadvertent effect of perpetuating a dangerous lack of awareness. "People believe it's no longer an issue if it's not in the media and that creates a false sense of security. It's like wearing a seatbelt. We don't hear of all the times a seatbelt saved someone's life. But it's still important to wear one," she explains.

LIAM Charitable Fund has ambitious plans for combating methanol poisoning in Indonesia in the future: "We're always going to push for a nationwide world standard procedure for methanol poisoning. It's been accepted in Bali. But we need to get it into hospitals all over the country," says Davies.

Indra had a mild case of methanol poisoning and made a full recovery. The reason why some people die and others survive, even if they have been drinking together, is that methanol is lighter than ethanol and floats to the surface of a bottle of bootleg alcohol. If the bottle is tainted, the person who takes the first drink is likely to get a glass of almost pure methanol and suffer the full consequences.

Until the healthcare practices developed by LIAM Charitable Fund are accepted nationwide, drinking bootleg liquor in Indonesia will always be a deadly game of chance.

CAMBODIA'S MINING INDUSTRY

YESENIA AMARO, SENGKONG BUN | 25 JUN 2018

A spate of deaths in Kratie province has drawn attention to Cambodia's problematic mining industry after reports that cyanide, used to flush gold mines, was found in the water.

The beleaguered mining industry in Cambodia is once again at the centre of controversy after cyanide—a highly toxic substance used to flush gold mines—was found in a stream in a northeastern province where at least 13 people died and nearly 300 others became ill in a span of days.

Minister of Industry and Handicraft Cham Prasidh first revealed on 17 May that cyanide had been found in the stream, but made a strange move later on 24 May when he signed a joint press statement with two other ministries. His ministry, along with the Ministry of Mines and Energy and the Ministry of Health, claimed in the statement that the deaths in Chet Borei district in Kratie province had been caused by the consumption of water contaminated with pesticides and herbicides, as well as high levels of methanol in local white wine.

On 25 May, Prime Minister Hun Sen, without mentioning names, shamed those who had made information about the cyanide public without reporting to him first. He also criticised them—essentially, Prasidh—for not sticking to the Ministry of Health's narrative that the water had only been contaminated by herbicides and pesticides. For Hun Sen's administration, the presence of cyanide as a potential factor in these deaths simply raises more questions about an industry already plagued with problems.

Silence from Cambodian officials

Observers "strongly" suspect that cyanide is behind the deaths in Kratie. In Prasidh's initial comments to journalists, he said that his ministry had deployed a team to the area to collect water samples from various points along the stream. Their analysis, he said, showed that villagers had been poisoned by wine and contaminated water, in which officials found chromium and cyanide. Following an investigation, officials identified illegal gold mining operations in the nearby province of Mondulkiri.

They also found a box of cyanide, but didn't specify which company had it. Rong Cheng Industrial Cambodia Co. Ltd was later suspected of being among the mining operations using and disposing cyanide.

"After using it, they have no protection system in place," Prasidh told reporters on 17 May. "After the rain… cyanide just floated away. When we measured the water in Mondulkiri, the level of cyanide was very high."

Cyanide has been used in mining for years, but is "strictly" regulated in most places around the world for the safety of humans, wildlife and the aquatic environment. "Cyanide prevents the body from taking up oxygen, resulting in suffocation, which may be fatal to humans and animals without prompt first aid treatment," says[1] the website MiningFacts.org.

Mother Nature, an NGO which has brought to light other scandals in the country's mining sector, was able to interview villagers in Chet Borei district, who said the fatal victims—all indigenous villagers—experienced strong headaches, dizziness, shortness of breath and repeated vomiting.

"Cyanide and other harmful substances that contaminated the water… not only [affected] people's health but also… livestock and [the] ecosystem of the river, which can be long-lasting," says Pech Pisey, director of programmes at Transparency International Cambodia, which has looked into practices of the country's mining sector in the past.

"The effects of [cyanide] have proven to be devastating and it will affect the livelihoods of people who are living in communities" nearby, if not properly cleaned up.

Speaking to *New Naratif*, NGO Mother Nature co-founder Alex Gonzalez-Davidson says that he found it odd that Prasidh was the one to reveal that cyanide was found in the water, while the Ministry of Mines and Energy, as well as the Ministry of Environment, have not said much.

"[It] is possible that [Prasidh] was bullied into back-pedaling and keeping quiet on the issue, most likely as a way by the government to try and solve the problem internally, in a way that the reputation of the Hun Sen dictatorship is not further affected," he says.

---

1 https://www.fraserinstitute.org/categories/mining

According to Hang Channy, governor of the Chet Borei district, the death toll has reached 13, although locals estimate that up to 18 died. Another 280 villagers have recovered after receiving treatment. Villagers were urged not to use water from the affected streams, and to avoid drinking white wine.

In his early comments to the media, Prasidh had warned that actions by the government were "forthcoming," especially against illegal mining operations.

So far, though, government officials have remained tight-lipped when asked for clarification or updates on the Kratie case. Several officials didn't respond to multiple requests to provide basic details, such as a breakdown of how many people died from contaminated water versus poisonous wine, the name of the laboratory in Singapore where victims' blood samples were tested, and whether any of the victims underwent official autopsies and toxicology examinations.

Multiple calls and requests for comment went unanswered by Yos Monirath, spokesman for the Ministry of Mines and Energy.

Tin Ponlok, an official with the Ministry of Environment, had spoken to the media prior to Prime Minister Hun Sen's blaming comments, but now says he's not in a position to comment. He referred questions to ministry spokesman Sao Sopheap, who in turn failed to respond to requests.

Ly Sovann, the spokesman for the Ministry of Health, would only refer the joint statement and prior press releases on the deaths. He did not respond to a message asking if officials were being pressured not to speak on the case.

The Pasteur Institute in Cambodia, which typically performs laboratory testing for the Ministry of Health, was not involved in this case, according to director Didier Fontenille. It's unclear why the Ministry of Health sent the samples to be examined in a lab in Singapore.

Mining, corruption and a lack of regulation

Cambodia's mining sector has been embroiled in scandals that experts have said were due to corruption and the government's failure to regulate the industry.

In 2016, United Nations trade data showed[2] USD752 million of sand imports to Singapore from 2007 to 2016, while Cambodia's figures only reflected about USD5 million in exports during that time. In 2017, Mother Nature engaged a Singaporean law firm to look into whether any Singaporean laws had been broken in relation to sand imports, but has since decided not to pursue the case after Singapore halted sand imports from Cambodia. The Singaporean government has denied[3] any accusations of illegally importing sand.

In September 2017, Mother Nature exposed[4] a similar discrepancy of more than USD30 million in imports of silica sand into Taiwan that Cambodia had not recorded. The only two companies[5] licensed to export silica sand are owned or chaired by tycoons and ruling party senators Mong Reththy and Ly Yong Phat. Both are closely connected to Hun Sen.

A large-scale gold mining operation in Preah Vihear province has been encroaching on indigenous villagers' lands, but is guarded by soldiers from the Royal Cambodian Armed Forces. The operation has been allegedly linked[6] to Hing Bun Heang, commander of Hun Sen's Personal Bodyguard Unit. Meanwhile, Hun Seng Ny, Hun Sen's youngest sister, is alleged to be behind an adjacent operation. Villagers have told Mother Nature they suspect those operations are also using cyanide.

Six miners—including four in Kratie province[7]—died in a span of a few months in 2017 due to the government's failure to oversee mining operations and halt illegal activities. In the same year, a number of villagers in Kandal province, near the capital Phnom Penh, lost their homes or portions of their homes after several riverbank collapses[8] near an area where four companies are engaged in sand dredging.

In this latest case of cyanide in the water, Gonzalez-Davidson says documents obtained by Mother Nature indicate that no companies are

---

2 https://m.phnompenhpost.com/national/sand-export-answers-sought

3 https://www.straitstimes.com/singapore/strict-rules-in-place-for-import-of-sand-mnd

4 https://m.phnompenhpost.com/national/fresh-sand-fraud-claims-ngo-mother-nature-sand-numbers-between-taiwan-and-government-appear

5 https://m.phnompenhpost.com/national/ministry-responds-mps-request-silica

6 https://m.phnompenhpost.com/national-post-depth/cambodian-gold-mine-shrouded-secrecy

7 https://m.phnompenhpost.com/national/miners-back-scene-fatal-collapse

8 https://m.phnompenhpost.com/national/official-visits-villagers-whose-homes-collapsed-near-sand-dredging-site

licensed to extract gold near the contaminated stream. There was no legitimate reason for cyanide to have been used in the area.

"So, if cyanide had been found, as some officials say was indeed the case, then of course top government officials will try and ensure that this is not made public," he says.

The problem continues

While cyanide's role in the deaths remains questionable, Gonzalez-Davidson says other troubling aspects of the mining industry are certain.

"What we can say for certain is that the mining industry in Cambodia is rife with corruption, is a major cause of environmental destruction, and that it is seldom, if ever, done in a way that local communities or the state sees any benefits, as most of the extraction is conducted under the façade that only exploration or prospecting is taking place," he says.

In 2017, a firm hired by Transparency International Cambodia to assess the country's mineral exploration licensing process found[9] 14 gaps that could potentially lead to risks of corruption and malpractice. One of those risks was that the application evaluation committee only consists of Ministry of Mines and Energy officials, who aren't required to declare any potential conflicts of interest with the companies applying for licences.

Pisey, with Transparency International Cambodia, says there are several actions that the government can take to clean up the mining sector, such as having robust legal frameworks and guidelines in place to safeguard the sector and provide an equal level playing field in the industry. Only credible companies with proven technical capacity and financial resources should be given licences.

He adds that an "effective monitoring and oversight mechanism must be in place to ensure not only compliance, but also accountability of the companies that are operating on the ground."

But Gonzalez-Davidson says that accountability and transparency are currently non-existent in the country's mining sector for one main reason. "It does not benefit those who benefit economically from the sector," he writes in an email to *New Naratif.* "Most so-called companies (in reality nothing more than criminal syndicates) involved in mining are operating with the aim of making a quick buck and moving on."

9 https://m.phnompenhpost.com/national/gaps-framework-open-mines-graft

"The only way the country of Cambodia can ever achieve a properly regulated mining sector, one that exists primarily to achieve higher standards of living for all Cambodians, [is] for the current government to take a step back and allow a new generation of politicians to take over," he adds.

It doesn't look like this will happen any time soon. With the country's only viable opposition party—the Cambodia National Rescue Party—forcibly dissolved last November, the upcoming election in July is a sure-win for Hun Sen. And, as the lack of answers over these deaths in Kratie has shown, it is likely to be business as usual for the problematic mining industry.

INDONESIA'S CAN'T-DO CLIMATE PLAN

WARIEF DJAJANTO BASORIE | 16 JUL 2018

Indonesia has set itself a target of reducing carbon emissions by 29% by 2030—a plan that, as things stand, is not achievable. Can the country correct its course on climate action, or will it be left to the next generation to pick up the pieces?

3 00 schoolchildren from the greater Jakarta area sat on a red carpet covering the cavernous Soedjarwo auditorium—named to honour the country's first forestry minister—at the Ministry of the Environment and Forestry in January this year. They were there to participate in the government-led Climate Festival; the theme was "Three Years of Climate Change Achievements".

Dr Nur Masripatin, the then-Director General of Climate Change (she stepped down in February 2018), tossed the kids a question on climate change: what will become of Indonesia if nothing is done about climate change by 2030?

An elementary schoolboy said the country would become hotter and drier. Another two students added to his answer, talking about global warming and the greenhouse gases that lead to climate change.

The director general beamed broadly. Dr Nur Masripatin, who has a PhD in forest biometrics from Canterbury University in New Zealand, has been a veteran negotiator for Indonesia at the annual United Nations (UN) climate conference since 2005.

Indonesia is a country of islands, with a majority of the population living along coasts vulnerable to climate change, she explained to the assembled pupils. The government hopes that such an event will equip children with information on climate change that they'll carry into adulthood.

Reaching Indonesia's targets

The event also sought to inform the public on the progress made in implementing international agreements and national policies, such as the Paris Agreement and the Nationally Determined Contribution, related to climate change. Government projects such as this one are only deemed successful if the people meant to benefit from the project feel that they have a stake in the issue, and commit to seeing it through.

The Paris Agreement[1], reached at the UN climate conference in Paris in 2015, is a legally binding international contract to limit global warming "well below" 2°C, through lowering carbon emissions from the burning of fossil fuels and the degrading of forests. The ultimate aim is zero carbon emissions worldwide by 2050.

In undertaking to realise the Paris Agreement, Indonesia's Nationally Determined Contribution, or NDC, sets a target of cutting emissions by 29% against a "business as usual" scenario (in which no planned action is taken) and by 41% with international cooperation. This climate action plan is due to be implemented from 2020 to 2030.

One of the many documents handed out to participants of the Climate Festival was the country's NDC Implementation Strategy, listing nine programmes with assigned activities spanning from ownership and commitment development to implementation and review. Also included was an academic paper on the draft government regulation for climate change.

The festival, and its accompanying books, talks, and handout material produced by the director general and her team, outlines an ambitious climate agenda. Yet what's not covered is interesting, too.

While the NDC Implementation Strategy cites projected greenhouse gas emission levels, it does not provide details on whether, or how much, emissions have already been reduced since 2011, when the government issued its national action plan to reduce greenhouse gas emissions by 26% by 2020. Nor does the NDC explain the formula it uses to reduce emissions in the five slated sectors: land-use, energy, IPPU (industrial processes and product use), agriculture and waste. The first two sectors alone produced 82% of the country's carbon emissions in 2010–2012.

Despite its absence in the Climate Festival's documents, information on emission reduction is provided[2] by the National Development Planning Agency (Bappenas). From 2010–2017, Indonesia has cut greenhouse gas emission by only 13.46%. It's a figure the Indonesian government aren't eager to publicise—it's a long way from their target. The government doesn't officially state how much carbon emissions has

---

1 https://unfccc.int/process-and-meetings/the-paris-agreement/the-paris-agreement

2 http://pep.pprk.bappenas.go.id/

been reduced because the NDC does not start until 2020, a government official explained.

"The government shall regularly provide emission reduction achievements in line with the NDC target it has committed to after Indonesia ratified the Paris Agreement. This is in line with our commitment to the NDC up to 2030. The information can be accessed in SIGN SMART[3] prepared by the Environment and Forestry Ministry," Dr Agus Justianto, Head of the Ministry's Agency for Research, Development and Innovation, tells New Naratif.

A major emitter of greenhouse gases

According to the World Resources Institute (WRI), Indonesia is the world's sixth largest emitter of greenhouse gases, and the largest contributor of forest-based emissions—an unsurprising fact if one thinks back to the devastating forest and peat fires in 2014 and 2015. Images from the United States' National Aeronautics and Space Administration (NASA) released in 2014[4] and 2015[5] show dense smoke blanketing parts of the country and its neighbours. Those two years were exceptionally bad, but such burning takes place annually.

In September 2017, WRI Indonesia published a 36-page working paper[6] on how Indonesia can achieve its climate change mitigation goal. The organisation found that existing policies in the land-use and energy sectors, even if fully implemented, are inadequate if the country is really serious about reaching the 29% target by 2030. Using its own methodology, WRI Indonesia estimated that the existing policies would only result in a 19% reduction.

A failure to achieve its mitigation target means that Indonesia won't be able to contribute its declared share in global fulfillment of the 2015 Paris Agreement.

---

3 http://signsmart.menlhk.go.id/signsmart_new/web/home/

4 https://earthobservatory.nasa.gov/images/83304/fires-in-indonesia

5 https://earthobservatory.nasa.gov/images/86681/smoke-blankets-indonesia

6 https://wri-indonesia.org/en/publication/how-can-indonesia-achieve-its-climate-change-mitigation-goal

Rethinking policies

Reaching the NDC goal would require revisiting existing policies, particularly in agriculture and energy.

In agriculture, the government wants to double the output of the highly lucrative oil palm by 2020. This would require the clearing of more forest and peatland to add to the 14 million hectares of oil palm plantations already present in the country—a move that would surely lead to more carbon emissions. The policy also undermines a forest moratorium, in place since 2011, on the issuing of permits to convert primary forest and peatland to oil palm plantations, pulp and paper estates and other land-use change activities.

Dr Agus denies any planned clearing of peatland, insisting that the moratorium is still in place. What the government wants to increase, he stresses, is productivity per hectare on existing oil palm plantations.

President Joko "Jokowi" Widodo also has a plan to boost the country's energy capacity by 35,000 megawatts during his current term, which comes to an end in 2019. Only 2,000 megawatts of that energy will come from renewable energy; 20,000 megawatts will come from coal-fired plants, another major source of greenhouse gas emissions. Oil and gas, as well as hydropower, will provide the rest.

This matter of generating 20,000 megawatts of energy from coal-fired plants was put to Bambang Brodjonegoro, Indonesia's Minister for National Development Planning and Head of Bappenas, at the Southeast Asia Symposium jointly organised by Oxford University and the University of Indonesia's School of Environmental Science in March 2018.[7]

The "best solution", advocated by environmentalists, would be to phase coal-fired plants out completely and embrace renewable energy sources. It's in line with the call of the "Powering Past Coal" alliance[8], a partnership of over 20 governments who intend to move away from coal. No Southeast Asian government has joined the alliance thus far.

Brodjonegoro, a former dean of the University of Indonesia's School of Economics, replied that Indonesia's plan relies on the "second-best solution": new coal-fired power plants will use clean coal technology,

---

7 New Naratif's Managing Director, Dr Thum Ping Tjin, was involved in the organisation of
   the Southeast Asia Symposium in his role of Coordinator for Oxford University's Project
   Southeast Asia.

8 http://sdg.iisd.org/news/countries-launch-powering-past-coal-alliance/

and that renewable energy, such as solar, wind or biomass, will be developed for isolated areas that are not yet part of the country's power grid. Energy is required for economic growth, he argued, and Indonesia has abundant coal deposits to meet that energy need.

But Indonesia might not need as much energy as policymakers initially thought. According to the Electricity Supply Business Plan 2018-2027 drafted by the Energy and Mineral Resources Ministry, a projection in Indonesia's additional power needs dropped from 78 gigawatts under the 2017–2026 plan to 56 gigawatts in the 2018–2027 plan. The decrease was due to overestimating the growth in demand; if the government had followed through with the initial plan, it would end up overspending by building unused power plants.

Plans are also underway to increase the portion of renewable energy—while renewable energy only provided 12.52% of Indonesia's energy in 2017, it's expected to rise to 23% in 2025. Coal is expected to decline as a source of energy from 58.3% in 2017 to 54.4% in 2025. But environmental groups say it's still not good enough.

"Many nations like India, China and even Saudi Arabia have altered their investment direction to renewable energy, whereas Indonesia still depends on coal for more than 50% of its power source," said Hindun Mulaika, Greenpeace Indonesia's climate and energy campaigner, in a recent press release.

Other organisations have called for more ambitious action from the Indonesian government. Germanwatch and Climate Action Network pointed out in their 2018 Climate Change Performance Index that Indonesia has the potential to further develop renewable energy, particularly since it has relatively large amounts of hydropower. WRI Indonesia recommended other mitigation actions, such as strengthening and extending the forest moratorium, restoring degraded forest and peatland, and implementing energy conservation efforts.

According to WRI Indonesia, increasing renewable sources in the energy mix will require implementing multiple policies, such as a carbon tax on fossil fuel power plants, the replacement of coal-fired plants with wind or solar sources, and the provision of subsidies for the promotion of renewable energy.

Indonesia already has bilateral and multilateral agreements for cooperation in climate change, such as an accord with Norway signed in 2010, where the Scandinavian country pledged up to USD1 billion for "significant reductions in greenhouse gas emissions from deforestation, forest degradation and peatland conversion". The financial contribution is made based on a verified emissions reduction mechanism. However, an influential coal lobby makes it difficult for the country to take bolder steps away from coal power plants.

A target that cannot be achieved

As it stands, Indonesia's 29% NDC target is not achievable, a government technocrat tells New Naratif.

"It is not based on what sectors knew, what the energy sector knew, what the road transport sector knew. No one has reliable data. Everyone has some sense of statistics," says the technocrat, who has asked to remain anonymous as he's not authorised to speak to the press.

The distinction between data and statistics is an important one—while statistics present a snapshot of one aspect of an issue, data is a real mapping of what exists, providing a more holistic picture. A good NDC should have reliable data from every sector, disaggregated to show the reality in each of Indonesia's 465 sub-national districts and town governments. While there might be a political aspect to this process, politics should not be dominant, the official added.

The lack of data is a big problem with a major impact on the way targets have been set. The government arrived at the 29% target via inter-sectoral meetings where each of the five mitigation sectors (energy, land-use, industry, agriculture, waste) stated how far they were willing to go in terms of reductions. But if the various groups only have "some sense of statistics" without actual reliable data, the targets set could easily be off the mark.

Hopes for a future generation

Indonesia's climate future is not bleak; there's still hope for significant progress moving forward. Beyond government policy and programmes, numerous civil society organisations are actively working on the issue.

One example is Climate Reality Indonesia, which had a booth at the Climate Festival. Its members, who have participated in Al Gore's climate course, are from all walks of life: students, academics, public officials, business people, homemakers, journalists, artists, clerics. They're committed to spreading climate awareness among their own circles to encourage a ripple effect that will increase public knowledge across the country.

"Climate change can be viewed from different angles: water, air, marine resources, forests, agriculture, energy, education, laws. Hence it's important to break down the issue of interest to understand the ground sentiment," says Amanda Katili Niode, manager of Climate Reality Indonesia.

There are signs that the public are interested. In 2015, a survey by the Pew Research Centre found that 63% of the country supported limiting greenhouse gas emissions as part of an international agreement. Climate Reality Indonesia is thus working on creating visual materials on specific climate change impacts and solutions to use in their outreach programmes.

Following Climate Change Director General Nur Masripatin's session, Hidayatun Nisa, a 24-year-old university graduate, delivered a rousing speech before the assembled schoolchildren. She told them about her work as a facilitator in the Care of Peat Village project run by the Peat Restoration Agency in a village in Jambi province on the east coast of central Sumatra, calling on students to study how to protect the environment for a better future.

"I do hope the children can learn to be sensitive to living things and protect the environment where they live. This also applies to their parents as the educational process that has the greatest effect is the education at home," Nisa tells New Naratif.

Without a change in gear for a more ambitious and robust emphasis on renewable energy and the safeguarding of the environment, Indonesia's climate change ambitions could end up amounting to little more than a can't-do plan. As it is, the current generation is already not on track to meet its own stipulated goals. If the country does not undertake a course correction soon, today's Indonesian children will find themselves having to pick up the slack in the future.

TURNING AWAY FROM TOBACCO

REYNOLD SUMAYKU | 03 SEP 2018

*Vaping may have economic and health benefits for smokers in Indonesia—
but the government is unwilling to show its support.*

The visibility is poor inside the vape shop and cafe in Tangerang, Banten Province. The vapour is everywhere, hanging in the air. Such vape shops are easily found in Indonesia's bigger cities, especially in Java and Bali.

Eight or nine young men are hanging out in the cramped shop, roughly the size of a garage. Some perch on bar stools facing the display table; others lounge on a set of rattan benches. They chat with one another, all puffing away on vaping devices.

The shopkeeper, 22-year-old Claudius Hans, stands behind the display table, handling the customers as they search for liquids or replacements for the cottons and coils in their vaping devices. Whenever there's a lull in business, Hans reaches for his own device and inhales deeply.

"People have leisure time here almost every night. Most of them are my friends, so I started to try [vaping]," he says. He's the only vaper in the room who had never actually smoked cigarettes. "It's been a year and half now. I wasn't even a smoker before. Vaping is now a kind of lifestyle, but I could stop any time. I'm not hooked on this."

Vaping: a replacement for smoking?

Generally considered a recreational activity, vaping uses e-cigarettes; a user inhales vapours produced by heating an e-liquid with a battery-operated device. Most e-cigarette liquids contain nicotine, and labels indicate the nicotine level: 0mg, 3mg, 6mg or higher. Other ingredients are also often added, including flavours like mango, banana, cream, blueberry or vanilla.

Often marketed as a replacement for smoking tobacco, vaping has been a controversial practice over the past decade, with critics arguing that e-cigarettes could be a gateway for children or non-smokers to eventually get on to real cigarettes.

Despite being vaguely known to Indonesians before 2010, the rising phenomenon of e-cigarettes can be traced to the start of 2014, when the first public fair was organised in Jakarta by vaping enthusiast Herwindo Prakoso and a friend. In that same year, the Association of Personal Vaporizer Indonesia (APVI)—an organisation of vapers who have since been seen as representatives of the industry—was initiated by a number of store owners, importers and users, including Prakoso.

Thousands of visitors attended that first e-cigarette fair, and the number of attendees has been significantly growing over the years. "There are several fairs each year. The biggest one is called Vape Fair, which is held annually and attracts hundreds of thousands of visitors," says Prakoso, now an events administrator with APVI.

According to APVI, the number of e-cigarette users reached over 950,000 by the end of 2017, including over 650,000 active users. The APVI also stated that, by the end of last year, there were approximately 3,500 vape entrepreneurs in Indonesia, which is good news for the local job market.

"If a vape shop owner employs a minimum of two or three staff members to run the business, we can say that there are over 10,000 job opportunities. The turnover could be trillions of rupiah," Prakoso adds.

Regulating e-liquids

The liquid used in e-cigarettes was regulated by the Indonesian authorities in July 2018, although an exemption was given to products that were manufactured prior to the start of the regulation and have yet to be labelled with tax bands. Full implementation of the regulation, to include all vaping liquids, will be put in place by October 2018. It's a profitable move: once all manufacturers are registered, the government expects[1] a revenue of IDR3 trillion (over USD207 million) a year from taxing e-cigarette liquids.

"Vaping liquids contain extracted nicotine," says Deni Sujantoro, head of communications and public relations for the Directorate General of Customs and Excise. Extracted nicotine, he explains, is among goods subject to tariffs in Indonesia.

---

1 http://jakartaglobe.id/business/govt-eyes-200m-additional-revenue-next-year-excise-vaping-liquid/

Sujantoro says that the issue was discussed extensively before the government's decree[2] that introduced taxes on vaping liquid last year. "We [heard] different perspectives and interests," he says. "Some emphasised the potential impact on public health, while others worried [about] its influence on children and so on. Therefore, it was decided that the products should be regulated by high taxes—the maximum."

The 57% excise tax slapped on to e-cigarette liquids is four times higher than the maximum tax levied on tobacco cigarettes. "The goal is clear… To make all kinds of e-cigarette products not too cheap so they will not be easily purchased by those underage," Sujantoro adds.

But it seems strange that local authorities are so circumspect about vaping, especially as Indonesia is one of the countries with the largest number of tobacco smokers in the world, along with China and India. Out of a population of 260 million, over 72 million people in Indonesia aged 15 and above are cigarette smokers—some 62 million of them smoke daily. According to data[3] provided by the World Health Organisation and the Global Health Observatory Data Repository, about 76% of the adult male population smokes; a sharp increase from the 61% in 2000.

"Today, tobacco consumption is a heavy burden for many households in the country[4]," said the Indonesian Consumers Foundation (YLKI) in a press release on World No Tobacco Day in May 2018. According to Indonesian Central Bureau of Statistics (BPS)[5], cigarettes are the second largest household expense after rice. A 2015 report by BPS has also shown that an average household where at least one family member is a smoker might spend three to five times more on cigarettes than on education. One would have thought that something to reduce cigarette addiction would be embraced with open arms.

The public health debate

Among developed countries, the United Kingdom was the first to see the potential of e-cigarettes in reducing the number of tobacco smokers. In August 2015, Public Health England (PHE)—an executive agency

---

2 http://www.jdih.kemenkeu.go.id/fullText/2017/146~PMK.010~2017Per.pdf

3 https://data.worldbank.org/indicator/SH.PRV.SMOK.MA?locations=ID

4 http://ylki.or.id/2016/05/siaran-pers-ylki-sehari-tidak-merokok-masyarakat-indonesia-
bisa-menghemat-rp-605-milyar-per-hari/

5 https://www.bps.go.id/news/2016/02/16/133/rokok-vs--kemiskinan.html

under the country's Department of Health—declared[6] that e-cigarettes are about 95% less harmful than smoking regular cigarettes. It also said that "there is no evidence so far that e-cigarettes are acting as a route into smoking for children or non-smokers."

In an explanation of the report, Professor Kevin Fenton, the Director of Health and Wellbeing at PHE said[7], "E-cigarettes are not completely risk free but when compared to smoking, evidence shows they carry just a fraction of the harm. The problem is people increasingly think they are at least as harmful and this may be keeping millions of smokers from quitting."

But the Indonesian government doesn't seem quite as convinced. Some vapers have protested the 57% excise tax rate, arguing that e-cigarettes could be good for public health by helping smokers quit, but to no avail. It doesn't help that some members of the government aren't fans of e-cigarette use, and think of it as being just as unhealthy—or even more so—than smoking regular cigarettes. In November last year, Minister for Trade Enggartiasto Lukita commented that e-cigarette users "should be tobacco smokers instead[8]."

In January 2018, Minister of Finance, Sri Mulyani, was quoted by the media[9] and said that a 57% excise tax imposed on e-cigarettes made sense, "since it's for health's sake."

A question of price

Deni Sujantoro considers e-cigarettes a "middle-class thing"; even if vaping does help some Indonesian smokers to quit, it'll mainly be confined to the middle class due to the high taxes that the government wants to impose on vaping products.

E-cigarette liquids currently cost between IDR100,000 (USD7) and IDR300,000 (USD21) per container, although shop owners plan to increase the price by at least 10% once the regulation is fully implemented.

---

6 https://www.gov.uk/government/news/e-cigarettes-around-95-less-harmful-than-tobacco-estimates-landmark-review

7 https://www.gov.uk/government/news/e-cigarettes-around-95-less-harmful-than-tobacco-estimates-landmark-review

8 https://www.liputan6.com/bisnis/read/3173006/ylki-minta-pemerintah-larang-peredaran-vape

9 https://www.liputan6.com/bisnis/read/3220602/sri-mulyani-vape-kena-cukai-57-persen-tidak-apa-demi-kesehatan

A pack of e-cigarette liquid—which comes in 60 millilitre containers—may last two to three weeks, depending on one's consumption level. When asked during a vape fair in Jakarta, one user said that, "Vaping is more affordable. I was a tobacco smoker consuming two packs of cigarettes a day."

Such a cigarette smoker, who goes through two packs of Marlboro Lights every day, will end up spending a total of IDR1.5 million (USD104) per month. On the other hand, a user consuming two packs of liquids priced at IDR150,000 (USD10.40) each could spend at least IDR600,000 (USD42) per month, inclusive of the device's maintenance. It's a significant saving.

But the numbers don't also work out this way for everyone. "Users must do the maths themselves," Hans says. "I would say it's not necessarily cheaper."

The type of vaping device, Hans explains, can often be a determinant in one's calculations. A user with a common device—without an e-liquid tank—needs to pay at least IDR25,000 (USD 1.70) for the cotton or coil replacements. "The cottons need a change every three or four days, and ideally once a week for the coils," he explains.

It also depends on how much one smokes, and *what* one smokes. While Marlboro Lights cost IDR25,000 (USD1.70) per pack, locally-produced tobacco cigarettes—mostly clove and tobacco cigarettes known as *kretek*—are priced between IDR15,000 (USD1) to IDR17,000 (USD1.18). Unless one smokes a huge amount, it could still be cheaper to stick with local smokes than switch to vaping. A survey done by the Centre for Social Security Study at the University of Indonesia (PKJS-UI) found that 66% of respondents said they would only stop smoking if the price of cigarettes went up to IDR60,000 (USD4) per pack. More (74%) would quit if the price was IDR70,000 (USD4.80) per pack.

National interests and harm reduction

Despite some of the benefits that vaping may provide, there seems little interest in trying to steer smokers away from cigarettes. Indonesia has long struggled to reduce the number of smokers in the country, but activists say there's no strong political will from the government to do so. Although Indonesia participated in the preparation of the Framework

Convention on Tobacco Control (FCTC)[10]—a document initiated by the World Health Organisation for tobacco control—it has not yet signed or ratified the agreement.

Last year, local media quoted the government[11] saying that it has chosen to prioritise its "national interests", despite planning to ratify the FCTC. Among these "national interests" is the welfare of tobacco farmers—the World Bank reported[12] that 43% of Indonesian households involved in manufacturing tobacco are poor.

However, the "national interests" also include government revenues. During the period from 2005–2015[13], revenue from tobacco excise increased from IDR33 trillion (USD2.2 billion) in 2005 to IDR140 trillion (USD9.7 billion) in 2015. Two years later, in 2017, this reached over IDR153 trillion (USD10.6 billion). This was excluding tax on other tobacco products and corporate tax on tobacco companies.

Konstantinos Farsalinos, a cardiologist and researcher with Onasis Cardiac Surgery in Athens, thinks that e-cigarettes should be pitched in terms of tobacco harm reduction. Currently conducting a survey among Asian vapers, including those in Indonesia, Farsalinos uses the analogy of using seat belts or helmets: "Not driving a car or not riding a motorcycle is the best option to eliminate the risk of accidents. Although not absolutely safe, the use of seat belts when driving cars or helmets when riding motorcycles are accepted as harm reduction approaches."

A former smoker himself, Farsalinos had tried nicotine gum and other products without much success before trying e-cigarettes. But he has also observed fear-mongering and bias in the discourse around vaping. "I can see there is a substantial predisposition against the use of nicotine in any form, even against a cleaner product such as e-cigarette," he writes in an email.

10 https://www.liputan6.com/bisnis/read/3220602/sri-mulyani-vape-kena-cukai-57-persen-tidak-apa-demi-kesehatan

11 https://nasional.tempo.co/read/779728/183-negara-setuju-fctc-jokowi-indonesia-jangan-ikut-ikutan

12 https://openknowledge.worldbank.org/bitstream/handle/10986/28567/120352-WP-P154568-10-10-2017-10-19-0-WBGIndoEmploymentFINALweb.pdf?sequence=1&isAllowed=y

13 https://openknowledge.worldbank.org/bitstream/handle/10986/28567/120352-WP-P154568-10-10-2017-10-19-0-WBGIndoEmploymentFINALweb.pdf?sequence=1&isAllowed=y

"We saw that a lot of research regarding e-cigarettes was driven by [this] predisposition, which has always been a less appropriate approach to research," he adds. "As a result, we saw many examples of misinterpretation, which led to incorrect conclusions and misleading arguments."

By 2017, according to the WHO's data[14], more than six million deaths were the result of direct tobacco use. In addition, around 890,000 deaths are the result of non-smokers being exposed to secondhand smoke.

"E-cigarettes are a special product for smokers, and should be used as an aid to quit smoking, by switching to a product that has lesser impacts," Farsalinos says.

"The problem with tobacco smoking is that any delay [in getting people to quit smoking] will cost millions of lives each day."

14 http://www.who.int/news-room/fact-sheets/detail/tobacco

HISTORY AND TRANSITIONAL JUSTICE

REMEMBERING COLDSTORE: FORMER DETAINEES SPEAK

KIRSTEN HAN, TOM WHITE, THUM PING TJIN | 01 MAR 2018

55 years after Operation Coldstore in Singapore, we photograph and talk to former detainees about their experiences.

It has been 55 years since Operation Coldstore, a major police operation in February 1963 in which over 110 anticolonial activists, union workers, students and politicians were arrested and detained without trial in Singapore. Carried out under the guise of fighting communism, the arrests severely undermined the left-wing anticolonial movement in Singapore and crippled the main opposition party, the Barisan Sosialis, who held 14 out of 51 seats in the Legislative Assembly (the governing People's Action Party, led by then-Prime Minister Lee Kuan Yew, had 25 seats). Some detainees would go on to spend over a decade behind bars without ever being formally charged with a crime. Operation Coldstore remains the largest round of arrests and detentions ever carried out in Singapore.

Over the years, the stories of these leftists have been largely obscured or erased from Singapore's official narrative. A survey done by the Institute of Policy Studies in 2015[1] found that Operation Coldstore was among one of Singaporeans' least remembered historical events. But the Old Left remembers: they gather every year during the Lunar New Year period for a big reunion lunch. It's an opportunity to catch up with friends and also commemorate events from their past.

This year, *New Naratif* spoke to some of the former detainees at the annual gathering. We present excerpts from short interviews with them

---

1 https://sg.news.yahoo.com/operation-coldstore---marxist-conspiracy--plot-among-events-least-known-and-important-to-singaporeans--ips-study-090329727.html

alongside their photographs below, juxtaposed against the entire Special Branch summary which Singapore's Internal Security Council (comprising seven members: the British Commissioner, two other senior British colonial officials, three PAP politicians including Lee Kuan Yew, and the Federation of Malaya Internal Security Minister, Tun Dr. Ismail) used to decide on their arrest and detention, along with commentary by *New Naratif.* These declassified Special Branch documents are found in the British National Archives.[2]

Chua Wee Puan
AGE AT TIME OF ARREST: 23

Chua Wee Puan was a member of the Singapore Bookshops, Publications and Printing Press Workers' Union. (Tom White)

---

2 http://discovery.nationalarchives.gov.uk/details/r/C13401921

"They wanted us to sign documents to 'renounce' communism; if you didn't sign they wouldn't let you out. I was part of the Singapore Bookshops, Publications and Printing Press Workers' Union. I was detained for about 10 years. I spent time in various prisons: Changi, Queenstown, Central [Police Station], Moon Crescent Centre [a detention centre, now closed, within Changi Prison]... I didn't get tortured, but I was kept in solitary for three months."

FROM THE BRITISH ARCHIVES:
Security Classification: Suspected Communist

Was first introduced to Communism as a student in the Chung Cheng High School. Later became an active member of the SCMSSU [Singapore Chinese Middle Schools Student Union] and was expelled from school for pro-Communist activities when the SCMSSU was banned in 1956. First entered the T.U. [trades union] field in 1959 as paid Secretary for the Singapore Spinning Workers' Union. Acting probably on the instructions of the underground CPM he was one of the sponsors of the move to field pro-Communist trade unionists as independent candidates in the 1959 General Elections in view of the split with the P.A.P. leadership at that time. For some unknown reason this was dropped although a number of candidates had already been selected. In June 1960 was advanced to a more responsible post in the Communist-controlled SGEU. He served on the Committee responsible for publishing the SUARA KESATUAN, the organ of the SGEU, and was particularly active in conducting cadre training classes teaching Communist theory to members of the SGEU. In November 1961 he conducted similar Communist training classes in the SBPPPWU in which he was by this time General Secretary. Throughout the Communist campaign of opposition to merger he consistently supported Communist United Front executives and afforded them an opportunity to put over their propaganda at cadre training classes within his own Union.

Chua's summary is a classic example of the smears, innuendo, and speculation used by Special Branch to dub many anticolonial activists as "communists". As anticolonial protests grew, and more and more Singaporeans demanded independence, the British colonial authorities responded by expanding the definition of communism to justify their suppression of the anticolonial movement. In August 1956, an internal memorandum by Special Branch Director Alan Blades and Colonial Secretary William Goode argued that all opposition to government policy, legitimate or otherwise, supported the Malayan Communist Party's aims, and therefore had to be classified as communist subversion and treated as such. Armed with this "definition", Special Branch proceeded to arrest numerous anticolonial activists. Yet Special Branch did not have a shred of evidence for its assertions above. Where it did have evidence, it was very quick to act and bring charges; where it did not, it was forced to detain the activists without trial.

Ang Eng Siong
AGE AT TIME OF ARREST: 23

Ang Eng Siong was a member of the People's Association. After the split in the People's Action Party, other People's Association workers—many of whom supported the Barisan Sosialis—chose Ang to be their representative to talk to Lee Kuan Yew. (Tom White)

"My arrest was because of Kuan Yew, because when I confronted him on behalf of the workers he told me he'd sent me to Japan [for education and training] and "now you come back you are against me." So I think [my detention] was because of Lee Kuan Yew's personal vendetta. I was detained for eight years and four months; I've been all over Singapore's prisons!"

FROM THE BRITISH ARCHIVES:
Security Classification: Suspected Communist Sympathiser

Became paid secretary of the Communist-controlled Singapore Textiles and General Merchants Employees Union (STGEU) in 1959 and General Affairs Officer of a pro-Communist Old Boys' Association in 1960. Resigned from the STGMEU in June 1960 when he was appointed Organiser in the People's Association. Played an active part in the Communist-inspired agitation of employees of the People's Association against the Government in 1961. Has disseminated Communist propaganda through lectures at cadre training classes of unions and played an active part in the Communist United Front agitation against merger, Malaysia and the Referendum in 1962.

Ang was arrested and detained for over eight years despite not being a communist, nor a communist sympathiser, but merely being a suspected communist sympathiser. Lee Kuan Yew had placed him in the People's Association in June 1960, thinking that he would be a reliable supporter of Lee's faction in the PAP. To Lee's surprise, Ang took his job of speaking up for workers seriously, and opposed Lee's attempts to undermine the independent trades union movement. One personal disagreement—and one single paragraph—drastically changed Ang's life forever.

Tan Kok Fang
AGE AT TIME OF ARREST: 23

Tan Kok Fang at the annual lunar new year lunch gathering of Singapore's 'Old Left'.

(Tom White)

"I'd just graduated from Nanyang University. I was a student activist with the Nanyang University Student Union—I was Chairman of External Relations for two sessions. I was detained for four and a half years. They accused me of being a Communist sympathiser. They didn't accuse me of being a Communist. But I considered myself to be an anti-colonialist."

FROM THE BRITISH ARCHIVES:
Security Classification: Suspected Communist Sympathiser

Expelled from school in 1954 for activities in support of the Communist-led agitation against National Service Registration. In SEP 57 was one of the leaders responsible for organising "Hsueh Hsih" indoctrination classes in the Chinese High School. Was

arrested on 25 SEP 57 but released on 9 OCT 57. In 1960/61 was
External Relations Officer of Nanyang University Students Union
and attempted to establish close relationship between the NUSU
and the International Union of Students (a Communist Front
organisation). Played an active part in the Communist-inspired
agitation against the 4-2 education system. Returned from a
NUSU tour of Australia in AUG 62 and was found in possession of
Communist literature.

The forced alteration of the Chinese education system from "3-3" (three
years of Lower Middle and three years of Upper Middle) to the English
"4-2" (four years of Secondary and two years of Pre-University) was hugely
controversial. This was not because of the principle of streamlining all
systems of education into a common system (which had widespread
support), but because the transition was incredibly rushed (Chinese
schools were only given a few months notice to prepare), it was extremely
poorly communicated (even then-Education Minister Yong Nyuk Lin
and his officials were bewildered by the speed of the changes, and
communicated inaccurate information at times), it was accompanied by
other fundamental changes to Chinese education (including the length
of the school week, teachers' pay, and educational standards), and there
was no policy formulated regarding what would happen to the Chinese
students left stranded by the changes. Naturally, the Upper Middle 1
students who were told in mid-1961 that they would suddenly have to
face school-leaving examinations at the end of the year were furious,
and angrily protested. Unfortunately, this happened at the same time
as the PAP split, leading Lee Kuan Yew to accuse the students of being
in league with the Barisan.

Yeh Kim Pak
AGE AT TIME OF ARREST: 27

Yeh was born in Malaya, and was stripped of his citizenship and banished under Singaporean law. He was not the only one; a 1976 Amnesty International briefing on Singapore noted that "[t]he usual pattern is for political prisoners to be detained without trial under the provisions of either the Internal Security Act or the Banishment Act." Detainees who were not born in Singapore lost their citizenship and were deported. *(Tom White)*

"They came to the coffee shop in Joo Chiat where I was working at 2am. About five or six officers came, and they took me to Outram [police station], where there were already many people. I was detained for four and a half years. I was a Singapore citizen but I lost my citizenship; they took me to the border. I couldn't return to Singapore for years, but now I can because I finally got Malaysian citizenship two, three years ago. [*To Kirsten*] You weren't even born yet; there were so many things happening at that time: independence, elections, organising… People like me are witnesses to history."

FROM THE BRITISH ARCHIVES:
Security Classification: Suspected Communist Sympathiser

In 1956 he strongly criticised Government's action in arresting Communists and gave full support to the Civil Rights Committee in its agitation for their release. He is a staunch admirer of Communist CHINA and consistently echoes the Communist stand in all current issues. He has served in various posts in the Singapore Coffee Shop Employees Union and associates closely with Communist suspects. He is actively concerned with ensuring maximum support for the Policies of the Communist controlled SGEU from members of his Union.

The irony of this summary is that in 1956, the People's Action Party were the leading opposition party, and led criticisms of the government's actions. From October 1956, then-Chief Minister Lim Yew Hock arrested and detained without trial many anticolonial activists, union workers, students and politicians, and banned numerous anticolonial associations. Many People's Action Party members were among those arrested. Lee Kuan Yew led the criticisms of Lim Yew Hock in the Legislative Assembly, accusing him of undertaking the arrests for political reasons and calling him a colonial stooge. Seven years later, Lee would use the same actions against his political opponents, justifying them the same way Lim had done in 1956—as an action against "communists", done in the name of "national security".

The hunger strike of 1970/71

There have been more discussions of Operation Coldstore in 1963 and Operation Spectrum in 1987 in recent years, but they aren't the only times where individuals have been detained. Deputy Prime Minister Teo Chee Hean stated in Parliament in 2011 that 1,045 people were detained under first the Preservation of Public Security Ordinance (PPSO, renamed the Internal Security Act (ISA) in 1963) between 1959 and 1990.[3] A list of political detainees from 1950 to 2015 compiled by

---

3 https://sprs.parl.gov.sg/search/topic.jsp?currentTopicID=00076651-WA&currentPubID

=00076180-WA&topicKey=00076180-WA.00076651-WA_7%2BhansardContent43a67

5dd-5000-42da-9fd5-40978d79310f%2B

Loh Miao Ping—herself a former detainee—counts over 1,300 names.[4] These include only people detained under section 8 of the ISA, which permits detentions (indefinitely renewable) up to 2 years. Approximately 1,000 to 1,500 more people have been held under section 74, which permits people to be held without a warrant by the Internal Security Department merely on suspicion of being a security risk for up to 28 days. Many such detainees were released after 28 days and immediately re-arrested when they stepped out of the ISD compound.

Conditions in detention are often described as poor. A 1976 Amnesty International briefing stated that "food is said to be poor, with only limited supplement by the families allowed."[5]

Toh Siew Tin, Sim Teong Hiok and Goh Peng Wah, detained in 1970, provided *New Naratif* with more details, some of which corroborates the description in the Amnesty International report: visits from family members were conducted by telephone, with a thick glass pane between them and the detainee. Conversations were monitored by prison officers, who would cut the call off the moment talk veered in a direction they did not approve of. Detainees would not be allowed certain books, even if those titles were not actually banned in Singapore. Newspapers would come to them with big holes where articles once were—a crude form of censorship to prevent them from receiving particular pieces of news from outside prison.

Then came another condition that was found to be unacceptable: the authorities wanted the detainees to work, doing menial labour for hours each day. "They wanted to soften our minds and make us cooperate with them," said Toh, who had been 20 years old when arrested.

The detainees sought to negotiate with those in charge. "We wanted dialogue for a long time, but it went nowhere," Goh said. She had been only 19 when detained.

---

4 https://remembering1987.files.wordpress.com/2015/08/political-detainees-in-singapore-10082015.pdf

5 https://www.google.com.sg/url?sa=t&rct=j&q=&esrc=s&source=web&cd=1&ved=0ah UKEwiQnoKClMnZAhUL148KHbzgA7MQFggmMAA&url=https%3A%2F%2Fwww. amnesty.org%2Fdownload%2FDocuments%2F204000%2Fasa360011976en. pdf&usg=AOvVaw1xSTRsbyB3L24ex5iCAjVR

From left: Toh Siew Tin, Sim Teong Hiok and Goh Peng Wah at the annual lunar new year lunch gathering of Singapore's 'Old Left'. (Tom White)

The detainees eventually decided to take drastic action in December 1970. Eight women, including Toh, Goh and Sim, began a hunger strike. A number of male political detainees in the men's prison did the same. "For the first week we drank water. After that, nothing," Toh said.

The hunger strikers were then subjected to brutal force-feedings, first once, then twice, and eventually three times a day. The three women still have clear memories of that experience:

"They'd stick a tube down your throat; if they couldn't get it down your throat they would stick a smaller tube through your nose. There would be a funnel on the other end and they would pour milk down the tube that way. Later, they would add a lot of supplements to the milk."

They recounted bruises all over their bodies; on their arms from being handcuffed to chairs, and their faces as prison officers forced their mouths open. Their throats would be rubbed raw by the tubes; Sim, who had been 25 at the time of arrest, recalled that there would sometimes be blood in their vomit when the hunger strikers threw up the milk being force-fed.

"We wanted them to agree to our requests [to not work in detention, and for better conditions]. We wrote to our parents telling them that we wanted to have a hunger strike because the conditions were so harsh," Goh said.

As the hunger strike wore on, the families of the detainees sought to put pressure on the government to improve conditions for their loved ones in detention. "Today if the lives of the political detainees should be seriously affected in any way, the LKY authorities would have to bear all the dire consequences. The LKY authorities must immediately stop all persecution and ill-treatment of political detainees, settle the reasonable demands of the detainees, unconditionally release all detainees," they wrote in a letter published in the *Journal of Contemporary Asia* in 1971.

Despite the painful and humiliating treatment, the hunger strikers persisted for over 130 days before the authorities relented. The detainees were no longer required to work, and some conditions were improved.

Today, members of the Old Left reminisce while surrounded by friends and family, but people are still being detained without trial under laws like the Internal Security Act and the Criminal Law (Temporary Provisions) Act. Without charges, trials, or access to the detainees, there is no way to verify the claims made by the Ministry of Home Affairs in its public statements justifying such detentions.

TO LEARN MORE

The 1963 Operation Coldstore in Singapore: Commemorating 50 Years (Petaling Jaya: SIRD, 2013), edited by Dr Poh Soo Kai, Tan Kok Fang, and Prof Hong Lysa, provides a diverse view of Operation Coldstore from the perspective of academics and former detainees.

"The Fundamental Issue is Anti-colonialism, Not Merger': Singapore's "Progressive Left", Operation Coldstore, and the Creation of Malaysia' by *New Naratif* Managing Director Dr Thum Ping Tjin (Asia Research Institute Working Paper Series No 211, 2013), provides historical context to Operation Coldstore, which was part of Singapore's contentious path to merger with the Federation of Malaya.[6]

If you're interested in the primary sources quoted above in the body of the article, you can view the Operation Coldstore summary case files (PDF, 14MB) retrieved from the British National Archives which were used by the Internal Security Council to decide upon the arrest and detention of 175 people.[7]

---

6 https://www.academia.edu/5320436/The_Fundamental_Issue_is_Anti-colonialism_Not_
Merger_Singapore_s_Progressive_Left_Operation_Coldstore_and_the_Creation_of_
Malaysia

7 https://newnaratif.com/wp-content/uploads/2018/02/British-Archives_Operation-
Coldstore.pdf

LOST HOMELAND: INDONESIA'S EXILE STORY

WARIEF DJAJANTO BASORIE | 26 APR 2018

The experiences of Indonesia's political exiles is little known, both within and without the country. Now, a veteran journalist has put together a collection of stories based on interviews with some of these exiles and their families.

Kadir Soelardjo, a 29-year-old medical student from Medan, North Sumatra, had been a guest at an event commemorating 16th anniversary of the founding of the People's Republic of China in Tiananmen, Beijing, when he received the news: there'd been an attempted coup back home.

In the early hours of 1 October 1965, six army generals in Jakarta, including Army Commander Lieutenant-General Ahmad Yani, had been abducted and assassinated by dissident members of the Indonesian Army who referred to themselves as the 30 September Movement. It was a fairly short-lived movement; Army Strategic Reserve Commander Major-General Suharto crushed the attempted coup that evening. The plot was blamed on the pro-Beijing PKI, triggering a large-scale anti-communist purge. Sukarno, Indonesia's first president, was politically weakened and forced to cede power to Suharto, who was formally appointed president in 1968.

A member of the Communist Party–affiliated CGMI (Concentration of the Indonesian Students Movement), Kadir became one of hundreds of Indonesians in Eastern Europe and China—mostly students, scholars and civil servants—who were exiled for their refusal to support Suharto's New Order.

Not all of them were affiliated to the Communist Party of Indonesia (PKI): I Ketut Putera was 23 when he got a scholarship to study economics in Bulgaria in 1963. Sukarno had pushed for higher education abroad for Indonesians, believing that they could help build the nation upon their return.

"I'm not a political person," said Putera. "Nevertheless, I took the risk to support Bung (Brother) Karno."

Kadir and Putera are among an estimated 500 *orang pelarian politik* (political fugitives) who had their Indonesian passports revoked after they refused to recognise Suharto's regime. These exiles include literary figures such as Utuy Tatang Sontani and Sobron Aidit, the younger brother of PKI chair D. N. Aidit.

The stories of these exiles are little known these days, both within and without Indonesia. A veteran journalist is trying to change this; Martin Aleida has compiled the stories of Kadir, Putera and 17 others in his book *Tanah Air Yang Hilang (Homeland Lost)*, published in Bahasa Indonesia in August last year.

Between March and June 2016, Martin travelled to cities like Amsterdam, The Hague, Berlin, Cologne, Paris, Prague and Sofia, where he interviewed 30 exiles about their experiences. "First, it's to give a picture to the people of Indonesia, particularly the young generation, that there are Indonesians who are treated unfairly whose citizenship has been invalidated," he tells *New Naratif*. "The second motivation is a drive within me as a journalist that their stories, the exiles, must be written."

Scholars in exile

In the early 1960s, Sukarno deepened ties with Communist-bloc countries. College degree programmes and scholarships, particularly to China and Eastern Europe, became available to young Indonesians.

The People's Republic of China and the Soviet Union had the most Indonesian students. After Suharto wrested power from Sukarno, Indonesia's relations with the Eastern-bloc states, particularly China, soured.

The students were able to continue their studies but were called in by the Indonesian embassies for what was termed a "screening". These sessions were essentially loyalty tests, with one dominant question: "Do you accept or not accept Suharto's New Order?"

Child psychology student Soejono Soegeng Pangestu at Charles University in Prague was defiant. He challenged the screening officer to explain what the New Order was, in relation to the news of widespread killings. For stating that he could not accept a regime that did not honour basic human rights, the Indonesian embassy in the Czech capital did not extend the validity of his passport. Others faced the same treatment: one either expressed support for the new president or lost the right to return home.

"[I]n their case, they did not get the opportunity to defend themselves," says Martin. "They were summoned to the embassy for interrogation. And basically, after interrogation, if they declared [that] they only accepted the old government, in this case it was President Sukarno who sent them abroad, it would be a major problem for them if they returned home to Indonesia. [They] could have been arrested or faced something worse."

Unable to return to their home country, some exiles were provided with jobs by their host country upon graduation, while others moved to Western Europe to seek asylum. After having rubbed shoulders with Chinese Communist Party officials, Kadir Soelardjo found himself moving to Amsterdam where he began working as a waiter in a Balinese restaurant. His wife, Melia Siregar, and daughter, Ita, joined him from Indonesia in 1976.

Strength amid adversity

Every exile profiled in the book has an exceptional story, presenting varied examples of persistence and resilience in the face of numerous hurdles.

Sobron Aidit moved to China to teach Bahasa Indonesia in the 1960s and prevented from returning post-1965. "But [then] the 1966 Cultural Revolution erupted. He was a prominent figure ostracised, isolated," Martin says.

After the death of his wife in 1981, Sobron flew to France with his two teenage daughters, Nita and Wita, and successfully sought political asylum. A year later, he and other political exiles opened the Restaurant Indonesia, serving Indonesian fare in a European city known for its sophisticated tastes.

Today, his daughter Nita runs the restaurant; her father passed away in 2007. Her customers, about 95% of whom are French, have their favourites—authentic Indonesian dishes like *nasi goreng*, *sate* and *rendang*—and the establishment has made it into the *Guide Michelin*. It's a level of success that belies the fact that, during the New Order years, the Indonesian embassy forbade Indonesians to patronise it. It was only after Suharto stepped down in 1998 that the taboo was shattered.

Another singular story is that of Waruno Machdi, born in Bogor in 1944. The son of a diplomat, he spent most of his boyhood overseas. He received his chemical engineering degree in Moscow and lived in the Soviet Union for 20 years. Although he states that he's not a Communist,

Machdi identifies himself as a Sukarno supporter. In 1977 he moved to West Berlin, using an exit visa issued by the Soviet Union to get himself to the American sector of the city; he hadn't been able to get along with the pro-Moscow Indonesian exiles in the Soviet Union.

He landed a job as an assistant researcher at the Fritz Haber Institute, a science research institute affiliated with the Max Planck Gesellschaft (Society) in Berlin. The institute needed someone with experience working with air-sensitive elements that couldn't mix with oxygen. There were twenty applicants, mostly Germans, but Machdi got the job; he'd worked in a similar field in the Soviet Union. This serendipitous result makes him one of the few exiles who has secured continued employment in the field of their academic study.

When asked for his impression of the exiles he'd interviewed, Martin swiftly zeroes in on what struck him the most: "Their strength. Meaning they could endure the political oppression. They could overcome it. And that oppression is not one layer in the sense that they are hounded by the New Order regime. But when they were in the People's Republic of China, they were banished to a place 200 kilometres away from Beijing. They had no freedom for contact with the outside. When they received visitors, the visitors had to be registered first. So, the oppression was layered."

Contributions and recognition (at long last)

When Abdurrahman Wahid became Indonesia's fourth president— remaining in power from 1999 to 2001—he invited the political exiles home. But the ship has sailed for many of these exiles and their families; they've adopted other nationalities and aren't officially Indonesian citizens any longer.

The future generations, too, might not recognise Indonesia as home. Nita, for instance, compared visits to Indonesia to going on "a stroll", as opposed to returning to her *kampung* (village). She's gone to Indonesia four times—once to bring her father's ashes to his birthplace of Belitung, an island off the east coast of southern Sumatra.

Martin says that these stories highlight the "presence of injustice", and that "to the present day this injustice prevails affecting a number of people despite regime change."

But some exiles have been more successful in bridging the gap and gaining the gratitude of the Indonesian government for advancing bilateral relations.

Putera's connection to Bulgaria, for example, has proven useful: in 2004, when a Bulgarian trade delegation travelled to Indonesia, Putera—who had worked at the Bulgarian Foreign Ministry after earning a PhD in economics in 1973—was asked to serve as the delegation's interpreter. He reprised this role in 2006, when Joko "Jokowi" Widodo, then the mayor of Surakarta, visited the Bulgarian city of Montana to sign a sister-city partnership.

His efforts have since been recognised. During an embassy function in 2015 marking the 70th anniversary of Indonesia's proclamation of independence, the Indonesian ambassador to Bulgaria presented Putera with the first serving of *tumpeng*, a ceremonial rice cone with beef, chicken and assorted side dishes. Putera was 75 years old then, the eldest in the reception, and the gesture of respect was a significant one: an official acknowledgement of an Indonesian in exile whose lost homeland has been regained.

But not all exiles have led successful, fulfilling lives: a sports reporter who had worked for the *Warta Bhakti* daily newspaper suffered from depression and ended up taking his own life in Amsterdam. His wife asked Martin not to use her husband's name in the book. Instead, Martin republished a fictionalised account of the journalist's life that he had written in June 2016. The story had been voted as the best short story published in the newspaper *Kompas* that year.

Further exploration

Producing *Tanah Air Yang Hilang* has been a labour of love. Martin's friends—some of them writers and poets themselves—donated money to fund his travels, while the exiles put him up whenever he visited.

There are many more stories to be told. There were, for instance, individuals who had attended the 1965 commemoration of the founding of the People's Republic of China—the same event that Kadir Soelardjo had been at—who had returned to Indonesia, only to suffer repercussions.

Wikana was one such person. He'd been a youth activist and a PKI member in the Provisional People's Consultative Assembly. A year after his return from China, Wikana was picked up by soldiers at his East Jakarta house and disappeared. His wife has had no word of his whereabouts, nor of his fate.

Martin's aware that there's much more to be said about this part of Indonesian history. He has no plans so far to release a second volume of the exile's experiences, but says he's planning to spend two to three years writing about the 30 September Movement: "In the past months I've been collecting books about the event abroad and domestically. But I'm looking for the testimony of victims. Their notes. Facebook has plenty of it. [...] There are blogs that bring together [such testimony]. I want to bring out the human side."

NORTH / SOUTH
WILL NGUYEN | 30 APR 2018

Growing up in the United States, Will Nguyen's knowledge of Vietnamese language and history had come from a firmly South Vietnamese perspective. His research has led him to interrogate the north/south divide in his journey to uncover multiple perspectives and truths.

I've always been into the idea of counterparts—"separate but equal", to borrow the politically dangerous phrase. *Captain Planet, Sailor Moon, The Mighty Morphin' Power Rangers*—these shows were always particular favourites of mine as a child because each contained an episode or arc where analogues to the good guys arose: Captain Pollution and his team of toxic "planeteers", the Four Sisters of the Black Moon, or the Dark Rangers. I find the inherent sense of balance in counterparts intensely satisfying, like yin-yang writ large.

As I've grown older, this affinity for correlates extended to international politics, in particular, ideologically-opposed, directionally-split countries, i.e. North and South Korea, or East and West Germany.

The time when the modern Vietnamese nation-state existed as two separate entities naturally possesses a particular gravity in my mind, as I'm sure it does in the minds of many overseas Vietnamese. After all, that pair's existence, its mutual antagonism, and one's annihilation of the other, is single-handedly responsible for the dispersal of Vietnamese people across the globe, a burst of human photons in one of many collisions between communism and anti-communism.

I was born in America; unbeknownst to me at the time, all the Vietnamese I ever encountered were former citizens of the Republic of Vietnam (i.e. South Vietnam) or as I'd known it, Vietnam. There was no alternative, no other. The yellow flag with three red stripes were ubiquitous and the only representation of Vietnam I knew.

The "right" and "wrong" anthem
Encarta Encyclopedia 97 provided me the first hint of another truth, of another "Vietnam"—the "evil" one, I would quickly learn. I remember doing a project in fifth grade which required us to produce a "country

profile" on a nation of our choosing. I referred to the CD-ROM encyclopedia and, without giving it much thought, copied out the red flag with yellow star, Vietnam's official flag as listed within the country's entry.

My grandmother was the first to "correct" me, scolding me as Encarta played "Tiến Quân Ca", the national anthem of North Vietnam from 1945-1975, and after the war, the official one of all Vietnam. That was not the "real" anthem, she told me. The information in that article was "wrong". When I asked her what the real anthem was, she hummed "Tiếng Gọi Công Dân"—the national anthem of South Vietnam from 1948–1975—a tune I was much more familiar with.

As I finished up my project, I asked my mother to look over my work. What she did, whether intentional or not, resounds with me to this day. Rather than make me remove my drawing of the yellow-starred red flag, she had me draw South Vietnam's red-striped yellow flag next to it, presenting both flags as equally valid.

It took me at least another two decades to realise this, but my mother's simple gesture was both an extremely powerful teaching moment and a representation of my intellectual angst with the overseas Vietnamese identity. It was my first taste of the concept of contradictory but co-existing truths.

Growing up, I never gave that distant land of Vietnam too much thought; the framework for that place and its people had been set up for me. We (the southerners) were the good guys; they (the northerners) were the bad. Everything we said was true; everything they said was lies. I never wondered why we were the ones living in another country.

College, membership in an active Vietnamese student association, and a kind-hearted Vietnamese professor ushered in a new era of knowledge for me. I began taking my first steps toward balance, and further steps towards the truth… or rather, truths.

North to South

In Vietnam, "nam tiến", literally meaning "march to the south", refers to the expansion of Vietnam southwards, from the Red River Delta down to the Mekong River Delta. This development shapes Vietnam's long-standing stereotypes between northerners and southerners. Contrary to people who like to compare the shape of Vietnam to a bamboo yoke or the letter 'S', I like to think of the state in more metaphysical terms: a past-oriented north that flows to a future-oriented south.

The Red River Delta is held up as the "birthplace" of Vietnam, the traditional seat of culture and politics. The northern region and its people are perceived as conservative, ascetic, and prone to resource and food shortages. This has bred a northern character that prizes resilience, indirect communication, the concept of "face" (linked to the concept of one's honour and prestige), and a muted cuisine that uses fewer herbs and spices.

As the state advanced into Cham and Khmer territory, a separate centre of power began developing in the south, attracting those drawn to "frontier" life and a multi-cultured existence. By virtue of self-selection, Vietnam's expansion south drew the free-wheeling, the forward-looking, the liberal, the cosmopolitan. The south was more abundant in food and resources; Saigon—formerly known by its Khmer name Prey Nokor and currently by its Sino-Vietnamese name Ho Chi Minh City—drew traders from the world over, and life was on the whole, easier and more prosperous.

These historical circumstances have defined what it means to be a southerner: we speak with a relaxed drawl and in a straightforward manner, we cook flavourful, vivacious, eclectic dishes, and we possess a progressive, open outlook that embraces global trends. It was no surprise that the south Vietnamese eagerly adopted American dress, customs, and culture during the 1950s–1970s.

But it isn't just a matter of character traits and cuisine; regionalism in its extreme form has repeatedly led to Vietnamese killing Vietnamese. Historian Huy Duc describes Vietnam as a home "whose walls are made of flesh and blood". It's not just a metaphor.

North versus South

A civil war in the 17th century proved to be an eerie foreshadowing of events three centuries later. The north and the south were split into two separate polities: "Đàng Ngoài" and "Đàng Trong", literally the "outside" and the "inside". The Trịnh lords ruled over the north, the Nguyễn lords the south. In 1802, the southern Nguyễn lords ultimately triumphed over their northern Trịnh rivals, uniting the country under its Southern aegis. Inklings of this contentious period still remain in our language: to this day, Vietnamese still say they are going "out" to Hanoi and "into" Saigon.

The 20th-century civil war between North and South was a reverse iteration. The 1954 Geneva Accords split Vietnam into directional counterparts once more—a communist north versus a democratic south—with nationwide elections set to unify the country in two years' time.[1] Ho Chi Minh was predicted to win. Knowing this, Ngo Dinh Diem declared the formation of an independent southern republic that technically was not signatory to the Geneva Accords and thus un-beholden. The United States supported the non-communist South Vietnamese government, pouring in financial aid. The northern victory in the Vietnam War in 1975 unified the country once more, but different perspectives persist. Depending on who you talk to, 30 April 1975—the day the People's Army of Vietnam and the Viet Cong captured Saigon—is described either as a liberation or an invasion.

My mother regularly reminds me I'm from the south. When I first began taking Vietnamese language classes in college and started pronouncing my v's, qu's, and final consonant n's, she and my eldest aunt jested that I'd "become a northerner". In class, I quickly learned that much of the Vietnamese I spoke at home was heavily marked by southern vocabulary used pre-1975. The enormous amount of south Vietnamese who had transplanted themselves in the 1970s and 1980s had led to the creation of communities that were essentially living time capsules.

The southernness of my spoken Vietnamese comes and goes depending on how inebriated I am, but the pride is palpable. On the first day of my advanced Vietnamese class at the College of Humanities and Social Sciences in Ho Chi Minh City in 2012, the professor asked me where I was from—"Will là người gì?"

Without thinking, I responded, "Will là người nam (I'm a Southerner)."

Taken aback but pleasantly surprised, the professor said that, in her 30 years of teaching, she'd never heard such a response from a "foreign-born". I quickly corrected myself—"Will là người Mỹ gốc Việt (I'm a Vietnamese-American)"—but the identity ambiguity persists.

Conversations

My investigation of the history between the north and south often involved prodding fellow southerners with sensitive topics. Once, I asked my Vietnamese professor in college in the United States about one of the war's alternate names in Vietnam—"Chiến tranh chống Mỹ cứu nước (The war to resist America and save the nation)"—which

1 https://www.history.com/this-day-in-history/geneva-conference-begins

heavily implied that we southern Vietnamese were imperialist collab-
orators. (For the record, the first South Vietnamese president, Ngo
Dinh Diem, and his brother, Ngo Dinh Nhu, were both assassinated
with tacit American support for not being compliant enough.) It was a
mind-blowing experience to later see the phrase in propaganda posters
on the streets of Saigon.

I had, of course, to thoroughly research the other side as well; I read
numerous books and watched countless interviews from individuals on
the Communist side, both those based in Hanoi as well as those hidden
away in the jungles of South Vietnam.

On my first trip to Vietnam in the summer of 2007, I took liberties
during my research project on gay culture in Saigon to randomly ask locals
their thoughts on the war, on life post-1975, on their current government.

"These colorful billboards… on every corner. They're so strange, aren't
they?" That was how I broached the topic with the motorcycle drivers.
Casual. Open-ended. The propaganda signs, with their blocky, solid-col-
ored, Soviet-style imagery, were a genuine curiosity to me. They were
government-sanctioned, overtly political signs, exalting the Communist
Party's leadership in history, in the South's "liberation", in developing
a "modern", civilised Vietnam. And they were literally everywhere. As
we drove by the myriad signs peppered around the city, I would use the
occasion to ask the moto-drivers their opinions of the political status quo.

"They're a bunch of liars."

"They don't really care about the people."

As one driver zoomed past a particularly large mansion, he told me
that it was the residence of a prominent Communist Party member. There
was a consistent sense of cynicism among these working class motorists.

An older, southern woman's story was particularly interesting, as she
was old enough to have experienced the "liberation" and the years that
followed. I met her through a family friend of my mother's. (My mother
had been terrified for my safety; I was the first family member to return
to Vietnam since they fled, and I would be traveling completely alone
as the child of a "collaborating" family.)

Upon arriving at the house, I was impressed by how large and modern
it was. It had granite countertops, hardwood floors, and classic, imposing
cherrywood furniture. This was luxury by Vietnamese standards; with
at least four motorcycles sitting in the spacious courtyard, it was clear
this family was relatively well off.

Auntie and I were sitting in the living room having a casual chat about our families, when the conversation turned to what life was like immediately after 30 April 1975.

At this point, she got up to close all the doors and windows, drawing the curtains. She whispered for the rest of the conversation. Her family had been businesspeople during the Republican era, accumulating a good deal of wealth. After the Communists came to town, local party members, aware of the family's affluence, found an excuse to confiscate the house. It was impossible to dispute the move, so the family decided to work within the new system, establishing enough political connections to eventually reclaim the house within a decade or so. There was a healthy dose of disdain for the powers-that-be in her stories, but her family's resilience, tenacity, and resourcefulness overshadowed all else for me. It was an injustice corrected through cunning manipulation of an alien political system. That she was still paranoid about being over-heard 20 years later speaks volumes of the pervasive and oppressive surveillance state the Vietnamese live under.

A different perspective came in the form of a Northern shopkeep at a propaganda poster shop. She'd noticed my many visits to her shop, and figuring out that I was Việt Kiều (overseas Vietnamese), took the initiative to engage me in conversation about history and politics.

I was taken aback but excited by her friendliness and eagerness to help me understand Vietnam. She told me to ask her anything I wanted. Aware that I was part of a Southern family that had fled after the war, she knew I'd been served a healthy dose of scepticism regarding Communism and the current political regime, and tried her best to argue for the other side. She'd moved to Ho Chi Minh City, she said, after its liberation.

I got straight to the prickly issues. Why had so many people from the South fled? What of the re-education camps? How can the pow-ers-that-be call the current system "democratic" when there's only one party in charge?

"People fled because they feared retribution," she said. "When you work against the victors, you are naturally apprehensive when they arrive."

The re-education camps, she went to on say, were not all that bad: "The ones I visited even had nice gardens and flower beds. And in any case, you have to understand the situation that the new government was in. You had an entire population grow up under an enemy's regime. When you come to power, you have to make sure this group cooperates, you have to make sure this group is educated in the ways of the new regime."

Her answers started to waver, though, when it came to the current "democratic" system. "We have elections. We have voting. We have representatives who form a national assembly," she said.

"Yeah, but all that stuff doesn't really matter when you can only pick representatives from one party," I argued back. "If everyone is forced to follow the same ideology, the same ideas, choice is a moot point. True democracy involves multiple parties." She disagreed, insisting that because the organs existed, democracy existed in Vietnam.

Conviction and democracy

To be sure, truth is a sensitive topic on both sides; I'd had just grown up entrenched in the anti-communist camp rather than the anti-capitalist one. Various attempts to remedy the situation have led to some rather awkward moments. I remember a conversation between my aunt and my mother where my mother said she had to give credit to the Communist government for keeping the country together and growing the economy at an appreciable clip, but my aunt quickly retorted that my uncle—who had served in the South Vietnamese army—would have maimed her if he heard her talking like that.

I'm still researching today, adopting a less polarised, more nuanced approach to the war and its competing ideologies than perhaps my mother would like. During a BBC interview, southerner Nguyen Thi Binh, former foreign minister of the Provisional Revolutionary Government of the Republic of South Vietnam and prominent Communist figure at the Paris Peace Accords, was asked for her thoughts on Vietnamese dissidents and their desire for a better nation. She retorted: "How are they any different from me?"

The dichotomy of "good versus evil" had been so deeply ingrained in the narratives of north and south that, until I heard that comment, I'd never really thought of it that way. These people, these Communists, laid down their lives for their ideals, for their country, and perhaps most meaningfully, for their countrymen. Can, or should, we cynically believe that those who fought on the northern side sacrificed the spring of their lives, and sometimes their lives altogether, simply to gain power at the expense of their fellow Vietnamese?

What, on the other hand, was the South fighting for? Trudging through American history books, one would be hard-pressed to find any real, fleshed-out answer beyond "the domino theory", a theory that argued that the fall of one country to Communism would lead to a domino effect among its neighbours. Reading such material, it was hard not to buy into the (Hanoian) idea that South Vietnam was a propped-up American creation. In fact, the more I researched, the more I realised that it was a deep sense of ambivalence among the southern population that lead to South Vietnam's embarrassingly quick demise.

When asked why they were fighting and what they were fighting for, South Vietnamese soldiers often turned out not to be very firm believers in their own cause. Boots and uniforms stripped off and abandoned in place by soldiers deserting on 30 April 1975 testify to that fact.

The wartime South Vietnamese population might not have been able to answer the question of "what are we fighting for?", but the next few decades of economic mismanagement and political oppression after unification would provide a resounding answer, especially for those not able to escape the country.

By the early 2010s, after nearly a decade of research and reading, my viewpoint had matured from "acknowledge that our side may have been 'wrong', and then find out what happened on both sides" to "never lose sight of the fact that democracy as the South attempted to espouse it trumps the totalitarian communism adopted by the North." Both were foreign, imposed ideologies, and the fact that one conquered the other has no bearing on virtue. As the Vietnamese author and political dissident Duong Thu Huong so eloquently put it: "Beauty does not always triumph."

Though film and media are thoroughly dominated by northerners, southern defiance is coming to the surface. "We only learn how to cherish things when we've already lost them," the 2017 trailer of Cô Ba Sài Gòn (The Tailor) begins. The southern voiceover is immediately followed by a close-up of Saigon's city hall, with the camera focused squarely on the flag pole—there the flag of South Vietnam flutters. Yellow with three red stripes. It is subtle but perceivable for those who look for it.

But of course, if that is too subtle for you, you can always rewind a few seconds and there staring you in the face from the very moment the trailer starts is the flag on the áo dài. The tailor's hand gently caresses a swath of yellow with three red stripes. Genuinely ask yourself if this is all coincidence. Of all the patterns in the world that the filmmakers could have featured on the dress, why this one? And why does the voiceover make the statements she does as this pattern is displayed?

A slow zoom-out is followed by shots of economic prosperity and vibrant displays of traditional áo dài to emphasise the blossoming of Vietnamese culture under a "fascist", "puppet" regime. That these scenes managed to make it onto the big screen directly undermines the communist narrative of Saigon needing to be "liberated". A particularly salient question asked among dissidents, both in and outside the country, is "who liberated whom?" Did the impoverished North really liberate the wealthier South? Or was it the other way around? Moreover, what exactly did the South need liberating from? A comfortable, prosperous, peaceful life?

The film champions the preservation of the áo dài—the traditional Vietnamese outfit—over Western fashions in 1960s Saigon, but the subversive message, wrapped in the garb of a innocent movie about fashion, is unmistakable. For South Vietnam, the loss is more political than cultural: no longer do citizens possess freedom, democracy, and a vibrant civil society. Even if imperfectly practised in South Vietnam, greater freedom of expression brought prosperity and a society of better quality than what Vietnam has today. Many Vietnamese, unable to express dissatisfaction with the status quo at the ballot box, vote with their feet. Leaving the country is the dream for those who have means to do so; Hanoi readily acknowledges that Vietnam suffers from brain drain.

Even so, it must be acknowledged that the war was a manifestation of North and South both wanting the best for the Vietnamese people while choosing drastically different paths. It would be unforgivably cynical to believe otherwise, to view either government as monolithic entities *not* made of Vietnamese individuals who loved their country. The root of the conflict stemmed from both sides competing to be the *only* good. Both the North and the South had causes they believed to be just—a fact which native and overseas Vietnamese have yet to fully accept.

On paper and in diplomatic circles, there is only one "true" Vietnam. Although the Republic of Vietnam ceased to exist after 30 April 1975, it lives on in the hearts and minds of millions of Vietnamese who abhor communist totalitarianism. It lives on in its enforced absence within Vietnam's national discourse. A silent, de facto ban of the yellow flag with three red stripes, of any positive mention of the southern republic, of anything related to the former state is, in a way, perpetuating South Vietnam's existence. And if history is any indication, the South remembers.

TIMOR-LESTE'S FORGOTTEN HEROES

SOPHIE RAYNOR | 22 JUN 2018

16 years ago, Timor-Leste reclaimed its independence after decades of brutal occupation. The world's attention turned away. But for the women whose contributions to independence go unrecognised, the fight never stopped.

In any of the hundreds of villages dotting the hills of Timor-Leste, you might meet a gentle, older woman, body wrapped tight in a sarong, selling vegetables, running a kiosk, or watching over grandchildren, sanguine as the day goes by. Her quiet stoicism belies the unresolved trauma many Timorese women carry with them—they were just children during Indonesia's 1975 invasion of Timor-Leste, but today they live with memories of forced starvation, torture, rape and death.

After the end of the Indonesian occupation in October 1999, the guerrillas who fought for the country's independence descended from mountain hideouts to a victor's welcome. They remain valorised and compensated by the country's government today. But for thousands of people who supported the resistance in secret as *clandestinos*—smuggling food to guerillas, passing messages through the country, sabotaging the enemy's weapons, vehicles, plans and efforts—recognition is much harder to come by, and compensation little more than a pipe dream.

And for the many women who suffered unimaginable violence as foreign forces swept their land, the glory of independence meant a return to the humdrum routine of cooking, cleaning, and child-raising. Their contributions remain unacknowledged and their fight for survival continues every day.

"Justice should be ongoing"

Josefa Adao da Silva was a nervous 12-year-old in 1975 when her family fled deep into the rocky mountains from invading Indonesian forces. Surviving for months in the makeshift mountain camps of Timor-Leste's independence fighters, da Silva watched both her parents die of starvation.

Da Silva recalls spending four years living in secret in the mountains. She helped the hiding guerrilla groups by teaching their children and patrolling the camp's perimeter until the day she was caught. She was captured, detained, interrogated and tortured. Soldiers kicked her, beat her, starved her, burned her skin, electrocuted her, took photographs of her naked, and dunked her head underwater in a tank filled with crocodiles. At three o'clock in the morning, an Indonesian soldier raped her in her cell.

He told her: "If you don't surrender your body, I will not shoot you—I'll cut your body into pieces right here."

Da Silva recalls his words in her story published in *Enduring Impunity*, a record by Indonesia's National Commission on Violence Against Women (*Komnas Perempuan*). Untold stories from Timor-Leste's fight for independence pad the fat book and present a stark picture of lives unresolved.

"I want a good life for me and my family," she says in *Enduring Impunity*. "I need something in return for what I have suffered."

In peaceful Timor-Leste today, da Silva runs a small kiosk. She left a forced marriage to an Indonesian soldier and lives with a son from that marriage and a new husband, whom she says accepts her despite the pervasive and dangerous belief that women raped by Indonesian soldiers chose to be with the men.

Timor-Leste voted for independence in 1999; after three years of administration by the United Nations, it emerged in 2002 as the 21st century's first new country. Public attention turned away from its struggle.

Now, former guerrilla leaders—almost all men—occupy powerful political positions and run the country, shrouded in the glory of days gone by, while many of the women have retreated into the background, a silent pillar of a sovereign state that may be peaceful but isn't yet just.

"Justice should be ongoing, because only with justice can we get truth about what we suffered," da Silva says. "There especially must be justice for all the women for whom independence cost them their dignity."

Today, the government of Timor-Leste provides generous pensions and strong support for veterans of the resistance. There's no question it's deserved. But veterans of armed conflict weren't the only contributors to the country's struggle for freedom.

The *clandestinos*

Despite the *clandestinos'* significant contributions to the fight at great personal risk, they're not classified as veterans for the purposes of the otherwise generous pension scheme[1]. To be eligible for a pension, veterans must prove their participation in the resistance as part of its "structures and organisation". But many *clandestinos* can't prove formal involvement, precisely because of the covert nature of their work.

The pension scheme is scaled to provide larger payments for veterans who can prove more years of "exclusive service" to the resistance cause. Again, the *clandestinos* are at a disadvantage: even if a *clandestino* could prove their involvement, the fact that their contributions were carried out in secret, undocumented, and masked by work and study, means they fail to meet the years of exclusive service required to achieve the economic security such a pension could provide.

According to officials, women made up over 60% of the *clandestino* population. Their activities, done under-the-radar, now go unrecognised and uncompensated. Women in Timor-Leste—systematically excluded from social, political and economic power—are again locked out of social and economic security, despite having risked their lives for their country.

A turbulent history

Long-neglected colonial outpost Timor-Leste, then known as Portuguese Timor, entered a decolonisation process following the Carnation Revolution that dissolved the Portuguese empire in the mid-1970s. As the dust settled in the tiny half-island country, a left-wing party known as the Revolutionary Front for an Independent Timor-Leste, or Fretilin, unilaterally declared independence on 28 November 1975.

The country enjoyed nine days of sovereignty before neighbour Indonesia launched, on 7 December 1975, a brutal land, sea and air invasion. The Indonesians justified the attack as a move to counter communism, and spread a belief that the nascent state wasn't equipped to self-govern.

Between December 1975 and March 1977 an estimated 50,000 to 100,000 Timorese were killed[2]. Invading forces systematically destroyed houses, stores and food sources, poisoning crops and water sources

---

1 http://bellschool.anu.edu.au/sites/default/files/publications/attachments/2015-12/SSGM_
IB_2014_13_KentWallis_Print%26Web.pdf

2 https://nsarchive2.gwu.edu/NSAEBB/NSAEBB174/710.pdf

with chemical weapons. Civilians endured countless atrocities and fled from their villages to the mountains, where they remained hiding until bombing and encirclement forced many to surrender.

Felismina de Araújo fled with her family from their village to the isolated mountains of Ainaro. They lived in the forest for three years, cooking and delivering food each night to rebel forces. She was caught one night and taken to the military subdistrict command, where she was kicked, interrogated and gang raped by Indonesian soldiers. She was four months pregnant.

"I told them I was pregnant, but they didn't care and said if I fought against them they would throw me in the river," she says in *Enduring Impunity*. "I just cried."

She was arrested again in 1982 and detained in the notoriously tough prison on barren Atauro Island, which today serves as a tropical holiday playground for expats in Dili. She never found out what happened to her husband.

Violence and independence

The conclusion of the Cold War and the 1998 end of Suharto's regime in Indonesia returned public attention to the question of Timor-Leste's independence. Suharto's successor, BJ Habibie, announced a referendum[3] for the Timorese, giving them a choice between special autonomy within Indonesia or independence. Despite intimidation from the militia, a staggering 98.6% of registered voters turned out, and 78.3% voted for independence.

The furious Indonesian forces retaliated, murdering citizens[4] as they retreated. In Bobonaro municipality, near the Indonesian border, a local women's organisation called FOKUPERS has worked with women widowed during the retreat to establish a support group called Nove Nove ("Nine Nine" in Portuguese), named for the month and the year in which their husbands were murdered, September 1999.

The group's coordinator, Teresinha Soares Cardoso, suffered through the death of her husband in the final days of the occupation, and the death by starvation of her 18-month-old baby in a refugee camp mere months later. Today, she runs a small kiosk, selling kitchen items and hand-woven *tais* (a traditional woven cloth) to support her children and

---

3 https://www.fmreview.org/kosovo/taylor

4 http://chegareport.net/Chega%20All%20Volumes.pdf

make ends meet. But she has to engage in constant arguments with her husband's family, who are trying to take over the land they'd bought as a married couple.

"My husband and I bought this land," she says in *Enduring Impunity*. "It was not inherited from his parents. However, my in-laws are secretly planting trees on the land without informing me so they can claim it, and are also dividing up the land to give to their two children. When husbands die, women have no rights to land."

Many women live far from urban centre; this distance compounds the barriers they face in accessing services and schemes available to them, including aged pensions and legal documents to land.

The *Chega!* promise

Post-independence, the United Nations established several transitional justice mechanisms in Timor-Leste, designed to draw a line between the country's violent past and hopeful future.

A Serious Crimes Court with jurisdiction over war crimes, genocide, crimes against humanity, and murder, torture and sexual offences committed in 1999 was established that year. A truth commission, known as CAVR, followed in 2002. Between 2002 and 2005 CAVR recorded approximately 1,600 statements from women survivors of violence, and published in 2005 a report of over 2,000 pages entitled *Chega[5]!*, or *Enough!*

Chega! painstakingly documented 835 counts of sexual violence and found clear evidence of the widespread and systematic way Indonesian forces engaged in rape, sexual torture and sexual slavery over the 24 years of the occupation, largely with impunity.

The report made specific recommendations for redress, and many hoped it would act as a framework for progress. But, more than a decade on, little progress has been made[6]. Parliamentary apathy and dwindling interest further curtail efforts.

Manuela Leong Pereira is the director of Assosiasaun Chega! Ba Ita, or ACbit, an NGO established in 2013 to implement the *Chega!* report findings. In her sunlit office in Dili, she shares some of the struggles the organisation has faced in securing political and financial support for its mandate.

---

5 http://chegareport.net/Chega%20All%20Volumes.pdf

6 http://ssgm.bellschool.anu.edu.au/sites/default/files/publications/attachments/2016-07/ssgmreportseries1chega10years.pdf

A national reparation scheme that would provide trauma counselling and financial compensation to women survivors has stalled. "Parliament just didn't have the political will to get the law passed," Pereira says. Without a champion in a high position of power, the needs of women survivors can easily fall to the wayside as the country's leaders grapple with other political questions.

Previously part of the local office of the Geneva-based International Centre for Justice, ACbit lobbied Timor-Leste's government to draft a reparations law that would provide financial compensation to women survivors. The organisation collected testimonies from victims to share women's experiences, but the Fretilin-led government took issue with an article of the law that would guarantee non-discrimination for victims.

"They just wanted the victims coming from [the] Fretilin party," Pereira explains. "We tried to explain to the advisors that's against international law, but they just postponed and postponed until their mandate finished." The government changed in 2012, forcing ACbit to start from scratch, but successive governments remain disinterested in the scheme.

A new government, a new hope

A minority government led by Fretilin took power after last July's parliamentary election. Pereira says that the government's Ministry for Social Solidarity, a long-term ACbit donor, cut funding to the organisation: "We don't receive [funding] anymore."

There's a chance that the situation might change. The Fretilin government was dissolved by President Francisco Guterres after failing to gain parliamentary support for its programme. A re-run election last month saw a new coalition of three parties win power. The People's Liberation Party, a member of the victorious coalition, campaigned on the importance of returning attention to the past conflict, and a previous government led by another coalition member, the National Congress for Timorese Reconstruction, gave ACbit consistent funding.

Pereira hopes the new government will revise the decision to cut ACbit's funding. But for now, without money from the Ministry of Social Solidarity, she says ACbit will drop its staff down to part-time roles.

Pereira seems frustrated by the block. "They don't need big money," she says of the survivors ACbit supports. "They just need attention, some specific programmes, some opportunities."

She cites university scholarships as an example of continuing discrimination against female survivors and their families. "They give scholarships to minister's children. [Children of survivors] already don't have education because they live very far from Dili, they have to compete with Dili children."

Around 70% of Timor-Leste's population lives rurally, and the country's universities are concentrated in the capital. The national university, Universidade Nacional Timor Lorosa'e, offers scholarships to the children of veterans, but no such initiatives exist for the children of other resistance survivors.

ACbit conducts participatory research with survivors and maintains a comprehensive database of stories and data, which inform advocacy and education work. The organisation supports six centres in four municipalities, where women survivors can gather to share stories and conduct business. "If we join them together they can support each other and understand," explains Pereira.

ACbit is the only organisation in Timor-Leste working directly and exclusively with women survivors of the conflict. Local non-government organisations FOKUPERS and Alola Foundation have also provided critical counselling, training and financial support to vulnerable women across the country, including survivors, and the women's NGO umbrella network Rede Feto has also conducted research.

Women's stories sidelined

In an interview[7] with the *Guardian* newspaper late last year, resistance fighter-turned-organiser Lourdes Alves Araújo identified the sidelining of women's contributions to the resistance movement as a key barrier to progress for conservative, patriarchal Timor-Leste.

"Since the war ended, it's been mostly men who have had their stories told and their images presented to the country," she said. "But many of our leaders and heroes were women, and it's important to recover that history and make it right."

Head of the women's branch of Organização Popúlar das Mulheres da Timor, a group with close links to Fretilin, Araújo says she and her colleagues are publishing a book to tell that story. ACbit and its regional sister organisation, the Jakarta-based Asia Justice and Rights (AJAR), have also published significant work and recommendations based on participatory research results and documentation.

---

7 https://www.theguardian.com/global-development/2017/dec/29/
female-guerrillas-denied-liberation-timor-leste-war-independence

"People just hear about veterans' stories, men's stories, not women's," says Pereira. "This is an opportunity to talk."

Life goes on for many women survivors of the conflict. For them, there is no wistful, charged ending to their story, no hero's reward or adulation. Pragmatic survivors getting on with their lives have little room for entertaining fancy. But there's a quiet determination to live a life bigger than trauma, to continue the fight, to have it mean more than it did.

"We have hope," Pereira says, more than once.

GENDER JUSTICE

PUSHING INDONESIA TO PROTECT WOMEN FROM VIOLENCE

KATE WALTON | 07 DEC 2017

With cases of violence against women in Indonesia still treated as sensa-
tional tabloid material, progress to protect women on a national level is
slow. But activists are slowly shifting the ground.

As women across the globe share their #MeToo stories of sexual harassment, Indonesia is facing a crisis of violence against women. Every year, a new story sparks heated debate and concern: in 2016, it was Yuyun, a 14-year-old girl raped and killed by 14 boys and men. In 2017, it's Putu, a 31-year-old Balinese woman whose left foot was cut off by her husband in a jealous rage.

These high-profile incidents drew outrage and horror from both the community and the government, but little progress on eradicating violence against women is being made in the country. The draft law on the Eradication of Sexual Violence has not only been stuck in parliament since 2014, but has also recently been dramatically reduced in scope—from 155 articles to just 59—by committee members debating its ratification.

The law aims to fill gaps in existing legislation by clarifying exactly what acts can be considered sexual violence, as current legislation often leads to different interpretations. In its draft form, it alters the concept of unwanted sexual acts from only penis-in-vagina penetration, broadening it to cover forced marriage, sexual exploitation, sexual slavery, sexual harassment, forced sterilisation and more. Importantly—and unusually for Indonesia— the law not only covers preventive efforts and punishment for perpetrators, but also provides psychological support and rehabilitation for victims. For example, the law offers victims the chance to have a closed court hearing, so that they do not need to meet their abuser face-to-face, as required under current law.

If the legislation isn't passed by the end of 2017, the drafting committee—led by Komnas Perempuan, Indonesia's National Commission on Violence Against Women—will have to once more lobby lawmakers to put the draft on the 2018 priority list of laws. Failure to achieve this would further reduce the draft law's chances of being passed.

"The biggest challenge has been to explain a new perspective to members of the legislative body [at the Indonesian parliament]," says Nihayatul "Ninik" Wafiroh, a member of parliament and part of the team who proposed the draft law. "By putting forward a law based on a new way of thinking—that is, suggesting that laws should defend the interests of victims—this is quite different from how the Indonesian Criminal Code was created."

This new victim-centric framing of the law triggered an incredibly long debate, with much back-and-forth, revision, and even deletion of key points. "Now it's even being suggested that the draft can only be made into law if the Criminal Code itself is revised," Ninik says. "So far, this has not happened. This means that we are required to change some of the articles within the draft law, so that they are in line with existing laws… some important points on victims' and witnesses' rights have even been erased totally."

Attracting media attention—and not in a good way

Many incidents of violence against women in Indonesia don't make the national newspapers, nor do they receive acknowledgment from the government. Unless the incident is particularly heinous or violent, most go undiscussed.

When Yuyun was raped and murdered in March 2016, only local newspapers from her home district, Bengkulu, reported the crime. It wasn't until my own project, Menghitung Pembunuhan Perempuan (Counting Dead Women Indonesia), stumbled across the news in April that activists became aware of the case and picked it up. A social media campaign was launched by singer-activist Kartika Jahja under the hashtag #NyalaUntukYuyun (#LightaCandleforYuyun), and a number of vigils and protests were held across the country. Only then did the government take notice. Unfortunately, the campaign did not lead to the national parliament ratifying the draft law, but instead resulted in a presidential decree that permits chemical castration for rapists and murderers—something activists consider to be both inhumane and ineffective.

"The media loves [stories of violence against women], and perhaps not in a good way," says Evi Mariani, editor of The Conversation Indonesia. News outlets, particularly tabloid newspapers and entertainment television shows, frequently share scandalous tales of women and girls raped or murdered—including photographs—to boost ratings or gain readers. "Research by Komnas Perempuan on the coverage of women in the Indonesian media shows that violence against women is the media's favourite."

"But not all cases make it to the press," she adds. "There are several reasons. The police don't report [cases] to the press unless it is gory, heinous... The other issue is that violence against women is underreported. The [stories] that make it to the press are the gory ones that the press can sensationalise."

There's a lack of sensitivity and care on the parts of the authorities, media and public when it comes to handling cases of extreme violence. One such case, undoubtedly only covered in the press because of the shocking manner in which the woman was killed, happened in 2016. EF, an 18-year-old girl from the Greater Jakarta area, was raped and killed in her *kost*, a kind of boarding house common across the country. Her murderers—a boy aged 15 and two 23-year-old men—raped her before shoving a large garden hoe, handle first, into her vagina. They reportedly even used their feet to push the implement further inside her body, so much so that the handle reached her rib cage. The hoe ruptured EF's internal organs, causing her to bleed to death. Her body was found the next day by a colleague.

Written and verbal descriptions of the assault are bad enough, but the widespread media coverage of EF's murder was further fuelled by leaked police photographs, likely after a police officer shared them with friends over WhatsApp. The photos were uploaded to social media, with nothing blurred out. 18 months after EF's death, photos of her naked body can still be found online.

Existing media coverage also tends to dwell on the sensational details of individual cases, without drawing connections between them as evidence of a broader culture of violence against women. Even when parallels—such as location, the age of the victim, or the relationship between the victim and their attacker—exist, these links are rarely made.

"The main source of information on cases of violence against women is the police," says Evi. "Masculine culture is deeply entrenched in the police force. They feed not only information to the press but also their perspective, [which is problematic because] many journalists do not use a gender [lens], especially those on the crime beat."

Understanding violence against women

Even the Indonesian Police Chief, General Tito Kanarvian, seems to have a poor understanding of violence against women. In October, he suggested that people reporting rape to the police should be asked whether they enjoyed being raped. "It's an important question," Tito told the BBC.[1] "If I was raped, how did I feel while I was being raped? Was I okay? If I was okay, then it wasn't rape." When pushed for clarification, Tito told journalists that it was a standard question and should be asked to weed out false reports.

Evi suggests that media coverage of violence against women would be better if journalists drew on women-friendly organisations, such as Komnas Perempuan or LBH APIK (Women's Legal Aid), as key sources. These organisations have been actively trying to contextualise the conversation by highlighting the prevalence of violence against women in Indonesian society.

In 2016, Komnas Perempuan recorded 259,150 cases of violence against women, mostly within marital relationships, but point out that this is likely to be only a fraction of all incidences across Indonesia. Many more go unreported, usually out of fear of reprisal from their abuser, social stigma, and because the police do not take violence against women seriously.

My own data recording project, Counting Dead Women Indonesia, recorded 193 cases of women killed in 2016. Only four of these cases involved female perpetrators; 50% of killings were carried out by the victims' husbands, boyfriends, exes, or men who were attracted to them. This is in line with global statistics that indicate that a majority of women are killed by their intimate partners. We count that another 150 women have been killed so far in 2017.

There is little that connects these women. The murders occur all over the archipelago, from urban centres to rural villages. The victims' ages range from as young as three to as old as 79. They are Muslim, Hindu, Buddhist, Christian, and followers of traditional religions. They span across the socio-economic spectrum. There is only one thread that cuts

---

1 http://www.bbc.com/indonesia/indonesia-41676366

across this diversity: these women were murdered by jealous male partners with anger and control issues.

"Social constructions cause men to feel as though they must be stronger and more powerful [than women]," explains Tunggal Pawestri, a women's activist based in Jakarta. "Many men feel they are superior and have control over women's bodies and lives. So, when even a tiny part of their masculinity is challenged, this can make them incredibly angry, because in their heads, men must always be respected."

It's a context that has recently been described by feminist theorists as "toxic masculinity", and it's not unique to Indonesia.

"Power relations between men and women are not equal, and the patriarchy remains strong worldwide, despite our best efforts to remove it," Tunggal says. "It's the same in Indonesia—patriarchy has strongly attached itself to and become symbiotic with our culture."

Work in progress

But there's still hope. There's a variety of organisations and communities fighting violence against women and sexual harassment across Indonesia, from small groups such as Hollaback! Jakarta and Lentera Sintas Indonesia to nationwide mass organisations like KAPAL Perempuan (Women's Boat) and Solidaritas Perempuan (Women's Solidarity). Energetic campaigns for 16 Days of Activism against Gender-Based Violence run every year—2017's program included a film festival, discussions, and a fun run—while Women's March 2017 attracted around 1,000 participants demanding rights for women and LGBTQ people.

Attitudes are slowly beginning to change. The President has encouraged Parliament to pass the Law on the Eradication of Sexual Violence; anti-catcalling initiatives are springing up across the archipelago and all over social media; and the daughter of the Sultan of Yogyakarta regularly takes to Twitter to rage about the patriarchy and what must be done to push for change. It's also invigorating to see teenage girls and boys expressing an interest in feminism and women's rights, with young women like anti-child marriage activist Sanita Rini and writer Asa Firda "Afi" Nihaya leading the charge for a more equal future.

"What makes me optimistic… is the increasing number of women who are aware that they must have an education, and that they can be powerful without having to rely on men," says Sanita, who managed to avoid marrying as a teenager by convincing her parents she could better provide for her family if she went to university. "There are more and more women pushing for change, and this means that more and more girls will be able to achieve their dreams," including living without the threat of violence, she says.

These shifts suggest that while little progress is currently being made on a national level to protect women from violence, there is a gathering momentum from the ground up. The movement's challenge now is to provide consistent engagement and mobilisation—not just of women, but men too—to build an Indonesia that protects and fulfils women's rights.

THE PERILS OF BEING AN SPG IN JAKARTA

KATE WALTON | 16 APR 2018

Working as a sales promotion girl (SPG) is one way for young Indonesian women to earn a decent income, but SPGs say they put up with daily sexual harassment.

D ev was promoting cigarettes in a mall in Yogyakarta when a middle-aged man walked up behind her and pressed his groin against her bottom. In her early 20s at the time, Dev says she froze and was too scared to even glance over her shoulder."I was shocked," she tells *New Naratif.* "I was doing something on the computer at our stand, and he just walked up and pressed himself against me. It felt like ages before my supervisor saw what was happening and yelled at him to go away."

Despite its status as a rapidly-developing metropolis, Jakarta remains conservative compared to some other Asian capital cities. Outside malls and clubs, it's uncommon to see women wearing skirts above the knee or tops that reveal their shoulders; those who do are stared at and cat-called. Yet most companies employing sales promotion girls (often known as SPGs) insist they must be scantily clad—many advertisements for SPG recruitment opportunities even specifically state "no jilbab", meaning they will not accept women who wear the hijab. It's a strange contrast in a city where more and more schools and universities, including public ones, are requiring female students to wear the headscarf.

Dev's experience is not uncommon. Working as an SPG in Indonesia brings with it many challenges: not only do the estimated 40,000 women working as SPGs[1] in Indonesia have high sales targets to meet, they must do so whilst remaining polite in the face of verbal and physical sexual harassment.

"It's a daily occurrence," 25-year-old Jakartan Nita Winoto says with a laugh. "We have to be clever and protect ourselves." She's worked for

---

1 http://wartakota.tribunnews.com/2017/12/19/kebutuhan-spg-di-indonesia-sekitar-40-ribu

multiple brands since she first started out in 2011 at the age of 18. She admits she never wanted to be an SPG; she wanted to go to university but couldn't afford it.

"My parents were getting older, so they needed me to financially support them," Winoto explains. "I applied for a job as an SPG, and they said I [physically] met the requirements. It turned out I was good at selling, too, so with all the commissions we get, my salary was almost as high as if I worked in an office."

Constant sexual harassment

It's a tough gig. Not only are the hours long and the conditions physically difficult—16% of SPGs interviewed in Medan[2] in 2016 had musculo-skeletal problems due to wearing heels higher than 5cm for hours on end—the sexual harassment is never-ending.

"Men stare at me; try to hold my hand; talk dirty to me; ask my telephone number; try to persuade me to be a nude model; invite me shopping by saying they'll spend lots of money on me; and once a middle-aged man asked me to become his second wife," Winoto says, shaking her head. "He said he'd give me my own shop, a house, a car, and a honeymoon overseas."

Even Winoto's own senior colleague from her head office tried to get her to send him nude photos. "He said he'd pay me per photo, but I didn't want to do anything like that, so I kept rejecting him," she says. "I had to do it politely, of course."

"Someone followed me when I left work, too, one night," she adds. The man followed her on his motorbike, and groped her breast before speeding off. "I felt so stupid," she says. "I was crying and ran home. I don't walk home alone anymore."

"I think it happens because people have a misunderstanding of what SPGs do," explains Mona[3], who worked as an SPG between the ages of 18 and 29. Many people think lowly of SPGs and believe they are available for sex work when this is often not the case. "All SPGs will have experienced this," Mona says. "It's just the way we each deal with it that differentiates us."

---

2 https://media.neliti.com/media/publications/14566-ID-keluhan-musculoskeletal-disorders-msds-pada-sales-promotion-girl-spg-pengguna-se.pdf

3 Name changed at the interviewee's request.

Mona is now 31 and quit working when she got married two years ago. She'd worked as an SPG for a private bank and a number of property companies, and says men were regularly inappropriate with her, teasing her and commenting on her body. Some offered her money to sleep with them or be their girlfriends, and one even followed her home.

"One man said to me, 'You're so pretty. Instead of exhausting yourself working hard like this, you should be with me. I'll pay you more than you earn now. All you have to do is satisfy me [sexually]'," Mona recalls. "Another man directly asked how much it would cost to spend the night with me."

"The man who followed me home did so because I rejected him," she says, adding that she felt very scared. "I asked my dad to take me to and from work for a week, but I couldn't tell him why. Now, I always carry a small folding knife with me. Just in case."

Danni Ludfi, a former promotional team leader who now runs his own SPG agency, regularly witnessed his female staff being harassed by male customers.

"[Some] men have negative thoughts about SPGs, they see them as socially lower than themselves," Ludfi says. "But there are some SPGs who do 'play sideways' as well, to earn extra money, and their minimalistic clothing doesn't help either—men see it as inviting. It's incredibly difficult as a team leader to deal with, because we have to be responsible for our staff's safety."

A wider problem

When asked why SPGs attract so much sexual attention from men, most of the women interviewed blame the clothing that their employers make them wear: short skirts or dresses, often skin-tight.

"I think they want us to wear this clothing because it makes people interested in buying our products," Winoto muses. "And the strategy works—men who weren't going to buy something do end up purchasing products after seeing us."

But many SPGs are groped even while fully covered up; Winoto had been wearing a jacket and long trousers when groped by the man on the motorbike. Mona points out that such harassment isn't just confined to on-duty SPGs, either. "Men say dirty things to us [when we are working], they try to hold our hands," she says. "But this happened to me when I was in primary school, too. My English and computing teacher used to hold my hand, sit too close, that sort of thing. In the end, I had to stop going to that class, because I was too scared to tell my parents. I was only nine years old at the time."

Even women who aren't technically SPGs, such as women doing front-line work for charities, aren't free from sexual harassment. Nurmufidha Muliana worked for two-and-a-half years in Surabaya for an international aid organisation; her job was to convince passers-by to sign up for monthly donations. She had no "sexy" clothing requirements but was still regularly harassed, as were two of the three friends she worked with.

"I remember one man in particular," Muliana says. "He kept looking up and down my body, even though I was fully covered. We chatted for a bit and I got him to give a donation, then he said 'Now I've helped you out. I've got two wives—would you like to be my third?' We are contractually obliged to make sure 100% of the people we talk to have a positive interaction, so all I could do was smile bitterly and pretend to turn away to talk to someone else."

Many of the SPGs *New Naratif* spoke to want to get out of the business but say that the money is too good to seriously consider working elsewhere. Smaller jobs such as selling shampoo start at around IDR175,000 (US$12.25) per day, in line with Jakarta's minimum monthly wage of IDR3.6 million (US$262). Bigger gigs, like those offered by big cigarette brands, can pay up to an impressive IDR500,000 (US$36.35) a day. Young women with demanding financial obligations and limited opportunities find it difficult to turn their backs on the job, no matter how much they hate the way they're treated.

Unlike domestic workers, there are there are no efforts to unionise or develop official networks. Women's activists, too, have paid little attention to the issue so far, focusing instead on broader anti-sexual harassment initiatives.

Winoto, though, maintains she would prefer to work in an office. "You know, wearing nice office clothes, so that no one stares at me anymore," she says. She admits that it's probably a pipe dream as employers prefer university graduates. For now, she continues looking for SPG work, while hoping that something better will come along one day.

REPORTING WHILE FEMALE IN MYANMAR

KIMBERLEY PHILLIPS | 18 JUN 2018

People in Myanmar often claim that there's gender equality, but women who decide to enter journalism tell a different story.

At first glance, Myanmar's newsrooms don't look too different from newsrooms anywhere else in the world. Rows of eager reporters hunch over their desks, punching at their keyboards. File that story. Edit that footage. Chase that source. It's particularly unglamourous in Myanmar, where journalists are routinely harassed, threatened and imprisoned for reporting.

But women in newsrooms across the country fight other battles on the sidelines—against a society that deems journalism a man's job, against harassment both in the field and in the workplace, and against a culture that holds women's expertise to be less reliable than men's.

People in Myanmar tend to confidently remark that women and men are already equals, thus negating the need for feminist action in the workplace or in the broader community. They point to the fact that Myanmar women gained suffrage in 1935—relatively early compared to regional neighbours. But a closer look at the rights and roles afforded to female staff members of local media organisations tells a different story.

Journalism: a man's job?

According to student journalists at the Myanmar Journalism Institute (MJI), the imbalances begin early.

When Hkawng Roi told her family of her intention to leave their home in Myitkyina, Kachin State, to study journalism in Yangon, her parents were "not really supportive". Her uncle threatened to cut her off entirely if she pursued her dream.

"Not a lot of parents will encourage their girls to be journalists. They think it's a man's job, and that [girls] should just choose a different career path," she says.

Sabae Hlaing, a seasoned journalist in her hometown in Mon States, agrees. She moved to Yangon to pursue further training at MJI, and says some of her peers leave the industry, reluctantly, due to pressure from their families or partner.

"The number of women in the industry is really low because they are not encouraged by their parents or their spouse. So many women journalists will quit their job after they get married or [some]... they like the job but some quit because their parents do not encourage them to stay in this industry," she says.

These stories stand in stark opposition to refrains about equality in work and life. Shortly after International Women's Day, an op-ed[1] in the state-owned daily *Global New Light of Myanmar* informed readers that "certain jobs, works and places are regarded as not suitable for [the] fairer gender. So these are marked only for men not because of discrimination but out of respect and regard for [the] fairer gender."

The op-ed serves as a concise example of the doublethink employed when considering women's status in the private and public spheres. The author notes several paragraphs later that, despite some occupations being unsuitable for women, "In public, Myanmar women are on par with men in every field, business, service, education etc. In addition to the domestic duties of their families Myanmar women prove in some cases with their feminine business acumen and gift better than their male counterparts."

Divisions of labour

Once in the workplace, many women say they don't enjoy the same upward mobility as their male counterparts.

Jane Stageman, who runs gender awareness training with international human development organisation FHI360, says women in the newsrooms aren't shy about airing their concerns. Once the sessions are underway, many complain about being saddled with domestic chores like clearing up mugs and plates. She says management teams must work to change the office culture.

"I think each organisation has to decide where it wants to start. Is it the culture it wants to tackle? Is it actually that there's no real voice

---

1 http://www.globalnewlightofmyanmar.com/status-myanmar-women-myanmar-history-culture/

for women in the organisation? Is it that the leadership style isn't quite right, in terms of actually hearing what's going on?" she says.

But when management teams in the industry are predominantly comprised of men, agitating for change can be an uphill battle. One of the strategies recommended by FHI360 is the formation of a gender committee tasked with advocating for structural reform of workplace policies around issues like harassment, promotions and parental entitlements.

Harassment and inappropriate comments are all too familiar to women in any workplace. Su Chay, a reporter for a local magazine, and Tin Htet Paing, a freelance journalist, both describe instances of harassment from colleagues and interviewees, including one high-profile government staffer.

According to Tin Htet Paing, she was dispatched by her editor to cover a press conference held by a municipal official. When she and her colleague approached him to ask follow up questions, he berated the pair for their clothing choices. Tin Htet Paing had been wearing black trousers and a blouse.

"When we approached he said, 'Don't you know how to dress formally? It is a conference and you are not dressed professionally,'" she says. He then went on to compare them to women from another broadcaster dressed in *htamein*, the traditional skirt for women in Myanmar.

"He wouldn't do it to any male reporter, he was more concerned with how we dressed than what kind of questions we were asking. It's already three or more years later but I still remember my anger at the time," she says.

But these challenges don't stop women from the business of newsmaking. Like most journalists around the world, Myanmar women see the job as a calling, a special role that allows them behind-the-scenes access as their country undergoes significant change.

Frontline war reporting remains largely the domain of men, and Su Chay says that's to the detriment of quality journalism. Women, she explains, have a knack for speaking to the victims of the country's myriad conflicts. On a recent trip to Kachin State, she found that families living in a displacement camp opened up to her.

"They [IDPs] are pretty fragile and not comfortable talking to people, especially men. As a woman journalist talking to the women there, in that kind of situation, I think they are comfortable talking to me," she says.

Cyclical messaging

Growing the number of female voices in the media landscape is a crucial element in the country's broader battle for press freedom and true democracy—and men in the industry are being put on notice.

The groundbreaking *Gender in Myanmar News* report, released in 2017 by the Myanmar Women's Journalists Society and International Media Society (IMS), highlighted the dearth of female sources cited in Myanmar-language media; only 16% of the sources in news coverage were women.

Su Chay thinks her male colleagues know they should be including women in their reportage, but "they just don't want to accept it. Because I think, they belittle women and women's ability."

It's a vicious circle: without female representation in the mainstream media, young girls and boys repeatedly absorb the notion that a woman's place is in the home—that women are not credible, professional experts.

There are parts of the media industry where women are better represented, although not necessarily for the right reasons. Broadcast organisations are proactive about recruiting women for presenter roles in news and entertainment: research conducted by IMS found that 66% of television presenters are women, far outnumbering the use of female sources.

"Most of the stations think that as a TV viewer, a woman's face will attract more [viewers] to watch the channel," says Sagawah Aung, a trainer at the Democratic Voice of Burma's Multimedia Academy. She adds that the risk of rumours and unwanted advances can deter female journalists from going into the field with male counterparts. Her current cohort at the Multimedia Academy, though, has an equal number of male and female trainees, so she's hopeful that diversity will increase.

A dearth of role models

One student at MJI, when asked who her role models are, struggled to name a single female reporter. She finally settled on a tutor.

It makes sense. It's hard for anyone to picture themselves in a job they've never seen done by someone like them. Research on the importance of role models indicates that young women benefit most from the presence of professional exemplars.

Myanmar's peace process is lagging, and press freedom is facing a decline[2] not seen under the previous administration. The role that female journalists have to play is key—without equal representation, there can be few meaningful strides made in the democratic transition.

Nowhere is this absence more stark than in the ongoing peace talks[3], convened between the government, the military, and the country's plethora of ethnic armies. Despite a stated goal of 30% representation, women accounted for only 7% and 20% of government and ethnic group delegates, respectively.

Women and children are disproportionately displaced by the country's long-running civil wars, yet their voices are not heard during the negotiations that are meant to bring peace to their communities. It's easy to lay the blame at the feet of the government, ethnic armies and the military for leaving women behind. But if reporters, with the support of their editors, know where to seek out the few women available, then their perspectives can be amplified.

To that end, Tin Htet Paing says women can, and should, assume their positions on the frontlines of the country's media and political landscape because "women's issues are everybody's issues."

"We always have different discussions and different perspectives. If you don't have women reporters or journalists all these different opinions and perspectives will be hidden and there will not be enough voices," she says.

---

2 https://newnaratif.com/journalism/decay-press-freedom-aung-san-suu-kyi/

3 http://www.dvb.no/news/womens-voices-at-latest-panglong-just-tokenism-say-critics/75737

VIETNAM'S FLEDGLING #METOO MOVEMENT

LAM LE | 21 JUN 2018

Recent testimonies of sexual assault and harassment have brought discussions surrounding #MeToo to Vietnam, but entrenched bias and mindsets have proven difficult to shift.

In the wake of the Harvey Weinstein scandal in the United States, Vietnamese freelance journalist Bao Uyen was encouraged last year by a male friend to share her own #MeToo story of sexual harassment in the workplace.

She didn't. She was afraid she'd be seen as using an overly friendly relationship with her boss to advance her career, and felt like she was partly to blame for not putting up more resistance.

A recent online survey[1] of 247 journalists conducted by Fojo Media Institute in Vietnam found that over 27% of female journalists and around 3% of their male counterparts have been sexually harassed. Perpetrators included sources and co-workers. The actual number is likely to be higher, the report says, as some female reporters interviewed in focus group discussions hadn't realised that harassment could also be verbal.

Despite its prevalence, most Vietnamese newspapers don't have a complaints mechanism in place, shifting the burden of dealing with the matter onto (potential) victims and supportive colleagues ready to come to their rescue whenever a source, colleague or superior goes too far.

Speaking out

Since she was still a student in Ho Chi Minh City, Uyen was told by colleagues and even a teacher that going to beer parties—"nhậu" in Vietnamese—and flirting with sources was a skill female journalists should master to help them get stories. The belief that women should somehow use their physical attributes and seduce their way into getting scoops has become entrenched; Dr Pham Ha Chung,

---

1 https://fojo.se/en/news/2347-vietnam-well-ahead-on-gender-issues-in-media

a lecturer at the Academy of Journalism and Communication in Hanoi said at the Fojo seminar in May that many young journalists have left the industry after being unable to "adapt" to these expectations, or having been on the receiving end of harassment.

When rumours circulated on Facebook on 18 April this year that an intern at Vietnam's most prestigious newspaper, Tuoi Tre, had attempted suicide after being raped by her boss, many comments online asked why the intern had not used her "reporting skills" to uncover the story.

24 hours after this story of sexual assault surfaced online, none of major newspapers in the country had covered it. It's an unspoken rule in the Vietnamese media industry: you're not supposed to criticise your colleagues. Their inaction led Uyen to share how her former boss had repeatedly asked her out for coffee and once touched her hair in an empty office.

The newspapers' silence on wrongdoings within the media industry "is not hypocritical. It is more like a failure of journalism," Uyen wrote[2] in a Facebook post which has been shared over 1,600 times.

Uyen isn't alone. She's part of a network of seven journalists who, for a week after the Tuoi Tre incident, wrote stories on Facebook about Vietnam's toxic media environment, where it's an open secret that some bosses extract sexual favours from interns in exchange for full-time positions. These #MeToo journalists refer to themselves as "nhóm phóng viên nữ (group of female journalists)"—more a reference to the issue they cover than an actual description, as one of their members is male.

Although the group's stories were widely shared by NGOs, groups for women's rights and young journalists who also invited them to speak at events, only two newspapers picked up their stories. The major newspapers didn't cover the Tuoi Tre case beyond reporting that the paper was looking into the allegations. But many started discussing sexual harassment and victim blaming, topics traditionally seen as too sensitive, more generally.

That might have been the end of it, but, in an unprecedented move, the University of Social Sciences and Humanities in Ho Chi Minh City—where the victim studies—demanded that Tuoi Tre investigate the matter. The university criticised the paper's denial of the attempted

---

2 https://www.facebook.com/adolfuyen/posts/1734112450010783

suicide, while not addressing available evidence that the student had suffered from prolonged distress. The alleged perpetrator has since resigned, and Tuoi Tre has transferred the case to the police, according to the paper's official statement.

More women come forward

On 27 April, just as Vietnam's first #MeToo case appeared to be losing steam, dancer Pham Lich claimed[3] on Facebook that Pham Anh Khoa, a famous rock singer, had sexually harassed her, adding that she had text messages[4] as evidence[5]. She had even communicated[6] with Khoa's wife in an attempt to resolve the matter privately. Not long after, two other women also came forward as Khoa's victims. Unlike the Tuoi Tre case, these allegations made it into the mainstream media.

Khoa initially threatened to sue his accusers for defamation, but was eventually forced to apologise amid heavy public backlash after he tried to dismiss the incidents as part-and-parcel of the Vietnamese entertainment industry. The United Nations Population Fund (UNFPA) dumped him as their ambassador, and several of his shows were cancelled.

More stories came forward on social media. On 19 May, nude model Kim Phuong said that she had reported Ngo Luc, a high-profile body painting artists, to the police for rape. She said on Facebook that she hoped other victims would come forward; fellow model Huyen Phuong did so, promising to testify in court if necessary. The case is ongoing.

Victim blaming and support

Such a turn of events is unheard of in patriarchal Vietnam, where male promiscuity is embraced as a reflection of "natural desires", while female sexuality is repressed and seen as little more than a reproductive tool.

There's been plenty of victim blaming with these recent #MeToo cases. When Kim Phuong came forward with her story, social media responses questioned her account and her motives. Some said they doubted her story as she hadn't had any bruises; others insisted that it isn't rape if the alleged perpetrator used a condom.

---

3 https://www.facebook.com/photo.php?fbid=1740308816063035&set=a.237945696299362.
  53303.100002517993448&type=3&theater

4 https://www.facebook.com/linkmieu.169/posts/1754026414691275

5 https://www.facebook.com/linkmieu.169/posts/1753888774705039

6 https://www.facebook.com/linkmieu.169/posts/1753915858035664

Such harmful misconceptions are widespread, and cut across genders; Fojo Media Institute's research found that female journalists' perceptions of what constitutes sexual harassment are as narrow as their male colleagues.

In March this year, UN Women released a report[7] saying that Vietnamese women and girls who report cases of rape and sexual assault are often not believed due to social and institutional bias. Interviews with policemen revealed cases in which families were advised to "protect" the victim's "honour" by keeping silent about the assault so as not to hamper her chances of finding a husband later.

But Uyen says there has also been an "unexpected wave of support". Even though someone cloned her Facebook account—then reported her original profile for being a fake account—after she shared her #MeToo story, the 29-year old journalist says she didn't receive any hateful messages: "It was all supportive."

Pham Lich and Kim Phuong report similar patterns—less shaming and more compassion than expected—in interviews with Uyen for an upcoming #MeToo Vietnam book to be published by the Vietnam Program for Internet & Society[8], a research programme at Vietnam National University Hanoi. Such encouragement, especially from male friends who went out of their way to amplify their stories, keep them going.

Public awareness

Khai Don, a popular writer who is also part of the network of #MeToo journalists, says the celebrity factor had a role to play in pushing some of the stories to the front pages of many newspapers. But there were other variables at play, too: in Khoa's case, the victims' perseverance, backed up by strong evidence, pushed the narrative along. Khoa also shot himself in the foot when he claimed that "in showbiz it's normal to pat each other's buttocks upon greeting"—a comment condemned by other celebrities and denounced as an insult to the entertainment industry.

---

7 https://e.vnexpress.net/news/news/ingrained-bias-prevents-female-rape-victims-in-vietnam-from-seeking-justice-un-3727101.html

8 http://vpis.edu.vn/welcome-to-vietnam-program-for-internet-society?lang=en

Also, by the time Khoa's case came to light, "the Vietnamese public was already better informed about sexual harassment and misconduct in the workplace," Khai Don tells *New Naratif.*

Vietnamese sexuality scholar Dr Khuat Thu Hong agrees. "Over the past few years, social awareness about violence, especially sexual violence against women and girls has seen significant changes," says Dr Hong, who wrote the book *Sexuality in Contemporary Vietnam: Easy to Joke About But Hard to Talk About* in 2009.

She attributes the change to the power of social media—used by more than half of Vietnam's population—and the ease with which waves of outrage in response to injustice against women and girls have spread, especially when lenient sentences are handed down to child molesters with powerful connections.

"But we can't ignore the hard work of agencies, organisations and the media over the past few years who studied and shared about gender based violence," she notes. "These activities have built a foundation for today's changes."

When the Tuoi Tre case broke, reliable data was ready for the #MeToo journalists to substantiate their stories, notably shocking data[9] from 2014 by NGO ActionAid showing that 87% of women interviewed in Hanoi and Ho Chi Minh City had been sexually harassed at least once in a public place. The study also showed that the majority of victims and bystanders had not acted upon the harassment.

Too soon to call it a victory

Despite this progress, Dr Hong says recent developments are simply signs that #MeToo could *eventually* become a movement in Vietnam. Both Uyen and Khai Don say it's too soon to call their campaign a success—they're still monitoring the police investigation into the alleged rape at Tuoi Tre.

Translating the growing support for #MeToo into structural change has in fact been hard. After a week of their #MeToo campaign, Khai Don "realised young newsrooms were open to it and wanted colleagues to understand they had the right to report sexual harassment."

But more traditional newsrooms—where power lies in the hands of male editors and upper management—still tend to blame the victim

9 http://www.actionaid.org/2014/12/safe-cities-women-and-girls-can-dreams-come-true

and see harassment at work as an internal matter not to be discussed publicly, lest it hurt the image of the media industry, Khai Don says.

The majority of lawmakers and powerful corporate bosses in Vietnam are not part of the social media-savvy generation that has been exposed to more progressive views on women's sexuality and rights from a young age. Many of these elite decision-makers are men who have grown old in a society that only recently started to question the validity of the Vietnamese proverb: "As a flower is meant to be nipped, a woman is meant to be teased".

Vietnam first acknowledged sexual harassment in its Labour Code just six years ago, but provided no definition, no prevention mechanism and no punitive measures. In 2015, the International Labour Organisation (ILO), together with the government, labour unions and local businesses, developed the Vietnam Code of Conduct on Sexual Harassment in the Workplace[10]. But Tran Quynh Hoa, communications officer at the ILO, says it's been difficult to convince local companies to adopt it.

"Those who have adopted the code of conduct are foreign-invested companies as they face pressure from abroad," she said at a seminar on gender equality in the Vietnamese media in May.

"When working with leaders, it's very hard to convince them that certain words or a certain look are in fact sexual harassment," she said, adding that they found the concept foreign and unsuitable for the Vietnamese context, where people love to joke.

While most Vietnamese companies do have internal protocols, these are primarily designed to increase the productivity of the workers, without much concern for employees' right to a harassment-free workplace, lawyer Nguyen Van Tu said during a talk show on #MeToo organised in April by CSAGA, an NGO that advocates for women's rights in Vietnam.

Unconscious bias

The issue also reveals unconscious bias that have been entrenched in Vietnamese social norms, media and laws for so long that even some of the men and women who openly support #MeToo are perpetuating harmful tropes.

---

10 http://www.ilo.org/hanoi/Informationresources/Librarydocumentationcenter/ WCMS_421220/lang--en/index.htm

Most notable was the case of above-mentioned CSAGA. In a now-deleted video11, CSAGA's effort to engage Khoa in a serious discussion of sexual harassment ended up normalising his mistreatment of women, blaming his actions on his naïveté as an artist working in an entertainment industry with no clear code of conduct, where he claimed it was "normal" for colleagues to get touchy-feely.

The problematic message was echoed by Nguyen Quang Vinh, director of the Performing Arts Department under the culture ministry. He called the public to forgive the singer after he had apologised. "Perhaps Khoa has been in an overly free environment and so failed to see that he had crossed the line," he told local newspaper *Lao Dong*. "There are actions deemed acceptable by one person but unacceptable by another. It depends on each individual."

As the Labour Code has no mechanism to impose penalties for sexual harassment, the Performing Arts Department didn't fine Khoa for sexually harassing Pham Lich while they collaborated on a show on national television. What the same department *does* have a mechanism in place for, though, is the imposition of fines—about VND5–10 million (USD220–440)—for dressing inappropriately, in ways that go against "Vietnamese values". Many female performers have been fined either for wearing skimpy outfits, or having wardrobe malfunctions. The local media reports widely on such cases.

More than just celebrating Women's Day

At the launch of the Fojo report detailing the prevalence of sexism and sexual harassment in the Vietnamese media, representatives of two well-known newspapers, *Vietnam News Agency* and *The Thao Van Hoa* (Sport and Culture), claimed their newsrooms were harassment-free. They confidently declared that there was no need for a code of conduct as they have more female reporters than male. They also have women in management positions, special benefits for women and big celebrations on Women's Day.

These features, however, are typical of a Vietnamese newsroom, according to the Fojo report. Vietnam consistently ranks highly worldwide in female participation in the workforce; the high number of women present in a company doesn't mean that gender is no longer an issue.

---

11 https://www.facebook.com/CsagaVietnam/posts/2555959761221838

"I hope the trade union doesn't just organise Women's Day parties but is also capable of protecting female employees," Hoa of the ILO said in response to the two newspaper representatives. "What if the female victims simply haven't told you yet about being harassed?"

As Uyen and Khai Don put it, #MeToo is not about forcing an equality of outcomes for men and women. Nor is it about smearing the media industry or the reputation of any man.

"[#MeToo] fights for respect for women," Uyen says. As far as the #MeToo journalists are concerned, it's about time.

ARTS, CULTURE, AND THE MEDIA

CAMBODIA'S HIDDEN LANGUAGE CLASSES

JANELLE RETKA | 15 JAN 2018

For about a decade in Cambodia, learning English was a risky undertaking.

In 1979, Ker Mao Chhommaradh, then 19 years old, moved onto Street 184, tucked behind the Royal Palace in the Cambodian capital Phnom Penh. 10 years later, it would be known as "London Street", accented by a slew of vibrant signs advertising language classes that turned it into a temporary hub of English-language learning in the city.

But there was no way Mao Chhommaradh could have known this back then. Quite the opposite; he says a ban on foreign language learning during that time meant eager students, including himself, were forced to study in secret.

"If you wanted to learn [English], you had to wake up at 3am," the 57-year-old recounts with precise diction as he stands outside his house in the heat of day. "You'll be learning in a dark place, so there was candlelight." Electricity was not an option, as it risked the class being raided by the authorities—a fate he had been lucky to avoid.

"We were very scared. They said, 'If you do something wrong, we will arrest you.' We thought, 'Oh, if they arrest us, they will step on our freedom.' We weren't interested in asking for details," says 49-year-old Chan, who also studied under the radar during the ban, and has since contributed to the creation of an online English-Khmer dictionary.

The ban on English

According to Chan, English had been the most popular language to study in the early 1970s, when Prime Minister Lon Nol's US-backed government was in power, because it was seen as the connection to modernity and Westernisation.

This changed after the government was overturned in 1975 by the Khmer Rouge regime. Education was banned and teachers were targeted as threats to communism. The government's ruthless anti-intellectual bent meant that knowing a foreign language or simply wearing eyeglasses—which were assumed to indicate a degree of higher learning—could get one condemned to death. Phnom Penh was evacuated and the country's population was pushed to the countryside to work in rural collectives.

"If someone spoke French, even one word, they would be killed… during the Khmer Rouge" because it was a sign of their education and class, says Cambodian political analyst Meas Nee. When the regime was overthrown by a rebel group with help from Vietnam in 1979, education was reinstalled in the country, but only on the government's terms.

"We could learn Russian and Vietnamese because it was from the communist bloc," says 53-year-old Lim Phai, who studied in secret before teaching his own English courses in 1983. But the learning of all other foreign languages were banned, with a particular focus on English.

There were political motivations behind the specificity. "English was from the free world, so they considered this counter-revolutionary because you could see the propaganda from the West, so that was the intention behind the ban," he explains.

But it was precisely this connection to the "free world" that made English so attractive. Proficiency in the language was seen as the key to fleeing the country and finding a better life after the destruction and violence of Pol Pot's Khmer Rouge—historians estimate that the regime oversaw between 1.7 and two million people's deaths. So English lessons went rogue.

Learning in secret

Classes were tucked into quaint apartments down alleys across the city. Groups of four to five students were organised among friends by word of mouth and taught in the dead of night by a handful of teachers willing to risk the ambiguous fate of a police raid.

"You would have to go searching and hunting [for classes], or find out from friends," Phai recalls.

While there had been no way of knowing how many classes were being held, Phai remembers that the students had been determined to both find willing tutors and master a new tongue. One woman achieved fluency studying privately under Phai for six months before fleeing the country. He never heard from her again.

Mao Chhommaradh and Phai used different textbooks—"Each Enjoy English" and "Essential English" respectively—that had survived the Khmer Rouge and helped lead the academic charge. But these books,

and the speaking of English itself, could only be found in the secrecy
of private rooms, for fear of discovery.

There was no clear punishment upon getting caught; Chan had heard
that some teachers and students faced fines and jail time, while Phai had
only heard of those caught paying fines and putting their thumbprints
to documents promising never to engage in them again. "The ban was
not really consistent," he says. When it came to vigilance, enforcement
and punishment, the local authorities had plenty of power and leeway.
    Still, some people went to lengths to avoid finding out what pen-
alty might have awaited them. Chan recalls his sister had friends who
jumped off a classroom balcony to escape a police raid.

A gradual shift
The ban lasted for about a decade before the authorities began to relax.
Phai puts the beginning of the change in 1984, when advertisements
for classes could finally be openly posted in Phnom Penh. His classes
were in full swing by then, but aside from photocopied editions of
"Essential English," he made sure to only use English-language materials from Russia to avoid any accusation of pushing Western ideologies
in his classroom.

But Chan thinks that the lifting of the language ban came closer to 1989. "When they started to allow it, they did not announce it. To me, I think they never officially lifted the ban," he said.

Despite the lack of any official policy change, the reason for the gradual shift toward tolerance was clear. Hun Sen's government had begun receiving more foreign aid from Western countries and soon signed the 1991 Paris Peace Accords to end the Cambodian-Vietnamese war. The United Nations later sent forces to Cambodia in an attempt to set up a new government and election.

Those who had learnt English in hidden corners found that their skills were suddenly in great demand. "There was a lack of people who spoke English to work with the foreign aid, so most of the people who could work with [the United Nations Transitional Authority in Cambodia] were people who returned from overseas," says Nee.

Interest in English lessons increased and vibrant advertisements shot up all along Mao Chhommaradh's "London Street". "In 1991, there were lots of classes on this street," he says.

Today, English is offered in state schools and "London Street" is back to being referred to simply by its number. Teaching English has shifted from a banned activity to a common attraction for young foreigners who visit or move to Cambodia to teach in private schools. As a result of the various learning opportunities now available—as well as increasing access to international entertainment and media—many of the capital's youth and young adults today are conversational or fluent in the language.

But private apartment-side classes are also still available; Mao Chhommaradh points to a sign above an alleyway written in Khmer script, guiding students toward a nearby classroom. It's a constant reminder of how things have changed in modern Cambodia: within a single lifetime, English language education has transformed from a risky undertaking to a thriving industry.

LEARNING MEDIA LITERACY IN SINGAPORE
KIRSTEN HAN | 22 FEB 2018

Media literacy has emerged as one of the ways with which Singapore can tackle "fake news". But how are Singaporeans' taught media literacy, and how does the country's political context and top-down education model make an impact?

Even before Donald Trump's candidacy turned from joke to reality, people were worried about social media and its many problems. Pundits and commentators fretted about polarised views, echo chambers, clickbait reporting and more. Then, out of the turmoil of the 2016 US presidential election and Trump's victory, came the latest buzzword(s): "fake news".

A term catches on

Suddenly, the term was everywhere, applied to situations ranging from malicious and petty to valid and worrying. While Trump gleefully labelled any news coverage he didn't like as "fake", governments elsewhere grappled with the spread of misinformation online, and how it distorted people's worldviews and affected communities.

Singapore has been no exception. "As a multi-racial and multi-religious country, disinformation campaigns and fake news can erode trust between various groups, and this can be exploited by external parties," said Amrin Amin, Parliamentary Secretary to the Minister for Home Affairs, during the budget debate in March 2017.

In June 2017, Law and Home Affairs Minister K Shanmugam gave the opening address at a forum on truth and trust in the media. He outlined foreign interference, racial and religious tensions, and confusion spread by WhatsApp rumours as part of the problem. "Legislative action… seems a no-brainer," he concluded. "Hopefully, we will have it in place next year or so."[1]

But Shanmugam did not present a new bill to Parliament in January 2018. Instead, he introduced a Green Paper on deliberate online false-hoods[2] put together by the Ministry of Law and the Ministry of Communications and Information. A Select Committee has been convened to examine the issue and is inviting public feedback until February 28.

Individuals as the "first line of defence"

Legislation has not been the only solution offered up in the discussion of "fake news". In that June 2017 speech, Shanmugam identified the need to "make society more resilient" via media literacy education and critical thinking. This echoed the speech made by Senior Minister of State for Defence Mohamad Maliki bin Osman during the 2017 bud-get debate, where he described individuals as the "first line of defence" in combatting "fake news" by being "discerning and responsible with what we read and decide to share online."

Media literacy education has been on Singapore's radar for quite some time; it was identified in 2003 as an important aspect of turning Singapore into a "global media city". Yet researchers point out that holistic media literacy education might still be lacking. "Regardless of its presence in the recent policy discourse and the emphasis given to the twenty-first century teacher education in the NIE, media literacy is still an unclear concept given the various operating interpretations in the local educational setting," wrote Lin Tzu-Bin, Intan Azura Mokhtar and and Wang Li-Yi in their 2013 paper "The construct of media and information literacy in Singapore education system: global trends and local policies" in the *Asia Pacific Journal of Education*.[3]

There is no media literacy curriculum in Singaporean schools. Instead, skills relevant to media literacy exist as components of other subjects and lessons. Social Studies teachers, for example, drill students in answer-ing source-based questions. Through these exam-oriented exercises,

---

1 https://www.mlaw.gov.sg/content/minlaw/en/news/speeches/opening-address-by-mr-k-shanmugam--minister-for-home-affairs-and1.html

2 https://www.mlaw.gov.sg/content/dam/minlaw/corp/News/Annexe%20A%20-%20Green%20Paper%20on%20Deliberate%20Online%20Falsehoods.pdf

3 http://www.tandfonline.com/doi/abs/10.1080/02188791.2013.860012?journalCode=cape20

students are taught to compare and corroborate different sources, analyse semiotics and consider hidden (or not-so-hidden) agendas. The English language syllabus also includes the teaching of competencies, such as critical reading, that fall under the umbrella of media literacy.

Then there's the focus on cyber wellness, which highlights the risks and dangers of digital spaces while encouraging individuals to adopt responsible practices. "Be a smart digital citizen," says the government-appointed Media Literacy Council (MLC) on its website.[4] The Council goes on to emphasise values like empathy, graciousness, respect and integrity. Resources provided include advice on combating cyber-bullying, online safety, dealing with trolls and dealing with screen addiction.[5]

"[P]ublic education seems to be infused with a protectionist rationale that aims to educate citizens, especially youth, about the harmful or hurtful experiences that their engagement with media can trigger, either for themselves or for others through their behaviour. Such ethical considerations are one important aspect of media literacy as espoused by leading scholars and educators internationally. However, they seem to predominate the spirit of public education initiatives led by the MLC, with the majority of their resources and programs targeting responsible media use and cyber wellness," writes Csilla Weninger, an assistant professor at the National Institute of Education, in her 2017 paper "Media literacy education in Singapore: Connecting theory, policy and practice".[6]

"The problem here is that media literacy education becomes too narrowly defined, thus restricting education initiatives that target media use as an avenue for expression and collaborative action," she adds.

What about participation?

The concept of media literacy has evolved, with many scholars shifting their attention towards the use of media as an everyday social activity that facilitates involvement in wider civic and political life. But in Singapore, an overly-narrow focus on cyber wellness and civility online positions individuals as consumers of the media, while neglecting their role as active producers in an era where smartphones and gadgetry make it easy to snap photos, shoot videos and author posts.

---

4 https://www.medialiteracycouncil.sg/Best-Practices/Values-and-Social-Norms

5 https://www.medialiteracycouncil.sg/Resources/Educators

6 https://www.academia.edu/27323564/Media_literacy_education_in_Singapore_
Connecting_theory_policy_and_practice

This cannot be divorced from the national political reality. Singapore was ranked 69 out of 167 countries in the Economic Intelligence Unit's (EIU) 2017 Democracy Index.[7] Described by the EIU as a "flawed democracy", it has a government that wields significant influence over many aspects of its citizens' lives, including over the media that they consume and the setting of "OB (out of bounds) markers" in national discourse.

"These political factors [top-down political decision-making as well as limitations on press freedom and free speech] favour a media literacy approach that aims to protect rather than empower, one that appeals to the social values of responsibility and harmony as opposed to rights and contention. In other words, mediated forms of agency and expression are supported insofar as they reinforce social and political stability... but not as potential sites of an alternative public," Weninger writes.

The result is a country whose people are adept in media production, but who produce content that fails to engage with current affairs. "Most of my students, when they first come to me, are not even interested in any kind of reading beyond what they gorge on via their preferred social media platforms," says Kevin Seah, a private tutor specialising in English, English literature and the A Level General Paper. "Their social media experience is a consciously frivolous one—their friends who engage with socio-political issues on social media are seen as a little bit strange."

This disconnect between media production and political participation was made particularly stark when the government paid prominent Instagram users to promote the country's upcoming budget. The result was a series of posed photos with prepared #sponsored captions calling for public feedback; an awkward juxtaposition of Insta-pretty pensive portraits with efforts to get people interested in a serious political issue. The campaign attracted widespread mockery.[8]

"[H]ow can you get someone that doesn't even understand the fundamentals of your product to explain it to the masses?" asked public relations director Wesley Gunter on LinkedIn.[9]

There are, of course, opportunities for young Singaporeans to gain

7 https://www.eiu.com/topic/democracy-index

8 https://sg.news.yahoo.com/singapore-sparks-mockery-instagram-influencers-budget-114937218.html

9 https://www.linkedin.com/pulse/mof-bloggergate-wesley-gunter/

production skills that would enable participation in public discourse via various media. Singaporean students are encouraged to achieve competency in activities like producing videos or coding. Yet these activities are often framed in the context of particular national goals.

In 2011, Lim Sun Sun, Elmie Nekmat and Shobha Vadrevu did a case study[10] of the N.E.mation! competition, an animation competition linked to Singapore's National Education programme, which is open to Singaporean and Permanent Resident students from secondary schools, junior colleges and centralised institutions. They found that while the competition encouraged media production, emphasis continued to be put on messages the government sought to communicate through the National Education curriculum.

"[V]ideos that explicitly convey policy-friendly messages are privileged over those that are more technically superior with less explicit national education messages," they observed. In this way, the participatory potential of media production is subsumed under over-arching state narratives. What's missing, then, is a critical engagement with society and politics.

It doesn't help that students are often conscious and wary of the limitations on free speech in the country. "I've... seen too many students who have a remarkable fear of getting the 'wrong answer' in whatever academic setting they're in," says Seah. "When thinking about politics, they are even more afraid: some of them ask me whether they'd 'get in trouble' if they write 'the wrong thing', whatever that is, in their essays."

Moving forward

While Singapore has neither been the target of entrepreneurial (if morally agnostic) Macedonian teenagers running "fake news" content farms nor well-resourced misinformation campaigns, the issue has already entered the public consciousness. The government asserts that Singapore is an attractive target for foreign meddlers, arguing that measures need to be put in place *before* any such incident occurs. "The [g]overnment's fear is very real, particularly since the next General Election is less than three years away," says media consultant and trainer Lau Joon-Nie.

It's a complex situation with no obvious solution. The need for

---

10 https://www.researchgate.net/publication/274721269_Singapore%27s_experience_in_

   fostering_youth_media_production_-the_implications_of_state-led_school_and_public_

   education_initiatives

legislation is controversial; while Law Minister Shanmugam might think of it as a "no-brainer", others have raised concerns of greater curbs on free speech. "We do not want a heavy-handed approach that will root out constructive, though at times disagreeable voices," said Nominated Member of Parliament Kok Heng Leun in his parliamentary speech. That the country already has laws dealing with inciting hostility, defamation, hoaxes and even "wounding religious feelings" has not escaped notice.

The call for better media literacy is much less contentious and could form common ground from which to proceed.

"While institutions of higher learning are already offering courses on digital literacy and 'fake news' tools, more can be done in the younger age groups from as young as pre-school," says Lau. "While there are external training providers which offer talks and courses to primary, secondary schools and junior colleges, media literacy topics such as media discernment, safe surfing and online etiquette ought to be incorporated into the school curriculum as a life-long skill."

It's a shift in pedagogy that might require a more fundamental reform in the education system. "[M]edia education production programmes should not be dominated by activities that transmit technical skills but pay equal emphasis to both technical competencies and critical literacy," wrote Lim, Nekmat and Vadrevu. "However, such efforts need to proceed in tandem with overarching institutional changes in the educational system where the top-down, transmission mode of instruction is gradually transformed into a more level, participatory style of learning."

WRITING THEIR OWN STORIES

VINCENT MACISAAC | 21 MAY 2018

While a lot of English-language literature and writing tends to hark back to the country's tragic history of violence and genocide, young Cambodian authors are taking charge of their own narratives—and finding success.

Suong Mak is still astonished by the excitement his latest novel generated at the sixth Cambodia Book Fair last December. Queues disintegrated as customers scrambled for copies of his long-delayed novel about a romantic relationship between two young men.

"Some of them became quite angry when we ran out of books," he recalls before sharing a video on his mobile phone of the boisterous scenes that erupted in front of his booth. Those who managed to buy copies of *High School in Love*—a novel for young adults—waved their copies like prizes, while those left empty-handed stared in exasperation.

"I've only see that kind of reaction for celebrities," he says. Suong Mak is only 32 years old but has already published 40 novels and novellas and over 100 stories—making him Cambodia's most prolific author. Most of his work has been published in the ground-breaking literary blog he launched while studying Lao literature in Vientiane.[1]

He's made an out-sized impact, but his success is not unique; other young Cambodian authors are making waves in the local and regional literary scene. Three of the last SEA Write Award winners for Cambodia were under 30.

Sok Chanphal—who won the award in 2013 when he was 29—sold 2,000 copies of his latest collection of short stories, *Romance*, in less than four months. Set Hattha, 26, published her first book, *The Test of Life*, in December last year. She's now waiting for a second print run, after selling 2,000 copies. Suong has lost track of how many copies *High School in Love* has sold, but 600 were snapped up within three days of its debut.

---

1 http://archphkai.wordpress.com/

The numbers might seem small when compared to international English language bestsellers but the rising popularity of fiction has caught the eye of businesses here. Sabay[2], which runs a variety of Cambodian news, entertainment and lifestyle portals, was one of the first to capitalise on it, introducing Sabay Enovel[3] in December 2012. According to editor Thavy Uch, it now sells stories and serialised novels to more than 60,000 monthly readers, has five full-time editors and almost five million followers on its Facebook page.

"Interest in fiction is surging," she says, noting competition from rival e-publishers is intensifying.

The revival of Khmer-language fiction—or books in general—is partly the result of demographics and education. According to official data, two-thirds of the Kingdom's 16 million people are under the age of 30 and the adult literacy rate is the highest it has ever been, slightly more than 80%.[4]

Cambodian writers say these new readers want stories that reflect their lives.

A colonised narrative

This outpouring of contemporary Khmer literature has yet, however, to reach Phnom Penh's largest bookstore, Monument Books, where the Cambodia section still overflows with histories by western academics and journalists, or biographies about narrow escapes from the Killing Fields written by the children of refugees. The accumulation of bleak titles—such as *Cambodia's Curse: The Modern History of a Troubled Land* or *Pol Pot: Anatomy of a Nightmare*—can feel overwhelming, creating an indelible impression of Cambodia as a tragic, dystopian kingdom stuck in its past. One consequence is that the present is often viewed solely through a funereal lens.

Sok has a different view. "A new Khmer literature is emerging," he says. "Young Cambodians want fresh, topical stories with real characters, and exciting, playful and creative writing."

25-year-old Hang Achariya—whose novella *Blood from Hell* has been adapted into a radio play—agrees, but stresses that technique is critical. Readers do not want stories that are derivative, he says.

2 http://sabay.com/

3 http://enovel.sabay.com.kh/

4 https://www.phnompenhpost.com/opinion/literacy-target-sustainable-development-goal

What's most important is immediacy, says Suong. No subject is off limits; even the rules of grammar are no longer sacrosanct.

Older writers are more descriptive, carefully detailing the scenery and atmosphere before characters begin to speak, Suong explains. Younger writers opt for simplicity. "They use very, very short words, like they are communicating with friends on social media. Sometimes they do not follow sentence structure or grammar," he adds.

Cambodian writers are also becoming more assertive, with several pointing to the annual Kampot Readers and Writers Festival as a catalyst for action. In 2016 local writers were side-lined from the festival, which appeared to be more of a showcase for expatriate writers. "Most Cambodian writers couldn't even afford to attend it," Hang says. "Some writers got depressed. They wondered, why can foreign writers put on a literary festival in our country that we cannot attend?"

This frustration led the local writers to launch their own festival in September 2017 in Siem Reap. It was a watershed moment. "Before the festival I had given up on publishing fiction," Suong says. "After, I felt inspired again."

An improbable plot

Seen in person, Suong comes across as someone who has to, almost unwillingly, make an immense effort to fit in; he seems nervous, confused and remote. His writing, however, is praised by his peers for its brazenness, indifference to convention and taboos, and plot twists—traits that mirror the improbable launch of his literary career.

He wrote his first novel—a horror story called *The Spirit of Love*—to spook his cousins. After reading it in school, it became the talk of his remote village in northeast Cambodia. Classmates encouraged him to publish it as a book.

Suong and his mother—a single parent who supported her two sons by selling noodles—followed their advice, travelling to Phnom Penh by bus with a handwritten manuscript, USD10 and the address of a publisher they'd seen in a book. The publisher explained that they had to pay him to print the book, before giving them USD5 and suggesting that they try to sell the manuscript to a book vendor at Orussey market. They eventually sold it to a vendor there after several others rejected it because they refused to believe that a teenager from a village had written a novel.

Two-and-a-half years later Suong returned to Phnom Penh for the second time, on a scholarship to attend university. He saw his book in print, its title and his name emblazoned on the cover. Overwhelmed by a feeling of being exposed, he asked a friend to buy a copy from the vendor who sold it.

She quizzed the friend about Suong's whereabouts and asked to meet him. When he showed up the next day she paid him USD50 for his book. It was the first time he had ever earned money. And then she asked him to write another.

"It was the first time I felt like a writer," he recalls.

Village roots

Like Suong, Sok, Set and Hang hail from villages that lacked electricity, moving to Phnom Penh to attend university. They, and other young writers, first connected via social media, began meeting in person and discussed how to use blogs and Facebook to promote their books.

Facebook is critical for promoting books in a country where libraries are scant and literary agents and publishing houses even rarer, says Set. Literature was vacuumed out of Cambodia by the Khmer Rouge who turned the national library into a space for raising pigs.

Young Cambodian writers are reviving their country's literature without the infrastructure writers in many other countries take for granted.

"If you want to be a successful writer in Cambodia you have to be an entrepreneur," Set explains. "We have to do everything. Write the book, manage the printing, the distribution, the marketing, the sales… You have to really love it. This is not something you do just for money."

Lek Chumnor, vice-president of the Khmer Writers Association agrees.

Most young writers even register their own books at the national library to copyright them and obtain ISBNs. He says they can earn about 30% in profit on the first run, with the rate rising for a second printing.

Lek launched a new publishing house—Khmer Books Publishing[5]—last November, focused on novels by young writers. It has editors, a graphic designer and a distribution network, he says.

Set is planning to follow suit. She sold enough copies of her first book—a collection of inspirational vignettes—to quit her job as a digital marketer. She's now investing in writers who cannot afford to publish

---

5 https://www.facebook.com/khmerbooks.net/

themselves, taking a percentage of sales in exchange for printing, marketing and distribution costs.

Set sees an untapped market, but one lacking the data to make informed decisions. There are no bestseller lists or book reviews in Cambodia, making it difficult not only for readers to decide what to buy, but for publishers to understand the market and how to cater to it. In such a context, it becomes easy to make mistakes, aiming either too low or two high. She's had this experience herself; when she published *The Test of Life*, she printed only 500 copies. They sold out in two weeks, requiring her to print another 1,500 more. She plans to print another 2,000 copies next month.

Shifting points of view

Suong was the first Cambodian writer to market fiction online. The literary blog he launched in Vientiane had 100,000 regular readers at its height. He's also credited by other writers as the first Cambodian author to pepper dialogue with emoticons, emoji and slang from foreign languages. More importantly, Suong stresses, was the shift he made from single point of view narration to multiple and sometimes contradictory narrators.

He credits his study of Lao and Thai literature—he can speak, read and write in both languages—for inspiring him to find new ways to tell stories in Khmer. In his e-book *Meteor*, for example, the first characters to speak are sperm racing towards an ovum. The book ends a little more than nine months later with a new-born found in a dumpster. Other stories portray Cambodian women trafficked to brothels in Thailand, or—in his first story translated into English, *Hell in the City*—the rape of the disabled daughter of a noodle vendor. He also published *Boyfriend*, the first Cambodian novel to portray a gay couple, in 2010.

Boyfriend was a hit, selling 5,000 copies, but also raised eyebrows. Suong recalls young men wearing surgical masks to hide their faces when purchasing copies. He also faced awkward questions, such as: "Are you trying to turn Cambodia gay?"

Attitudes have changed dramatically since then, he says. There are pockets of acceptance even in villages.[6]

---

6 https://www.phnompenhpost.com/national-post-depth/despite-legal-hurdles-cambodias-lgbt-couples-are-adopting-and-changing-minds

Still, Suong was hesitant about publishing *High School in Love*. Friends warned him that readers would recoil from its cover depicting two young men embracing. When he finally decided to release it he began with teasers on Facebook—posting photos of the book placed everywhere from rice fields to coffee shops, till it felt ubiquitous.

He and other Cambodian writers are now looking at markets beyond Cambodia. An increasing number of them are being translated into English, and published in journals.[7] More translations are in the works. Lek says the focus now is on the quality of translation. Expectations are rising. A page is turning.

---

7 http://www.nouhachjournal.net/

IDENTITY POLITICS

REGARDLESS OF RACE, LANGUAGE OR RELIGION...

KIRSTEN HAN | 09 SEP 2017

Singapore's long-cultivated image of being colour-blind meets its greatest challenger with the country's first racially-predetermined presidential election.

T he idea of Singapore as a multi-racial and multi-religious utopia has been drummed into its citizens for decades, thanks to its history books and the countless less-than-subtle propaganda-tinged videos and ads.

The widely-accepted narrative for Singaporeans and the rest of the world is that of a nation built on meritocracy and a people who are colour-blind. But Singapore is hardly post-race, an unpleasant fact unearthed by this year's presidential election.

Following a high-profile review led by Chief Justice Sundaresh Menon, amendments were made to the country's elected presidency earlier this year. On top of more onerous qualifying criteria such as requiring candidates from the private sector to have been a senior executive managing a company with at least S$500 million in shareholders' equity, the changes also introduced a "hiatus-triggered" model: if a particular race—out of the Chinese, Malay and Indian/Others racial groups—has not been represented as president for five terms, the next election will be restricted only to members of that race. Under these changes, the 2017 presidential election is reserved only for Malay candidates.

This Malay-only ruling for the elections has raised questions about the criteria that needs to be met to qualify as Malay, and thrown up for public discourse the controversial topic of racial identity in this multi-cultural country.

The Malay-only presidential election has also "exposed the highly-constructed nature of 'race' and racial identity, that are often taken for granted and not questioned in Singapore," said Laavanya Kathiravelu, assistant professor in sociology at Nanyang Technological University.

"It affirms the primacy of race as a defining feature in our political landscape and encourages the citizenry to think in racial terms, rather than in more neutral ways about the leadership of our country."

Racial classifications

The Singapore government has long adhered to the CMIO (Chinese, Malay, Indian, Others) model, identifying these groups as the country's main races. These broad groupings have always been problematic in their failure to reflect the complexity of real life, but this recent change to the presidential election system has placed this penchant for racial categorisation under extra scrutiny.

Although race is often discussed in the context of a social issue, the political implications of race continue to manifest in daily life, particularly since it's often a factor in official policy-making.

Take, for instance, Singapore's much-praised public housing system. Under the Ethnic Integration Policy, introduced to require different races to live in the same neighbourhood, the government determines the percentage of people of different races living in a particular housing block in the name of racial integration.

"Once people live together, they're not just walking the same corridors every day, they're not just taking the same elevators up and down, their kids go to the same schools... and they grow up together," said Deputy Prime Minister Tharman Shanmugaratnam during an interview at the 45th St. Gallen Symposium in 2015.

Welfare groups, too, are set up according to race, such as the Chinese Development Assistance Council, the Mosque Building and Mendaki Fund, the Singapore Indian Development Association and the Eurasian Association. These groups raise funds from members of the racial group they represent, which are then supplemented by government grants, to be disbursed to the less-privileged members of the community.

"In this way, state policies make clear that the population's access and rights are differentiated, rather than all citizens having the same opportunities to make claims based on a shared belonging to the nation," NTU's Laavanya wrote in her article "Rethinking Race: Beyond CMIO Categorisations".

Four races and counting

The CMIO model has also long obscured greater diversity in Singapore, reducing citizens to four monolithic groups while ignoring the hetero-geneity that exists even within each individual category.

This over-simplification of ethnicity and identity was, in actual fact, a deliberate move by the British colonial administrators who—seeking convenience over accuracy—first introduced these categories. The first census carried out in 1871 included categories like "Klings", "Bengalees", "Bugis", "Javanese and Boyanese" and "Arabs", but by 1921 the bureaucrats had decided to categorise all native peoples of the Malayan archipelago as "Malay". The census report stated that "considerable difficulty was experienced in coming to a decision as to which of these races should be tabulated separately and which amalgamated under the heading 'Malay'."

In 2011, the government introduced the option for inter-ethnic cou-ples to double-barrel the race of their children, although policies such as the aforementioned Ethnic Integration Policy would only be imple-mented according to the first component (thus making it important for parents to consider if they wanted to, for instance, register their child as "Chinese-Indian" or "Indian-Chinese").

Race and identity had always been a source of confusion for Nabilah Husna growing up. Born to an Indian father and Malay mother, Nabilah is categorised as Indian in official documents, but was raised within Malay-Muslim customs and traditions, and personally identifies as Malay.

"I have vivid memories being super confused with what I am, and I have gone through 'phases' where I strongly identify with one more than the other, or neither, whether or not that identity is influenced by whatever social group I happen to be with," Nabilah told *New Naratif.*

This question of ethnic identity and belonging has long existed, not only in Singapore, but in much of the Malay world.

In one episode of *The History of Singapore* podcast, historian Nurfadzilah Yahaya said that the question of who could be considered Malay had already surfaced in the 1920s and 1930s, and could not be divorced from political considerations.

"Why is it that the Arabs, coming from so far away and fewer in num-ber, were less problematically regarded as… Malay in Malaysia and also Singapore, than say, the Chinese, who also frequently intermarried with local populations in Indonesia and Malaysia, but were always regarded as foreign?" she pointed out.

"One thing that has been argued is that these Arabs... were Muslims, and so they were more naturally included within the Malay world, which is predominantly Muslim. But that being said, there are Chinese Muslims who have also not been welcomed into this category of Malay or *bumiputra*, and one might argue that... Chinese Muslim influence in Southeast Asia has been around for longer than Muslim influence from South Asia and Middle East."

Political distinctions

Today, the politicisation of race has become even more stark. Confusingly, an individual's race stated on his or her official documents can be distinct from the race he or she is considered to represent in elections.

Under a system first introduced with the creation of Group Representation Constituencies in 1988—where candidates stand as teams in mega-constituencies in teams in a winner-takes-all contest—minority candidates are required to first self-identify as belonging to one of the four official racial groups. This identity is then evaluated by a government-appointed committee to determine whether that particular racial community "accepts" the individual as one of their own.

As such, the race listed on one's identity card isn't relevant when it comes to standing for elections: someone categorised as Malay in their official documents could still be rejected by the committee, while another person could be accepted despite being classified under another race in official documents. This was confirmed earlier this year by Member of Parliament Zainal bin Sapari, who wrote in a Facebook comment that "your race need not be stated as 'Malay' in your NRIC or birth cert to be considered as a Malay candidate."

Removing racial barriers to move forward

Far from making Singapore colour-blind, the limitations of the CMIO model has triggered concerns of hampering racial equality and representation in Singapore.

"The state must come to terms with the fact that classifying diversity in terms of four simple 'racial groups' is not sufficiently nuanced or representative, given the current migration from around the world and changing demographic realities within the population," wrote Laavanya.

Moving away from, or even abolishing, the CMIO model will not automatically solve the issue of racism and racialisation in Singapore. It could, however, be a first step, allowing people to stop seeing themselves as hyphenated citizens—Chinese-Singaporean, Malay-Singaporean, Indian-Singaporean—but simply as Singaporeans.

"IT WAS A POLITICAL ISSUE": RECALLING THE 1998 MEDAN RIOTS

AISYAH LLEWELLYN | 23 NOV 2017

Understanding the reactions of the Chinese-Indonesian community in Medan to rising ethnic tensions requires one to realise that the anti–Chinese violence in 1998 was more about politics than race.

Apek Cafe in Medan has been in business for 80 years. It's now run by Suyenti, who inherited it from her father. Suyenti, who declined to share her last name, is Chinese-Indonesian, and Apek Cafe hasn't changed much since her father first opened its doors after moving to North Sumatra from China.

The small front room is filled with several large communal tables made of wood; Suyenti is loathe to change them to anything more modern as they add to the atmosphere. "Because of the way the tables are set up, everyone has to share," she says. "Customers talk to the people on the same table as them and everyone is friendly. This is a multicultural area."

The city of Medan in North Sumatra is known as one of the most multicultural places in Indonesia. Around 60% of the population are Muslim while about 29% are Christian, with smaller Buddhist and Hindu communities, mostly made up of Chinese and Tamil-Indonesians.

But despite this relative ethnic diversity, Medan was also ground zero of the 1998 riots which targeted Chinese-Indonesian businesses, spreading across Indonesia and leaving over a thousand people dead. 20 years on, media coverage on the violence against Chinese-Indonesians tend to forget this fact, and that it was originally never about race, ethnicity, or religion. But this understanding is crucial at a time where there are concerns ethnic tensions might be on the rise once more in Indonesia.

Where it began

Medan, with its reputation as a hotbed of student activism, saw months-long student protests against the Suharto government in 1998. Most of these demonstrations were tied to rising prices across Indonesia, particularly the costs of gasoline and electricity. On May 4, 1998, the police moved in on the Institut Keguruan dan Ilmu Pendidikan Negeri (IKIP Negeri) to clear the student protesters. The resulting stand-off led to allegations that the police attacked and assaulted students, and over 50 people were said to be detained. The next day, the police station where those arrested had been taken was surrounded and attacked.

The violence escalated as students and civilians turned out onto the streets of Medan, ransacking buildings, setting them on fire and smashing cars. Angry mobs attacked Chinese owned businesses, scrawling "*milik pribumi*" meaning "property of indigenous Indonesians" on the walls. It's unclear how many fatalities there were, but some estimates put it at six, with hundreds injured. The violence then spread from Medan to Jakarta, and then to Solo. Estimates say over a thousand people died in these riots, with over 160 cases of rape reported. Thousands of Chinese-Indonesians fled the country.

Suyenti was lucky; both her coffee shop and neighbourhood weren't attacked. The shop was closed for several days, but reopened a few days later. "I had no problems in 1998," she says. "Everyone I knew in the neighbourhood was very kind to me."

Osma Halim had a different experience. He's 68 years old and retired now, but was a sauce salesman in 1998, selling wholesale bottled sauces to local shops and restaurants. He's the only person *New Naratif* approached for an interview who would talk about the 1998 riots and the violence in detail. The majority of those asked didn't want to discuss that dark period in Medan's history, saying they would prefer not to dwell on the past.

He recalls mobs of hooligans coming to the area around Jalan Asia, a district known for its large Chinese-Indonesian community, armed with sticks and rocks. When he heard about an impending attack, he went straight home and locked himself in. For the next month, he survived on instant noodles and didn't venture outside in the day. In the following weeks, he only left home when it was dark to guard the area with other local residents. They worked in shifts so there would always be a line of people guarding the perimeter of Jalan Asia.

The area was attacked several times between May 5 and May 8. Halim says he and other Chinese-Indonesian residents gathered piles of rocks and threw them at the attacking mob to defend the neighbourhood. He estimates that about 1,000 people tried to attack the area and storm the shops and businesses.

"They threw rocks at us, always aiming for our heads. One of my friends had his eye knocked out," he says, shaking his head. "We had nothing to defend ourselves with. At night I saw all the shops had been looted and smashed. They took everything. Nothing was safe."

Politics over race

"I always thought that it was a political issue, rather than a racial one," Suyenti says of the violence.

This distinction between politics and race is important to a narrative that has been muddled over the years. The student protests and subsequent riots are now almost always referred to as the "race riots" or "anti-Chinese riots" of 1998, but that was not how things began, nor was anti-Chinese sentiment the original focus of the student protesters. The protests made no mention of specific ethnic groups and had focused on the Suharto regime, which many saw as corrupt. Many however considered the targeting of the Chinese-Indonesian community in 1998 a throwback to 1965 and the anti-Communist purges in Indonesia that left an estimated 500,000 to a million dead, including many ethnic Chinese.

In the paper 'Explaining Anti-Chinese Riots In Late 20th Century Indonesia',[1] Samsu Rizal Panggabean and Benjamin Smith explain that the anti-Chinese violence was a result of attempts to deflect attention away from the incompetence of the security forces:

> It was not inevitable that violence would take an ethnic and anti-Chinese turn until the crucial uncontrollable events of May 5 [...] The inability of either police or army units to manage the events set the stage for their deployment of pre-man [local gangsters] to shift the frame of rioting from anti-regime to anti-Chinese.

Put simply, local hooligans had been deployed to transform a political issue into an ethnic one, and thus shift the spotlight away from the government—the original target of the demonstrations. Rather than a case of deep-seated racial tensions bubbling to the surface, the targeting of Chinese-Indonesians in 1998 was a cynical political move and carried out largely by organised hooligans and opportunistic youths.

---

1 https://www.academia.edu/6201956/Explaining_Anti-Chinese_Violence_in_Late_20th_Century_Indonesia

The violence, or lack thereof, could depend on the whims of the local gangsters; Chinese-Indonesians stayed safe in some neighbourhoods because the local *preman* refused to allow anyone to loot in their area or touch the Chinese businesses. As one Chinese-Indonesian resident of Kampung Madras in the centre of Medan, who didn't want to be named, told *New Naratif*: "[Their leader] wouldn't let the hooligans come down here. He protected us."

Andy, a Batak-Muslim who asked that his real name not be revealed, was one of the youths who participated in the looting. He was 13 years old in 1998 and remembers some small-scale robbery in his neighbourhood.

"I went out with my friends to see what was happening," he says. "Many of the shop windows had already been shattered. Everyone was running into the shops so I ducked into a shoe store and grabbed all the shoes I could find."

After he got home, he realised that he'd snatched all the display models and only had the right foot of each pair of shoes. When his mother learned what he'd done, she beat him and made him take them all back to the shop.

"I was just a kid, of course, I had no understanding of the political or racial situation," he says. "I just wanted some free shoes."

Tensions today

This context serves as a vital prism through which to look at the reactions of Chinese-Indonesians in Medan at a time when ethnic and religious tensions are noted to be on the rise in Indonesia. This is particularly true following the bruising gubernatorial elections in Jakarta in 2017, in which race and religion were said to have played a big part in Anies Baswedan, a Muslim candidate, sweeping to victory, over the then-Jakarta governor, Basuki Tjahaja "Ahok" Purnama.

Ahok—a Christian Chinese-Indonesian who inherited the position of governor after his running mate Joko Widodo was elected president in 2014—was jailed for two years in May this year on blasphemy charges after he was found guilty of insulting Islam by quoting a verse from the Qu'ran in a speech. The charge was widely considered as part of a political power-play in order to prevent Ahok election's as governor of Jakarta. In the lead up to his sentencing, thousands of Indonesians, organised by conservative Muslim groups, took to the streets in protest, calling for Ahok to be punished. The protests, although largely peaceful, sparked fears across Indonesia that riots targeting Chinese-Indonesians could happen again. Baswedan, in particular, was seen as deliberately courting Muslim voters in order to secure victory, and was accused of using race as a tool to cause divisions between the different ethnic communities in Jakarta.

Halim refuses to comment on the possible ripple effects of the Ahok trial, worried that any words of support for the former governor could be taken out of context, but shakes his head at the suggestion that it might reignite racial tensions in Medan; he feels safe now and says he isn't worried.

"We were never united, but we've always co-existed just fine," he says.

THE ROOTS OF THE HATE
MARCO FERRARESE | 02 APR 2018

The existence of a tiny supremacist Malay Power faction within the Malaysian underground music scene and the reasons behind its rise suggest that in Southeast Asia, the meanings of global subcultures sometimes get lost in cultural translation.

The existence of "Malay Power"—a term usually referring to Malay Neo-Nazis—is confounding. Members of Malay Power are brown, firmly outside the Nazi concept of racially superior Aryans, yet embrace one of the world's worst subcultural expressions of racial hate. Its development has grown out of a confused mix of Malaysian racial politics and selective interpretations of religion and history.

Malaysia is a multi-racial, multi-cultural and multi-religious nation, but Malay Muslims—who form the majority of the population—are accorded a special status, allowing them preferential treatment in areas such as employment and scholarships.[1] Malaysian politics has also been dominated by the United Malays National Organisation (UMNO), a founding member of the Barisan Nasional (BN) coalition currently in power. Shamsul Amri Baharuddin, a Malaysian scholar, once described Malaysia's social reality as caught between the "authority-defined" idea of society, shaped by those in power, and the very different "everyday-defined" reality of its multi-cultural street life.

This has seeped into Malaysia's predominantly Malay music underground, too. For Malay Power, "authority-defined" ideas of Malay privilege and supremacy have penetrated the imported global punk and metal ideologies that Malaysian musicians refer to. The results are interesting yet puzzling: hybrid identities that equally share racist, Islamic, and underground music ideologies.

---

1 https://newnaratif.com/journalism/malaise-malaysian-malays/

Separate but present

"Malay Power bands play their own gigs in places we don't know of,"
says Cole Yew, manager of Soundmaker Studio in Penang, Northern
Malaysia's most established alternative performing club. "In Malaysia,
the antifascist skinhead movement [has grown] quite big, and most of
the live houses support its anti-racial agenda."

But Nazi enthusiasts can sometimes still end up playing at regular
venues, at least until someone belatedly realises what's happened. Yew
points to a January 2018 show at the Muse Jamming Studio in Alma,
just off Penang island: the band Total Sick was banned from performing after some of its members were recognised in a photo taken outside
another underground club, in which the Malay men and women smiled
and posed with two swastika flags. Some had their right arms raised
in Nazi salutes.

This weird phenomenon is poorly understood and not often discussed. An article on "Malaysian Nazi skinheads" published by Vice
in 2013[2] ignited an uproar among antifascist Malaysian skinheads and
drew criticism for its misrepresentation of the Malaysian underground
music scene. "Boot Axe? We don't even know who they are," the late
Rozaimin Elias, one of the most dedicated and active antifascist skinheads in Malaysia[3], once told me about the band of "brown Nazis" the
publication had featured. To really gain an insight into Malay Power,
one needs to look deeper into the underground music scene, as well as
racial politics and identity issues in Malaysia.

Enter Nusantara

In general, contemporary Malaysian underground music follows the
standards of performance set by the Western genres they reference,
without too much localisation. But Malaysian hard rock bands from
the 1980s—mat rockers like Sweet Charity, Rocker and Bloodshed—
injected local themes into their lyrics. It was a move similar to the
thematic switch of second wave Norwegian black metal bands such as
Mayhem, Darkthrone or Immortal, who, from the mid-1990s, distanced
themselves from the Satanic imagery of the genre's early pioneers and
gradually embraced the folkloric themes, images of Vikings and pagan
worship of their Scandinavian identities. Some of the bands, however,

2 https://www.vice.com/en_us/article/jmv73p/the-malaysian-nazis-fighting-for-a-pure-race

3 http://sea-globe.com/skinheads-malaysia-marco-ferrarese-southeast-asia-globe/

quickly descended from Norse mythology into the bleak extremism of Nazi-fascism and homophobia.

Something similar—but thankfully without the church arson or the killing of bandmates and homosexuals seen in Scandinavia—happened in Malaysia. "Nusantara [refers to the] Malay Archipelago—Malaysia, Southern Thailand, the Philippines, Indonesia and Borneo—and in the early days of Southeast Asian extreme metal, it was bands like As Sahar, Langsuir, Zubirun and Hayagriva to come up first with eastern themes. It was mostly lyric-wise, since their music was still very much influenced by Scandinavian black and death metal," says Rammy Azmy, a metal musician and curator of historical Malaysian metal fanzine *Kemenyan*.

The early Malay metal bands used images of bomohs (traditional Malay healers and shamans) and local ghosts and vampires on their demo tape covers. For example, the 1993 debut tape of Langsuir, "Occultus Mysticism", depicts the Malay vampire who gave the band its name floating above a pentagram inscribed with symbols that look like Islamic calligraphy. Lyrics, however, remained in English, following global examples of black and death metal.

"The old bands very much borrowed Malay traditional melodies and then rearranged them into metal riffs, mixing [in] lyrics based on Malay black magic, myths and superstitions, but still mostly in English. It was a prototype of what we [hear] today," says Rammy.

Today, Bentara of the band Langsuir is a university professor based near Ipoh and hasn't been involved with the band since 2009. To him, black metal was about Satan or myths and legends, of which Malaysia has plenty to borrow from. "I chose a band name related to Nusantara: Langsuir, a Malay female vampire, was perfect, evil and catchy. Instead of adopting the global strands of black metal, I adapted them [to] my culture, even if I was only 14 years old [then]."

The Malaysian underground music scene also departs from its Western references in another significant way. Within the Anglo-American extreme music context, religion is generally frowned upon (with the exception of forms of Christian heavy metal). It's considered an authoritarian tool, used to control the conservatism that metal and punk was born to contest. Yet most Malays in the Malaysian scene are practising Muslims.

Wan, the former leader of the Singaporean Eastern black metal band As-Sahar, who currently plays with another Singapore-based band Phenomistik, doesn't see any conflict. "[T]here's nothing wrong with

Muslims liking heavy music," he says. "As long as it's limited to just liking, and doesn't go beyond that—I mean, without incurring in any acts of blasphemy or forbidden by Islam. In my view, there is absolutely no correlation between music and your own faith."

To Malays, their religious and underground identities are separate yet constantly co-existing. But the close correlation of ethnicity and religion—particularly for Malays, who are defined under the Constitution of Malaysia as people who adhere to Islam, among other characteristics—can blur the lines.

Steering towards hate

According to Rammy Azmy, the whole Neo-Nazi faction within Malaysia's underground scene evolved out of the Nusantara metal bands. "At first, we metalheads didn't care that much about the fascist symbols and racist ideologies, because everything 'bad and evil' is welcome in extreme metal," he explains. "But eventually, it became a real thing, and developed into this circle called 'Darah dan Maruah Tanah Melayu (Blood and Honour of the Malay Land)'. They support each other, have their albums and demos released under this moniker, and even [have] a secret annual gig featuring all the Malay Power bands".

A Blogspot page, last updated on 10 September 2012, promotes a mix of skinhead and black metal bands such as Maruah, Singhasari and Brown Attack. It's difficult to get members of the group to talk to outsiders. Malay Power is kept hidden among a very closed-knit group of people who don't like sharing their opinions and are shunned by members of the regular scene who want little to do with them.

I eventually managed to get in touch with one musician, Daeng (a pseudonym) of the Selangor-based band Jugra. The band plays an interesting mix of Oi! Skinhead punk and National Socialist Black Metal; their name hints at the royal town of Jugra in Selangor, once the seat of ruling monarch Sultan Abdul Samad. I ask how he and his peers, as Malaysians, justify the use of Nazi symbols in their lyrics and associated artwork; Malaysia, historically and culturally, had nothing to do with Nazi ideology.

"National Socialism is for all who believe in a nation for one race, one leader and one nation, not only Germans or Aryans," explains Daeng. "If you search deeper in the history of National Socialism, there were lots of non-white [Schutzstaffel (a paramilitary force under Adolf Hitler and the Nazi Party)] recruits and political parties from ethnic groups such as Arabs, Indians, Chinese, blacks, and even Nusantarans. The usage of Nazi imagery and symbols in some of our bands is simply a tribute to the Third Reich as one of the most glorious empires [that] ever existed. It was also the best symbols to represent our radical views."

Coming to Islam, Daeng agrees with most other Malay underground musicians, stating that music and religion are two well separated identities that have nothing much to share. "Islam is a spiritual belief and it has nothing to do with being a nationalist or having a heavy metal band," he adds. But unexpectedly, Malay Power proponents vehemently disagree with those who similarly play the racial card. In fact, they see the Malay political elite as a nemesis to be fought.

"I hate UMNO and BN," Daeng says. "They are our sworn enemies, we will never ally with them. This worthless party only thinks for themselves whilst masquerading as [a] Malay nationalist party. Malaysia was formed this way because of these people, thanks to these betrayers who desperately signed with the British in order to take control of this country, and see what happened: racial issues and corruption everywhere. I never believed in democracy and all those Zionist-loving discourses. This country must be revived as an absolute monarchy and it shall! Revere the sultanate, expel the barbarians."

Malay Power may represent just a small part of Malaysian youth and society, but it's existence, as well as its isolation, tells us about the sentiments some contemporary Malays harbour towards their own citizens and state. On the one hand, the existence of a strong antifascist skinhead community that embraces the positive values of a global musical movement demonstrates a willingness to fight racism and supremacy, at least within the Malaysian music scene. But on the other hand, the presence of Malays who identify as both Muslims and "national socialists", points to a confused sense of identity in Malaysia's post-colonial and highly globalised context. It's a hybrid they've created for themselves, cherry-picking from history and global subcultures to suit their own pre-existing formulation of Southeast Asian identities.

It's an inconsistent position that, Azmy argues, transforms Islam into a non-universal "tribal cult", mixing the religion with "Malay paganism and illogical customs": "All Malays should know that Prophet Muhammad is not a nationalist, as he banned asabiyyah (racism)… The Nusantara spirit is not approved by Islam, because those who glorify Nusantara put racism on top. A Muslim should unite under tawheed (Oneness of God), not some racist idea."

A CELEBRITY WEDDING REVIVES IDENTITY ISSUES

TEGUH HARAHAP, AISYAH LLEWELLYN | 09 APR 2018

Following the high-profile wedding of the Indonesian president's daughter, a Mandailing association in North Sumatra is lobbying for greater recognition.

"The Mandailing people do not want to be called Batak because Mandailing is not Batak. There is no relationship between the two groups," says Paruhuman Sah Alam Lubis, chairman of Himpunan Keluarga Besar Mandailing (HIKMA), or the Association of Mandailing Families, in Medan.

The Mandailing, an indigenous group in North Sumatra, are usually referred to as Batak, an umbrella term for a number of North Sumatran ethnic sub-groups including the Batak Mandailing, Batak Toba, Batak Pakpak, Batak Simalungun, Batak Angkola and Batak Karo. Despite being grouped under the same ethnic label of Batak, these sub-groups speak different dialects, have different cultural traditions and originally come from different parts of the province. Around 44% of the population of North Sumatra are classified as Batak.

It's a label that HIKMA feels is historically inaccurate. The association hosts events across the province to raise awareness of the differences between "Mandailing" and "Batak". It's a cause that some Mandailing have championed since 1922, but is now having its day in the sun thanks to a celebrity wedding involving the President of Indonesia.

A celebrity wedding and a murky history

The question of whether the Mandailing should be classified as Batak has been a long-standing topic of discussion for local Mandailing groups, or fodder for gossip in Mandailing coffee shops. But the 2017 wedding of Kahiyang Ayu, daughter of Indonesian President Joko "Jokowi" Widodo, to Batak Mandailing Bobby Nasution, though, has now brought the issue to the fore.

The wedding featured a range of traditional Batak customs, from the outfits to the dances performed. It also highlighted the confusion between the use of the terms "Mandailing" and "Batak Mandailing"; even the president himself was nonplussed.

"In the beginning Jokowi did not understand our position, because when he met with our group in preparation for the wedding reception, he kept saying 'Batak Mandailing' so he got some complaints from those who know the Mandailing history," explains Lubis.

"At first he was amazed and confused. But after he was shown some references on the history of Mandailing by officials and traditional leaders, then he understood that the Mandailing are not part of the Batak group."

Indonesia is built on the national slogan "Unity in Diversity"; there are more than 300 ethnic groups across the archipelago. While a sense of national unity is central to Indonesian society, the issue of asserting one's own ethnic identity is equally significant. And HIKMA has been at it for a long time: the association, founded on May 4, 1986, is made up of families who belong to the Mandailing group and has been at the forefront of separating Batak and Mandailing culture.

"Mandailing will never admit that they are Batak. If some Mandailing don't mind being called Batak then they only make up a small portion of the population," Lubis claims. "The fact is [that] we consider Mandailing to be closer to a nationality than an ethnic sub-group".

For HIKMA treasurer Ahmad Raja, the Mandailing's refusal to be classified as Batak is largely a rejection of the categories imposed by the Dutch colonisers who controlled Indonesia from the 1800s to 1945: "When the Dutch entered Indonesia, they saw people in the Toba region who moved around often so they called them 'Batak' or 'the wild'. The Dutch then used the word Batak to mean a culture or a tribe."

But things aren't so clear-cut. While it's true that the Dutch used the term, the term might have pre-dated their arrival. Other sources, such as the Encyclopaedia Britannica, say that the term was "likely coined during pre-colonial times by indigenous outsiders (e.g., the Malay) and later adopted by Europeans." Pre-colonial texts like Zhao Rugua's 13thcentury *Description of the Barbarous People* make references to the 'Ba-ta' of the Srivijaya Kingdom while the *Suma Oriental* from the 15thcentury mentions a kingdom known as 'Bata'.

Disagreements persist, with local experts weighing in. On October 23, 2017, a focus group discussion in Medan on the issue was attended by dozens of participants, including researcher and historian Phil Ichwan

Azhari, anthropologist Usman Pelly, and Erron Damanik, a researcher from Medan State University (UNIMED). At the event, Pelly claimed that the word "Batak" can't be found in ancient Indonesian manuscripts. "For example, in the seal of King Sisingamangaraja XII it is only written Ahu Si King Toba, there is no 'Batak King'," he said. "Batak does not exist, especially Mandailing."

For HIKMA Chairman of Education and Training, Syahian Zukhri Nasution, it's a matter of perception. "If you look at the traditional Mandailing customs that always used objects made of gold, do you still think that Mandailing should belong to a Batak tribe which means 'a wild man'?" he asks. "Batak branding is harmful to the Mandailing."

A golden opportunity

HIKMA sees the term "Batak" as a derogatory slur, a term used by the Dutch to paint them as wild, uncivilised natives. It's a term they want to dissociate with as soon as possible, and Kahiyang Ayu's nuptials have given them a "direct line" to the president to lobby for their cause. It's a rare opportunity to put their issue on the map in a large country where smaller ethnic communities often go unheard.

Indonesia is a sprawling archipelago of some 13,000 islands containing hundreds of ethnic sub-groups, all speaking different languages and with myriad traditions. Despite this, political power in Indonesia is often perceived as being overly focused on Java or, even more narrowly, as Jakarta-centric. Almost all of Indonesia's former presidents have been Javanese—even Bacharuddin Jusuf Habibie, born in Sulawesi, was half-Javanese—contributing to a sense that Javanese interests have always come first in the country. HIKMA now sees the Mandailing as having the chance to stand out and distance themselves from other Batak groups. And all of this comes not a moment too soon.

The celebrity wedding coincides with a time when money from Jakarta is pouring into North Sumatra at an unprecedented rate. The government has made plans to increase the number of tourists to the Lake Toba region to one million by 2019; a huge jump from the 300,000 who visited in 2017. Silangit Airport in Siborong-Borong was turned into an international airport in October 2017 and effort is also being put into making other parts of the province more attractive to tourists. Jokowi is also the first Indonesian president in the 72-year history of the republic to visit Batak areas like Lake Toba, thus elevating the region's national visibility.

As the money flows in, the Mandailing are using their history to make a name for themselves—literally. They say they're simply claiming what's been rightfully theirs for centuries. HIKMA hopes that all this will bring greater recognition of Mandailing culture (and funds to promote it), which would in turn open up more political opportunities for Mandailing candidates in regional elections. That Jokowi's daughter has been given the traditional Mandailing family surname, or marga, of Siregar is meant to further cement the relationship between the ethnic sub-group and those at the top of Indonesian politics.

According to Ian Wilson, a research fellow at the Asia Research Centre at Murdoch University, this is common practice across Indonesia: "There are lots of instances of this. For example, in Jakarta the 'Betawi' groups try to use their apparent indigenous status as social and political capital, and many politicians are receptive to this."

As Wilson explains, if local groups can gain the ear of a sympathetic politician in Indonesia by using their indigenous heritage, then there can be a number of benefits. "Exclusivist rights, representation or access to resources are all things these groups are looking for," he says. "It is all about mobilising ideas of indigeneity and authenticity as a means to gain things not accessible to others."

This wouldn't be the first time local Batak groups have tried to curry favour with politicians for economic and political reasons. One of the current candidates for the 2018 governorship of North Sumatra, Edy Rahmayadi—originally from Sabang in Aceh—was bestowed the traditional Batak surname Ginting when he visited Karo Regency in 2017. This, apparently, was in honour of his love for the Batak Karo and his support for villagers who had been evacuated from around Mount Sinabung, an active volcano. Interestingly, the marga was given to Rahmayadi by Himpunan Masyarakat Karo Indonesia (HIMKI), a sister group of HIKMA set up by the Batak Karo.

Lili Ginting, the head of the women's branch of HIKMI, was quick to explain the rationale for the happy occasion, which coincided with plans for a Bon Jovi concert in Karo Regency. "We hope that the Bon Jovi concert will open the door for more foreign tourists to visit Berastagi[a town in Karo Regency]which is in line with Edy Rahmayadi's plans for Berastagi to become a world tourism destination," she told the press.[4]

4 http://sumutpos.co/2017/04/03/pangkostrad-edy-rahmayadi-ditabalkan-marga-ginting/

Other high profile gubernatorial candidates from outside the region have also been claimed and given surnames by local Batak groups. Djarot Saiful Hidayat, the former governor of Jakarta, was given the surname Nababan—a typical marga of the Batak Toba—in January 2018 in a traditional ceremony.

Plans for the future

HIKMA currently operates on a provincial scale in North Sumatra but has plans to increase its presence to all Indonesian provinces. The group is involved in religious and cultural activities across North Sumatra in order to get their message to as many people as possible. "We have held events such as breaking fast together during Ramadan and have held soccer tournaments, as well as attending cultural events such as participating in the annual celebration of Sumatra Province," says Lubis. "And, of course, we also attended the wedding of the president's daughter".

But despite the Mandailing's objections, there's no consensus among the other ethnic groups who share the Batak classification. As Erron Damanik explained during the focus group discussion, the Mandailing have rejected the term "Batak" from as far back as 1922, but other groups such as the Batak Toba and Batak Angkola are still comfortable using it, and cite evidence of the term being used in pre-colonial times.

According to former journalist Budi Hutasuhut, who is Batak Angkola, the Mandailing are insisting upon breaking away from the umbrella group while still following traditional Batak customs. He, too, references the wedding, which appears to have become the flashpoint for renewed conflict about this issue.

"From the perspective of traditional customs, the Mandailing can't say they are not Batak," he said in an interview in November last year.[5] "Look at Jokowi's daughter's wedding to Bobby Nasution. Nasution is Mandailing. So why did they wear ulos [traditional scarves] from the Batak Angkola? Angkola clothes. Angkola dances. The Angkola are Batak. If the Mandailing are not Batak then they need to let go of all the traditional Batak customs like clothes and everything else."

If the Mandailing don't want to be known as Batak, Hutasuhut adds, then they need to do more research to prove a distinct difference

---

5 http://www.medanbisnisdaily.com/news/online/read/2017/11/08/12316/
mandailing_bukan_batak_sejarah_dan_mitologi_jangan_dicampur_aduk/

between the two terms; their arguments can't just revolve around the assumption that the word "Batak" is based on colonial bias.

It's criticism that Syahian Zukhri Nasution tends to just brush off. To him, the matter is clear and those who disagree are simply misinformed. "Let them resist this if they want to. They are only saying this because they don't have any proof or other strong evidence to back them up," he says.

This tension between the groups just goes to show how convoluted Batak history has become over the years; there are details and specifics that no one can agree on. But the Mandailing aren't going to let go of their newfound proximity to the country's leadership; for a small ethnic minority group, this opportunity to be heard on a national political level is simply too good to pass up.

INEQUALITY

DO MULTI-LEVEL MARKETING SCHEMES HELP WOMEN?

AISYAH LLEWELLYN | 05 FEB 2018

Companies like Oriflame promise Indonesian women financial success from the comfort of their own homes. But achieving that dream can prove more difficult than advertised.

L ike all good sales people Rachel[1] speaks mostly in jargon and is vague when pressed for details. Her account is currently inactive, but for the past four years she's worked as a freelance consultant for Oriflame Cosmetics in Medan. She makes it sounds like a great proposition for working women in Indonesia: "If you work hard then you can go abroad once a year for a free trip and you get a car. Oriflame also teaches you how to improve yourself and grow your own business."

Oriflame Cosmetics is a Swedish company that has been in business for 45 years, and operates as a multi-level marketing scheme, or MLM. This is how it works: men and women sign up, not only to sell beauty products, but also to recruit others to work as consultants, creating a sales chain that looks like a pyramid. Oriflame has some three million members across 60 countries.[2]

But Oriflame claims to be about so much more than just makeup; it says that it's really in the business of empowering people to make their business dreams come true.

"We believe in dreams. A dream is individual and personal," it gushes on its website.[3] "Oriflame is, and always has been about fulfilling dreams. This is what we do. Every day. For people all over the world." The company also pitches itself as a staunch believer in sustainability and helping the "most vulnerable in society".

---

1 Name changed to protect her identity.

2 https://mlmcompanies.org/oriflame/

3 https://uk.oriflame.com/about

Being a part of this involves signing up to be a consultant. In Indonesia, this means that you get a salary and money from the products you sell, and the attractive prospect of financial security for women who may otherwise struggle to earn an income.

Limited opportunities

According to its 2016 Annual Report, Oriflame's operating profit from Asia and Turkey skyrocketed from 9% in 2010 to 44% in 2016.[4] Indonesia, along with Turkey, China, India, Mexico and Russia, is identified as a strategic market in the company's global operations.

Rachel is an example of the kind of person that Oriflame appeals to. She's struggled to find work since graduating with a degree in communications from Universitas Islam Sumatera Utara (UISU) in 2009. She's not alone; according to data from the World Bank, there are 7.2 million people unemployed in Indonesia. She has a four-year-old daughter and, until recently, her husband worked outside the home; even if Rachel could find a job, the logistical and financial burden of arranging adequate childcare would place a strain on the family. It's what makes Oriflame seem like such a good fit—it allows her to work from home and earn money while taking care of her daughter.

But information about the actual sign-up process on Oriflame's Indonesian website is sparse and confusing. According to Rachel, signing up as an Oriflame consultant in Indonesia requires an initial payment of IDR50,000 (USD4), plus the purchase of a welcome pack which starts at IDR119,000 (USD8). This comes with IDR200,000 (USD14) worth of starter products and a "free" gift, which in Rachel's case was a handbag. Consultants then need to purchase more products to get an Oriflame account, which allows them access to free online business and marketing tutorials, as well as in-person seminars at Oriflame's Medan offices. Oriflame produces a new catalogue of beauty products every three weeks.

Buying new products costs between IDR200,000 (USD14) to IDR900,000 (USD63) every month; the more you buy, the higher your level within the company, and the more you earn per recruit. It's a potentially significant amount in a country where, based on figures from the World Bank, 27.7 million live in poverty and the median starting salary for a university graduate is IDR3 million per month.

---

4 http://vp233.alertir.com/sites/default/files/report/2016_annualreport_screen_0.pdf

The rate of return is also not particularly encouraging. At the time of writing, a lipstick is priced at IDR129,000 (USD9) online, and sellers are not allowed to mark up the price. Consultants earn between 10%–30% from their sales, depending on their status within the company and how many people they recruit. All in all, they tend to make between IDR20,000 (USD1.50) to IDR270,000 (USD18) in profit every month depending on the amount of products they purchase. At Rachel's level, in the "Business Class" division, she had to pay IDR900,000 every month for new products.

According to Rachel, many who have signed up to Oriflame don't try that hard to sell anything. "I use the products for personal use. You can sell them or give them to your friends and family and let them use them," she says.

How, then, does anyone make money? Once asked, Rachel enthusiastically launches into an explanation of the second phase of the company's marketing strategy: recruitment.

Consultants are encouraged to recruit others to sign up as Oriflame consultants. The company promises that doing so will help with "increasing your earnings" and also "developing your beauty, business and management skills through Oriflame Academy training courses." Rachel explains that she recruits others by posting Oriflame promotions on Twitter and Facebook pages, but is reluctant to engage with the economics behind this. When asked how much she earns per recruit, she's at first evasive: "It is not about the money. In Islam we are duty bound to help people to better themselves and get rewards."

When pressed further, she explains that Oriflame's base salary structure—which starts at around IDR100,000 (USD7)—is also tied to the number of people you've recruited. The more active consultants you recruit, and the more people *they* recruit, the more your base salary increases. The most Rachel has ever made in a month is IDR1,000,000 (USD70).

Considering the IDR900,000 she had to pay upfront for the products, it still doesn't seem like a good deal. But Rachel isn't necessarily being disingenuous; she's been well-coached by Oriflame to make the scheme sound attractive. Rachel explains that the free training seminars push the women to work hard: "They tell us that if people ask why the base salary is so low we have to explain that they need to work hard to make more money. The trainers explain that if we are not diligent then we won't make any money. The people who are successful are the ones who build networks." "Building networks", of course, refers to recruiting more members.

The glamour of success stories

For those struggling to increase their income, there are role models to look up to. Vonita Bermana Wickasono is a big success story for Oriflame in Indonesia. Once, at a conference for Oriflame's biggest stars, the company proclaimed her its sixth best consultant in the world.

"I decided to resign from my job when my husband had to go and work in Kalimantan. So I had to choose between going out to work [in Jakarta] and leaving my children or resigning from my job," Vonita says in a YouTube video where she talks about how Oriflame changed her life.

For aspiring earners like Rachel, Vonita's videos are amazing. They depict a life of ease and luxury: getting a foot massage[5] at a fancy salon while working on her laptop, receiving a free car[6] from Oriflame as a reward for her sales portfolio, taking free trips to the Leaning Tower of Pisa or the River Thames on the company's dime.

To achieve this, Vonita must be either selling huge amounts of makeup every month or recruiting large numbers of sellers. But something doesn't quite add up.

"Almost all of these schemes tell you that you can make money by just recruiting three or four or five, let's say five [new sellers]. Then you let the five do their five which gives you twenty-five," Robert Fitzpatrick, President of the anti-MLM consumer organisation Pyramid Scheme Alert, told CNBC in 2013.[7] "What they don't show you is that you can only do that thirteen cycles, and you would exceed the population of the earth."

Spending to earn

Remaining an active Oriflame member also comes with a monthly cost. This is where Rachel's dreams hit a wall. Her husband, who was working as a casual labourer for a construction site, kept getting hurt as he was not provided with any safety equipment. Fearful that he would

5 https://www.youtube.com/watch?v=lZUPHMxvfnc

6 https://www.youtube.com/watch?v=a4j-milWxfl

7 https://www.cnbc.com/id/100366687

one day seriously injure himself or be killed falling off a roof, Rachel begged him to quit.

"Without his salary, I can't afford to buy IDR900,000 [worth] of products every month so my account is now inactive," she says. "Vonita was lucky when she started because her husband was working in Kalimantan and she used his salary to pay for the products. She was never stuck."

Rachel isn't the only one who has faced problems. When asked if her friends have been successful selling Oriflame products or recruiting new members, she admits that none of them have, but insists it's because they didn't work hard enough, didn't have the right attitude, or were "just not right for Oriflame". Oriflame's seminars heavily emphasise the need for hard work; Rachel recounts a session she attended where she was told that consultants were "lucky" to have access to the online training course (which they had paid for upon signing up) and that "you should spend all your time in front of your laptop studying until your hair falls out". The implication, it seems, is that failure is the result of shortcomings on the consultants' part, and not a reflection upon the company's business model.

New Naratif visited the Oriflame head office in Medan on a Saturday. It was packed with members and the front lot was a sea of cars and motorbikes. The building houses a "Beauty Room" where members can try products and learn how to use them, a sales counter where they can buy makeup, and several back rooms used for seminars. On the day we visited, there was a free seminar for consultants on giving facials. The cashier counters, where sellers queue to pay for their new products and membership fees, were by far the busiest part of the whole enterprise.

When New Naratif asked to speak to an Oriflame representative, a customer service staff member said that the head of Oriflame Medan was out of town giving a seminar in Surabaya. He agreed to call and fix up an appointment in the next few days, only to send a text message saying that he would need to reschedule. Follow up calls, over several days, to try and confirm a meeting went unanswered.

Multi-level marketing: a good opportunity?

For women in developing countries with limited opportunities, multi-level marketing schemes like Oriflame's seem like a path to success and a better life; a way to achieve financial well-being while also fulfilling responsibilities at home. Endorsements from success stories like Vonita add to the allure. Efforts to contact and interview Vonita went unanswered even while she continued to be active uploading Oriflame promotional videos on to her Facebook page.

Serious doubts remain over whether such schemes really empower and benefit their participants. Large amounts of money—sometimes beyond the means of the women who sign up—are required up front, with meagre financial return. Based on the figures put forward by Rachel, Oriflame sellers only earn a small profit on their sales even if they move huge quantities of product every month, and constant recruitment is simply not feasible as a sustainable way of raising one's salary.

In fact, studies suggest that almost no one makes any money out of a multi-level marketing scheme; a scathing report published on the US Federal Trade Commission's website stated: "Failure and loss rates for MLMs are not comparable with legitimate small businesses, which have been found to be profitable for 39% over the lifetime of the business; whereas less than 1% of MLM participants profit. MLM makes even gambling look like a safe bet in comparison."[8] The companies themselves might do well, though; in 2016 Oriflame's gross profit totalled EUR882.9 million, or almost USD1.1 billion.

Rachel can no longer afford the IDR900,000 a month required to be an active member of Oriflame. She's been working on another plan: building a new business selling clothes online. It's work that she enjoys, and she says it's going well. But she's still not ready to give up on Oriflame's promise.

"I'm just trying to make my clothing business successful so I can save as much money as possible," she says. "Then I can use the money to go back to Oriflame."

---

8 https://www.ftc.gov/news-events/blogs/business-blog/2018/01/ftc-staff-answers-questions-about-mlms

INDONESIA'S "SMALL FRY" DRUG DEALERS
TEGUH HARAHAP, AISYAH LLEWELLYN | 28 JUN 2018

For those in Indonesia with few employment options and limited capital, selling drugs can be a lucrative and easy way to earn extra money—thanks to surprising support from the local community.

It was two o'clock in the morning and Marjo[1], his wife and their 4-year-old son were fast asleep at home when someone started banging on the front door. Marjo knew without even getting out of bed that it would be one of his "patients"—the term he uses for clients who come to his house to buy drugs.

Marjo is 37 years old and has worked as a chicken seller in Simpang Limun Market in Medan, North Sumatra, for three years—or at least that's what most of his neighbours think he does for a living.

The money he gets from selling chickens doesn't all go into his own pocket—he has to share some of the proceeds with the wholesaler who provides him the birds in the first place—so he's started supplementing his income by dealing drugs. He's been selling illicit substances, mainly cannabis and crystal meth, out of his home for almost a year.

"Who aspires to be a drug dealer?" asks Marjo, looking weary, "But if I just rely on my wages from selling chickens then how can I provide for my family?"

Indonesia's drug problem
Indonesia is a country with a well-known drug problem. Speaking to the media in 2017, Sulistiandriatmoko, the chief representative of the National Anti-Narcotics Agency who only goes by one name, said that there were around six million drug users in Indonesia[2].

---

1 Names have been changed at interviewees' request.

2 https://www.scmp.com/lifestyle/article/2120688/why-indonesias-drugs-problem-getting-worse-despite-shoot-sight-orders-and

The island of Sumatra—and North Sumatra in particular—is famous in Indonesia for its drug culture. According to a 2016 report[3] by the Transnational Institute, North Sumatra, and particularly Aceh, has a long history of cannabis use, which only started to be restricted under the Dutch in the 1920s. Despite state efforts to outlaw it, cannabis is now "the most widely used illicit substance in Indonesia, with approximately two million users in 2014." Other drugs of choice across the archipelago include crystal meth, ecstasy and heroin.

A lack of opportunities

It wasn't supposed to work out this way for Marjo. He studied law at a private university in Medan and dreamt of being a lawyer, but his parents lost the ability to pay for his education. He tried to hold on as long as he could and finish his studies, working part-time in order to pay his university fees.

When asked what his side job was, he just smiles. Then he explains that he sold marijuana on campus—many of the "patients" he has now were students who bought his drugs back in the day. According to Marjo, selling drugs on campus was much safer than selling them outside.

"When I was at university, selling drugs was easy—I never had to worry about getting caught by the police because there was an unwritten rule that said that they weren't allowed on campus. If they tried to come onto the campus grounds and arrest anybody then the students would hurl rocks and chairs at them," Marjo says, laughing at the memory. But it ultimately still wasn't enough to put him through school.

Marjo's wife, Warni*, knows about his "side job". She was against the idea in the early days, when he started selling drugs, and the two argued often. She's since come round and learnt to accept her husband's choice, especially when their financial worries mounted and they needed to provide for their child.

Early in their marriage, Warni sold sold traditional Indonesian breakfast dishes like *lontong* and *nasih gurih*, and they didn't have any serious financial issues. They still lived in Marjo's parents' home—thus saving on rent—and Marjo's mother took care of their son when Warni went to work. But things took a turn for the worst, for reasons that Marjo refuses to explain, and the small family moved out.

---

3 https://www.tni.org/en/publication/cannabis-in-indonesia

Having lost both free accommodation and childcare, the family's options became more limited. It didn't help that things were tense with Warni's side of the family as well; her parents had not approved of their daughter's choice of husband.

Small fry drug dealers

In Indonesia, low-level drug dealers like Marjo are known as *kelas teri*—which translated to something like "small fry"—as they only sell marijuana and crystal meth in small quantities. He refers to them as "budget packages".

The money that Marjo gets from selling drugs is relatively modest; there are times, depending on the higher-level dealers that he has to buy from, when he doesn't make a profit at all.

"If it's marijuana then I buy five ounces at a time at about IDR150,000 (USD10.65) per ounce. An ounce is enough for fifteen packets and I sell one packet for IDR20,000 (USD1.42) which can be made into two or three joints depending on the user," he explains.

"If it's 'white' [crystal meth] then I take one sack [five grams] from another dealer. The dealer sells it to me for IDR800,000 per gram (USD58)," he continues. "I mostly sell it in small packets that cost IDR150,000 (USD10.56) and quarter gram packages for IDR250,000 (USD17.50)." From five grams of crystal meth he's able to earn up to IDR500,000 (USD35) gross profit.

Marjo says that some people know about his side profession, but they don't give him any trouble or report him to the police. On one occasion two women came to his house to find out if it was really true that Marjo dealt drugs. He told them the truth.

When asked why they didn't report him to the police, Marjo gives a surprising answer: "My wife and I confided in them about the struggles we've experienced in our family. When my wife started to pour out her heart, she began to cry, and the women also cried when they heard our story, so they tried to help us by keeping quiet."

This silence, however, came with certain conditions: "I promised I wouldn't sell drugs to anyone in the area or who was still at school."

According to the United Nations Office on Drugs and Crime (UNODC), Indonesia's drug problem[4] has changed over the years:

---

4 http://www.unodc.org/indonesia/en/issues/counter-transnational-organized-crime-and-illicit-trafficking.html

"While cannabis continues to be the most prevalently used drug, the use of amphetamine type stimulants (ATS) is growing rapidly. There has been a five-fold increase in undefined ATS production facilities busted over the last four years and a three-fold increase in methamphetamine related arrests in 2009 compared to 2006".

While only a few years ago crystal meth was mostly imported from Europe, or from other countries within Asia, the rising demand has meant that "the domestic manufacture of ATS has increased to meet the growing demand for crystalline methamphetamine and ecstasy (MDMA)".

With the rise of locally produced crystal meth, and cannabis grown across North Sumatra, small fry drug dealers like Marjo have sprung up to fulfil demand. For many people struggling to make ends meet—such as those with low education levels, childcare issues and limited capital—selling drugs looks like a lucrative and easy option. As Marjo's experience shows, such low-level dealing also comes with relatively little risk as local communities are willing to cover for them. It may sound strange, but an empathetic society has allowed small fry drug dealers to flourish across the archipelago.

A culture of empathy

Irna Minauli, a psychologist from Medan, explains the social and psychological aspect of small fry drug dealers within local communities: "Indonesia, and especially North Sumatra, is a place that has a strong sense of collectivity. This collective culture also makes for deeper feelings of solidarity. The desire to help each other is part of daily life here. This means that people are more empathetic about what happens to other members of society."

Despite his illegal side hustle, Marjo says he's known in his area for being friendly, and enjoys participating in communal activities and events near his home. "Warni also often helps cook the food for ceremonies or parties with the other women in the neighbourhood," he says proudly.

There are other examples of local populations protecting the small fry drug dealers in their midst. On the 1 May 2018, a police officer in Ogan Komering Hulu Timur in South Sumatra was conducting an operation to catch a drug dealer known for dealing crystal meth. When he tried to make the arrest, the dealer started screaming and pleading for help from his family and neighbours. They sprang to his aid.

"The neighbours tried to detain the officer by putting plastic barrels and trees along the road and throwing rocks at his car," Erlin Tangjaya, head of police of Ogan Komering Hulu Timur, Erlin Tangjaya, told[5] local media.

So strong is the support for local small fry drug dealers—who are perceived as individuals doing all they can to get by rather than as criminals—that when conducting drug eradication programmes and arrests, the police often keep the operations under wraps so that even members of the teams involved don't know where and who the target is.

"If we announce it, the criminals will be able to escape ahead of the operation, and we also map out the target area and know all the entrances and exits that the targets may use to try and hide," said the director of the police narcotics division in Jakarta, Kombes Eko Daniyanto, in a statement[6] *(link in Bahasa Indonesia)* to the media in 2016.

"Maybe in the future I will quit"

When asked what he makes on average from selling drugs in a single month, Marjo chuckles, stands up and walks to the cupboard in his living room. "This is the profit," he says, showing off five mobile phones. "It's been three weeks and the owners still haven't come back to collect them; it's like I'm a pawnshop to some people. Someone told me that he would leave the phone as a guarantee and come back and pay me for his drugs in two days at the most, but he wasn't being real. Two of these phones left by customers don't even work."

Marjo says some customers give him their phones as a guarantee when they want to buy crystal meth on credit. He doesn't have any strong feelings about the drug abusers who come to him and doesn't think about how he is helping feed their addictions. It's just a way to make money. He says he has to be "clever" when dealing with "patients" as not all of them are the desirable clients. "Sometimes, if people want to get credit by leaving me their phone, yeah… I have to be clever about it, some I give credit to and others I don't. If all of them didn't pay me upfront then how would I survive?"

5 https://kabarokutimur.com/2018/05/01/saat-ditangkap-polisi-bandar-narkoba-lakukan-hal-ini/

6 http://mediaindonesia.com/read/detail/25869-bnn-curigai-bandar-narkoba-hasut-masyarakat

Selling chickens, cannabis and crystal meth was not the plan Marjo had for his life. He doesn't know how much longer he'll continue to be a small fry drug dealer. It all depends on his reason for selling drugs in the first place: his family.

"Maybe in the future I will quit selling drugs," he says. "But when my son has stopped drinking milk and doesn't need to wear nappies anymore".

DYING YOUNGER IN KELANTAN AND TERENGGANU

AIDILA RAZAK | 30 AUG 2018

The discussion of inequality in Malaysia usually proceeds on racial/ethnic lines, but geography, history, class, and policies play a massive role in determining the opportunities available to a young man at birth.

By the time the British transferred power to a local elite in 1957, nearly two centuries of colonial exploitation had left her in a sorry state. Unsurprisingly, the newly-independent Malaysia[1] of the 1960s had a life expectancy that far trailed her former colonial master Great Britain. A baby born in Malaysia in 1960 would be expected to live 59.48 years, according to World Bank data[2]. In contrast, the UK's life expectancy the same year was 71.13 years.

Malaysia's development in the ensuing decades, however, has closed the gap. Today, a baby born amid the gleaming skyscrapers of Malaysia is expected to live 72.7 years - 22% more than two generations before, according to the latest data from the Department of Statistics Malaysia (DOSM)[3]. In the UK the life expectancy for a baby boy at birth is 79.5 years.[4] But this success story is far from uniform: people living in some

---

1 Malaysia was formed in 1963 by a merger of the Federation of Malaya with the British colonial territories of Singapore, North Borneo (renamed Sabah), and Sarawak. Singapore left Malaysia in 1965.

2 https://data.worldbank.org/indicator/SP.DYN.LE00.IN?end=2016&locations=MY&start =1960&view=chart

3 Department of Statistics Malaysia: https://www.dosm.gov.my/v1/index.php?r=column/ pdfPrev&id=dkdvKzZ0K1NiemEwNlJteDBSUGorQT09, accessed 18 July 2018

4 UK Office of National statistics: https://www.ons.gov.uk/peoplepopulationandcommunity/ birthsdeathsandmarriages/lifeexpectancies/bulletins/lifeexpectancyatbirthandatage65b ylocalareasinenglandandwales/2015-11-04#national-life-expectancy-at-birth, accessed 13 June 2018.

parts of Malaysia live far longer than their fellow citizens in other parts of the country.

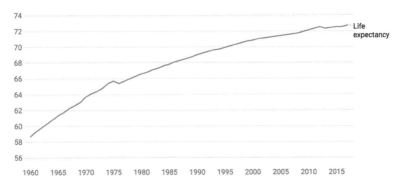

Figure 1: Life Expectancy in Malaysia. (Source: Department of Statistics Malaysia and the World Bank)

According to 2017 DOSM figures, males in the northeastern eastern state Terengganu are expected to only live up to 68.8 while those in neighbouring Kelantan have a life expectancy of 69.2. This is an average 8% lower than national figures—a disparity which may not immediately strike one as remarkable. But to look at it another way, the life expectancy for Terengganu males today matches the national figure in 1986. In other words, life expectancy for males in the east coast states are lagging an entire generation behind.

Uneven development is not new, of course. During the colonial period, Malaya's development was very unequal. The states on the west side of the Malayan peninsula (including Kedah, Perak, Selangor, Negri Sembilan, and Johor, along with the Straits Settlements of Penang and Malacca), which contained the vast majority of ports, tin mines, and rubber plantations, had better infrastructure, better facilities, and greater development. By contrast, the states on the east side (Kelantan and Terengganu) were far less developed. By 1909, one could travel via the West Coast railway from Johor Bahru to Penang, uninterrupted. The first stretch of the East Coast line from Gemas to Tumpat did not open till 1910, and the railway has, to this day, never reached Terengganu. Likewise, Federal Route 1 and its successor North-South Highway run through Western states.

But what's surprising about this unequal lifespan is that it doesn't come from the country's colonial legacy. It was created in independent Malaysia, long after the colonial period was over. In the early 1990s, life expectancy for males on the east coast states was comparable to the national figure at about 69 years. In 1991, life expectancy in Kelantan and Terengganu were 69 and 69.3 respectively, while the corresponding national figure was 69.2.

But while other states progressed, these two east coast states remained in the 60s range, even falling throughout the 1990s before recovering in the early 2000s. A look at life expectancy overall (see graph 2) shows a massive divergence between the national level and the states of Kelantan and Terengganu starting from the early 1990s.

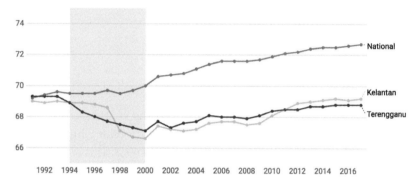

Figure 2: Life Expectancy for Males in Kelantan & Terengganu. Life expectancy for males in these two states were comparable to national levels in the 1980s. They dipped in the 1990s and never recovered. (Source: Department of Statistics Malaysia)

Most curiously, this phenomenon only afflicts men in Kelantan and Terengganu. When it comes to life expectancy, women in the two states march almost in lockstep with their national sisters.

Perhaps the strangest thing: we don't know why.

Diet: The orthodox explanation

Diet has long been blamed for poor health among east coast residents. The cuisine of the east coast, stereotypically, has a higher sugar content compared with the rest of Malaysia.

The Malaysian Diabetes Association's Kelantan branch secretary Ab Aziz Al-Safi Ismail once told *Utusan Malaysia* that the local diet causes high rates of the disease in the state, with 95.3% of loss of limbs there attributed to diabetes.

"The answer to why Kelantan has a high rate of diabetics is very easy: because they love sweet foods, and this has been going on for generations," he said.[5]

To illustrate his point, he said, the Kelantanese are the only ones who add sugar when they eat the flatbread breakfast staple of roti canai and with curry.

But the numbers don't match.

According to the National Health and Morbidity Survey 2015 (see graph 3), the east coast states have middling prevalence of diabetes and obesity.

A high-sugar diet may affect life in Kelantan and Terengganu, but it is not an explaining factor for lower life expectancy.

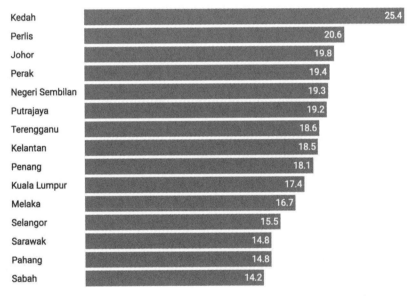

Figure 3: Prevalence of Diabetes by State (%). The high sugar content in Kelantan cuisine is perceived to be the cause for the residents' poor health, but the state does not have the highest diabetes prevalence in Malaysia. (Source: The National Health and Morbidity Survey)

---

5 Utusan Malaysia, "Ramai hidap kencing manis di Kelantan", 8 February 2006, http://ww1. utusan.com.my/utusan/info.asp?y=2006&dt=0208&pub=Utusan_Malaysia&sec=Dalam_ Negeri&pg=dn_08.htm, accessed 18 July 2018

Income: A Class Explanation

One measure frequently used to understand divergence in life expectancy is income, where household income and life expectancy are compared to look for possible correlation. Plotting this for Malaysian states, however, does not show a clear picture.

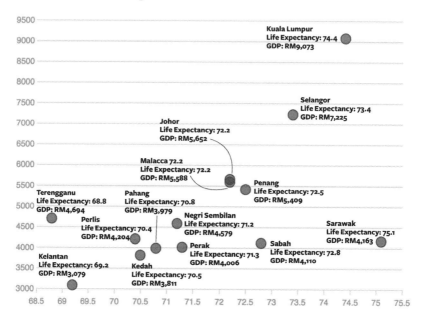

Figure 4: Life Expectancy vs. Median Income by State (2017). (Source: Department of Statistics Malaysia)

Kelantan, which has the second lowest life expectancy, has the lowest median household income. However, Terengganu, which performs the worst in life expectancy, has a mid-range median income. This means at RM4,694 a month, Terengganu's median household income surpasses states with better life expectancy.

Here's what Kelantan and Terengganu have in common—they have the highest concentration of poor households in Peninsular Malaysia, according to two separate academic studies which used different measures.[6]

A 2016 study[7] mapping concentration of poor households in the peninsular found the "prominent poverty hot spots" to be Northern Kelantan and Northern and Middle Terengganu. The researchers from Universiti Teknologi Malaysia, University of South Florida, and University for Development Studies, Ghana, looked at districts in all states and measured the number of households who earn below the poverty line. They found that the northern parts of Kelantan and Terengganu have the highest concentration of "extreme poverty" where household earn RM520 or less a month.

"The heads of poor households in these rural areas are simply not making enough money," they said.

So is poverty killing east coast men? Such a suggestion may seem jarring in a country like Malaysia with a robust welfare system and where universal access to healthcare is guaranteed. All Malaysians can access walk-in GP services for as little as RM1 (18p), and these services act as referral points for more specialised care in public hospitals at almost 100% subsidy.

But access does not only mean low financial barriers.

Universiti Malaya (UM) academic Dr Noran Hairi is a co-author of a study published last year[8], which found that poorer Malaysians are dying younger. And like the 2016 mapping study, the UM researchers found most of those dying younger were concentrated in Terengganu and Kelantan.

---

6 Jeevitha Mariappun, Noran N. Hairi, and Chiu-Wan Ng. "Are the Poor Dying Younger in Malaysia? An Examination of the Socioeconomic Gradient in Mortality." Ed. Andrew R. Dalby. *PLoS ONE* 11.6 (2016): e0158685. *PMC*. Web. 18 July 2018; M. Rafee Majid, Abdul Razak Jaffar, Noordini Che Man, Mehdrad Vaziri and Mohamed

Sulemana, *Mapping Poverty Hot Spots in Peninsular Malaysia using Spatial Autocorrelation Analysis,* Universiti Teknologi Malaysia, Johor Bahru, Malaysia, 12-14 August 2015, Accessible online: http://eprints.utm.my/id/eprint/61717/2/MohammadRafeeMajid2015_ MappingPovertyHotSpotsinPeninsularMalaysia.pdf, accessed 18 July 2018.

7 Ibid.

8 Jeevitha Mariappun, Noran N. Hairi, and Chiu-Wan Ng

Instead of measuring income, Dr Noran and her team used a deprivation index which measured things like a household's type of dwelling, whether they had access to infrastructure like water and electricity, availability of transport and even if they own a television set.

Deprived districts bear higher burden of premature mortality

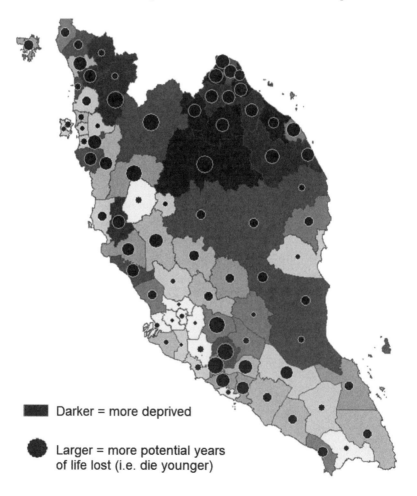

Darker = more deprived

Larger = more potential years of life lost (i.e. die younger)

Figure 5

The index was then compared to infant, child and adult mortality rates in Peninsular Malaysia. What they found was people in regions with higher concentration of deprived districts were dying younger.

Dr Noran said the deprivation index helped capture determinants which are beyond the residents' control—like infrastructure and government policy.

"What we are looking at are issues. A simple example is the Titanic. When we map out the death rates (from the sinking of The Titanic), we see that it follows a social status.

"Not as many of the 'haves' die as the 'have-nots'. We try to explain why there are more survivors from a certain social class. Firstly because there were not enough lifeboats so women and children were prioritised but even then there were more from higher classes who survived.

"So we look at the situation of the ship. The passengers in the first and second class cabins had easier access to the lifeboats. So it is mainly about the policies and conditions, and not what the individual could have done," she said.

In 21st century Malaysia, the UM researchers found that higher mortality rates in poorer districts reflected an environment where there were less opportunities for better quality of life.

They observed that Malaysia's development has been driven by industrialisation, which was concentrated on the peninsular west coast.

In 1960, agriculture made up 37% of the economy and produced 66.2% of jobs. In 2015, it made up only 7% of the economy and 12.7% of jobs.

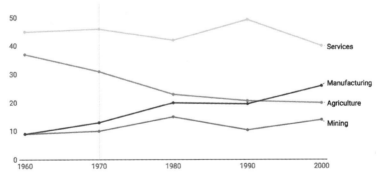

Figure 6: Share of GDP by Sector (%): The role of agriculture in the Malaysian economy continues to shrink. (Source: Jomo (1990) and Bank Negara Malaysia Annual Reports)

East coast states, like Kelantan and Terengganu, relied heavily on agriculture and fisheries and the national shift away from this has left an impact on health outcomes there.

"All districts regardless of average wealth of its population have groups of people who are disadvantaged and therefore susceptible to poorer health outcomes. However, if the district itself is wealthy, it will have better infrastructure, healthcare and social services which are able to alleviate the burden of disease across its population," they said.

Dr Noran said Malaysia's public healthcare is "among the best in the world" with the vast majority living within 5km of a health clinic.

	Public clinic	Public hospital	Private clinic	Private hospital
Q1	5.7	23.6	14.2	172.3
Q2	4.7	17.7	7.9	108.3
Q3	4.5	14.9	5.8	79.7
Q4	4	12.8	4.6	56.2
Q5	3.7	10.9	2.8	41.3

Figure 7: Distance (km) to Medical Facility by Income Quintile. Those in the lowest income quintile (Q1) live furthest from medical facilities. (Source: Rozita Halina Hussein (2000))

But the researchers found respondents in the deprived districts were more inclined to use alternative healing methods, leaving medical treatment to a later stage of illness, thus impacting treatment and mortality outcomes.

A recent study by Raja Perempuan Zainab II Hospital in Kelantan[9] found that more than half of cancer patients in the states trust alternative treatments including visiting bomoh (shamans). 54% cited fear as a factor behind not consulting doctors. To mitigate this, the hospital holds awareness roadshows, which include bringing diagnostic and prevention services like mammograms into communities.

But fear of modern medicine is far too simplistic an explanation, and plays into negative stereotypes of rural and poor households wreathed in ignorance and superstition. Access is a far more predictive, and measurable, explanatory factor.

9The New Straits Times, "Worrying: Cancer patients trust bomoh more," 15 March 2018, https://www.nst.com.my/news/exclusive/2018/03/345302/worrying-cancer-patients-trust-bomoh-more

By recording a household's access to transportation, Dr Noran and her colleagues found that living 5km away to a public GP clinic does not mean much if a household is located in districts with poor roads and public transportation.

"It may cost a day's income to (go to a clinic)," she said. The local healer is thus a more convenient option.

GP clinics also do not have the capacity for advanced diagnostics, referring patients to public hospitals even further away—and correspondingly, more expensive to get to and requiring time off from work.

This matched findings of a separate study[10] which found that Malaysian households with the lowest income live furthest from health facilities.

The wealthiest respondents lived an average 10.6 km from a public hospital while the distance was more than double at an average 23.6 km for the poorest respondents.

Correspondingly, those who do not seek care in hospitals tended to concentrate in Kelantan (36.2%) and Terengganu (36.5%).

Even if a patient makes it to a public hospital on the east coast, the queue to see a specialist is likely to stretch further than those on the more affluent west coast states, a report by the World Health Organisation shows[11].

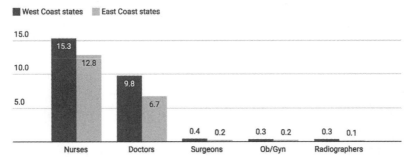

Figure 8: Medics per 10,000 Population (2010). There are fewer medical professionals on the east coast states compared to the other states in the peninsular. (Source: World Health Organisation)

10 Khoo Boo Teik ed. Policy Regimes and the Political Economy of Poverty Reduction in Malaysia, Palgrave McMillan, 2012.

11 World Health Organization: http://www.moh.gov.my/penerbitan/Laporan/WPR%20 Country%20Profile.pdf, accessed 18 July 2018

(WHO defines west coast states as Johor, Negeri Sembilan, Melaka, Selangor, Perak, Penang, Kedah, Perlis and the federal territories of Kuala Lumpur and Putrajaya, while east coast states are Pahang, Kelantan and Terengganu. However, it should be noted for the purpose of our analysis that Pahang's income levels are much higher than Kelantan and Terengganu. At RM32,244, its GDP per capita in 2016 places it at the top half of Malaysian states in terms of income. Terengganu is 10th (RM27,268) while Kelantan is last (RM12,812). This means private healthcare is more accessible to Pahang residents, as is travel to other states for medical purposes.)

Using ministry data, the 2013 WHO report shows there are fewer doctors and nurses in the east coast region, compared to the more affluent west coast region. This trend is consistent for other types of medical professionals, compared to the population.

The WHO said regional discrepancy is most marked when it comes to medical specialists in Malaysia, in both public and private service. West coast states had twice as many specialists compared to east coast states, in both public and private service.

Similar trends persists when it comes to hospital beds and the number of public health clinics for GP services in the east coast states.

Dr Halim Salleh, who retired from as associate professor at the medical faculty at University Sains Malaysia in Kelantan in 2014, said the lower numbers of health professionals in the east coast states reflects higher levels of privatisation of healthcare in the country.

In a paper published as part of United Nations journal, he noted that the number of doctors in public service outnumbered those in the private sector in 1970s. The balance tipped in the 1980s, in line with rapid neoliberal industrialisation.

He said while all medical graduates in Malaysia undergo a three-year mandatory public service, an "obviously large number" leave the service once they attain senior positions.

"To some extent, the trend of doctors' leaving government service is to be expected: by one estimate for early 2000s, doctors in the government services were earning only about 10% of the salaries enjoyed by their private sector counterparts," he said.

The number of specialists in the east coast states would not differ so markedly if there were opportunities for private sector growth there. However, the states' median income indicates that private healthcare is beyond the reach of most Terengganu and Kelantan residents, making it a less viable market.

Contacted recently, he is reluctant to say if this is the reason for lower life expectancy in the two states.

He said while the link between poverty and health outcomes has been long established through various academic research, a deeper study taking into account the social, economical and political factors is needed to truly establish why men on the east coast states of Kelantan and Terengganu die younger than their cousins in the other parts of Peninsular Malaysia.

The Mysterious Gender Gap

Further study is also needed to understand why life expectancy for females in Kelantan and Terengganu far surpass the males.

Although still at the bottom of the table, life expectancy for females in Kelantan (75.2 years) and Terengganu (74.6 years). This is comparable to national figures for females in 2004 (75.5 years)—a lag less severe than their male counterparts. (Recall that life expectancy for males in Terengganu in 2017 is on par with national figures from 1986.)

So why are women in Kelantan and Terengganu living much longer than the men that despite facing the same conditions of income, healthcare and infrastructure? One theory might be childbirth. Kelantan and Terengganu have the second and third highest crude birth rate in the country, behind Putrajaya.

As crude birth rate is the rate of birth by population, the federal territory Putrajaya ranks high due to its miniscule population of 90,000 people. Kelantan and Terengganu have 1.718 million and 1.125 million people respectively.

High birth rates and the fact that 99% of Malaysian births are attended by a skilled health professional indicates that women in these states are more likely to access healthcare, regardless of their circumstances. That postpartum care in rural areas includes up to eight home visits also indicates that a greater proportion of women access healthcare.

Politics: Not An Explanation

Politics is an important factor when it comes to Kelantan and Terengganu. Kelantan has been governed by Islamist party PAS since 1990, while Terengganu was under PAS rule for two terms, in the 1970s and the early 2000s, and once again following the 2018 general election.

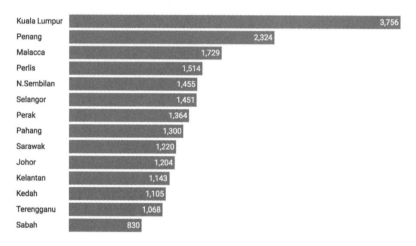

Figure 9: Healthcare Spending per capita (1997-2015). Figures are in MYR. (Source: Malaysia National Health Accounts)

Both are oil producing states but oil royalties from the federal government—or the lack of it—has been used as evidence of marginalisation along political lines.

When the PAS wrested power from BN in Terengganu in 1999, the 5% oil royalty paid to the state was replaced with *wang ehsan*, a discretionary contribution to the state channeled through federal agencies and not directly to state coffers.[12] This was reversed on request of the state government took over Terengganu in 2004.

Kelantan, however, is still embroiled in a long court battle over the matter. It says the federal government wrongfully denied the state the royalties, using technicalities over the distance of the oil wells and the Kelantan coast.

---

12 Utusan Malaysia "Terengganu minta Kerajaan Pusat kembalikan royalti minyak", 21 April 2008, http://ww1.utusan.com.my/utusan/info.asp?y=2008&dt=0421&pub=Utusan_Malaysia&sec=Muka_Hadapan&pg=mh_02.htm

One way to check if a state's population have indeed been punished for voting against the ruling coalition is to look at healthcare spending per capita. According to the Malaysian Federal Constitution, all spending on public health comes from the federal coffers. As such, healthcare expenditure per capita figures could show if there has been elements of deprivation on political lines. A look at the latest figures released by the Department of Statistics, however, suggests otherwise.

While Terengganu and Kelantan have among the lowest healthcare spending per capita, the reason is unlikely as simply as mere political calculation. Selangor and Penang—both states held by the then-opposition coalition from 2008 until the recent election—are in the top half in the list of healthcare spending per capita. Conversely, the BN's stronghold states Johor and Sabah are among the bottom four.

We Need More Data

But as Dr Noran and her team established, multiple factors determine deprivation. In this case, it could include spending on industrial infrastructure, public transportation and education, for example. A more robust measure would take into account total federal spending for each state.

Partisan politics means that federal ministers have often times touted how much the federal government has spent on "opposition states" like Kelantan, but getting into the details is a little more complicated.

Public policy researcher Tricia Yeoh said state allocations are difficult to quantify as the Treasury's budget documents only provides spending per ministry, and ministries do not conventionally provide tabulations of its spending per state.

Of course, it would have been possible for the office in charge to extract the values of grants allocated to each state to facilitate detailed analysis, she wrote in her column in the magazine Penang Monthly[13], but with the right to information not enshrined in Malaysia, public access to such data remains a challenge.

Such figures, however, are more readily available in healthcare, where measures are frequently reported to international bodies like the WHO and the United Nations.

---

13 Penang Monthly, "What's in the budget for state governments?" November 2011, http://penangmonthly.com/article.aspx?pageid=7321&name=whats_in_the_budget_for_state_governments, Accessed July 18, 2018.

These statistics have helped academics like Dr Noran to continue their research into health and socioeconomic determinants in Malaysia as the nation progresses into a developed nation.

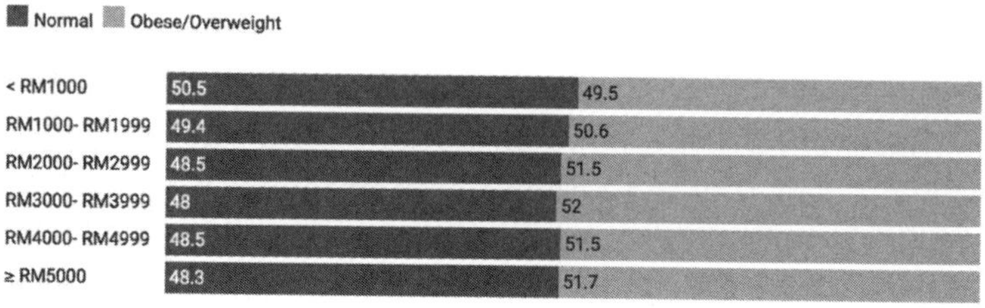

Figure 10: Obesity/Overweight Prevalence by Income 2015 (%). Prevalence of obesity among the lower income groups almost paces the higher income groups. This means lifestyle illnesses are affecting the lower-income to a higher degree. (Source: National Health and Morbidity Survey)

Following their study on deprivation and life expectancy, the team looked at obesity rates across the nation over the years. This time, the team matched it to income levels.

They found that while obesity rates are still relatively higher among the rich, there is evidence of a shift towards higher concentrations among the lower income.

In fact, the latest National Health and Morbidity Survey shows that prevalence of obesity among the lower income groups almost paces the higher income groups. This means that lifestyle illnesses are now affecting the lower-income to a higher degree, Dr Noran said.

Coupled with challenges of healthcare provision in the lower income east coast states, and without direct intervention to boost mortality figures in these states, the story of life expectancy disparity in Malaysia may remain fairly grim.

Conclusion

Our analysis shows that while ethnicity or even diet are frequently blamed for poor quality of life indicators in states like Kelantan and Terengganu, access to healthcare is a better predictor of life expectancy. Overall, it appears federal policies have lead to the underdevelopment of these states, with correspondingly adverse health outcomes.

A change in federal government may bring some positive changes for Kelantan and Terengganu. Weeks following the election, the PAS-led state governments announced that the new Pakatan Harapan government will channel oil royalties directly to the state government's coffers—a move which could help the state roll out measures to attract investments for economic development.

Having lost almost every seat it contested in Kelantan and Terengganu, Pakatan Harapan has also vowed to boost its showings in these states in the next general election. This could mean channeling federal funds into these states to boost development and support the livelihoods of its residents, convincing voters there it could better govern than PAS.

The focus to court voters through better economic outcomes could be the turning point for life expectancy in Kelantan and Terengganu. But whether it will retain momentum to catch up with the nation would require long-term federal investment and commitment beyond the next general election.

DEVELOPMENT AND URBANISATION

CAMBODIA'S SHOWCASE ISLAND

BEN PAVIOUR, BEN SOKHEAN | 08 JAN 2018

Wealth, hope and heartbreak take shape on Phnom Penh's Diamond Island, a cautionary tale for the city and the country.

On Sunday evenings in Phnom Penh, all roads lead to Diamond Island. By sundown, traffic along the routes to Koh Pich, as it's known in Khmer, is gridlocked with USD70,000 Range Rovers and USD150 Daelim motorbikes. The drive to the island passes some of modern Cambodia's dazzling new temples. One entrance to the 100-hectare island borders NagaWorld, a casino with video billboards whose glare can be seen from the stilt houses and dirt roads on the other side of the Mekong River. Another falls under the shadow of The Bridge, a newly completed 45-storey, USD300 million luxury condominium project that has the distinction of being the second-tallest building in the city. A third sits near Aeon Mall, where teenagers guide elderly grandparents up their first escalator.

Koh Pich inspires its own kind of awe. In architecture, atmosphere, and infrastructure, it seems to take inspiration from everywhere but Cambodia. The island features a towering replica of Paris' Arc de Triomphe, a neoclassical City Hall fronted by dolphin statues, a carnival with bumper cars and a haunted house, streets named after Ivy League universities, a bar that serves cocktails out of baby bottles and syringes, and a convention centre where Prime Minister Hun Sen regularly uses university graduation ceremonies to dress down his critics.

The island's singularity has not been lost on Phnom Penh's roughly two million residents, many of whom live in cramped conditions in the city's mushrooming periphery. They come for Diamond Island's neon-hued novelty and rare public spaces: its riverwalk for family strolls, its fat roads for teenage motorbike cruises, its parks for cheap dates of barbeque and beer.

For visitors like 30-year-old Nam Tang, the island is a break from reality. Tang moved to the capital from his rural home in November to study Korean. It has been a rude awakening; the city feels big and dangerous, he's in bed by 10pm to avoid thieves, and pays USD16 a month for a room he shares with nine strangers. He escapes it all by going to Koh Pich to watch shows on his tablet. To him, the island is beautiful, and the contrast between it's luxury condominiums and his rental room are "opposites like sky and earth."

Growing alongside Phnom Penh

Over the last decade, Koh Pich has transformed from a spit of marshy farmland to a towering symbol of Cambodia's lopsided development. When developers first proposed changes to the island in 2004, central Phnom Penh was a low-slung capital known for its crumbling colonial villas and simple Chinese shophouses; some of its side streets hadn't been resealed since the 1960s. The country spent decades recovering from the doomed agrarian experiments of Pol Pot and the ensuing civil war, which continued in bursts until the Khmer Rouge put down arms in 1998. According to the World Bank, 54% percent of the country still lived in poverty as late as 2004.

Over the last ten years, and particularly over the last five, foreign investors have pumped billions of dollars into Cambodia's construction, garment, and tourism industries, driving a consistent 7% annual growth in gross domestic product. Real estate investors hungry for a new frontier—or a place to park ill-gotten cash—were pulled towards Phnom Penh. The city went from a few hundred condominium units in 2009 to 4,794 units by the end of June 2017, according to real estate firm Knight Frank, encouraged by a 2010 law that allowed foreigners to own property above the ground floor. The offerings have proven particularly attractive to Chinese buyers priced out of more expensive foreign cities, with most local sales offices marketing their offerings in Mandarin as well as Khmer and English. To Prime Minister Hun Sen, who has led Cambodia since 1985, the boom is proof of his oft-repeated pledge to turn "battlefields into marketplaces."[1]

The investment is especially dramatic on Diamond Island. The island's developer, Overseas Cambodia Investment Corporation (OCIC), hatched plans with the government to develop Koh Pich in 2004, paying off residents with cash, land, rice, and fish sauce, according to the Phnom

---

1 http://pressocm.gov.kh/en/archives/17744

Penh Post[2], and evicting a few who refused to leave. OCIC has since set to work transforming the site into a sprawling collection of luxury housing and retail developments.

Sales of the units on the island are booming. As of mid-November, sales representatives at the 33-storey Casa Meridian said they had only a dozen of its 512 units—priced between USD135,000 and USD285,000—available for sale. At D.I. Riveria, a five-tower project modeled after Singapore's Marina Bay Sands, investors from China, Taiwan and Japan, as well overseas Cambodians, have already snapped up 90% of units, priced up to USD700,000, in the first building set for completion early next year.

For the islands' backers, the project is emblematic of Cambodia's leap toward a more prosperous modernity after decades of war and poverty. "It went from fields to skyscrapers," says Va Kun, a 65 year-old who has overseen OCIC's construction sourcing since 2004, and who has lived on the island since 2008. Relaxing on a bench near the Bassac River with his grandson, Kun says the development has been a boon to neighborhoods adjoining the island, where fires, buyouts, and evictions transformed poor communities into a mall, clubs, and other towers. "Before I saw the areas outside here were slums, and now they are villas."

Kun's vision of progress is blueprinted into Koh Pich, where names like Elite Town and Elite Road make no bones about their target demographic. Cities across the world are grappling with extreme inequality, but there are few places quite like Phnom Penh, where Maserati-driving elite pass noodle vendors surviving on a few dollars a day. Cambodia's per capita gross national income was just USD1,302 in 2016. If Koh Pich's rise suggests a new prosperity, its backstory of evictions, cheap labour and preventable tragedy also hints at the costs of getting there.

For Tang, the island is an unfulfilled promise of future prosperity. "I think it's only proven true for the wealthy," he says. "And as you can see, the poor people come here only as construction workers."

That evening, hundreds of the workers stream from the island to the tin barracks where they live in makeshift dorms. The men and women appear exhausted and are cautious in front of reporters; wages in the industry hover around USD5 to USD7 per day for unskilled labor and most don't want any trouble. But Suos Piseth, a 40 year-old migrant

---

2 http://www.phnompenhpost.com/national/koh-pich-island-stream-greed

who has spent three months constructing one of Koh Pich's towers, interrupts a shy colleague.

"I think it's just a small part of the city," he says. "It doesn't represent the development of our country. I see so many Cambodian people are so poor. And here's a place where rich people come and live."

"I don't want to see many Cambodian workers here," he adds.

The making of Koh Pich

The four water ways that converge and branch out from Phnom Penh have a knack for spitting up and swallowing land mass. Steven Boswell, who authored the local historiography *King Norodom's Head*, places a short-lived 17th century royal capital on a now-submerged island called Koh Slaket near Koh Pich's current location at the mouth of the Bassac River. When Cambodia declared independence from France in 1953, Koh Pich literally wasn't on the map.

Longtime residents remember Koh Pich as little more than a gathering of sand that began accumulating alluvial silt in the 1960s. Farmers and migrant Vietnamese fishermen settled on the island after the fall of the Khmer Rouge regime in 1979. Boswell's Cambodian wife, Ham Dany, said Koh Pich was a no-go for many city residents, who feared what might be lurking in the darkness of the island's tall grasses. According to Boswell, residents reached the city in small canoes.

In 2004, the OCIC sent Hun Sen a proposal to bring massive change to the island. Plans called for infilling the marsh and adding a 600-meter observation tower, university, hospital and high-rise office and residential developments, the *Phnom Penh Post* reported. Later plans added a 555-meter tower that would have topped any in Asia, though this has yet to come to fruition. (Different developers have since announced plans for a 133-storey twin tower project at an adjoining site that will be among the tallest in the world).

The OCIC's origins remain murky. Ministry of Commerce records list Pung Kheav Se, a Sino-Cambodian who also serves as chairman of Canadia Bank and advisor to Hun Sen, as the company's chairman. A leaked 2006 U.S. Embassy cable called Kheav Se a "banking pioneer" and listed him as one of the ten most powerful tycoons in the country, a group whose symbiotic relationship with senior government officials it said "reinforce the culture of impunity."[3]

---

3 https://wikileaks.org/plusd/cables/07PHNOMPENH1034_a.html

The government approved the plans and OCIC and local authorities told the 300 or so families on the island they had to leave. The *Phnom Penh Post* reported that the farmers accepted buyouts at as little as a tenth of the market price and took plots of land on the outskirts of the city; the farmers who talked to the press felt as if they had no other choice. Larger landholders fared better; a few even became rich. In February 2006, military police armed with AK-47s and shotguns stormed the island and kicked out the last three families. The soldiers attempted to capsize the boats of journalists, attorneys, and NGO workers who looked on, according to the Cambodia Daily.[4]

Yeng Virak, former head of the Community Legal Education Center which worked with the farmers at the time, says the remaining families took their case to court and lost. The government and OCIC argued that the farmers were squatters on state land and had no land titles—a common and convenient position for the powerful to take given the Khmer Rouge's destruction of property records during their rule.

"During all of the years of our legal case and advocacy, the court said [the farmers] have no right to claim possession rights for state or public land," Virak says. "But you know later, [the government] ended up giving private ownership rights to the businessmen."

By the standards of Phnom Penh property development, this process was cordial. Housing rights organisation Sahmakum Teang Tnaut (STT) identified 77 eviction sites across the city by 2011, involving many thousands of residents. Though the government and developers often argue that evictions are necessary to promote economic growth, a report released by STT last year[5] found that only a third of the sites have shown any sign of construction, and the vast majority of evictees reported getting little to no compensation. Evictees were sometimes put up in relocation sites upwards of 30 kilometers from the city centre.

"Most of them—99 percent—move back because it's too far," says Sia Phearum, head of the Housing Rights Task Force. "They return to Phnom Penh to [become] a construction worker or moto [taxi] driver."

As central Phnom Penh has gentrified, lower and middle class Cambodians have been pushed farther and farther from the city's core. Unremarkable houses in central neighborhoods like Boeung Keng

4 https://www.cambodiadaily.com/archives/dozens-of-police-evict-3-koh-pich-families-52665/

5 http://teangtnaut.org/wp-content/uploads/2016/12/1PK-Final-Report_V12.1_final-edits_ formatted518907-1.pdf

Kang come with price tags clearing USD3 million—enough to buy a Tribeca loft or a refurbished two-bedroom in Notting Hill. The small but growing middle class have found more reasonably-priced places farther out. Phearum says he paid about USD70,000 for his house 10 kilometers from the city. He was able to afford it because of his relatively well-paying NGO salary, but others are not so fortunate.

"The majority make only USD1,500 per year, so what can they do?" he asks. "Since 1993 until now, the government and the developers just favor the rich or the upper-middle class… I have found one or two or three companies who develop affordable housing. It's just a start."

City Hall spokesman Met Measpheakdey says citizens should alter their expectations rather than blame the government for the housing prices charged by private developers.

"If you have only USD50,000 and you want your family to live somewhere, it's true that you won't be able to find a place in the middle of the city," he says. "You should change your mind and look at the outskirts."

"It's up to their ability [to pay]," he adds. "It's up to the free market."

Tragedy on the bridge

It takes about 45 minutes in light traffic to reach Khat Chhorn's house from Koh Pich. The most direct route, along Veng Sreng Boulevard, passes through a dusty urban oblivion of factories, repair shops, and convenience stores. The area houses many of the city's thousands of garment workers, most of whom live in crowded dorms. On January 3, 2014, the street turned into a fiery battlefield when hundreds of military police armed with AK-47 assault rifles opened fire on protesting workers who had blockaded the street. Five people were killed and dozens more injured in what rights groups called the worst state-sponsored violence since the 1990s.

Chhorn lives several blocks away from a factory, in a room he shares with his daughter, son-in-law, and grandson. The concrete floor of the space is covered in blue tarp and a banner advertising a nearby school. Paint fumes from the motorbike detailing shop on the ground floor occasionally reach the room, but Chhorn doesn't seem to notice.

The family moved into the space shortly after his youngest son, Chhoel Chhat, was killed and two of his other children, injured, in one of the worst tragedies in modern Cambodian history. The accident, which occurred on a bridge to Koh Pich, destroyed the 53 year-old's marriage and robbed him of his peace of mind. Today he won't go near the island.

"I hate Koh Pich so much," he says. "Even if a billionaire gave me tens of thousands of dollars to visit Koh Pich, I would turn him down."

On the morning of November 22, 2010, Chhorn caved to his 12 year-old son's pleas and allowed him to join his brother and sister in downtown Phnom Penh for the Water Festival, a three-day event that revolves around boat racing along the Tonle Sap River. Hundreds of thousands of people go to the festival, and Chhorn was worried about his son's safety in the crowds. "He was too small to go there," Chhorn says.

That afternoon, the siblings set off for a concert on Koh Pich. They were just starting to cross the bridge when a commotion broke out on the other side, sparking panic. Chhat's brother Aun hoisted his sibling onto his shoulders, but the force of the crowd toppled the pair over. Aun lost consciousness. He awoke in pain but dragged himself up to find his brother and sister. Both were badly injured and ambulances, caught up in the chaos of the stampede, were slow to arrive. At the hospital, a doctor told Aun that they were busy with urgent cases. Chhat died in his brother's arms. Chhorn says his daughter Chanthy survived but sustained her own serious injuries.

The stampede claimed 353 lives in all, a tally Hun Sen described as the worst loss of life on any single day since the fall of the Khmer Rouge in 1979. The government and OCIC initially blamed each other for the accident, and Cambodia's opposition party called for an independent investigation. The only investigation conducted by authorities ultimately concluded that the stampede had been sparked by panic that the suspension bridge was about to collapse. Victims were paid compensation—Chhorn received about USD12,000 from various sources—and the case was closed. Few expected more from a government that rarely delved too deep into unexplained deaths.

"No one has been held responsible yet for my son's death," Chhorn says. "I just got some compensation. But the money can't solve my heartache."

Measpheakdey, the City Hall spokesman, says the government had done everything it could to aid healing from the accident, including an annual blessing ceremony held for family members. Since the stampede, authorities have increased security at the Water Festival to prevent accidents, he says.

This increased security was on full display during the 2017 festival, with military police and members of Hun Sen's personal bodyguard unit stationed with Chinese assault rifles at intersections across the city. Their presence came at a tense political moment, with the Supreme Court on the cusp of dissolving the opposition Cambodia National Rescue Party (CNRP). The party nearly unseated Hun Sen in the 2013 elections, and seemed poised to do so in next year's vote. The dissolution, approved by the Supreme Court on November 16, followed a several months-long crackdown that has seen independent media shuttered, politicians jailed, and NGO workers surveilled and harassed. The government sees the crackdown as a small price to pay for peace and economic stability. "To protect the peace for millions of people, if necessary, 100 or 200 must be eliminated," Hun Sen said in June.[6]

Against that backdrop, City Hall now sees the Koh Pich stampede as another example of the anarchic possibilities of large gatherings.

"After going through this accident, we took it as a lesson," Measpheakdey says. "So that's why for any rally in the city… we think about security first."

Hope and alienation

In the 1960s, Phnom Penh's garden thoroughfares and modernist Khmer architecture made it among the most pleasant capitals in the region. Then-Prince Norodom Sihanouk ruled the country with an iron fist but also built some of the country's first public schools, universities, and hospitals. Driven by an expanding middle class, Phnom Penh turned into a cultural hotspot. Architects, bands and filmmakers borrowed and recast Western influences, creating novel genres of music, buildings and art. Set against the savagery that followed, the era is now remembered as a cultural golden age.

Phnom Penh's upward skyline and economic growth have rekindled a guarded sense of a city on the rise. The capital feels young; UN statistics[7] show that almost two-thirds of Cambodians are under the age of 30. A small but visible middle class has emerged, drafting architectural plans in coffee shops lit with hanging bulbs and dancing to Korean pop and Justin Bieber in Wat Botum Park.

For foreigners living in the capital, the youthful energy can be contagious. French filmmaker Davy Chou, whose grandfather was a leading producer during Sihanouk's reign, saw cinematic potential in

---

6 https://www.cambodiadaily.com/news/prepare-coffin-hun-sen-repeats-bloody-power-promise-131626/

7 http://cambodia.unfpa.org/sites/default/files/pub-pdf/Flyer_Cambodia_Youth_Factsheet_final_draft_%28approved%29.pdf

the moment, but it wasn't until he set foot on Koh Pich in 2013 that his film came together.

"Everything I wanted to convey, explore, portray, was somehow here on Koh Pich," he says. The island's concentrated ideas of what modernity should be, its visible social chasms, "the gigantism and kitschism of the place itself" had obvious big screen potential, he says.

Chou's *Diamond Island* debuted last year. It follows Bora, a young Cambodian who moves to Koh Pich as a construction worker only to an encounter his inexplicably wealthy and estranged older brother. As he is presented with new opportunities—a girlfriend, a new job, a shot at going to the US—Bora sifts through the murkiness of young manhood, settling into a mood between hope and alienation.

Phnom Penh has shuttled between those two extremes in the last five years. Optimism in the capital, an opposition stronghold, crescendoed in the aftermath of the 2013 election, when tens of thousands of city dwellers took to the streets calling for Hun Sen to step down. A 2014 political deal between the prime minister and his rivals diffused the movement, and the last few years—and especially last six months—have neutered it entirely. The government now frames the 2013 protests as a failed, US-backed attempt at a color revolution led by the opposition. With the CNRP gone, few outside observers expect a credible national election next year.

State-affiliated TV stations have run footage of war drills in preparation for revolution and war, but there's little sign of anarchy in the streets of the capital. Unlike the previous mass demonstrations, public protest has been limited to a farmer who was arrested for handing out leaflets outside the Supreme Court in November. Hun Sen's bodyguards still laze in hammocks outside his house near Independence Monument, drinking beer and charging their phones. The city feels as calm as it has ever been.

Cham Bunthet, a political analyst who conducts leadership training for young Cambodians, says the youth are showing a maturity and restraint their leaders lacked. "I'm very hopeful for the new generation," he says. "I see them as having a more solution-oriented mentality." At the moment, however, they are defenseless against powerful political elders. "If they pull young people in the wrong direction, it would destroy everybody. Even themselves."

Bunthet sometimes takes his students on river cruises that skirt Koh Pich. He sees the island not as a model for the country's future, but a cautionary tale.

"Koh Pich is just a balloon," he says. "Bring the balloon and tell the world, 'This is Cambodia.' But a small scratch could explode it."

A NEW MODEL FOR HO CHI MINH CITY'S SIDEWALKS

MICHAEL TATARSKI, DAM XUAN VIET | 09 JUL 2018

Amid a resumed clearing campaign, some of Ho Chi Minh City's sidewalk vendors have embraced changes. But questions remain over what might be lost if the city is turned into a "little Singapore".

For ten years, Le Thi Thuy sold *bánh cuốn* (rice noodle rolls) in front of the Saigon Zoo and Botanical Gardens. She and her husband remember it as a busy, but also tense, experience. "Back then, if there was a policeman or urban security officer in sight I would tremble in fear and get ready to run away," she recalls in Vietnamese. As an unregulated street food vendor, law enforcement officers could have made her life difficult, even confiscated her stall.

Ho Chi Minh City, the largest urban centre in Vietnam, is home to an ever-growing array of modern skyscrapers and glitzy hotels—a visual manifestation of the country's growing economy. Amid the glass and steel temples to commerce, however, the city's traditional sidewalk culture remains a vital part of daily life. Street vendors like Thuy are go-to breakfast, lunch and dinner stops for everyone from sanitation workers to suited-up professionals opting to squat on stools while enjoying quick meals.

But this culture has faced increasing pressure from city leaders, especially in District 1, the commercial heart of Ho Chi Minh City. Doan Ngoc Hai, the district's vice-chairman, has been so committed to an aggressive sidewalk clearing campaign that he is sometimes referred to as "Captain Sidewalk". His efforts are aimed at ridding the area's pavements of cars, motorbikes and street vendors obstructing walkways. The vision is to create a clean, orderly "little Singapore"; a nod to the neighbouring city-state often held up by governments and administrators as a model metropolis.

Mixed reactions

The initiative was at first met with applause. Although sidewalks are meant for pedestrians, they've long been appropriated by traffic in Ho Chi Minh City—vending carts set up shop on them, cars use them as extra parking lots, and motorbike drivers treat them as a shortcut to get around traffic jams. Walking around this hyperactive city can be a nightmare.

However, enthusiasm for the campaign waned once images of crying street vendors hit social media. Hai's policy has been criticised as cold and heartless, robbing low-income hawkers of their livelihood.

"What will I do for work if they force me to stop?" an elderly vendor told *Saigoneer* in 2017.[1] "I have a heart condition and need to work to afford medicine. Older people like me can't get other jobs."

Hai has also come up against his own colleagues, with warnings[2] to watch himself when dealing with vehicles sporting diplomatic plates and the setting up of a task force[3] that essentially undermined his authority. Such incidences, among others, have turned Hai's crusade into an on-again, off-again effort struggling against controversy and entrenched interests. After a hiatus of about half a year, he resumed his work in mid-May after withdrawing his resignation from the vice-chairman position.[4]

Working in a designated zone

One of the more permanent results of Hai's campaign has been the creation of two "street food streets" in District 1. It is at one of these zones—a 15-minute walk from her original location—that Thuy now sells her *bánh cuốn*. She's been operating a stall, with official permission, for seven months.

It hadn't been a voluntary choice: Thuy at first resisted the idea of moving. "We had a lot of customers back when my wife was still selling food at the zoo, therefore she didn't want to go," her husband Phu

1 https://saigoneer.com/society/society-categories/9716-chasing-pavements-in-defense-of-saigon-s-sidewalk-economy

2 https://e.vnexpress.net/news/news/captain-sidewalk-told-to-tread-carefully-around-diplomatic-cars-as-cleanup-campaign-continues-3644973.html

3 https://e.vnexpress.net/news/news/more-red-tape-could-make-you-see-less-of-captain-sidewalk-on-saigon-streets-3655769.html

4 https://e.vnexpress.net/news/news/saigon-s-sidewalk-campaign-resumes-after-months-long-break-3751860.html

explains. "She kept up the same life, being chased around for a while, and then the police caught her and brought her into the ward office and basically made it compulsory for her."

The zone, located on Nguyen Van Chiem Street, hosts 20 stalls, but not anyone can get permission to set up shop.

"You have to be a resident of Ben Nghe Ward and living in a poor household with a certificate of poverty," Thuy explains in Vietnamese. "Then you'll get a spot here, and there are 40 households here already." (Administratively, Saigon is broken up into districts, which are further divided into wards—Ben Nghe Ward is part of District 1.)

The food zone operates in shifts, with one set of vendors working from 6am–10am, then another serving from 11am–3pm. Those in the morning shift push the carts, kept in a nearby parking lot, into position. The afternoon crew puts them back in the lot when they're done for the day.

Ward officials oversee all the administration work in the zones. "The registration process came with a card, name tag, and food hygiene and safety training," Thuy shares. "There are also health checks, and there's no way someone else can work here without being registered."

She's now happy to be in the vending zone, saying the security of an officially sanctioned space is good for her business. Unregulated street vendors routinely play cat-and-mouse with the authorities—scattering at the sight of law enforcement only to resume their position once the coast is clear. In comparison, Thuy says her new setup is "better and more stable, and I don't have anything to be afraid of." Because each vendor is only allowed to sell a specific dish or beverage, she also doesn't have to worry about competing with another *bánh cuốn* stall in the same zone.

Phu agrees. "You could only stand there and keep an eye out," he says of their previous spot. "You wouldn't even dare to sit. The nervous feeling was draining."

"I'm not even talking about them catching you and confiscating your stall; just the thought of running from them while pushing the stall is already painful," he adds dryly.

Now, he says, there are frequent and thorough hygiene checks by the city and clinics. "It's a tight system, but it's good in that way," he says. "You know, if something happens, if something goes wrong while we're working, they'll come and help us handle it."

It's far cry from before the food area was established, when vendors had minimal support. "Back then, everyone was on their own, with no organisation, no nothing," Phu says. "It was like living in the wild…

no one would help you! But now, if there's just something you have a question about, you give the ward a call, and they'll come and help you figure it out. That's what I like most about this whole thing."

Scaling up?

While Phu feels like the establishment of this specific street food zone has been a success, he also acknowledges that there's a long way to go. The zone is merely a small part of District 1—the sheer number of street vendors working around town is a challenge for the city's leaders. Beyond that, Ho Chi Minh City has 23 other districts in which many street vendors continue to run rings around the officials.

"The city can't even fully manage Ben Nghe Ward, not to mention the whole district!" Phu exclaims. "And then there are people from north and central Vietnam, since everyone comes to this city to make a living. Those people have either gone back to their hometown [since the campaign began] or accepted the fate of being chased and captured on the street. In a city like this with that volume [of vendors], it's impossible to manage."

The apparent success of the Nguyen Van Chiem street food zone, along with that of the similar zone in nearby Bach Tung Diep Park, has led officials in other parts of District 1 to express the desire to create other designated vending areas.[5] Thus far, however, no other such zones have opened.

A desirable change?

For some, however, the question isn't whether Ho Chi Minh City *could* create more street food areas, but whether the city *should*. Annette Kim is an associate professor and director of the Spatial Analysis Lab at the University of California and a leading expert on Ho Chi Minh City's pavement culture. She wrote the 2015 book *Sidewalk City: Remapping Public Space in Ho Chi Minh City*, in which she argues that planners should embrace this aspect of urban life, instead of trying to regulate it into something unrecognisable.

"One Singapore is enough," Kim says in an email. "Vietnam has something else to offer the world that I hope it will consider how to express value for. My research has shown that people from around the

5 https://e.vnexpress.net/news/travel-life/travel/more-street-food-zones-in-the-making-for-downtown-saigon-3673623.html

world who come to Vietnam love its beautiful, humane and delicious approach to life in public space."

Phu, for his part, fully endorses the new system. "I feel really great about this, it's really civilised," he shares. "Not only does it solve the problem for us of where to work so we can provide for our children, but the leaders also help to solve any problems while keeping a positive relationship between sellers and customers through health and food hygiene checks. We didn't know any of that back then!"

COMICS

MALAY WEDDING
ADI NAZRI | 09 SEP 2017

Malaysian cartoonist Adi Nazri takes a look at the dos and don'ts of a traditional Malay wedding for a modern-day couple.

FIRST, THEIR FAMILIES NEED TO MEET UP, SO THE FUTURE IN-LAWS CAN TO GET TO KNOW EACH OTHER AND DISCUSS THE ARRANGEMENTS FOR THE WEDDING.

NEXT, THEY HAVE TO ATTEND A MARRIAGE COURSE IN ORDER TO GET A CERTIFICATE REQUIRED WHEN REGISTERING THEIR MARRIAGE WITH THE LOCAL AUTHORITIES.

HOW TO TREAT YOUR FAMILY 101

THEN IT IS TIME TO FIND... A WEDDING RING!

(A MATCHING PAIR IS NOT ACTUALLY REQUIRED... BUT, WELL, THAT SEEMS TO BE THE COMMON PRACTICE.)

NEXT: THE WEDDING DRESS .

FORTUNATELY THE GROOM'S OUTFIT IS A MUCH LESS COMPLICATED AFFAIR!

FOOD IS ON THEIR MINDS NOW, THE MOST DELICIOUS PART OF THE LIST!

DISCUSSIONS WITH THE CHEF, THEIR OWN AUNTIE MOSTLE, WILL HELP DECIDE WHAT WILL BE SERVED AT THE WEDDING.

AND THEN THERE IS THE NEED TO SUDDENLY ACQUIRE DESIGN SKILLS IN ORDER TO COME UP WITH THE INVITATION.

WEDDING INVITATION

ALI & SITI

GIFTS ARE EXCHANGED ON THE WEDDING DAY, SO THE COUPLE NOW HAS TO FIND SUITABLE ONES.

SOME ITEMS HAVE A LOT OF TRADITIONAL SYMBOLIC MEANING.

THIS YELLOW STICKY RICE, OR *PULUT KUNING*, FOR EXAMPLE, REPRESENTS THE INTENT TO BUILD AND STRENGHTEN THE RELATIONSHIP BETWEEN THE COUPLE AND THEIR FAMILIES.

THE ENGAGEMENT RINGS ARE INCLUDED AS PART OF THE GIFTS EXCHANGED - THESE USED TO BE PRESENTED BY ELDER RELATIVES, BUT NOWADAYS IT IS OFTEN THE GROOM'S PARENTS WHO DO SO.

THIS IS CASH CHEQUE

ALONG WITH THE GIFTS, THE GROOM WILL ALSO PRESENT THE BRIDE'S PARENTS WITH *DUIT HANTARAN*, A MONEY GIFT THAT ACTS LIKE A DOWRY.

ANOTHER TYPICAL GIFT IS A COPY THE QUR'AN, WHICH THE COUPLE CAN READ AND RECITE FROM IN THEIR COMING DAYS AS HUSBAND AND WIFE.

BETEL LEAVES PLAY AN IMPORTANT ROLE IN THE EXCHANGES. FOR EXAMPLE THERE IS THE *TEPAK SIREH*, WHICH CONTAINS THE LEAVES AND OTHER INGREDIENTS LIKE CLOVE AND GAMBIER.

AMONGST OTHER THINGS, IT REPRESENTS THE RECOGNITION THAT COUPLE ARE IN A FORMAL RELATIONSHIP - THAT THE MAN IS "MARKED" AND THE WOMAN "BOOKED".

SIMILARILY, *SIREH JANJUNG* IS USED TO COMMUNICATE TO THE GROOM THAT HIS OFFER OF MARRIAGE HAS BEEN ACCEPTED.

BESIDES THESE, BOTH SIDES CAN ALSO INCLUDE MANY OTHER BETROTHAL GIFTS...

...SHOES, PERFUMES, FOOD... WHATEVER THE OTHER HALF FANCIES!

A FEW NIGHTS BEFORE THE WEDDING, THE CANOPY IS SET UP. THIS IS WHERE THE RECEPTION, OR *MAJLIS PERSANDINGAN*, WILL TAKE PLACE, WHERE FRIENDS, RELATIVES AND GUESTS WILL GATHER TO OFFER THEIR BLESSINGS AND CONGRATULATIONS TO THE COUPLE.

WHILE THIS IS HAPPENING, THE FAMILIES GATHER TO FINALIZE THE DETAILS OF THE UPCOMING CEREMONY...

...SUCH AS THE SEGREGATION OF VARIOUS RESPONSIBILITIES TO ENSURE THAT THINGS RUN SMOOTHLY.

BACK AT THE TENT, EGGS ARE BEING BOILED. THESE WILL BE USED TO MAKE *BUNGA TELUR*, OR FLOWER EGGS, WHICH WILL BE GIVEN TO GUESTS AS AN APPRECIATION OF THEIR ATTENDANCE, AND SYMBOLIZE FERTILITY.

TODAY, MANY COUPLES GIVE OUT CHOCOLATES, SWEETS OR CAKES INSTEAD, BUT THOSE WHO WISH TO BE MORE TRADITIONAL STILL PREPARE *BUNGA TELUR*.

IN SOME CASES, THE BRIDE WILL HAVE TO BE PREPARED TO RECITE SOME *SURAH* OF QUR'AN.

THIS IS KNOWN AS THE *KHATAM QUR'AN* CEREMONY.

ON THE DAY OF THE CEREMONY, THE COUPLE'S BED IS DECORATED WHILE THE COUPLE PREPARE THEMSELVES FOR THE BIG OCCASION.

THE WEDDING TEAM IS ALSO BUSY PREPARING THE BRIDAL DIAS - AFTER ALL, THE HIGHLIGHT OF THE CEREMONY WILL BE WHEN THE COUPLE SIT ON THE DIAS, OR PELAMIN, IN THEIR WEDDING FINERY, TREATED AS KING AND QUEEN FOR THE DAY.

THE BRIDE'S FINGERS AND NAILS ARE STAINED WITH HENNA BY HER BRIDESMAIDS, IN A CEREMONY CALLED THE BERINAI CURI.

TRADITIONALLY THIS IS ONE OF THREE BERINAI CEREMONIES, THE OTHER TWO OF WHICH, CALLED THE BERINAI KECHIL AND BERINAI BESAR, ALSO INVOLVES THE GROOM.

EVERYONE PITCHES IN - FAMILY MEMBERS AND NEIGHBOURS, TO MAKE SURE ALL THE PREPARATIONS ARE IN ORDER, FROM FOOD TO DOORGIFTS.

THIS COLLECTIVE ACT OF HELPING EACH OTHER, CALLED MEREWANG, HAS TRADITIONALLY HELPED BUILD STRONG SOCIAL TIES IN THE COMMUNITY.

IN THE PAST, THE FOOD WOULD BE BROUGHT TO GUESTS BY BOYS AND GIRLS CARRYING LARGE ROUND TRAYS.

BUT NOW IT IS MORE COMMON FOR THE GUESTS TO SERVE THEMSELVES BUFFET-STYLE.

WHEN THE GUESTS ARRIVE, THE HOSTS WILL GREET THEM AT THE ENTRANCE OF THE EVENT HALL OR CANOPY.

THE GROOM SOON APPROACHES WITH HIS ENTOURAGE.

IN MANY INSTANCES (DEPENDING ON THE CULTURE OF THE STATE), THE GROOM WILL BE PREVENTED FROM REACHING THE BRIDE UNTIL HE PAYS A "TOLL FEE" - WHICH CAN INVOLVE GIVING PACKETS OF MONEY OR A CLEVER EXCHANGE OF PANTUN, A TRADITIONAL MALAY POETIC FORM.

AFTER THAT, THE GROOM WILL SIT IN FRONT OF TOK KADI, THE MAN APPOINTED TO MARRY THE COUPLE.

THERE WILL ALSO BE AT LEAST FOUR WITNESSES PRESENT TO MAKE SURE THE VOWS ARE RECITED CLEARLY AND PROPERLY.

A DAY IN THE LIFE OF A MALAY DAD

ARIF RAFHAN OTHMAN | 26 SEP 2017

A day in the life of a freelance illustrator in Malaysia.

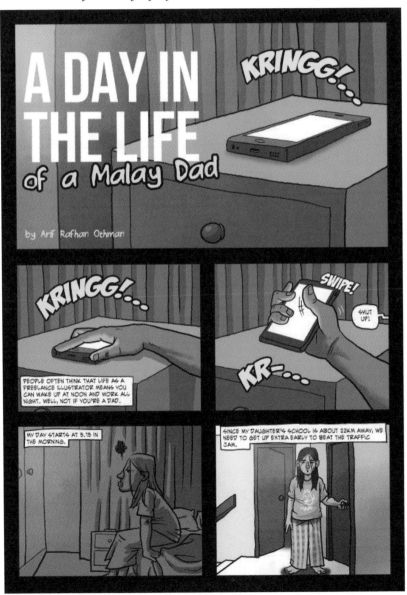

THE SELECT COMMITTEE ON ONE TIGHT SLAPS

SONNY LIEW | 30 MAR 2018

A rare Select Committee on One Tight Slaps promises to consult a range of stakeholders. Upon arrival, witnesses find a very different reality.

"NO ONE SHOULD HAVE TO BE SUPER IN ORDER TO BE HUMAN"

JAMES TAN | 14 MAY 2018

The story of a Singaporean family, adapted from Teo You Yenn's book of essays "This Is What Inequality Looks Like".

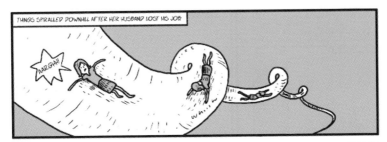

THE SUMMIT
SONNY LIEW | 11 JUN 2018

A historic meeting takes place between US President Donald Trump and North Korean leader Kim Jong Un.

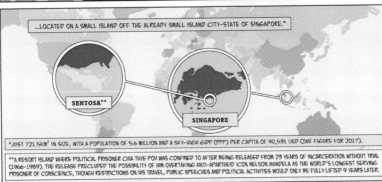

INVISIBLE INK
JANELLE RETKA | 27 JUL 2018

As Cambodians nationwide prepare to head to the polls for the country's sixth general election this month, one woman says she won't be in the crowds.

"SIXTY DOLLARS PER MONTH", 48-YEAR-OLD LANDLORD **KY POV** PROCLAIMS PROUDLY AS SHE LEADS ME INTO THE VACANT STUDIO APARTMENT ON THE SOUTHERN END OF CAMBODIA'S CAPITAL. SHE FEELS SAFE TO TALK ABOUT POLITICS IN HER FLAT, WELL OUT OF EARSHOT OF POTENTIALLY NOSEY NEIGHBOURS, IN A PROPERTY THAT CONSTITUTES THE MAIN SOURCE OF HER LIVELIHOOD.

POV HAS RECENTLY REGISTERED AS
A VOTER FOR PRIME MINISTER HUN
SEN'S RULING CAMBODIAN PEOPLE'S
PARTY (CPP), AHEAD OF THE GENERAL
ELECTION ON JULY 29, THE
COUNTRY'S SIXTH SINCE CAMBODIA
BECAME A DEMOCRACY IN 1993.

SHE IS, HOWEVER, QUICK TO POINT
OUT THAT THIS WAS NOT BY
CHOICE. "I WAS INVITED TO A
MEETING WITH THE VILLAGE
CHIEF, AND *THEY* REGISTERED ME
AS A CPP VOTER. I DON'T WANT TO
VOTE FOR THEM."

BEFORE MOVING TO HER CURRENT
PROPERTY IN 2009, POV HAD BEEN A
RESIDENT AT **DEY KRAHORM** - OR RED
EARTH - A SOCIAL LAND CONCESSION
SETTLEMENT THAT HAD BEEN
FORCIBLY RAZED TO THE GROUND
EARLIER THAT YEAR BY A
DEVELOPMENT COMPANY AND
GOVERNMENT AUTHORITIES. THE
PAINFUL EVICTION LEFT
HER WITH A BITTER
TASTE FOR THE

RULING PARTY...

AND AN AFFINITY FOR THE LONGTIME- AND THEN-OPPOSITION LEADER **SAM RAINSY**, WHO'D CONDEMNED THE EVICTIONS.

RAINSY, HOWEVER, HAS BEEN LIVING IN SELF-IMPOSED EXILE SINCE LATE 2015. THE OPPOSITION LEADER IN HIS STEAD HAS BEEN IMPRISONED AND THEIR PARTY, THE CAMBODIA NATIONAL RESCUE PARTY (CNRP), RECENTLY DISSOLVED, LEAVING ITS 3 MILLION FOLLOWERS LARGELY **ADRIFT**.

SITTING ON THE TILED FLOOR OF
HER VACANT FLAT, POV TELLS ME
SHE'D VOTED FOR SAM RAINSY
IN EVERY ELECTION
SINCE 1993, BUT THAT
HUN SEN HAD ALWAYS
REMAINED IN POWER.

THE COUNTRY FACES ITS **SIXTH
GENERAL ELECTION** AT THE END OF
THE MONTH - THIS TIME AROUND,
MINUS THE OPTION TO VOTE FOR
RAINSY, AND INDEED, ANY PARTY
THOUGHT TO HAVE A SHOT AGAINST
THE INCUMBENT CPP.

IN ORDER TO BOOST VOTER TURNOUT,
HOWEVER, VOTERS HAVE, FOR THE
FIRST TIME EVER, BEEN GIVEN A
HOLIDAY SO THAT MORE MAY BE
ABLE TO RETURN TO THEIR HOME
VILLAGE TO CAST THEIR VOTES.
IN THE ABSENCE OF ANY REAL,
MEANINGFUL COMPETITION FOR
THE CPP, SOME SEE THIS MOVE
AS AN ATTEMPT BY THE RULING
PARTY TO SECURE A MORE
CONVINCING MANDATE AND TO LEND
GREATER LEGITIMACY TO THE
ELECTION RESULTS.

"I DON'T KNOW WHAT TO TICK ON THE BALLOT PAPER NOW," SAYS POV. "I NORMALLY VOTE, BUT THIS YEAR I'M NOT SO SURE. MAYBE I'LL JUST STAY HOME."

"PEOPLE SAY THAT IF WE DON'T VOTE, IT MEANS WE SUPPORT THE REBELLION," SHE SAYS, CITING RUMOURS THAT NON-VOTERS WILL BE DUBBED "TRAITORS" FOR SUPPORTING RAINSY'S CALL FOR A BOYCOTT. THE EVIDENCE OF INDELIBLE INK ON VOTERS' INDEX FINGERS WILL OSTENSIBLY HELP REDUCE VOTER FRAUD—AND ALSO MAKE IT OBVIOUS WHO *HASN'T* VOTED.

"MANY PEOPLE SAY THAT THEY'RE GOING TO DIP THEIR FINGER IN THE INK BUT NOT VOTE FOR ANYTHING... IN ORDER TO INVALIDATE THE BALLOT AND, THEY HOPE, THE ELECTION."

ACCORDING TO LOCAL MEDIA,
HOWEVER, "PRETEND VOTERS" MAY
JUST RISK BEING SENT TO PRISON.
POV LAUGHS AT THE
QUANDARY FACING NON-
CPP SUPPORTERS: EITHER
RISK BEING SEEN AS
"TRAITORS" WITH CLEAN
INDEX FINGERS - OR BE
FOUND OUT FOR FAKING
THEIR VOTES.

"BUT I DON'T FEEL SCARED. I ONLY
WANT TO VOTE FOR THE CNRP. NO
CNRP MEANS I STAY HOME."

"THE INTERNATIONAL COMMUNITY
WON'T ACCEPT THE RESULTS. THE
PEOPLE ALREADY KNOW THAT THIS
ELECTION IS WRONG. THE RESULT
WILL BE THE SAME - HUN SEN'S
CPP WILL WIN - WHETHER WE
SHOW UP OR NOT."

NEVERTHELESS, SHE'S NOT DETERRED. "I'M NOT SCARED AT ALL. I'M GOING TO *SHOUT* IT ALL THROUGH MY VILLAGE: I WILL **NOT** VOTE FOR THEM."

REGARDLESS OF THE INEVITABILITY OF THIS ELECTION, POV MAINTAINS HOPE THAT **CHANGE** CAN STILL COME TO CAMBODIA.

BUT RIGHT NOW, SHE CONCEDE, "I'M NOT QUITE SURE HOW."

BY
JANELLE RETKA
TRANSLATION BY
OUCH SONY

AUTHOR BIOGRAPHIES

Adi Nazri is a Malaysian comic artist and editor born in Kuala Terengganu, and currently working in Subang Jaya, Selangor. He has published several independent comic magazines, including entitled Anthologykapalooza (2014) and Kapalooza Komik (2015) and is the President of PeKOMIK (Malaysian Comic Enthusiast Organization).

Aidila Razak is a journalist. She is temporarily based in London, pursuing an MA in Digital Journalism at Goldsmiths, University of London. She has spent almost a decade writing about Malaysian politics and society, and can usually be found musing about these topics on her Twitter account @aidilarazak.

Aisyah Llewellyn is a British freelance writer based in Medan, Indonesia, and New Naratif's Regional Editor, Deputy Editor for Bahasa Indonesia, and Consulting Editor for North Sumatra. She is a former diplomat and writes primarily about Indonesian politics, culture, travel and food. Reach her at aisyah.llewellyn@newnaratif.com.

Ainur Rohmah is freelance journalist with four years' track record in reporting general news, politics and finance for Anadolu Agency. She has also written stories for publications like The Jakarta Post and The Globe Post. She's interested in women's issues, refugees, and radicalism in Islam.

Arif Rafhan bin Othman is a comic artist, a mural artist, an animator, a doodler and a neighborhood art teacher in both digital and analog medium. His work has spanned from paintings, book illustrations (for MPH & Fixi), graphic novels, (MPH & Maple Comics), graphic facilitation (BNM & PruBSN), corporate comics and art installation for corporate offices. He was the Creative Director in his previous e-Learning company for 11 years before embarking into servicing the wider industry and established himself as a true artist. He obtained his Bachelor's Degree in IT (Hons) in 2000 with minor in Multimedia from PPP/UiTM, Shah Alam, Malaysia.

Ben Paviour is a freelance reporter formerly based in Phnom Penh, where he led politics coverage for the Cambodia Daily.

Ben Sokhean is one of Cambodia's leading politics reporters and currently is on staff with the Phnom Penh Post.

Brennan O'Connor worked for Canada's leading media publications before dedicating himself full time to cover self-generated under-reported stories in the mainstream press. In 2010, he left his native country to move to Southeast Asia to follow a long-term photo project on Myanmar's ethnic minority groups. O'Connor's photography was recently projected at the prestigious Visa Pour l'image in Perpignan and honoured with the 2017 Prix Lucas Dolega Award in January. As part of the award, the series was exhibited in Paris this January. His work has been published in Foreign Policy; Paris Match; L'Obs; Al Jazeera; The National; Burn Magazine; and The Walrus and screened at Angkor Photo Festival and Yangon Photo Festival in 2015 and the Fotograf Vakfı 3rd Documentary Photography Days in 2016.

Calum Stuart is a Scottish-Welsh journalist who was previously the Vietnam correspondent for Thomson Reuters based in Ho Chi Minh City and briefly a copy editor at the Democratic Voice of Burma in Chiang Mai. He has worked in both print and broadcast journalism.

Charis Loke is an illustrator and educator based in Penang, Malaysia. Drawing upon literature and visual culture, she makes pictures that evoke wonder and curiosity. As a member of Arts-ED, Charis also works on community arts and culture education programmes for youth. Her work can be found at http://charisloke.com.

Dam Xuan Viet is a freelance press assistant and aspiring photojournalist, based in Ho Chi Minh City, Vietnam. A Harry Potter fanatic and committed cat owner/butler, he tries to live everyday according to the Ellen Degeneres quote "Be kind to one another."

Deborah Germaine Augustin is a Malaysian writer and researcher. Previously, she worked as a Parliamentary Assistant for the MP of Kelana Jaya. She recently graduated from Western Michigan University's MFA in creative writing program, and is currently working on a cross-genre chapbook about immigration in the United States.

Febriana Firdaus is an independent investigative journalist based in Jakarta, Indonesia. She has reported on politics, corruption, human and LGBT rights, the 1965 purge, Papua, and ISIS. She is an editor of Ingat65, an online project for young people's perspectives on the legacy of Indonesia's 1965–66 massacres, and manages the Voice of Papua newsletter. She has previously worked at Tempo and Rappler. Her freelance work has appeared in TIME, BBC Indonesia, Jakarta Post, VICE Indonesia, etc. In 2017, she received the Indonesian Oktovianus Pogau Journalism Award in Courage for her fearless reporting on human rights, including on LGBT issues.

George Wright is a British freelance journalist based in Phnom Penh covering politics, rights abuses and migration among other issues for the likes of the Columbia Journalism Review, VICE and The Diplomat. He was an associate editor at The Cambodia Daily for four years until it was shuttered amid a crackdown on independent media last year.

Godofredo Ramizo Jr is a PhD candidate at the University of Oxford, studying the social impact of digital technologies and the platform economy. An Oxford Clarendon scholar, his dissertation investigates the effects of ride-hailing technologies in Southeast Asia's gridlocked megacities.

Born in Singapore, **James Tan** works as an illustrator and comic artist. He likes to draw and gets his inspirations while watching people and stirring his kopi siew dai at the kopitiam.

Janelle Retka is a Phnom Penh-based illustrator and journalist.

Jeamme Chia is an independent political economist interested in geo-spatial, environmental, and socio-economic issues, especially where they intersect with questions of sustainability, equity, and development in Southeast Asia. She grew up immersed in Penang's civil society and activist scene, which is where she cultivated a strong sense of justice and interest in public policy. Her current work is focused on understanding the issues related to the global palm oil supply chain by analysing trade flows, tropical deforestation in key production zones, and socio-economic conditions in primary production zones in Indonesia and Malaysia. Jeamme completed her bachelor's degree at Sarah Lawrence College, where her concentrations were Economics, Environmental Science, and French.

John Lee is the pseudonym of the author, who wishes to remain anonymous. He is an artist and teacher, and has been active in the LGBT community for over a decade. He is interested in human rights and other social issues.

Joshua Carroll is a freelance reporter based in Myanmar. His work covers human rights, development and media freedom. He tweets at @jershcarroll

Jules Rahman Ong is a freelance writer, fixer, producer and an award-winning independent documentary filmmaker. He holds a permaculture design certificate and is passionate about creating a world where humans live sustainably with animals, plants and mineral.

Kate Mayberry has lived and worked as a journalist in Southeast Asia for two decades. Now freelance, she was a member of the launch team for Al Jazeera English, and was previously a correspondent with Bloomberg.

Kate Walton is a queer feminist activist living in Jakarta, Indonesia. She is the founder of the Jakarta Feminist Discussion Group, and one of the organisers of Women's March Jakarta and Feminist Fest 2017. Kate is on Twitter at @waltonkate.

Katharine Ee is a freelance journalist based in Kuala Lumpur.

Kenneth Cheng Chee Kin is an analyst at Political Studies Programme at Penang Institute. He researches on political economy, democratization and local elections in Malaysia.

Kimberley Phillips is a multimedia journalist based in Myanmar. She edit and reports for Democratic Voice of Burma. Find her on Twitter @kimberleyphps.

Kirsten Han is Editor-in-Chief of New Naratif, and a Singaporean journalist whose work often revolves around the themes of social justice, human rights, politics and democracy. Her bylines have appeared in publications like The Guardian, Foreign Policy, Asia Times and Waging Nonviolence. As an activist, Kirsten has advocated for an end to the death penalty in Singapore, and is a founding member of abolitionist group We Believe in Second Chances. Reach her at kirsten.han@newnaratif.com.

Lam Le is a freelance journalist based in Hanoi, Vietnam. She previously worked for two years as editor at VnExpress International.

Leonie Kijewski is a German freelance reporter based in Cambodia. In her reporting she focuses on the intersection of human rights, social justice, and politics.

Marco Ferrarese is an expert on Malaysia and Borneo. He co-authored guidebooks on Malaysia, Brunei and Thailand for Rough Guides, and published a novel, Nazi Goreng, which is banned in Malaysia, and several non-fiction books. He has written more than 100 articles on travel, culture and extreme music in Asia for a variety of international publications including Travel + Leisure Southeast Asia, CNN Travel, BBC Travel, The Guardian, and National Geographic Traveler (UK). He also blogs about Penang (at http://www.penang-insider.com/guide-48-hours-in-penang/) and his adventurous travels around Asia and the Middle East (at http://www.monkeyrockworld.com).

Mech Dara is a Cambodian freelance reporter covering predominantly politics and human rights issues. He joined The Cambodia Daily in 2012 before switching to The Phnom Penh Post four years later. He decided to go freelance this month after the Post was sold to an investor who had previously done work for Prime Minister Hun Sen's government.

Michael McLaughlin is a producer, writer and educational/business consultant in Hanoi. Before coming back to what began as a 2004 flirt with Vietnam, Michael produced urban and design planning videos and wore many hats in documentary distribution for Gathr Films.

Michael Tatarski is a journalist based in Ho Chi Minh City, Vietnam. He focuses on the environment, urban development and social issues. Find him on Twitter @miketatarski.

Oliver Slow is a Southeast Asia-based journalist.

Ooi Kok Hin is Monbukagakusho scholar and research student at the Graduate School of Political Science, Waseda University and research affiliate at Penang Institute.

Patrick Beech is a senior editor and writer in Malaysia.

Reynold Sumayku is a freelance photographer, journalist, writer, editor, photo editor, educator based in Indonesia with over 20 years working as a freelance contributor and editorial staff with national and international print/online media. Website: https://reynoldsumayku.com

Samantha Cheh is a freelance journalist based in Kuala Lumpur. She has previously worked as a staff writer for Tech Wire Asia. Her work can also be found in South China Morning Post, Salaam Gateway and Art Republik magazine.

Sara R Moulton is a freelance writer and editor based in Ho Chi Minh City, Vietnam. Find her on Twitter @smoult.

Sengkong Bun, formerly with the Phnom Penh Post, is a Cambodian freelance journalist, fixer and translator based in Phnom Penh. He is a winner of an award from the Society of Publishers in Asia for excellence in reporting. Follow him on Twitter at @sengkong_bun.

Sharmilla Ganesan is a radio producer/presenter, features journalist, and culture writer based in Kuala Lumpur, Malaysia. She has previously written for The Star (Malaysia), The Atlantic, South China Morning Post, and ArtsEquator.

Sol Iglesias has a PhD in Southeast Asian Studies from the National University of Singapore (NUS). Her research focuses on patterns of political violence in the post-Marcos, democratic period of the Philippines. She has a MA in international affairs from the Fletcher School at Tufts University, MA in political science from NUS and BA in public administration from the University of the Philippines. Sol was the first Filipino, Asian, and woman to be Director for Intellectual Exchange at the Asia-Europe Foundation (2009 to 2012).

Sonny Liew's New York Times bestseller The Art of Charlie Chan Hock Chye is a winner of 3 Eisner Awards, and was the first graphic novel to win the Singapore Literature Prize. He was a recipient of the National Arts Council's Young Artist Award in 2010, and his works include The Shadow Hero (with Gene Yang), Doctor Fate (with Paul Levitz) and Malinky Robot, along with titles for Marvel Comics, DC Comics, Disney Press and First Second Books. Born in Malaysia, he lives in Singapore.

Sophie Raynor is a freelance writer based in Dili, Timor-Leste, interested in gender, youth and politics in Southeast Asia. She is on Twitter @raynorsophie.

Stanley Widianto is a Jakarta-based journalist who writes primarily about culture, politics and how they sometimes intersect.

Teguh Harahap is a freelance writer and translator based in Medan, Indonesia. Previously he worked as the editor of Koran Kindo, a weekly newspaper for Indonesian migrant workers based in Hong Kong.

Thum Ping Tjin ("PJ") is Managing Director of New Naratif and founding director of Project Southeast Asia, an interdisciplinary research centre on Southeast Asia at the University of Oxford. A Rhodes Scholar, Commonwealth Scholar, Olympic athlete, and the only Singaporean to swim the English Channel, his work centres on Southeast Asian governance and politics. His most recent work is *Living with Myths in Singapore* (Ethos: 2017, co-edited with Loh Kah Seng and Jack Chia). He is creator of "The History of Singapore" podcast, available on iTunes. Reach him at pingtjin.thum@newnaratif.com.

Originally from Bradford, West Yorkshire in the north of England, **Tom White** is currently based in Singapore where he works as a freelance photographer. His photography has been published and exhibited internationally. Editorial clients include The New York Times, The L.A. Times, The Wall Street Journal, TIME magazine, The Guardian U.K, Thompson Reuters and The European Press Photo Agency.

Tran Vi is a Vietnamese human rights advocate and a journalist with a background in law study. Her works focus on the promotion of human rights, democracy and the rule of law in Vietnam through independent journalism and research. Her projects include thevietnamese.org and luatkhoa.org, and she is also an anti-death penalty advocate working specifically on the issues of fair trials and wrongful convictions in Vietnam. She is available at vi.tran@luatkhoa.org

Victoria Milko is a multimedia journalist based in Myanmar. She is currently an editor at Frontier Myanmar, with her work also found in The Washington Post, NPR, and others.

Vincent MacIsaac is an editor, reporter and researcher based in Southeast Asia.

Warief Djajanto Basorie reported for the domestic KN I News Service in Jakarta 1971-1991 and concurrently was Indonesia correspondent for the Manila- based DEPTHnews Asia (DNA, 1974-1991). DNA is a feature service reporting on development in Asia for Asian media in English and the vernacular. English-language subscribers included the Bangkok Post, Hong Kong Standard, Asian Wall Street Journal, Indonesia Times, Philippine Daily Inquirer. In 1991 he joined the Dr. Soetomo Press Institute (LPDS, Lembaga Pers Dr. Soetomo), a journalism school in Jakarta as an instructor and convenor in thematic journalism workshops. Most recently he was project manager for three cycles of workshops on covering climate change since 2012. More than 600 journalists in provinces in Sumatra, Kalimantan (Indonesian Borneo), Sulawesi and Papua prone to forest and peat fires have participated. The latest cycle ended December 2017.

Will Nguyen considers himself a "Schrödinger's cat" of East and West. He is Vietnamese or American, depending on who's looking. Will graduated from Yale University in 2008, with a Bachelor's in East Asian Studies. He is currently completing his Master in Public Policy at the Lee Kuan Yew School of Public Policy (NUS), where he has pursued topics of Vietnamese history, culture, and politics.

Yen Duong is a multimedia journalist and feature writer currently based in Hanoi, Vietnam. She holds a Master's degree in Communication at University of Vaasa (Finland), with a focus on semiotics of contemporary culture and media.

Yesenia Amaro is a freelance journalist and former Phnom Penh Post reporter. Before joining the Post, she covered social issues and immigration for the Las Vegas Review-Journal, where she was named journalist of the year in 2015 by the Nevada Press Association and also won the organisation's community service award. Follow her on Twitter at @YeseniaAmaro.

Zaina Abdul is a Bruneian writer and feminist working on expanding sources of the people's narrative.

```
 120
 100
 260
  65
 290
-----
 835
```